CAMBRIDGE LIBRARY COLLECTION

Books of enduring scholarly value

Archaeology

The discovery of material remains from the recent or the ancient past has always been a source of fascination, but the development of archaeology as an academic discipline which interpreted such finds is relatively recent. It was the work of Winckelmann at Pompeii in the 1760s which first revealed the potential of systematic excavation to scholars and the wider public. Pioneering figures of the nineteenth century such as Schliemann, Layard and Petrie transformed archaeology from a search for ancient artifacts, by means as crude as using gunpowder to break into a tomb, to a science which drew from a wide range of disciplines - ancient languages and literature, geology, chemistry, social history - to increase our understanding of human life and society in the remote past.

A Study of the Bronze Age Pottery of Great Britain and Ireland and Its Associated Grave-Goods

The fifth Baron Abercromby (1841–1924), a soldier and keen archaeologist, published this two-volume work in 1912. His especial interest was prehistoric pottery, and he introduced the word 'Beaker' as a term to indicate the late Neolithic/Chalcolithic western European culture which produced these characteristic clay drinking vessels. His aim was to produce a chronological survey of British and Irish ceramics from the late Neolithic to the end of the Bronze Age, to classify these by type and geographical area, and to examine the goods associated with dateable pottery in burials and cremation urns. This heavily illustrated work also puts the British beakers into their European context and considers the possible indications of movements of people given by variations in style. Volume 1 examines burials, the associated grave-goods and skeletal remains, especially skulls, which may provide ethnographic information.

T0381728

Cambridge University Press has long been a pioneer in the reissuing of out-of-print titles from its own backlist, producing digital reprints of books that are still sought after by scholars and students but could not be reprinted economically using traditional technology. The Cambridge Library Collection extends this activity to a wider range of books which are still of importance to researchers and professionals, either for the source material they contain, or as landmarks in the history of their academic discipline.

Drawing from the world-renowned collections in the Cambridge University Library and other partner libraries, and guided by the advice of experts in each subject area, Cambridge University Press is using state-of-the-art scanning machines in its own Printing House to capture the content of each book selected for inclusion. The files are processed to give a consistently clear, crisp image, and the books finished to the high quality standard for which the Press is recognised around the world. The latest print-on-demand technology ensures that the books will remain available indefinitely, and that orders for single or multiple copies can quickly be supplied.

The Cambridge Library Collection brings back to life books of enduring scholarly value (including out-of-copyright works originally issued by other publishers) across a wide range of disciplines in the humanities and social sciences and in science and technology.

A Study of the Bronze Age Pottery of Great Britain and Ireland and Its Associated Grave-Goods

VOLUME 1

JOHN ABERCROMBY

CAMBRIDGE
UNIVERSITY PRESS

CAMBRIDGE
UNIVERSITY PRESS

University Printing House, Cambridge, CB2 8BS, United Kingdom

Cambridge University Press is part of the University of Cambridge.

It furthers the University's mission by disseminating knowledge in the pursuit of
education, learning and research at the highest international levels of excellence.

www.cambridge.org
Information on this title: www.cambridge.org/9781108082556

© in this compilation Cambridge University Press 2015

This edition first published 1912
This digitally printed version 2015

ISBN 978-1-108-08255-6 Paperback

A STUDY OF THE
BRONZE AGE POTTERY
OF
GREAT BRITAIN & IRELAND
AND ITS ASSOCIATED GRAVE-GOODS

BY THE
HON. JOHN ABERCROMBY
LL.D., F.S.A.Scot.

WITH 1611 ILLUSTRATIONS OF POTTERY, 155 EXAMPLES OF GRAVE-GOODS, AND 10 PLATES SHOWING ORNAMENTATION

IN TWO VOLUMES
VOL. I

OXFORD
AT THE CLARENDON PRESS
M DCCCC XII

HENRY FROWDE, M.A.

PUBLISHER TO THE UNIVERSITY OF OXFORD

LONDON, EDINBURGH, NEW YORK

TORONTO AND MELBOURNE

PREFACE

THE time has arrived when an attempt should be made to arrange the chief types of British and Hibernian pottery in chronological order. Dr. Thurnam in his well-known monograph, published forty years ago, described very accurately all the typical forms of British pottery then known. But he had not the material at his disposal to place these in their relative order of time. Indeed by a regrettable slip he gave it as his opinion that cinerary urns were earlier than beakers or drinking cups. From a merely descriptive point of view all that he wrote about our Bronze Age pottery still holds good and requires but little change.

To prevent confusion with true neolithic pottery, I have adopted the terminology of Dr. O. Montelius and treated the pottery, here dealt with, as belonging to the Bronze Age. What might be termed a 'Transition' or a 'Copper' period is therefore classed as Period I of the Bronze Age.

A valuable adjunct to the study of the different classes and types of pottery is gained by subdividing Great Britain and Ireland into various zones or areas and studying each separately. By this means it is possible to watch the changes that took place in a particular type as it moved gradually from south to north.

One result of the study is to show the influence exerted by Hibernia at a very early time on the food-vessel class of ceramic in the northern half of England, and the probability that the most elaborate type of this class is derived from a Hibernian prototype. Another result is that the 'overhanging rim' type of cinerary urn may, with great probability, be derived from a food-vessel form. Further, that north of the Thames Valley and in Hibernia there is no visible break in the sequence of ceramic types from the beginning to the end of the Bronze Age. South of the Thames foreign types appear in Period IV, but there is no evidence to show that these new comers ever advanced northwards, and their influence on the history of the country appears to have been *nil*.

Finally, an attempt has been made to accommodate Dr. O. Montelius's Chronology of the Bronze Age in Britain to one that seems more in accord with the evidence derived from a study of British ceramic.

In previous papers I have expressed my thanks to many Curators of Museums at home and abroad for allowing me to obtain photographs of some of the specimens preserved in their Museums. For many new illustrations, made for these volumes, I have more especially to tender my best thanks to Mr. R. Mortimer for very generously allowing me to have photographs taken of a very large part of his collection at Driffield.[1] They have been of the utmost use, indeed, indispensable. I am greatly indebted to the Rev. Ed. H. Goddard and Mr. Howard Cunnington, Curators of the Devizes Museum, for photographs of bronze daggers and other objects, some of which have not been published before; to Captain J. Acland, Curator of the Dorchester Museum, for bronze blades and other objects now published for the first time; to Mr. St. George Gray, Curator of the Taunton Museum, for many photographs; to Mr. Arthur Wright, Curator of the Colchester Museum, for photographs and other communications; to Mr. C. Bradshaw, Assistant Curator of the Sheffield Museum, for many photographs. I am not less indebted to M. du Chatellier[1] of Kernuz for allowing me to photograph urns in his large collection; to M. Champion of the Museum of St. Germain for photographs of urns from the collection of M. Piette; to Dr. Sophus Müller of Copenhagen, and Herr C. Rothmann of the Kiel Museum, for permission of getting photographs taken of several examples of Continental pottery.

Finally, I am under a great obligation to Dr. Robert Munro, M.A., M.D., LL.D., for reading the MSS. and proofs besides suggesting alterations.

EDINBURGH,
April 20, 1911.

---

[1] Since the above was in type I have learnt with the greatest regret of the death of Mr. R. Mortimer and of M. du Chatellier.

CONTENTS OF VOLUME I

CHAPTER I. INTRODUCTORY

CHAPTER II. BRITISH CERAMIC

CHAPTER III. CONTINENTAL AND BRITISH ORNAMENTATION COMPARED

CHAPTER IV. OBJECTS FOUND WITH BEAKER INTERMENTS

CHAPTER V. ETHNOGRAPHICAL AND HISTORICAL

CHAPTER VI. COLONIZATION AND DIFFUSION OF THE INVADERS (see Maps)

CHAPTER VII. THE FOOD-VESSEL CLASS

CHAPTER VIII

CHAPTER IX

CHAPTER X

CHAPTER XI. ORNAMENTATION (v. Plates of Ornament)

CHAPTER XII. OBJECTS FOUND WITH FOOD VESSELS

CHAPTER XIII. ETHNOGRAPHICAL SECTION

CHAPTER XIV. ETHNOGRAPHICAL

LIST OF ABBREVIATIONS

Anderson = Dr. J. Anderson, *Scotland in Pagan Times ; Bronze and Stone Ages.*

Ar. Arch. = *Archaeologia.*

Arch. Cambr. = *Archaeologia Cambrensis.*

A. W. = Sir Richard Hoare, *Ancient Wilts*, vol. i.

B. = Barrow.

B. A. H. = *Boletín de la real Academia de la Historia.*

B. B. = Canon W. Greenwell, *British Barrows.*

Bateman (1) = J. Bateman, *Vestiges of the Antiquities of Derbyshire.*

Bateman (2) = Bateman, *Ten Years' Diggings.*

Bruce = Bruce, *Catalogue of Antiquities in Alnwick Castle.*

Cat. Dev. = *Catalogue of the Devizes Museum.*

Colini = Colini, *Il sepolchreto di Remedello sotto.*

C. T. = Warne, *Celtic Tumuli of Dorset.*

D. = Diameter.

Diggings, s. v. Bateman.

Du Chatellier = *La Poterie aux époques préhist. et gauloise en Armorique.*

E. R. = East Riding of Yorkshire.

Evans A. S. I. = Sir John Evans, *Ancient Stone Implements of Great Britain.*

Evans A. B. I. = Sir John Evans, *Ancient Bronze Implements of Great Britain.*

H. = height.

J. A. I. = *Journal of the Anthropological Institute.*

J. B. A. A. = *Journal of the British Archaeological Association.*

Jewitt = Ll. Jewitt, *Ceramic Art in Great Britain*, vol. i.

J. R. H. A. A. I. = *Journ. Royal Historical and Archaeol. Assoc. Ireland.*

Matér. = *Matériaux pour l'histoire primitive de l'homme.*

Montelius = O. Montelius, *Chronologie d. ältesten Bronzezeit in Nord-Deutschland.*

Mortimer = R. Mortimer, *Forty Years' Researches in British and Saxon Burial mounds of East Yorkshire.*

Much = Dr. M. Much, *Die Kupferzeit in Europa* (1893).

N. C. = Borlase, *Naenia Cornubiae.*

N. O. = Dr. W. Pleyte, *Nederlandsche Oudheden.*

N. R. = North Riding of Yorkshire.

Paris = P. Paris, *Essai sur l'art et l'industrie de l'Espagne primitive.*

P. A. I. = *Proceedings Archaeological Institute.*

P. R. = Pitt Rivers, *Excavations in Cranborne Chase.*

P. R. I. A. = *Proceedings Royal Irish Academy.*

P. Soc. Ant. ⎫ = *Proceedings Society of Antiquaries of*
P. S. A. L. ⎭   *London.*

P. S. A. S. = *Proceedings Society of Antiquaries of Scotland.*

Rev. Ar. = *Revue Archéologique.*

S. A. C. = *Sussex Archaeological Collections.*

Ten Years ⎫ s. v. Bateman.
Vestiges ⎭

Vic. Hist. = *Victoria Histories of Counties.*

W. A. M. = *Wilts Archaeological Magazine.*

Wosinsky = Wosinsky, *Inkrustirte Keramik d. Stein- u. Bronzezeit.*

W. Z. G. = *Westdeutsche Zeitschrift für Geschichte und Kunst.*

Z. E. ⎫ = *Zeitschrift für Ethnologie.*
Z. f. E. ⎭

CHAPTER I

INTRODUCTORY

BEAKER TYPES OF THE CONTINENT

PLATES I TO III.

In Great Britain the researches of craniologists have demonstrated that the appearance of bronze and of the beaker types of ceramic coincides with the advent of a new race characterized by a brachycephalic skull distinctly different from the dolichocephalic head of the earlier neolithic inhabitants. Before attempting to arrange our British beakers chronologically, it is therefore necessary to direct our attention to the Continent, whence came the invaders, in order to learn something of the pottery which most resembles what is found in this country.

What Dr. A. Goetze and P. Reinecke regard as the oldest class of neolithic pottery in Central and Northern Europe is known to German archaeologists as 'Cord-ceramic', from the specimens being usually, though not invariably, decorated by impressions made with a cord upon the moist clay. This kind of ware occurs in Northern and Central Europe north of the Danube; to the west it scarcely passes the Rhine. Although this class of pottery has several forms, such as the amphora and the cord-beaker (*Schnurbecher*), it is only necessary to mention the latter. Originally this type of vessel was composed of two parts, consisting of a globular body out of which rose a cylindrical or conical neck, such as we see in figs. 1*, 2*, both from Thuringia. But in course of time the well-marked separation between the body and the neck became obliterated and smoothed over, so that forms arose such as figs. 3*–6*, also from Thuringia. The five following specimens from Holstein and Holland, figs. 7*–11*, and the three from Jutland, figs. 12*–14*, all seem to be derived from a form like fig. 1*, and are also known as curvilinear beakers (*geschweifte Becher*), a term first applied to them by Tischler. Other examples from Denmark and Rügen are figured by O. Montelius.[1]

It will be noticed that in the typical cord-beaker the ornament does not cover the whole vessel, and in many well-made examples the neck alone is decorated. When the ornament of the cord-beaker is arranged in alternate plain and decorated zones or bands, figs. 5*, 6*, Dr. Goetze supposes the maker of the beaker has been influenced by seeing examples of the bell- or zone-beaker, in which the ornamentation is always so arranged. On this account he considers these two classes of ceramic to be partly contemporary. In an example from Hebenkies, Wiesbaden, with an angular shoulder as in fig. 38*, but more slender than the latter, the whole surface of the vessel is decorated, but it is evidently a latish specimen, as the ill-formed amphora, which accompanied it, shows.[2]

---

[1] *Chronologie d. alt. Bronzezeit in N.-Deutschland*, figs. 241, 242, 245, 289, 291.

[2] Schumacher, *Alterth. uns. heid. Vorzeit*, V. Band, Tafel xlix, Fig. 852.

B

Vessels of the cord-ceramic have been found with faceted stone hammers, with small, nearly rectangular, stone celts of rectangular section, and once only with metal in the shape of a small finger-ring of bronze, poor in tin. With few exceptions the mode of interment was by inhumation, the body being laid in a pit-grave and then covered by a low tumulus.[1] The examples from Holstein and Jutland, figs. 7*–14*, were found singly in graves under tumuli, sometimes with a stone axe, and belong to the last part of the Neolithic Period.[2]

Dr. Goetze has further published the account of a recently explored neolithic tumulus near Poserna, Weissenfels, in Thuringia. It contained a cord-beaker like fig. 13*, a flat stone celt, a flint saw, a spiral cylinder of flat copper or bronze wire with a diameter of three-quarters of an inch, and making three and a half turns, also a small spiral ear-ring, making a turn and a half, of the same metal. In another tumulus near the last there was found a late amphora and a cord-beaker in form not very unlike fig. 11 from Somerset, though the former is rather more angular at the greatest diameter. (*Praehist. Zeitschrift*, i. 191–5 (1909).)

THE BELL- OR ZONE-BEAKER.

This type of vessel from its form is often called a bell-beaker, but from its scheme of ornament Goetze terms it a zone-beaker. For purposes of decoration the cord technique was no longer used, and for it was substituted that made by an instrument such as a cogged wheel or a notched and curved slip of wood, which when pressed upon the wet clay, left small square depressions at short intervals. These small holes were often filled with a white substance, which greatly enhanced the appearance of the vessel by making the design stand out in white against the darker ground of the surface. Yet the ornament, as was also the case with the cord-beaker, was sometimes incised with a pointed instrument.

The bell-beaker has a wide range, though very different from that of the cord-ceramic. Examples are known from Spain, Portugal, the south and north-west of France, Sardinia, Sicily, N. Italy, the Middle and Lower Rhine, Holland, Great Britain, the Upper Danube, the neighbourhood of Buda-Pest, Moravia, Bohemia, Thuringia, and Saxony. Specimens have also been found, though rather rarely, in Prussia, Pomerania, Mecklenburg, and Hanover.[3] Perhaps Holstein should be included, as figs. 45*–47* seem to belong to the type, especially the latter, which is ornamented with the 'square notch' technique.

Where this type of ceramic first came to light and where was the focus from which it spread over a large part of Europe are not known for certain. Dr. O. Montelius has no doubt that it is of Eastern origin. For the form he cites several curvilinear vessels from Troy, and with regard to the form and scheme of ornament he supposes that the alternate plain and ornamented zones which characterize the type are imitations of the alternately painted and plain zones seen on Egyptian pottery of the twelfth dynasty. But if we accept the recent dating of the Egyptian dynasties, the period of the twelfth dynasty from 2000–1800 B.C. falls rather too late. In Sicily, the south-east of Spain, and the south of France we find specimens such as figs. 15*–18*, all very similar in form, with the greatest diameter placed low down and

---

[1] Goetze, *Z. E.* (1900), pp. 260–3; P. Reinecke, *Westdeutsche Zeitschr. f. Geschichte u. Kunst*, xix, Hefte iii und iv, pp. 223–8.

[2] Montelius, *Chronologie*, p. 119.

[3] Reinecke, *op. cit.* pp. 231–2.

characterized by a very simple scheme of ornament arranged in alternately plain and ornamented zones. Hardly anything could be simpler. On this account it may be presumed that these are earlier than examples in which triangles or the 'metopic'[1] motives appear, or in which the greatest diameter is removed to a higher position. The specimen from Sicily, fig. 15*, is certainly exotic, and like those from Spain and the south of France belongs to the aeneolithic period. In Central and Northern Europe this style of zone ornament is confined to a single form of pottery and on that account it leaves the impression that this type of vessel is foreign and not native in the soil. But in a grotto near Cagliari in Sardinia, with a fragment of a bell-beaker bearing the same decoration as fig. 15*, was found a handled cup ornamented with similar zones, showing that this style of decoration was not there confined to a single kind of vessel.[2]

Some years ago Dr. Arthur Evans recorded his opinion on a label attached to a caliciform vessel from Los Minares (grave 18), in the Ashmolean Museum, that this type diffused from the Iberian Peninsula to West Gaul, Britain, and other parts of North-western Europe. And that it may have originated in a textile form of Esparto grass, like a basket of this form from an early Andalusian cave.[3] M. Louis Siret has arrived at a like conclusion and pointed out to me in his collection some fragments of true Neolithic Age which are ornamented in zones alternately plain and decorated, the lines being made with a notched instrument precisely in the same way as is found on caliciform vessels in Spain. Two fragments decorated in this way have been figured by M. L. Siret.[4] Recently Dr. Hubert Schmidt has also arrived at the conclusion that the original home of the bell-beaker or caliciform vessel is to be looked for in the south-west of Europe, that is to say in the Iberian Peninsula.[5] This seems highly probable, for in Spain we find many examples of neolithic round-bottom pottery with a cavetto neck from which such forms as those represented by figs. 15*, 16*, could easily be derived by merely flattening the base and rounding a little the angle at the shoulder.[6]

Certainly this style of decoration took firm root in the Iberian Peninsula where it arrived at great perfection and was applied to a considerable number of forms. Two examples from the celebrated find at Ciempozuelos in the province of Madrid are shown by figs. 20*, 21*. Other specimens of this ware, richly ornamented, were discovered by Mr. George Bonsor near Carmona in the valley of the Guadalquiver.[7] On the whole, then, there seems to be a great probability that the bell-beaker originated in Spain and, in company perhaps with copper, first spread eastwards to Sardinia and Sicily and then north and north-westwards into Central Europe where its eastern limit is the longitude of Buda-Pest. The type appears to have reached Brittany at a fairly early period, for some of the examples from there (figs. 22*–26*) show the same arrangement of plain and simply decorated zones as on the specimen from Sicily.[8]

---

[1] This term is applied to a zone divided into fields or panels by several vertical lines, an arrangement which recalls a Doric frieze composed of alternate metopes and triglyphs.

[2] *Bull. Pal. Ital.* xxiv, tav. xviii, figs. 3, 4, 7.

[3] A modern African basket with almost the form of fig. 19*, with alternate dark and light coloured zones is figured by Herr C. Schuchhardt, *Praehist. Zeitschr.* i. 42, fig. 1.

[4] *Anthropologie*, xx. 318, fig. 64, *b, c.*

[5] *Praehist. Zeitschr.* i. 131 (1909).

[6] H. and L. Siret, *Les premiers âges du métal etc.* pl. lv, nos. 41, 45 ; pl. lvi, no. 592.

[7] *Revue Archéol.* xxxv (1899), figs. 117, 121.

[8] Dr. A. Schliz seems to make Brittany the focus from which bell-beakers were spread over a large part of Europe, but he does not support this assertion by any proof (*Zeitschr. f. Ethn.* xxxviii (1906), p. 334).

Although Erd, a little south of Buda-Pest, lies far away to the east, fig. 27* is not very different in form from fig. 23* from Carnac in Brittany. Both, however, differ a good deal from figs. 15*, 16*, which seem to represent the oldest form. It is sometimes supposed that this form of vessel was exported from some centre or other, but another Hungarian example is ornamented with two zones each composed of a single row of small circles, a motive found frequently on other forms of pottery in Hungary but not elsewhere.[1] This piece must therefore have been made in the country and not imported, though of course the first example was introduced from abroad. In Bohemia, several well-formed specimens like fig. 27* have been figured by Dr. Pič,[2] but the motives of ornament often show a considerable development when compared with the simple diagonal shading of fig. 15 and on that account are no doubt of later date (v. *Tables of Ornament*, Pl. iv).

In figs. 28*–47*, the last three from Holstein, we see specimens of the bell-beaker and the gradual decay of its forms in Germany, a result for which a considerable length of time must be assumed. The first three examples from Rottleben near Rudolstadt and Bitterfeld, about twenty miles north of Leipzig, are excellent specimens and do not differ much in form from the Hungarian vessel, although the 'metopic' motives on the two from Rottleben and the 'false relief' technique upon the other, show that they have been made under local influences and were not imported from Western Europe. In these three examples, which seem the earliest of those here figured, the greatest diameter lies rather low down, but in the next four (figs. 32*–35*) it has a tendency to rise and the lower part of the vessel begins to flatten. This development ends with figs. 37*–39*, from Andernach and Urmitz on the Rhine, for in these the profile at the greatest diameter is nearly angular and its position is higher than before. Fig. 42*, also from Urmitz, is much better formed than fig. 39*, but the height of the greatest diameter seems to betray its later date.

It was mentioned above that the cord-beaker from Hebenkies near Wiesbaden, though more slender, has a profile quite similar to fig. 38* and the former is doubtless descended from a normal cord-beaker such as figs. 1*, 2*. With the Hebenkies vessel another cord-beaker was found not differing much in form except that the body is more rounded and the profile shows a continuous undulation from base to lip. The neck expands towards the lip as in fig. 4* but in a much greater degree. On the same plate as these two vessels Dr. Schumacher illustrates two other cord-beakers (figs. 866, 867), from near Bingen and from near Giessen, with nearly angular profiles much like figs. 37*, 38*, but more slender. A doubt may therefore arise whether figs. 37*, 38*, and the links which lead up to them (figs. 32*–35*), are really derived, as suggested, from genuine bell-beakers or not. Using the 'square notch' technique as a test, we find it certainly on figs. 35*, 37*, 39* and perhaps on fig. 34*, and that circumstance coupled with their ornamentation in zones makes it extremely probable, if not quite certain, that this series was derived from a bell-beaker prototype. The explanation therefore is, that starting from two different points the same goal was reached. At a certain stage in their development the cord-beaker and the bell-beaker had each a tendency to flatten the curve between the base and the greatest diameter, but the different origin of these later examples can still be detected, if other criteria fail, by the relative stoutness of the offshoots of the bell-beaker and the great slenderness

---

[1] Wosinsky, *Inkrust. Keramik*, Taf. lxxviii. 3.   [2] *Čechy predhist.* tab. i. 2 ; xxxv. 9 ; xxxix. 1, 3, 4, 5.

of examples descended from a cord-beaker prototype. For instance, the lower part of fig. 46* from Holstein is plain, as in cord-beakers, and the zones are not normal; and yet, owing to its stoutness and outline, this example seems to be derived from a bell-beaker. It does not follow, however, that though these two types of ceramic reached the same goal that this event happened at the same time. The probability is that the cord-beaker arrived first, as it seems to have begun earlier in time, though both were to some extent contemporary.

Vessels like figs. 43*, 44* are so formless and pot-like that we must consider them as a late phase in the evolution of the beaker.

On reaching Holland we find a Batavian type (figs. 49*–53*), the forms of which differ decidedly from those of Central Europe. All show a well-marked constriction at the base of the neck. A certain tendency in this direction is seen on two cord-beakers from Holstein (figs. 10*, 11*) and on a bell-beaker also from Holstein (fig. 47*) as well as on the pot-like fig. 44* from Andernach on the Rhine. The neck is short and sometimes upright, and the examples in which this is found are probably later than the others in which it is everted. In the scheme of ornamentation the plain zones have generally disappeared and the lower part of the vessel is sometimes left plain. The metopic motives survive, but the lines which formed the crosses are replaced by bars. Everything points to the Batavian type being later in time than the bell-beakers considered hitherto, and if we compare it with the examples from Sicily and Spain (figs. 15*, 16*) we may feel convinced that the two series must be separated by several centuries.

The Date of the Bell-Beaker Type.

Hitherto the bell-beaker has been considered from a typological view, and the changes in form and ornamentation which it underwent in its slow migration from south to north have been traced. It remains to learn what objects of stone and metal have been found associated with this type, in order to see if any corroboration can be obtained in support of the view that southern examples are really earlier than those of Central Europe.

Fig. 15 * was found in a cave at Villafrati near Corleone in Sicily. The cave was not explored under proper supervision, but Mr. Peet considers the contents of the cave to be late neolithic.[1] Dr. O. Montelius assigns to this bell-beaker a date of about 2500 B.C. or earlier.[2] If this dating is approximately correct it also covers fig. 16 * from Millares in the province of Valencia, Spain. From a circular bee-hive chamber with a diameter of $2\frac{1}{2}$ m., entered by a short passage, at Purchena, Llano de la Atalaya (Almeria), M. Louis Siret showed me three caliciform vessels. One of grey colour, of hard paste, $6\frac{1}{8}$ in. high, is like fig. 16 *. The other two of soft paste are somewhat different. In one of these of brown and black colour, $5\frac{1}{2}$ in. high, the angle at the greatest diameter is a little more rounded, as in fig. 19 *. In the other of red and black colour, $4\frac{3}{4}$ in. high, the curve is still greater, like the lower part of fig. 23 *. The rest of the grave-goods consisted of a shallow, round-bottomed bowl with an ornamented zone, and several plain bowls; part of a flat axe, two knives, two awls of copper, a copper arrowhead of spatula form, a flint arrowhead with concave base and some shells. As the paste of the vessels is different, it is possible all three were not deposited at the same time and that the pair made of soft paste is later than the other.

A bell-beaker much like fig. 16 * in form, but with a row of hanging triangles along the uppermost zone, a mark of later date, was found by M. Casalis de Fonduce in an *allée couverte* at Castellet in Provence. Among other objects with it were a good many lance heads and lozenge-shaped arrowheads of flint and one with barbs and tang, a fine chisel-axe of green porphyry, beads of limestone and *callaïs*, a bead of gold $1\frac{3}{4}$ in. long, and a small plaque of the same metal.[3]

---

[1] Peet, *Stone and Bronze Age in Italy*, p. 125.   [2] Montelius, *Chronologie*, p. 88.   [3] *Matériaux*, xii. 446–63, pl. xv.

Figs. 17 *, 18 *, 19 * were found by M. Piette in the *allée couverte* La Halliade (H. Pyrénées) together with a polished flat axe of stone, a necklace of disc-shaped beads of *callaïs*, and an oblong plaque of gold formed by hammering several very thin leaves together.[1]

Figs. 20 *, 21 * were found near Ciempozuelos in the province of Madrid, some few miles to the south of the city. Eleven pieces of pottery were unearthed, consisting of various sorts of bowls, dishes and beaker-like vessels, the designs upon which were filled with a white matter. A copper arrowhead and an awl or pricker of the same metal were found with three of the vessels. None of the human bones found with any of the pottery had been burnt.[2] With very similar pottery from near Carmona in Andalucia, Mr. G. Bonsor found about thirty awls or prickers of copper, quite like the last mentioned.[3]

Fig. 22 * is quite plain and undecorated. It was found at Kerallant, St. Jean Brévelay, Brittany, with two other vases of different types, a fragment of gold, a worked flake of flint, and a small oblong plaque of schist. It is preserved in the Museum at Vannes.

Fig. 25 * from the dolmen of Er-roh, La Trinité sur Mer, was found with a barbed flint arrowhead, a bead of agalmatite over an inch long, and a fragment of a wooden bracelet.

Figs. 28 *, 29 * from Rottleben, Rudolstadt, were found with a stone bracer or wrist-guard of slightly curved section, with two perforations at each end. Similar bracers are known in Great Britain, Thuringia, Bohemia, Moravia, Italy, Sardinia and France.

A bell-beaker from Eisleben very similar in form to the last two was found with a rudely made triangular dagger, apparently of copper, measuring $4\frac{1}{8}$ in. long, with a broad tang. In outline it resembles a rude copper dagger from near Cagliari and a better formed one, also of copper but with a shorter tang, from Remedello in the province of Brescia.[4]

A bell-beaker from Stelchoves in Bohemia, in form not unlike fig. 35 * but with a rather more rounded and globular body, was found with a rude bronze or copper dagger $4\frac{3}{4}$ in. long including the tang, the edges of which are beaten up so as to curl over, a stone bracer with three perforations at each end and a fragment of a flat stone celt. These objects are figured by Dr. Pič.[5]

Figs. 39 *, 40 *, 42 * from Urmitz, and figs. 37 *, 38 *, 44 * from Andernach, were found on inhabited sites, I believe, and not in graves.

Fig. 46 * from Edeberg, Lensahn, in Holstein, was found with a flint axe.

Fig. 49 * from Wageningen, Gelderland, though found by itself, is stated by Dr. Pleyte to belong to the same time as two bronze daggers, each with three rivets and with a groove parallel to the cutting edge, a bronze flat axe considerably expanded at the cutting edge, and a bangle of thin bronze wire, all of which he figures.[6]

Fig. 48 * from Brummen, Gelderland, was discovered with burnt bones.[7]

Fig. 50 * from Beekbergen, Gelderland, belongs to the same period as the beaker from Brummen.[8]

Figs. 51 *, 52 * from Epe, Gelderland, were found in a tumulus with an axe-hammer of diorite $6\frac{7}{8}$ in. in length and a plate of hard slate with a hole at each end.[9]

Fig. 53 * from near Epe, Gelderland, was found full of ashes and bones, on the top of which lay a bronze pin with a semi-conical head, a bronze bracelet with expanded ends and a socketed bronze celt.[10]

The result of this review of the finds made with bell-beakers confirms what was suggested at the beginning of the chapter, that the southern examples of the Mediterranean area are older than those of Central Europe. Though the small bronze dagger from Eisleben might well be earlier than that from Remedello, the cemetery of which Montelius dates between 2100 and 1950 B.C., its date could not be pushed back to 2500 B.C. or earlier, the date assigned

---

[1] *Matériaux*, xvi. 528–33.

[2] *Boletín de la R. Acad. de la Historia*, xxv. 437.

[3] *Rev. Archéol.* xxxv. 88, 89 117.

[4] Colini, *Bull. paletnol. ital.* xxiv, tav. xvii. 1 and tav. ix. 1.

[5] Pič, *op. cit.* i. 83.

[6] *Nederland. Oudheden*, pl. xi and p. 49 (text).

[7] *Op. cit.* pl. xii. 2, p. 50.

[8] *Op. cit.* pl. xxii. 2, p. 78.

[9] *Op. cit.* pl. xxiv. 1, 2, text p. 88.

[10] *Op. cit.* pl. xxiv. 5–8, text p. 89.

to the Sicilian example. Though the Eisleben specimen is a fairly early one, there is reason to assume that all the bell-beakers of Central Europe are later than figs. 15*, 16*, and that the latest examples reach down to about 2000 B.C. Evidently none of the Batavian examples can be placed earlier than that date, and the last specimen, if really descended from a bell-beaker, belongs to the later part of the Bronze Age.

From the above it follows that merely from their geographical position the British beakers about to demand our attention must be later on the whole than those of Central Europe, and yet not so far apart in time as to make it difficult or impossible to derive one from the other. It is doubtful, I believe, if any British beaker can be dated earlier than 2000 B.C.

At the beginning of the chapter it was mentioned that the invaders of Britain, who brought beakers with them, were brachycephalic, although, since a certain mixture of cranial types began early in Europe, it is quite probable that among them were persons with dolichocephalic and mesaticephalic skulls. In this connexion may be mentioned a brachycephalic skull with a cephalic index of 87.43, found with a bell-beaker at Wahlwies on the Stockach in Baden, and described and figured by Dr. A. Schliz.[1]

A map shows the position of the German and Batavian bell-beakers of which illustrations are given, and also the position of Wahlwies in Baden.

THE ORNAMENTATION.

On Plate IV are shown eight examples of motives from cord-beakers. We may observe the shaded hanging triangles; the bar-chevron brought out by horizontal shading; and the panels or fields by the vertical lines which bound them. The fields are left blank, and this arrangement seems to be the beginning from which the more advanced 'metopic' motive developed by filling in the metope or panel with some simple design.

On the same Plate are exhibited twenty-six examples of motives found on bell-beakers in Bohemia and Germany. The very simple motives of oblique or crossed lines on vessels from Sicily, Spain, and France are best seen on the illustrations of the vessels themselves. In the south and north-west of Gaul the ornamented zone might occasionally be composed of triangles or of lozenges, but never of bar-chevrons or metopic motives. Although tradition taught that ornamentation should be applied in zones, we find some infringement of the rule at a fairly early time, for instead of leaving blank spaces at intervals the whole body of the vessel was marked with a cord wound spirally round it, as in fig. 17*,[2] or with parallel lines made with the 'square notch' technique.[3]

In Bohemia we find the shaded lozenge, the chequer surface pattern, the bar-chevron on a shaded ground, and varieties of metopic motives in use for decorative purposes.

In Germany, where some of the vessels are later, there is a greater variety of design. The motives that found favour were hanging triangles shaded horizontally, line-chevrons, the trellis motive, various metopic combinations, the hatched lozenge and the shaded bar-

[1] *Z. E.* xxxviii (1907), pp. 338–41.

[2] The absence of plain zones on fig. 17* results from the technique of the ornamentation. This was evidently produced by winding a cord round the vessel, and it would have been manifestly inconvenient to interrupt the winding in order to form several plain zones.

[3] P. du Chatellier, *La Poterie etc.*, pl. ii. 1; pl. viii. 2

chevron. These last two designs are on a larger scale than in Bohemia, and are intersected by a narrow plain band. This intersection is a more recent innovation, for we see it on vessels with an angular profile from Andernach, which we have found reason to believe are of later date than those with well-rounded body.

In the Batavian type the plain bands were reduced to a minimum of depth, and sometimes the lower part of the vessel was left plain. The leading motives employed were the lozenge border with the lateral triangles shaded, metopic designs in which the cross is represented by two cross bars instead of two cross-lines, and the bar line-chevron which is seen on fig. 52*.

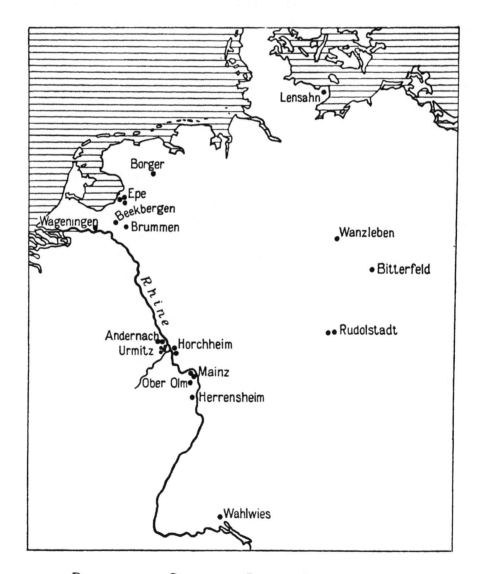

DISTRIBUTION OF GERMAN AND BATAVIAN BELL-BEAKERS.

CHAPTER II

BRITISH CERAMIC

As far back as 1871 the late Dr. Thurnam published an admirable and learned monograph on 'Ancient British Barrows',[1] in which he discussed the structure of round barrows and their contents. This led to a description and classification of all the sepulchral pottery known to him in great Britain and Ireland [2] and to an account, profusely illustrated, of the objects of bronze, stone, bone, &c., that have been brought to light in connexion with British interments. Owing to Dr. Thurnam's great learning and to the generous number of illustrations with which his monograph is provided, it will always remain, though no longer up to date in some respects, a valuable storehouse of information.

In describing the various classes of pottery he seems to have taken them in what he believed to be their chronological order. A number of rudely made vessels are arranged under seven headings as *Culinary Pottery*. Then follow *Sepulchral Pottery—Cinerary urns* of various types, Incense Cups, *Food vessels* of different types, and lastly *Drinking Cups* of three types. These he supposed to belong to a late period when, from different causes, as the influence perhaps indirect of Roman culture, the burial of weapons had become rare.[3] But the idea that beakers [4] or 'drinking cups' were late in time was certainly erroneous; the sequel will show that this class of ceramic must take precedence of the other classes in order of time.

THE BEAKER CLASS

Vessels of this class are hand-made, usually from 6 to 9 in. high, with thin walls made of clay tempered with sand or finely pounded stone. The surface of the vessel has often a polished appearance from being smoothed and rubbed with a stone or a piece of bone. The vessels were fairly well baked in an open fire and assume a yellowish, light brown or drab colour, though a few are red or reddish. The ornament is profuse and arranged in horizontal zones with plain bands between, as in Continental bell-beakers. This class of pottery is found almost invariably with skeleton interments [5] under barrows, though a few instances have been noted where there was no indication that a tumulus had ever existed.

---

[1] *Arch.* xliii. 285–552.

[2] *Op. cit.* pp. 331–400.   [3] *Op. cit.* p. 389.

[3] For 'drinking cup', a term introduced only at the beginning of the last century by Sir R. Hoare, I have substituted the term 'beaker' as being (1) more compact and (2) international—corresponding with Becher, Bägere, Bæger, Bicchiere, words used by the archaeologists of Germany, Sweden, Denmark, and Italy to designate a class of vessel very similar to the 'drinking cup', but with reference to its form, not to its supposed purpose.

Furthermore there is every reason to believe that this vessel, as Canon Greenwell pointed out long ago (*B. B.* p. 102), served the same purpose as a food vessel.

[5] Exceptions are only found in five places; with beaker 93 b from Glamorgan, with beakers 136, 137 from same grave at Rudstone, with figs. 166–71 in two adjoining cists at Hexham, with fig. 161 from Aberdeenshire, with fig. 267 from Banffshire. Figs. 16, 203 from Devonshire and Stirlingshire were both secondary interments, and the primary ones were with cremation.

Thurnam distinguished three principal types and named them after the first three letters of the Greek alphabet. I have retained the three types and his description of them below, but for typographical reasons have substituted A, B, C.

A.   High-brimmed, globose cup.

B.   Ovoid cup with recurved rim.

C.   Low-brimmed cup.

A.   *High-brimmed globose beaker.* This is the prevailing type in South Britain, to which probably four-fifths of known examples belong. The body is more or less globular; the upper part, separated from the body by a constriction, frequently very defined, spreads out like the calyx of a flower and forms a brim or neck that almost equals the body in height. The sides of the neck or rim, whether more or less erect or sloping, are straight and not recurved at the lip.

B.   *Ovoid beaker with recurved rim.* In this there is no distinct demarcation between the body and the rim, but the one glides into the other by a gradual curve. The brim is of slight elevation and in the Wilts. examples is curved outwards at the lip. The body, instead of being globular, is oval. More attention seems paid to the fabric than to decoration. The walls are thinner than in any other variety of British fictile vessels and as they have been well fired the colour is red, almost as bright as that of Samian ware.

C.   *Low-brimmed beaker.* This form, which prevails in Scotland and Northumberland, north of the Roman Wall, may be regarded as a debased variety of our first type. As compared with A the body is rather oval than globular and the brim much lower, not more than one-third or one-fourth of the height of the body.[1]

Thurnam's descriptions of the three types into which he divided the beaker class are excellent in their way, but a number of specimens exist the form of which is not covered by them. I have therefore found it necessary to add the sub-type B2 and the varieties AC, AB, BC. The only difference between A and AC is that in the latter the constriction lies higher than in A and therefore approximates its position in C.

AB is a variety of vessel which appears to be derived from A, but yet has a general likeness to B.

Similarly BC is a compound variety which sometimes is, or seems to be, derived from C, but in which the angle between the neck and shoulder has become a curve, giving the profile a resemblance to type B.

As the object of this study is to arrange the beakers as near as may be in chronological order, so as to form a rough time-scale that will subserve the purposes of history, the best plan is to study the pottery in geographical order, noting local differences as they occur in our peregrination from south to north; for it must be assumed, not without reason, that the course of the new comers took that direction. This method will show better than any other that the advance of the invaders was not rapid and that to know the geographical position of the place where a beaker was found often gives us at once a general idea of its date with respect to the first arrival of the new colonists. With this end in view I have divided Great Britain into seven provinces :—

[1] *Arch.* xliii. 391–4.

PROVINCE I. THE AREA SOUTH OF THE THAMES

TYPE A.

After inspecting the examples of type A, figs. 1–18 *bis*, the first thing that attracts our attention is the fact that the type cannot be recognized in any pottery east of the Rhine.

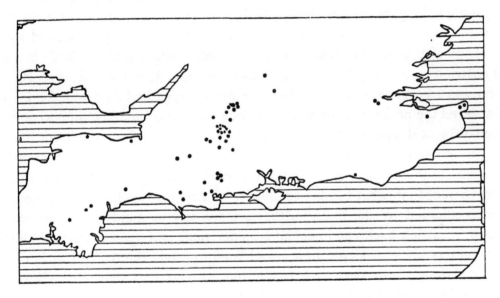

PROVINCE I.

The scheme of ornament and the motives that compose it are quite similar to those on the bell-beakers and cannot be separated from them, but the form of the vessels is different; the essential distinction being the constriction at the base of the neck in type A.   In a paper on 'The oldest Bronze Age ceramic type in Britain',[1] published in 1902, I hazarded the opinion that the beakers with globular bodies, like figs. 7, 2, 3, might be derived from cord-beakers such as figs. 1*, 2*, 3*, though they took their scheme of ornament from the bell-beaker.   But further consideration has convinced me that such an origin is unlikely, for though the date of the cord-beakers is not certain, it appears to be too early for our purpose and the vessels seem never to have developed in the direction of our type A in respect of their ornamentation.   We must therefore look elsewhere for its origin.   It is true that the Batavian type shows a constriction at the base of the neck, but the resultant vessel corresponds with type C, which in

---

[1] *J. A. I.* xxxii. 391–2.

Britain, as the sequel will make manifest, is certainly later than the beginning of type A. The nearest analogy then to this type is to be found in Central Spain, figs. 20*, 21*, vessels which are undoubtedly older than the Batavian examples. Consequently we have to suppose that at a period intermediate between the Ciempozuelos and the Batavian types, a third parallel development—though the second in time—took place among the people who invaded Britain, very near the time when the invasion occurred.

Figs. 1–18 *bis* seem to form a series from shapely to shapeless forms and the question remains—Which end of the series is the earliest?[1] The answer is not doubtful. A comparison of fig. 1 with figs. 20*, 21*, and fig. 18 with fig. 53*, makes it clear that in fig. 1 the well-rounded body, the splayed neck, and the well-preserved tradition with respect to the zone-ornament are early features characteristic of the Ciempozuelos type, but entirely wanting in figs. 17, 18, these being as shapeless and pot-like as fig. 53*. The lower half of the older bell-beakers east of the Rhine is well rounded, and it is probably to forms like fig. 27* from Hungary and fig. 30* from Bitterfeld that the constriction which gave rise to type A was first applied.

Having settled the point that a globose body was an original feature, we observe that as time went on the lower part of the body gradually flattened, leaving a rounded shoulder, till the original shape of the beaker ultimately disappeared. Still a globose body is not of itself a necessary criterion of an early beaker; it is true for type A, but not for type C, where the globular form was long preserved, even after the former type had died out, for in judging of the date of a vessel the ornamentation and technique must also be taken into account.

Yet it may be said, granted that fig. 1 has the appearance of an old form and fig. 18 of a pot, what proof exists that this deterioration of form took place progressively in order of time and not accidentally in any part of the beaker period, in such a way that specimens can be picked out and arranged in what has the semblance of a regular evolution? No help to answer this question is afforded by the finds, for they are too few in number and too indecisive in character, so we must fall back upon general considerations and upon analogy. Although it is probable that potters when making a new vessel tried to retain the traditional form, they were naturally inclined to perform their task easily and without excessive expenditure of effort. Rounded forms being more difficult to mould by hand were naturally and unconsciously flattened a little; another generation having only these to imitate flattened the curves still more, and so on in succeeding generations till the beaker became a mere pot. This process of course was not quite uniform all over the country and some potters naturally were better and more conscientious than others, but as they were always working under the restraint of tradition which hindered without quite stopping invention, the forms they reproduced did not deviate much from those forms current in their generation and in their locality. For when two or more beakers of rather different shape have been found with the same interment, the difference between them can always be explained by supposing they were made by women of different ages or who came from different parts of the province. That the revival of old forms which had passed away was impossible is shown by the fact that type A becomes rarer the further north we travel, and never passed beyond the Tay. If archaizing had been possible—in

[1] It must be understood that though we may be sure of the general course of the development the actual position in time of one piece with respect to its imme- diate neighbours is uncertain. For instance, figs. 2, 3, 5 may be a little older than or contemporary with fig. 1, yet it is certain all belong to the early part of the series.

other words, if any form of beaker could be produced at any part of the beaker period—this fact could not have occurred. It is well known that spoken languages are in a state of movement and subject to gradual morphological change, and that every uneducated man speaks the language of his own generation and not that of several generations ago. Although the changes that take place in language are very much slower than those observable in beaker forms, there is, I believe, this analogy between them, the movement advances steadily forward in one direction, not backwards and forwards in a chaotic and lawless manner. Hence it is reasonable to suppose that the changes of form in the beaker were stages in an evolution steadily advancing in one direction and that potters reproduced the forms current in their generation just as they spoke the language of their own time and not of any other.

After this prelude to justify a belief in an orderly evolution of beakers as they succeeded each other in time, we can begin to examine more closely the series of type A from fig. 1 to 18 *bis*, which embraces twenty-six beakers, though only twenty-three are here reproduced. To form a time-scale with large divisions it may be divided into three phases. Phase I, figs. 1–8; Phase II, figs. 9–16; Phase III, figs. 17–18 *bis*.

In all examples of Phase I the constriction is nearly at the middle, and at first is sharply defined, but afterwards the angle becomes rounded ; the body is nearly globular, the neck has an outward splay and with one exception there are at least three plain bands or zones. It might be supposed that a very globose beaker like fig. 6,[1] where the body passes into the neck with a sweeping curve, illustrated a transition from the bell-beaker to type A, but I believe that its relative height is opposed to such a suggestion, and that the curve is due to effacement of the original angle just as in fig. 8.

In Phase II the curvature of the lower part of the body flattens by degrees, leaving a rounded shoulder which passes with a slight curve into the neck, and this near the end of the series is hardly splayed outwards, becoming nearly vertical. Figs. 11, 12, and 20 of type B 1 were found by Mr. St. George Gray as secondary non-central interments in different parts of the same barrow and are not separated by any great length of time, probably by not more than a generation. The first of these beakers was found at a depth of 3 ft. 3 in. from the top of the barrow, the second at a depth of 3 ft., and the example of B 1 at the depth of 2 ft. This important find proves that the two types A and B 1 were at any rate partly contemporary. Dr. Thurnam cited fig. 16 as an example of type B,[2] but the inward curve of the neck, seen also in fig. 15 and in a much slighter degree in fig. 13, have induced me to regard it as a late example of type A. It is well to note that it belonged to a secondary interment, the primary one consisting of cinerary urn (fig. 458), of food-vessel type, inverted over a deposit of burnt bones.

Phase III consists of three specimens which show but slight traces of their origin and descent; there are no plain zones, the whole surface being covered with punctures and incisions made with a pointed instrument. Fig. 18 was found with the skeleton of a child, a fact which may partly account for the negligence displayed in the workmanship. The last of all, fig. 18 *bis*, shows a slight raised moulding about an inch below the lip.

---

[1] On the vessel is written Brenley, Kent, a name which I cannot find, and suppose it is intended for Brendly near Faversham in north Kent.

[2] *Arch.* xliii. 393.

Finds made with type A are mentioned in detail below, so it is sufficient to state now that bronze in the shape of a bronze dagger appears first in Phase I with fig. 4a[1]; in Phase II with figs. 10, 13, 13 *tris*. The objects that accompanied figs. 1, 4, 4 *bis* belong to an early period, but they are of a kind which lasted so long that they afford no real assistance in dating the beakers with respect to each other. With figs. 4, 12 was found a fine flint dagger.

Type B.[2]

Sub-type B 1.

This subtype contains nineteen beakers from fig. 19 to 35, two of which are not reproduced, and may be divided into two phases; Phase I, figs. 19–24; Phase II, figs. 25–33. What we have learnt from observing the evolution of bell-beaker forms on the Continent makes it probable that beakers in which the greatest swell lies comparatively low are older than those in which it is near the middle, and that a flattening of the curves indicates a later date in the series. Figs. 19, 21 from Wilts. may both be compared with figs. 33*, 34* from Horchheim, and fig. 24, also from Wilts., with fig. 42* from Urmitz on the Rhine. The angularity at the line of the greatest diameter seen on figs. 37*, 38* from Andernach on the Rhine recurs on figs. 25, 26, 28, 30 from Dorset and Wilts. The parallelism therefore between the Rhenish and the British beakers is complete and they only differ in one respect, viz. that on the latter ornamented zones are narrower and composed of simpler motives, more analogous to what is found in Brittany and Holstein, (fig. 47*.)

In Phase I the greatest swell of the body lies comparatively low, though, with the exception of fig, 23, not so low as in the older Continental specimens. Fig. 20 is a very well formed example, but the absence of plain zones makes me hesitate to set it before fig. 19. It belongs to about the same time as figs. 11, 12, both of which are placed in Phase II of type A.

In Phase II, figs. 25–33, the greatest diameter lies rather higher than in Phase I, the curve of the walls flattens and becomes angular; at the end of the series the beaker is nearly formless. The decoration is very simple, more so than in Phase I, and in the main consists of several narrow zones, alternately plain and ornamented. Figs. 34, 35, from north-east Kent, seem to belong to B 1, though to which phase is uncertain; so, partly from that uncertainty and partly from their small size, I have not ranged them with the others. They only measure 4 in. in height and appear to belong rather to domestic than to sepulchral pottery. That beakers were used for ordinary domestic purposes will be proved later on when we have reached Province V.

Sub-type B 2.

This small group, consisting of four examples (figs. 36–8) one of which is not reproduced,[3] is characterized by a somewhat ovoid body passing into a very short neck. The general form

---

[1] This beaker is only known from an old and probably not very correct illustration. The body is bulbous but the neck is rather short, as in fig. 4.

[2] Since this was in type I have received from Mr. Herbert Druitt a photograph of a very fine specimen of type B found near Christchurch, Hants. Height 5⅝ in. It is better formed than fig. 19, is more slender and

shows six narrow ornamented zones. Unfortunately it is too late to reproduce this early beaker.

[3] It is 4½ inches high, was found near Canterbury and is figured *Vict. Hist. Kent*, i. 324. For figs. 36, 37, I am much indebted to Mr. W. M. Newton of Dartford, Kent, who sent me the photographs.

recalls that of fig. 43* from Herrensheim in Rhein-Hessen. None of these examples exceeds 5½ in. in height and their chronological position with respect to type A is uncertain, though a necklace of thin bronze leaf rolled into small cylinders, which was found with fig. 38, makes it possible that this example is later than the beginning of A.

No flint daggers have been observed as yet with this type, though one had been deposited with fig. 12 of type A in the same barrow as fig. 20 of type B 1. Metallic daggers, however, were found with figs. 19, 21, 24. The first two of these have quite recently been analysed by Prof. Gowland and found to be of pure copper. On this account it is not impossible that these two beakers are contemporary with Phase I of type A.

Variant BC.

The body presents a fine oval curve and passes with a curve into a relatively short neck, which generally appears to be flat, though sometimes a slight curve may be observed.

This variant embraces six beakers, figs. 39–42 *bis*, one of which is not here reproduced.[1] Its nearest analogue on the Continent is fig. 42* from Urmitz on the Rhine, and it is evidently derived from type B, but the constriction lies so high and the neck is so apt to become straight that it soon passes into type C. Naturally Thurnam regarded fig. 41 as an example of type B, but the absence of plain bands shows that it is a late specimen, dating from the time when the old tradition was enfeebled, and the curve of the neck, measured from the constriction, was already comparatively flat. In fig. 42 on the other hand the neck shows a slight inward curve which quite detaches it from B. Fig. 42 *bis* from Somerset perhaps belongs to this group. It shows that a very simple motive, such as bands of parallel lines made with the point, is not necessarily a sign of superior age, for this example is evidently a very late one.

Type C.

This type seems to be represented in Province I by a single example, fig. 43, from Abingdon, Berks. No doubt in the future more specimens will be brought to light.[2]

PROVINCE II

This province extends from the Thames to the Humber, and includes Wales.

Type A.

There are twenty-seven examples of this type, see figs. 44–69, one of which is not reproduced. The development of type A is on the same lines as in the south.

Phase I includes the beakers from fig. 44 to 54.

---

[1] It was found near Lancombe, in the valley of the Plym, Devon. *Trans. Devon Ass.* xxxii. 46–51, fig. 1.

[2] Since this was written a very fine example, 9⅝ inches high, from Mortlake, has been published by Mr. Reginald A. Smith of the British Museum in *Ar.* lxii, pl. xxxviii, fig. 2. It has a tendency in the direction of the variety BC, and yet it is apparently contemporary with a neolithic round-bottomed vessel, *op. cit.* p. 340. This is not surprising, as the original inhabitants were in the neolithic stage when the invaders arrived, and their pottery remained unchanged for some time afterwards.

Phase II from fig. 55 to 66.

Phase III from fig. 67 to 69.

Although the general development is the same as south of the Thames, an interesting local variety occurs in Norfolk (fig. 44), the squat form of which may be compared with fig. 48* from Holland, though the position of the constriction is different. The East Anglian forms (figs. 44–7) all appear to be rather later than the earliest Wiltshire examples, though they belong to the same Phase. For instance, the lip of fig. 46 from Suffolk is bevelled and a similar bevel is found on three beakers from Staffordshire (figs. 55, 59, 60 of Phase II). In the last two the base of the bevel is accentuated by a raised moulding, while in fig. 66 from Northamptonshire the bevel is dispensed with, and only the raised moulding remains.

PROVINCE II.

Comparing the Derbyshire and Staffordshire examples of Phase I (figs. 48–54) with the similar Phase in Province I, it will be noticed that in the former the body being flatter near the base is less well rounded, the outward splay of the neck is generally less marked, the ornament on the whole is less well rendered, and the vessels leave the impression of inferior and less careful workmanship.

In Phase II the development of a raised moulding below the lip on figs. 59, 60 has already been noticed. On fig. 64 it will be observed that except near the top of the neck the ornament covers the whole vessel; on fig. 65 there is also no plain band. In these examples, which show deviations from the old tradition in the matter of ornament and are therefore relatively late, it will not escape notice that the form of the vessels has deteriorated greatly from the forms of Phase I.

Phase III, fig. 67, is not very unlike fig. 66 as regards its scheme of ornament, and there is some uncertainty as to where it was found.[1] Fig. 68 belonged to a secondary interment discovered at a considerable distance from the centre of the barrow and at no great depth below the surface, facts which of themselves make it likely that the beaker cannot be a very early example of its type.

Variety AB.

This variety consists of figs. 70, 71, and only differs from A in the fact that the profile forms a freer and more regular curve from the base to the lip whereby it approximates type B. There can be no question concerning its origin and its true affinities. The position of the smallest diameter and the straightness of the neck from that line upwards, make it quite clear that AB is a variety of A, and the curve between the body and the neck is only a slight exaggeration of the curve seen on other examples of A (figs. 52, 55, 63). Fig. 71 was found in the same barrow as fig. 56 and though from different graves they are of the same clay and fabric, and are probably contemporary. If the latter beaker is properly placed, then this variety belongs to the early part of Phase II. In Province I, fig. 6 might equally well be reckoned a member of this variety.

Type B.

Sub-type B 1.

This sub-type includes ten beakers, figs. 72–81, so diverse in form and with such gaps between them that they cannot be said to constitute a series. The first three, figs. 72–4, all of small size, with a height of $3\frac{3}{4}$–$4\frac{1}{2}$ in., are evidently related both by size and form to figs. 34, 35 from E. Kent. They came from near Taplow in Bucks., and the special interest attached to them is that they were discovered in removing several circles belonging to pit-dwellings and are apparently not sepulchral.[2] Fig. 75 from Oxford is an example of the taller kind ($7\frac{3}{4}$ in.) and is not very different from others in Wilts. and Dorset, though the absence of plain bands is to be observed. Fig. 76 from Huntingdon is a giant among beakers, measuring 10·8 in. in height, and the ornamentation shows that it cannot be considered an early example; so, too, the absence of plain zones of ornament on fig. 77 from Oxford tells the same tale. In fact, all the beakers of this sub-type seem to belong to a late date in the history of the beaker, though there is nothing to prove it, for with the exception of the Taplow vessels there is no record of the discovery of any of these beakers, and they were not accompanied by any grave furniture.

Sub-type B 2.

This sub-type seems to include five specimens, figs. 82–7, but the forms are so divergent and irregular that nothing can be done with them. Figs. 82, 83 from Brandon in Suffolk were

---

[1] In the Catalogue of the York Museum it is said to have come from Woolstone, Lincolnshire, but as I can find no place of that name in the county, I suppose it was found at Woolston on the Mersey, $2\frac{1}{2}$ miles from Warrington in South Lancashire. The abbreviation Lanc. has been misread as Linc. and then wrongly expanded.

[2] *Maidenhead Natur. Field Club, 8th ann. report* (1890–1), p. 46.

found together with a flat stone wrist-guard having three perforations at each end. The former much resembles fig. 38 from the coast of Sussex, though an inch shorter. All the specimens of this sub-type are under 6 inches in height—the first is only four inches high, and with the exception of fig. 84 the decoration is of the simplest kind. It is not impossible that they represent the domestic pottery of East Anglia at a latish period in the history of the beaker.

Fig. 88.

This beaker came from Derbyshire and is figured by Dr. Thurnam as an illustration of type B. It stood 7 in. high, was the only example of type B in that county or in Staffordshire, and the engraving of it is quite unlike any other beaker in Province II. As regards height and form it somewhat resembles fig. 20 from Somerset. But comparing it with two examples of AB, figs. 70, 71, and taking into consideration that woodcuts are rarely quite accurate, I suppose that, though in appearance it belongs to type B, it is really another example of the hybrid variant AB.

Type C.

This type consists of six examples, figs. 89–93. In what seem to be the older specimens, the oval body forms an angle with the neck, but this angle is very apt to become rounded and if this change is carried too far the variant BC is the result. When the body is ovoid it is natural to derive it from the variety BC, where this feature is characteristic; when it is more globular, as in fig. 90 from Norfolk, it may have originated from type A by raising the position of the constriction. Fig. 90 *bis* is figured by Thurnam, who considered it as an example of type B,[1]—the illustration is far from correct—but I have taken the straightness of the neck as the decisive test and perhaps it would be more accurate to class it under BC, certainly not under B. From the rarity of the type in the two southern provinces it seems evident that its evolution is comparatively late, though as yet there is no direct evidence to support this view nor to correlate it with the other types. But on reaching the next province we shall be in a better position to clear up several doubtful questions.[2]

[1] *Arch.* xliii. 393.

[2] Since this was written, a highly interesting find of beaker fragments in connexion with a prehistoric settlement and refuse pits on the River Nene near Peterborough, has been made by Mr. Wyman Abbott. (*Arch.* lxii. 333–9.) Most of the sherds from the pits belonged to beakers. One, that seems to have been found entire, is hardly 4 ins. high and belongs to type A (pl. xxxvii, fig. 1). Fragments that have been restored are of types A, AC, and their ornamentation agrees with what is found elsewhere.

With the beaker fragments were also found sherds of a different kind of ware. One fairly complete vessel is round-bottomed and of neolithic type. Mr. Reginald A. Smith, who comments on this vessel (*op. cit.* pp. 340–52), connects it with other neolithic vessels from Argyll, East Riding, Somerset, and with three vessels from the Thames, figured for the first time. From these neolithic vessels he would derive, quite rightly, some of the forms of the Bronze Age food vessels.

It does not follow that these beakers do not belong to Bronze Age I, because they are contemporary with the neolithic pottery of the older inhabitants. When the short-headed invaders arrived at the Nene, about two generations after the invasion of the South coast, they found the natives in that stage of civilization, and were themselves very scantily supplied with bronze or copper.

WALES.

There do not seem to be many examples of beakers in Wales, and I have only been able to learn of eight.

TYPE A.

A fragment of this type in the British Museum was found in a cist with a cinerary urn on the banks of the Alau in Anglesea, though the urn was evidently intrusive and secondary. A row of large bar-saltires runs round the upper and lower halves of the beaker which seems to belong to this type, but as the ornamentation covers the whole vessel it cannot be placed in Phase I. The two examples from Glamorganshire (figs. 93*b*,[1] 94) belong to Phase II, and fig. 94*a* from Rhosbereio in Anglesea to Phase III.

TYPE B 1.

Fig. 94*b*[2] from Plas Heaton in Denbigh is 8 in. high and has much the same form as fig. 75 from Oxford. The skull found with it has a ceph. index of 78, and is figured in *Crania Britannica*, no. 23. In form, fig. 95 from Denbigh resembles fig. 19 from Wilts., but the absence of plain bands and the deep grooves below the neck show that it is later.

TYPE C.

Fig. 96 from Montgomeryshire is only 4 in. high and resembles fig. 44 of type A from Norfolk, but here again the absence of plain bands and the grooves round the neck show that it is not so early a form as it looks, though it is probably older than fig. 97 from Carnarvon.

PROVINCE III

This province consists of the county of York.

The records of the discovery of beakers in Wiltshire, made over a hundred years ago by Sir R. Hoare and at a later date by Bateman in Derbyshire and Staffordshire, leave much to be desired by reason of their incompleteness. But for the ceramic of the East Riding we have very abundant and reliable records in the volumes of Canon Greenwell and Mr. R. Mortimer of Driffield.[3] The latter in particular has enormously facilitated the understanding of the text by giving plans of most of the barrows excavated, and by faithful drawings of every object discovered. These detailed accounts are so valuable to students of British prehistoric pottery and the finds have been so considerable that, although the area explored is less than one-eleventh part of the whole county, Yorkshire may well be taken as a distinct province. As

---

[1] Of fine clay, brick-red, almost glossy surface. Found with a cremated interment. Height 7½ in. Figured *Arch. Cambr.* Jan. 1902, pp. 25–8.

[2] Height 8 in, fine paste, reddish brown, walls thickish. Figured *Arch. Cambr.* 3rd ser., xiv. 273.

[3] I am particularly indebted to Mr. R. Mortimer for most generously allowing me to get photographs taken of any piece of pottery in his collection which I thought necessary for this work.

eleven barrows have yielded multiple interments, all beakers found in the same barrow are placed together, so that the differences between contemporary beakers of the same or of different types may be more easily examined and compared.

The beakers contained in these mounds are as follows :—

Barrow I,[1] figs. 112–14.   Barrow VII, figs. 130–1.
  ,,   II, figs. 115–17.   ,,   VIII, figs. 132–4.
  ,,   III, figs. 118–21.   ,,   IX, figs. 135–9.
  ,,   IV, figs. 122–4.   ,,   X, figs. 140–1.
  ,,   V, figs. 125–7.   ,,   XI, figs. 142–3.
  ,,   VI, figs. 128–9.

As the changes that took place in the evolution of type A are more regular and more easily traced than in type B, and as the place that C occupies has still to be found, type A

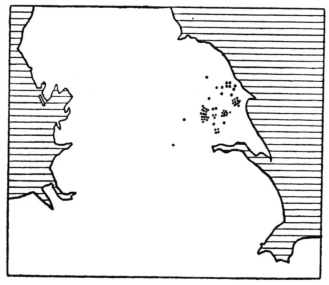

PROVINCE III.

forms the best chronological scale, and I therefore refer the other types and variants to its different phases in order to fix relatively their approximate position in time.

TYPE A (AC).

On comparing the earlier beakers of type A in Yorkshire with those of Wilts., it is evident that they are separated by a certain space of time. In the northern province there are only two specimens of Phase I (figs. 98, 99) ; in all the others that seem to belong to it (figs. 100–4, 114 (?), 116), the position of the constriction is no longer so central as in the south but is placed higher up, though not so high as in type C. This feature only occurs once in Province II, in fig. 62 from Derbyshire, a beaker that belongs to A, Phase II. This variety can be termed AC, but as it follows the same development as type A in Provinces I, II, it is more convenient to treat the beakers as if there was no difference between A and AC.

[1] By means of the beaker-number the actual number of the barrow and the references will be found in the List of Illustrations (pp. 87–91).

Phase II includes seventeen examples, figs. 105–9, 113, 118, 121, 126–8, 130, 131.[1]

Phase III appears in two examples, figs. 110, 111.

Barrow I.—Fig. 112 of the variety AB and fig. 113 of Phase II were found on the floor of the central grave and are therefore contemporary. The first shows the same relaxation of the constriction as figs. 70, 71 from Staffordshire and Derbyshire, and like them it belongs to the earlier part of Phase II. Fig. 113 of Phase II has followed the more normal development, and judging from the right-hand curve the body was intended to be more bulbous than is actually the case. The constriction in fig. 114 of AC, Phase I, is placed so high that the beaker almost belongs to C. It is probably contemporary with the other two vessels and therefore belongs to Phase II of the southern Province. The explanation is, either that Phase I lasted longer in Province III than in the south or, what is more probable, that this vessel is really an unusual variety of type C.

Barrow III.—Figs. 118, 121, both of Phase II, were found in different parts of the barrow and from the record there is nothing to show which beaker was deposited first. But as the latter, though found 26 ft. from the centre, lay in a grave 4 ft. below the floor of the barrow, while the former, though deposited nearer the centre, lay on the natural surface of the ground, fig. 121 is probably the earlier of the two.

Barrow V.—Figs. 126, 127 both belong to the later part of Phase II. The former lay in the central grave 6 in. above fig. 125 of type C, while the latter had been deposited several feet from the centre and is therefore somewhat later.

Barrow VII.—Fig. 130 lay in a grave 3½ ft. below the natural level, at a distance of 9 ft. from the centre; fig. 131 had been deposited with a child at 12 ft. from the centre and may therefore be somewhat later, as its form seems to show. Both belong to the later part of Phase II.

THE VARIETY AB.

This variety includes figs. 112, 124, 149, 150.

Under the heading Barrow I, fig. 112 has already been mentioned.

Barrow IV.—Fig. 124 was found in the same grave as figs. 122, 123 of type C, but three feet higher.

Two other examples are afforded by figs. 149, 150. The first was found with a stone bracer having two gold-headed rivets at each extremity, and part of a thin, flat, bronze knife-dagger. The raised bead-moulding round the neck we have already seen on late beakers from Staffordshire and Northamptonshire.[2] Fig. 150 was a secondary interment, but the primary burial had also been accompanied by a beaker, so crushed as to be past repair, a 'pulley ring' and a button with the V-shaped perforation, both of jet. All the evidence therefore tends to show that this variety is contemporary with Phase II.

TYPE B 1.

This type includes figs. 120, 139, 142, 143, 151, and perhaps figs. 133, 134. It is very sparsely represented in Province III, consisting as it does of only five certain examples, and these, as in East Anglia, are of small size.

Barrow III.—Fig. 120 is only 2½ in. high and was found on the floor of the same shallow, non-central grave as fig. 119 of type C. Both these vessels may belong to the period of Phase II, like figs. 118, 121, which were unearthed from the same barrow.

---

[1] Figs. 107, 108, 110, 128, 130 appertain to A, not to AC.   [2] Figs. 60, 66.

Barrow XI.—Fig. 142, with a height of 4⅞ in., had been placed with the body of a child at 16 ft. from the centre and 6½ ft. above the natural surface ; fig. 143, with a height of 4¼ in., lay beside the remains of a woman at 21 ft. from the centre and 6 ft. above the natural surface. These circumstances of burial all point to a late part of the beaker period.

Fig. 151 is only 4½ in. high and accompanied a secondary interment. It may be contemporary with four flat bronze axes which were unearthed close together in the same barrow, and appear to have been deposited at the time of the erection of the mound. In size and form these four examples resemble those from Bucks.[1] in Province II and Kent[2] in Province I.[3]

Barrow IX.—Fig. 139 measures 6¾ in. in height and accompanied the remains of a woman as a secondary interment. It is certainly later than three beakers of the variety BC, of which presently, and as regards height and general form it may be compared with examples from Norfolk and Suffolk.[4]

Barrow VIII.—Formally, it is perhaps necessary to include figs. 133, 134 under the head of type B, although it seems more likely that they are derived from a variety of A approximating type C. Although the profiles of these vessels have a general likeness to those of type B, such as figs. 19, 20, a closer examination shows that they are quite different, and there appears to be no real relationship between them at all. The two beakers are both comparable with fig. 149 of the variety AB, with this difference, that the lower position of the least diameter in the latter shows that in figs. 133, 134 the evolution started from a form very near type C and not from A. Again, on both figs. 149, 133 we see raised mouldings round the neck, which makes it unlikely that the latter can belong to type B. In time, figs. 133, 134 are contemporary with fig. 132 of type C.

The Variety BC.

This variety consists of ten examples, figs. 140, 135–7, 152–7.

Barrow X.—Fig. 140 was found in the same grave as fig. 141 of type C, but at a lower level; the grooves below the lip, also to be observed on figs. 123, 125 of type C, show that it is closely connected with that type.

Barrow IX.—Figs. 135–7 are contemporary, and though found at the centre were not the primary interments. All differ from each other in some respects, in others they are united. The first two show a considerable flattening and consequent angularity of the originally oval body, which points to a rather late time ; the third, though preserving better than the others the oval curve of the body, betrays its late date by the absence of any plain zone in the scheme of ornament, so that all three must be placed in the second half of the beaker period.

Fig. 152[5] seems to belong to this variety and is of special interest because it was found by Canon Greenwell in the same barrow as three remarkable cylindrical objects of chalk on which are carved the eyes and eyebrows of a human face, about which more will be said below. The raised moulding below the lip of the beaker shows that it cannot be placed very early.

Fig. 153 was dug out of a sandpit together with a very dolichocephalic skull having a cephalic index of 66.5 ; the femur had a length of 19¾ in. showing that the skeleton was that of a tall man. With it were deposited several objects, including a flint dagger 6½ in. long.

Fig. 154, which presents no plain bands and is therefore late, was found as a secondary interment close to the edge of the barrow, which had a diameter of 60 ft.

Figs. 155, 156 both occurred with secondary interments.

Fig. 157 was classed by Thurnam under type B, but comparing it with fig. 62 from Derbyshire, it would seem to be a weakened form of type C and should therefore be more properly ranged under BC. Its whole appearance leaves the impression that it is of late date.

---

[1] Figs. 72, 73.   [2] Figs. 34, 35.   [4] Figs. 81, 78.
[3] O. Montelius does not allow that the beaker and the   [5] The illustration is taken from *Arch.* lii. 16.
axes can be contemporary (*Arch.* lxi. 128).

Type C.

This type contains fifteen examples, figs. 115, 117, 119, 122, 123, 125, 129, 132, 138, 141, 144–8.

Barrow II.—There was no grave exactly central, but near the centre was a grave containing fig. 115. At the bottom of another grave nearly touching the first lay a male skeleton (fig. 116 of AC, Phase I) and a fine polished flint axe 3 in. long; in the same grave had been deposited the body probably of a woman (fig. 117) and a bronze pricker. All three vessels are probably nearly contemporary. The absence of a plain zone on fig. 116 and the rounded angle at the line of the constriction, thereby bringing the beaker nearly into the variety AB, make it evident that these three beakers belong to the later part of Phase I, nearly at the end of it.

Barrow III.—Fig. 119, only $4\frac{5}{8}$ in. high, was found in the same grave as the diminutive fig. 120 of B 1, which we have already learnt belongs in time to Phase II.

Barrow IV.—Figs. 122, 123 were found together on the floor of the central grave without any trace of a skeleton. They must be older than fig. 124 of the variety AB, which lay 3 ft. higher, and like figs. 115, 117 may belong to the end of Phase I or to the beginning of Phase II.

Barrow V.—Fig. 125 was found on the floor of the central grave and fig. 126 of type AC, Phase II, lay 6 in. higher. The former may be placed near the beginning of Phase II and the other somewhat later.

Barrow VI.—Fig. 129 lay on the floor of the central grave, while fig. 128 of A, Phase II, had been deposited at a level 4 ft. higher at a later date.

Barrow VIII.—Fig. 132 is contemporary with figs. 133, 134, which seem to simulate rather than belong to type B. All three may be placed in Phase II.

Barrow IX.—Fig. 138 belonged to a secondary burial and is probably later than figs. 135–7 of the variety BC, for all three of which we have found reason to assign a date later than the middle of the beaker period. The roundness of the body is striking and is not met with elsewhere in Province III, but both as regards size and rotundity of body it may be compared with examples from East Anglia of types A[1] and C[2]; and probably from there this local form penetrated into the East Riding.

Barrow X.—Fig. 141 is rather small, with a height of $5\frac{1}{2}$ in., and lay in the same grave as fig. 140 of the variety BC, but 5 ft. higher. It was therefore deposited later, and the comparative angularity of the body shows that it is not an early example of type C and probably belongs to the end of Phase II or even later.

Figs. 144–8 exhibit other examples of the type, which were found separately. It should be remarked that fig. 146, the form of which is abnormal from the wide though not high moulding round the neck, is ornamented all over and devoid of plain bands. The angularity of the body in fig. 148 is evidently intentional, and this feature may be regarded as a later development from the oval-shaped body of the early examples of this type. It is no doubt the latest of all the beakers found hitherto in Province III.

Conclusions.

It has already been remarked that the difference between type A in the two southern provinces and in Province III is so considerable that a measurable space of time must be allowed between the manufacture of the earliest beakers in Province I and of those in Province III. This statement is corroborated by comparing the relative number of beakers of the different types and varieties in Province II with those of Province III, for the total number of specimens in each is not very different. I only count the beakers that are reproduced in this volume.

---

[1] Figs. 44, 46.   [2] Fig. 20.

	A	B 1	B 2	BC	C	AB	AC	Total
Province I.	23	17	4	5	1	—	—	50
„ II.	28	11	5	—	8	3	—	55
„ III.	7	7	—	10	15	4	19	62

Here we observe that although the number of type A in Province I is nearly the same as of A and AC in Province III, as many as nineteen beakers in the latter area belong to AC, which is not represented in the two provinces in the south. Type B has progressively lost ground in passing from south to north, while type C on the contrary has increased in numbers. The variants BC, AB, AC, most of which are derived from older forms by obliteration of their distinctive characteristics, are also on the increase after passing the Humber.

These differences cannot be attributed entirely to chance; the element of time must certainly be taken into account and the change of taste which favoured type C at the expense of B. The interval that separates the earliest part of A, Phase I, in the south from the earliest part of A in Province III, cannot, I imagine, be set at less than about five generations.

In the southern provinces no clue was found in the relative age of type C with regard to A, but the multiple interments throw light upon this important point. The evidence they have yielded shows that in Province III type C appears first near the end of Phase I and is also contemporary with Phases II, III, but lasted longer than either. From early examples of the type, such as figs. 115, 117, 122, 123, we see that the body was more or less oval, and any decided angularity in the profile must be a sign of later date.

With regard to the variant BC, we have found no reason for dating it specially early, and the group may be considered contemporary with Phases II and III of type A; and the same may be said of type B 1.

PROVINCE IV

This province includes England north of the Humber, with the exception of the county of York.

Although the area covered by this province is considerable, I have only been able to learn of thirty-four local beakers, most of which were found casually, so that details of their discovery are wanting. This series of beakers is therefore smaller than in the other provinces, but taking it as it is and comparing it with the series in Province I, the difference between them is remarkable, even after allowing that in the future more specimens of type A will be brought to light. The number of specimens in each of the three types is reversed. In Province IV there is at present only one certain example of type A, Phase I, and it belongs to the variety AC; Phase II is not represented at all, its place being taken by type C, of which there are sixteen examples. Of type B there is only one doubtful specimen, but there are nine examples of the variety BC. This change has not been sudden, for at each successive stage in our progress from south to north we have observed changes in the *facies* of the beaker types. Type A has been gradually losing ground and the same may be said for type B. On the other hand type C, which was only just beginning to appear in the two southern Provinces, has received a great accession of strength in the two northern areas. The increasing number of examples of the variant AB, which does not appear in Province I, and of BC which is not represented in Province II, points to a gradual weakening of the old tradition, caused by the want of good models, or by an increasing carelessness on the part of the potters, some of whom may have belonged to the older neolithic population to whom the beaker ceramic was strange and novel.

Type A (AC).

The only certain example is fig. 158 from Northumberland, a beaker which is not unlike fig. 98 from Yorkshire, and both are nearly of the same height. But as the latter belongs to A, not to AC, and the junction between the body and neck is less emphasized in the former, the Northumberland example must be regarded as the later of the two.

Fig. 159, also from Northumberland, is only a fragment of uncertain type but is of interest, having been found with a flint dagger, thus making the tenth weapon of this description discovered in the four provinces, with a beaker interment.

PROVINCE IV.

Fig. 159a is distinguished by a horizontal raised moulding round the vessel at the position of the greatest constriction[1] and perhaps belongs to Phase I of AC.

The Variant AB.

Fig. 160 from Northumberland has three slightly raised mouldings round the neck, such as we have seen before in Yorkshire.[2] The absence of any plain band shows that this example is a late one.

Fig. 161 from Cumberland has been so much restored that it is hard to say whether it belongs to this variety or not.

Fig. 161a from Northumberland is derived from AC and has a bevelled lip, the inside surface of which is also ornamented.

Type B 1.

Fig. 162 from Northumberland has been so much restored that the original profile has nearly disappeared, but if the reparation is correct it may as a matter of form be placed in type B 1. I believe, however, judging by the curvature of the body when compared with the profiles of this type of beaker in Province I, that it is really an exaggerated example of the variant BC.

---

[1] Figured by Bruce, *Cat. of Antiq. at Alnwick Castle*, pl. xiii.   [2] Figs. 133, 149.

THE VARIANT BC.

There are nine examples of this variant, of which eight are reproduced in figs. 163–70.

Figs. 167–9 were found in the same cist near Hexham, Northumberland, and figs. 170, 171 came from another cist lying about 2 yds. from the first.[1] The last beaker belongs to type C.

Fig. 163 from Clifton, Westmorland, is a very fine example, measures 7 in. in height, and belongs almost to type B, but the want of curve in the short neck shows that it must be classed with BC. Fig. 165 is from the same place, but I know nothing of the conditions under which the vessels were found.

Fig. 166, probably from Northumberland, possesses a form which appears sometimes to be assumed by type B. For instance, it resembles figs. 75, 76 from Oxon. and Hunts.; but the first of these at any rate has manifest analogies with genuine examples of type B south of the Thames and may be classed under that head. With fig. 166 it is different, for it is rather to be compared and connected with figs. 165, 169 from the same province as itself, both belonging to the variant BC but more nearly related to C than to B. Both form and ornament show that it is a very late example, nearly at the close of the beaker period in Northumberland.

The four examples of this variant from Hexham are also late, as is shown by the absence of plain bands on two of them, but not so late as the last beaker. Figs. 167, 170 simulate type B, but do not really belong to it; grooves similar to those round the neck of the first are to be seen on beakers of types C, BC in Province III,[2] and the ornamentation on both vessels is more appropriate to types C and BC than to B. All four are evidently the handiwork of persons who had never seen a good model, though the careful and laborious ornamentation on figs. 167, 168, 170 is proof that the potters were not careless, but merely ignorant of the older tradition which was fast dying out. In this connexion it may be noted that these four beakers seem to have been deposited with cremated remains, as a few burnt bones were observed in both cists, but none unburnt.

TYPE C.

This type comprises sixteen examples, of which fourteen are here illustrated (figs. 171–84).

Fig. 172 from Northumberland is a fine example measuring 9¾ in. in height and much resembles fig. 123 from Yorkshire, which is only half an inch shorter, and contemporary with a good example of AB. It was found in the same cist, though separated by a compartment, with fig. 172a, a much smaller vessel only 5 in. high ornamented all over and belonging to the variant BC.[3]

Fig. 174 from Northumberland, fig. 175 from Cumberland, fig. 176 from Westmorland, and fig. 177 from Durham, although they vary a little in height and profile, are much like fig. 129 from Yorkshire, which was deposited earlier than an example of type A, Phase II.

Figs. 178, 179 were found with the body of a girl in a cist at North Sunderland, in Northumberland; the former is 8 in., the latter 5 in. high.

Figs. 180–4 evidently belong to a time when the tradition of good form was lost. In the first the body has become angular, as in fig. 148 from York. In the remaining four the old technique, the use of a notched instrument for making the lines of ornament, has been abandoned and replaced by a pointed instrument, while the forms of the vessels are entirely decadent.

The modifications that took place in the *facies* of the beaker ceramic between its first appearance in Province I and in Province IV respectively, are matters of fact which can scarcely be disputed seriously. It is otherwise with regard to the length of time necessary to effect this change, a secondary question about which there must necessarily be difference of opinion. Under any circumstances we should naturally expect that a small body of invaders

---

[1] For the photographs of these very interesting beakers I am indebted to Mr. J. P. Gibson, who has written an account of them in *Arch. Æliana*, 3 ser., vol. 2, pp. 136–46.

[2] Figs. 123, 125, 140, 144, 156.

[3] Bruce, *Cat. Antiq. Alnwick Castle*, pl. xii.

landing in South Britain would require a considerable space of time to push their advance as far north as the Tweed. Roughly speaking, I estimate that about two centuries should be allowed. The variant AC no doubt prolonged type A in the north, and the beginning of the beaker period in Province IV may be placed fully 200 years after the invasion. The earlier examples of type C coincide in time with part of Phase II, and the later specimens may probably be brought down later than the time when beakers had nearly disappeared from the province south of the Thames.

PROVINCE V

This province includes the area from the English Border to the Tay as well as the northern half of Ireland.

The further we proceed northwards the more the *facies* of the pottery differs from that of the Southern Province. As time goes on it becomes more and more difficult to classify the

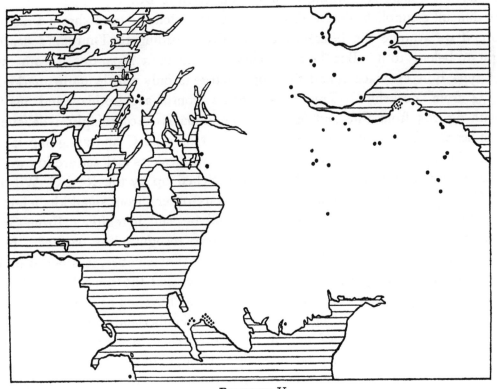

PROVINCE V.

different vessels owing to their divergence from the typical forms of the south, and to the convergence of distinct types. This blurring of the forms leads or seems to lead to the result that a beaker which formally belongs to one type has only simulated it, and really, as it seems to me, belongs to another. We have already come across examples of this phase in the evolution of beaker forms, but now it becomes more common and more difficult to deal with.

There is nothing astonishing in this and it is no valid argument against the classification of the beaker types as set forth in this volume. It resolves itself into a matter of interpretation. In bad handwriting it is impossible to distinguish between *n* and *u*, *um* and *mu*; yet the writer knew what he intended to write and if the words in which these syllables occur are known to us there is no difficulty in deciphering them. So when confronted with what seems to be an example of simulation we have to inquire what was the probable intention of the potter. To take a concrete example such as fig. 198; did the potter intend to make a vessel like fig. 19 of type B with which Canon Greenwell has compared it,[1] a type in which it was formerly included by myself,[2] or is it an example of BC and really descended from type C? In the first instance, forms ought to be compared with others in the same province before going further afield in search for analogies. Now neither in this province nor in the three provinces that intervene between it and Province I is there any beaker that can be placed alongside fig. 19 of type B. Examining fig. 198 a little closer on the least-repaired side, it is evident that the relatively short neck is quite straight, and that though it has a stouter body its profile may be reasonably compared with other examples of BC, such as figs. 205 and 208, which are manifestly variations of type C. From this it may be inferred that the potter, never having seen any vessel like fig. 19, intended to produce a beaker approximately like type C, which at the time she made it was already weakened in the direction of BC.

A more difficult example to deal with is fig. 197, in which the neck shows a distinct curve, and therefore, if we arrange the beakers mechanically according to Thurnam's description of type B, ought to belong to it. But the ovoid curve of the body separates it from the typical examples of type B in Province I, and the upper curve is only a little more marked than in figs. 133, 134 from Yorkshire. This beaker came from East Lothian and may also be compared with fig. 205 from Fife and fig. 208 from Lanark. Accordingly, I believe there is sufficient justification for regarding fig. 197 as a variant of type C and assigning it a place in group BC. Including incomplete vessels, about forty-two beakers at least are known from this province, besides fragments of two or three dozen picked up by the Rev. G. Wilson on the sandhills of Glenluce Bay in Galloway,[3] and numerous others from small kitchen-middens at Gullane Bay and North Berwick, of which more will be said hereafter. From Stoneykirk, Wigtonshire, comes an interesting fragment not hitherto recognized as part of a beaker, for Mr. L. Mann, who figures it, describes it as an urn.[4] When entire, it stood 9 in. high and must have much resembled fig. 150 from Yorkshire, which has the same height, but differing from it in having no ridge round the neck, while the lip was bevelled as in fig. 46 from Suffolk, figs. 55, 59 from Staffordshire, and fig. 161a from Northumberland. The peculiarity of the ornament lies in this, that the incised motive of cross-hatched lozenges is applied directly on the surface of the vessel without being bounded by horizontal lines or enriched by additional motives. The same thing is seen on fig. 111 from Yorkshire, where the central motive consists of hexagons rudely made and cross-hatched. The fragment probably belongs to group BC, and was found with 187 perforated lignite discs and a triangular pendant which formed a neck-lace of early type.

Another beaker, about 9 in. high and elaborately ornamented but of unknown type, is recorded to have been found in a cist on Carnwath Moor, Lanarkshire, the cap-stone of which was sculptured with concentric circles, triangles, and lozenges.[5]

---

[1] *P. S. A. S.* vi. 345.   [2] *P. S. A. S.* xxxviii. 333.   [4] *P. S. A. S.* xxxvi. 584, &c.
[3] *Arch. and Hist. Coll. Ayrshire and Galloway*, vi. 103.   [5] Figured in *P. S. A. S.* x. 62; Anderson, p. 88.

Type A.

Fig. 185 from Kilmartin in Argyll is the only example of this type and belongs to Phase II.

Variant AC.

This group includes figs. 186–94. Although fig. 188 from Roxburghshire has a well-rounded body, the absence of plain bands shows that it is not an early example; it may be compared with fig. 114 from the East Riding.

Fig. 190 from Fife was found in a cist in a sandpit with four flint arrowheads with stems and barbs but not of specially fine workmanship. The exact locality where fig. 191 was found is not known, but as it belongs to the Poltalloch Collection it was probably found on or near that estate (in Argyll). Where fig. 193 was discovered is also unknown, but as it is in the Stirling Museum I have marked its position on the map near Stirling, though perhaps it came from South Perthshire.

Type B 1.

Fig. 195 from West Lothian and the fragment (fig. 196) from near St. Andrews, Fife, are both good examples of this type; much better than fig. 143 from the East Riding. They most resemble fig. 225a from Aberdeenshire. I have described a fragment of a beaker, seemingly of type B, though perhaps of the variant BC, which when entire may have had a height of nearly 9 in. It was found in a short cist while digging a drain near Largs in Ayrshire. The skull of the skeleton beside it has been fully described by Dr. R. Munro, who states that it had a cephalic index of 84·6 and belonged to a male individual.[1] The motives of ornamentation resembled those seen on an example of type B from Denbighshire (fig. 95).

Variant BC.

This group includes figs. 197 to 203, 205, 208, 211.

The first two examples of this variant have already been discussed. The third (fig. 199) is also very difficult to place. Its height (9 in.) is greater than any certain example of type B, and a raised moulding below the lip is only seen on one doubtful example from Hunts.,[2] otherwise this feature occurs only on examples of type A and the variant BC. The absence of any plain band shows that this is a late specimen, too late to compare directly with any example from Province I, which is several generations earlier. My impression is that the angularity of the body arose in the same way as in figs. 198, 207, and that the upper curve was produced by gradual increments, attaining its maximum in fig. 197, a stage in this transformation being apparent in fig. 207 of type C. The same reasoning applies to figs. 200, 201.

Figs. 197, 199 are so well formed that if the beaker class had lasted much longer a new type might have arisen characterized by a continuous curve from base to lip, but the Fates were against it, so that the gradual evolution from ruder specimens in Provinces III, IV having reached its highest pitch in these two examples collapsed and went no further in that direction.

Fig. 203 can unfortunately be studied only on a photograph, as the original was lost on its journey from the Bridge of Allan to Edinburgh. It seems to have the curves of type B, but the ornamentation belongs to type C and may be compared with that upon fig. 209 from Lanarkshire. The rows of horizontal lines below the lip are also found on specimens of types C and BC in Provinces III[3] and IV.[4] On that account it appears better to place the specimen in group BC. It was found only 2 ft. below the summit of a large tumulus 21 ft. high, apparently without any interment. The primary interment was contained in a small stone cist on the floor of the tumulus, and consisted of fatty black earth mixed with charcoal and small bits of human bone. Whether the interment was after incineration is not stated, but the small dimensions of the cist (2½ ft. × 1½ ft.) seem to imply that the body had been burnt.[5]

---

[1] *P.R.S. Ed.* xxvi. 292, 305–9.　　[2] Fig. 76.　　[3] Figs. 123, 125, 140, 141.　　[4] Figs. 177, 182.　　[5] *P.S.A.S.* vii. 519–21.

TYPE C.

In this province there are four examples of multiple interments, viz. figs. 204, 205 from Collessie, Fife; figs. 206, 207 from Caik Muir, Midlothian; figs. 208, 209 from Lanark Moor, and figs. 210, 211 from the Berwickshire coast.

Fig. 205 of the variant BC was found in a stone cist placed on the natural surface, nearly at the centre of a large cairn about 120 ft. in diameter and about 14 ft. high. About 12 ft. from the centre, fig. 204 of type C was found in a pit 6 ft. deep, and about 25 ft. from the centre was another hole of less depth containing a thin triangular bronze knife-dagger 6 in. long, and near it the gold mounting of the handle. Probably both these interments and also the bronze knife-dagger are contemporary. The angularity of the body of fig. 204 shows that the interment belongs to a rather late part of the beaker period.

There are no details regarding the finding of figs. 206, 207, beyond the fact that each was found in a stone cist on the top of a hill. Both are probably contemporary or nearly so and like the pair from Fife, they are of rather late date.

Fig. 208 of group BC and fig. 209 of type C are said to have been found together, which is not unlikely, but no details are recorded.

Figs. 210, 211 from Cockburnspath, Berwickshire, were found in the same cist under a barrow; the second beaker belongs to variant BC, and is much like fig. 172a from Lesbury in Northumberland.

Fig. 213 from South Lanarkshire was found under a cairn in a central cist, with a bronze ring 3 in. in diameter. There is no beaker like it in the province, but it may be compared with fig. 138 from the East Riding, which is in all probability later than three examples of BC.

Fig. 217 from the Island of Mull was found with fragments of a bronze blade and a bracer of greenstone having a perforation at each end. It is much repaired, and has lost so much of its form that it may well be regarded as belonging to the last phase of the beaker period in Province V.

DOMESTIC POTTERY.

The fragments of beakers (figs. 219–22) from the kitchen-middens at Gullane Bay and North Berwick, of which more hereafter, are of the greatest interest, for they prove that both types A and B or their derivatives were used for domestic purposes, and that they were profusely ornamented with shaded triangles and other motives. The triangles and the lattice band on fig. 221 from Gullane recur on the fragment (fig. 218) from a cist found near the golf links at North Berwick, and the example of B1 from North Berwick (fig. 222) is like fig. 195 from Bathgate in West Lothian, and fig. 196 from near St. Andrews in Fife. These beaker fragments from the kitchen-middens are therefore contemporary with similar vessels found with interments in Province V.

IRELAND

Dr. Thurnam states positively that beakers do not occur among the sepulchral antiquities of Ireland. Yet he took note of one figured in the *Dublin Penny Journal* (1838, p. 108), though he regarded it as doubtful. In fig. 223 I reproduce from the above Journal this beaker, now unfortunately lost, together with two other vessels, all found under the same cairn at Mount Stewart, Co. Down. The general accuracy of the illustrations of the two food vessels, when compared with their photographs (Food vessels, figs. 233, 234), warrants confidence in the general accuracy of the representation of the beaker. The curved arrangement of dots below the lip of the globular urn, fig. 233, is exaggerated, though there is some ground for their appearance. Otherwise, considering the very small scale of the woodcut, the ornamentation on the body of the vessel is sufficiently well interpreted. The height of the small vessel behind it appears too great, but probably it had been placed on a block of wood to allow it to be seen at all. That the exact profile and ornamentation of the beaker is correctly rendered I do not maintain, though I assume that the draughtsman had before him a beaker from $7-7\frac{1}{2}$ in. high, probably of the variant BC, ornamented all over like fig. 199 from Ayrshire, and that he copied it with some success. For, as this vessel is quite unlike any Irish vessel that has been preserved entire, and as it is extremely improbable that the Dublin draughtsman in 1838 was acquainted with Sir R. Hoare's heavy tomes, it seems unnecessary to suppose that the vessel figured in the *Penny Journal* is the invention of the draughtsman.

If this were the only beaker known in Ireland there might be some ground for suspecting its authenticity, but in the Museum at Dublin there are fragments of perhaps three beakers from Moytura in Co. Sligo which may be seen in fig. 224. These fragments were found in a half-demolished tumulus in the Townland of Moytura West.[1] It contained two central cists, an upper and a lower one. The upper cist contained the skeleton remains of two adults and a child, a thin piece of bronze, and fragments of pottery of at least three distinct vessels—one piece having bands of dotted lines alternating with a diamond pattern. The pottery was of light drab colour on the outside and red within.[2]

PROVINCE VI

This area includes the counties of Forfar, Kincardine, and Aberdeen.

There are at least forty-four examples of the beaker class in this province, and when compared with the specimens in Province I they show the greatest contrast. Type A has now disappeared entirely. There are two examples of type B 1; all the rest belong to type C or to its variant BC. None of the specimens of type C are so well formed as in Provinces III and IV; sometimes it is hard to say whether a beaker should be classed under C or BC, and it is evident that the type is getting worn out, like a die that has been too long in use.

Type B 1.

The fine example of this type, fig. 225a,[3] from near Torphins in South Aberdeenshire, may be compared, as regards form, ornament, and height, with fig. 195 from West Lothian. A later and small example, in which the curvature of the body is replaced by an angle, is shown in fig. 225 from an unknown locality in Aberdeenshire. The chronological position of this type with regard to the other types in Provinces V and VI cannot at present be decided.

Multiple Interments.

There are six instances in which two beakers have been found together in the same cist or in such close proximity that the pair may be considered contemporaneous.

---

[1] Borlase corrects 'West' and replaces it by 'North'.   [3] Figured by Mr. Coles in *P. S. A. S.* xl. 313.

[2] Borlase, *Dolmens of Ireland*, i. 187–8.

Fig. 226 of type C was found near Kintore in Aberdeenshire with fig. 227 of the group BC. The first may be compared with fig. 213 from Lanarkshire, found with a stout bronze arm-ring, and the second with fig. 197 from East Lothian and fig. 256 from Aberdeenshire.

Figs. 228, 229, from Ardiffrey in Cruden parish in the north-east of Aberdeenshire, both belong to the later part of type C. From their difference in height and from the different technique with which the ornament is executed, they are evidently the handiwork of two persons very likely of different ages. The latter vessel was found with a stone bracer, a flint axe, and seven flint arrowheads.

Figs. 230, 231 of type C, from Ellon in the same part of the county, were found with four flint arrowheads and are probably by the same hand. In both, the ornament covers the whole surface and in both there is a slight moulding or the suggestion of one at the base of the neck, as well as the rudiments of a base ring at the foot. The deep bevel forming a sort of shelf on the inside of the lip is probably imitated from a food vessel. On account of these features, both beakers must be considered as belonging to the later part of the beaker period.

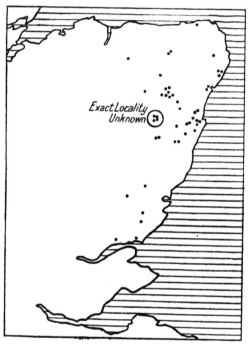

Exact Locality Unknown

PROVINCE VI.

Figs. 232, 233 from Skene in South Aberdeenshire are very dissimilar in appearance. The first belongs to group BC and in form resembles fig. 264 from Turriff in the northern part of the county; the second is a later version of a beaker like fig. 216 of type C from East Lothian and may also be compared with fig. 261 of the variant BC from near Aberdeen. The band of parallel lines below the neck occurs on several beakers of type C in Provinces III, IV, and V, and the motives on the ornamented zones below it may be observed on beakers from Lanark and Kinross,[1] the latter of which also belongs to type C. Both these beakers from Skene were found with a single male skeleton having a brachycephalic skull, the cephalic index of which is 86·1. The man was short, with a stature of about 5 ft. 4 in.

Figs. 233a, b, from Pittodrie in the centre of Aberdeenshire, are not very dissimilar in profile, though one is taller than the other, and both belong to the group BC.[2]

Figs. 234, 235 are from near Durris in Kincardine. The first belongs to the variant BC, the second to type C.[3] This last shows an undercutting at the base of the neck, not unlike what is to be seen on the two beakers from Ellon, an innovation which differentiates these three beakers from others of type C.

---

[1] Figs. 186, 214.
[2] Figured by Mr. Callander, *P. S. A. S.* xl. 26, figs. 1, 2.
[3] Figured on a larger scale by Mr. Coles, *P. S. A. S.* xl. 306.

Type C.

There are eighteen examples of this type, of which seven have already been mentioned. Further specimens are seen in figs. 236–46. Although fig. 237 from Cruden in north-east Aberdeenshire has a well-rounded body and a relatively long neck for the type, the foot ring at the base and the technique of the ornament prevent its being considered a really early beaker from the point of view of Province I. The geographical position of Cruden alone is sufficient evidence that it must be later than the earliest examples of this type in Province V. And not only that, but the structure of the cist in which it was found was abnormal. It was formed of two long stones lying north and south, the ends being packed with small stones.

In spite of the confused and inadequate narrative relating the discovery of fig. 241, some notice should be taken of it. At Freefield near Aberdeen, a mound 60 ft. in diameter and about 15 ft. high was explored by driving a trench through it from south-west to north-east, at a level a little above that of the field in which it lay. At the centre of the cutting a small cairn of stones was found, and in it or below it 'a dreadfully rusted piece of iron, somewhat in the form of a chisel', also a smoothish stone like a whetstone. Later on, at a point near the north-east end of the trench and about 5 ft. above the ground-level, this beaker was found embedded in clay.[1] It was therefore a late secondary interment as its form suggests. To account for the presence of iron we must suppose that during the excavations it had fallen among the stones of the cairn from a higher level and was not perceived till the workmen began to remove them.

The Variant BC.

This group consists of twenty-four examples, of which five have been already noticed.[2] The earlier specimens of this group (figs. 247–51) are well formed and offer a great contrast to some of the later ones. Fig. 249 was found with a horn spoon, which is good evidence that the beaker was not a drinking cup but a receptacle for something more solid than a fluid. These objects were contained in the same cist which held the skeleton of a tall man and of a female child.

Fig. 261 from near Aberdeen was found in a cist with burnt bones, and this is the only beaker in Province VI recorded to have been associated with a cinerary interment.

Fig. 262 is ill-formed and very rudely ornamented, yet it was found in the central cist under a large cairn at Linlathen in the south-east corner of Forfarshire, with a small bronze knife-dagger 4½ in. in length, though originally a little longer. In height and form this beaker resembles fig. 282 from Lesmurdie in Banffshire.

PROVINCE VII

This Province includes the counties west and north of Aberdeenshire.

The *facies* of this pottery, consisting of about twenty-nine beakers, is quite similar to that of Province VI, though it seems to show more late forms. With one exception all the specimens belong to type C or its variant BC, and there is no trace of a revival of type A. In the formation of the body, too, of type C, the well-shaped curves, such as we found in Provinces III and IV, have disappeared and are replaced by a less-elegant bulge. The exception (fig. 265) is the sole representative of type B, though not of the same variety as in Provinces V and VI, but resembling in form fig. 82 from East Anglia in Province II. This specimen was found near Dornoch, Sutherland, and its appearance so far north, with no intermediate

---

[1] *P.S.A.S.* xv. 193–4.

[2] Fig. 259*a*, of a very unusual form, is figured by Mr. Eeles, *P.S.A.S.* xxxvi. 628. It has a double

constriction, one at the base of the neck, another above the base of the vessel. Fig. 288 is a less exaggerated example.

example between it and that from Suffolk, may be explained by supposing that it is one of the shapes of vessels used mainly for domestic, rarely for sepulchral purposes. Although larger than the Suffolk beaker, it is comparatively small, with a height of 5½ in., and it is precisely the small vessels of from 4 to 5 in. high that seem to have been preferred for household use.

Type B 2.

Fig. 265, from a cist found in a gravel bank near Dornoch, as has just been mentioned had only its upper half ornamented, and it appears to have hard solid walls suitable for domestic use.

Province VII.

Type C.

Fifteen specimens of this type are seen in figs. 266–76, 277–9, 281.

Fig. 267 from Buckie on the Banffshire coast was found in a cist in a field, but there was no trace of a mound. In one corner of the cist lay a quantity of charred and burnt human bones.

Fig. 269 from near Evanton in the county of Ross was found in a cist with a bracer of greenish stone having four perforations. The skull of the male skeleton found with these objects had a cephalic index of 80·8.

Multiple Interments.

Figs. 277–9 were found in the same cairn at Forglen, Banff, and figs. 280–2 were taken from three adjoining cists at Lesmurdie in the same county.

The first three are all of type C, but on the verge of the variant BC. Fig. 277 is an interesting specimen, as it shows a transition in the direction of fig. 282, thus confirming my belief that forms like figs. 227, 199, 200 are variants of type C and not true examples of type B. Fig. 277, like fig. 199, shows a raised moulding immediately below the lip, but in a more exaggerated form. With it was found a small barbed and stemmed flint arrowhead one in. long. All three beakers evidently belong to a late part of the beaker period and they were deposited in the cairn in the order in which they are here given, though probably not exactly at the same time.

In the triplet from Lesmurdie, fig. 281 belongs to type C, figs. 280, 282 to the variant BC. Fig. 280 was found at a rather greater depth than fig. 281 and may have been deposited earlier, but it is quite uncertain. What is most certain is that all were made by different persons each using a different technique and style in making the ornament.

VARIANT BC.

Eleven examples of this group are seen in figs. 280, 282–91.

Both figs. 283, 284 might be placed in type B, as I have done on a former occasion, if the description of that type is too blindly followed and no attempt is made to discover the intention of the potter. The ornamentation in both instances shows that the potters were acquainted with the style of decoration found on type C. The roundness of the body, especially in the second example, strengthens the impression that the vessel belongs to type B, but we have seen a similar roundness on true specimens of type C,[1] and one of these from Cruden in Aberdeenshire has a foot ring like that on fig. 284. Hence, we need not hesitate to infer that the women, who made these and other vessels of the group, did not intend to make beakers of type B but of the variant BC.

Perhaps fig. 285 in the Elgin Museum is not a true beaker but only a food vessel.

Fig. 286 from Dunrobin, Sutherland, was found in a cist containing the skeleton of a brachycephalic young woman with a cephalic index of 82·4. Beside her lay 116 small shale discs, about the size and thickness of a threepenny bit, of which six were perforated ; and also eighteen beach-rolled pebbles.

Fig. 286 *bis* from near West Watten in Caithness is the most northerly beaker hitherto discovered in Britain. It was found in a cist while removing gravel from a pit along with a male skeleton, the skull of which had the high cephalic index of 85·8.[2]

---

[1] Figs. 236, 237, from Forfarshire and North Aberdeenshire.

[2] Since this was written, Mr. Alex. Curle, Secretary to the Royal Commission on Historical Monuments of Scotland, informs me that he saw the fragment of a beaker obtained from a cist at Bettyhill, Strathnaver, on the north coast of Sutherland, and therefore a little further north than West Watten. The decoration was composed of diagonal lines in bands, alternating in direction, with a slight ridge or moulding between them. The latter feature shows that the beaker is of late date, as might reasonably be expected, considering its geographical position. A similar feature combined with a similar motive of ornament may be observed on the neck of fig. 245 from Banchory in South Aberdeenshire, also a late specimen.

TABLE OF THE BEAKERS ARRANGED IN TYPES

Province	A	B 1	B 2	BC	C	AB	AC
I	*Ph. I.* 1–8. *Ph. II.* 9–16. *Ph. III.* 17–18 *bis*	*Ph. I.* 19–24. *Ph. II.* 25–33. *Extra* 34–5	36–8	39–42 *bis*	43		
II	*Ph. I.* 44–55. *Ph. II.* 55–66. *Ph. III.* 67–9	72–81	82–7		89–93	70, 71, 88 ?	
Wales	*Ph.II.* 93*a,b,*94. *Ph. III.* 94*a*	94*b*–95			96–7		
III	*Ph. I.* 98, 99. *Ph. II.* 105–9, 113, 118, 121, 126–8,130,131. *Ph. III.* 110, 111	120, 139, 142, 143, 151—perhaps 133, 134		140, 135–7, 152–7	115,117,119, 122,123,125, 129,132,141, 144–8	112, 124, 149, 150	*Ph. I.* 100–4, 114, 116
IV		162 ?		163–70	171–84	160, 161, 161*a*	158, 159*a*
V Ireland (North)	*Ph. II.* 185	195, 196		197–203, 205, 208, 211 223	204,206,207, 209,210,212, 213–17		186–94
VI		225, 225*a*		227, 232, 233*a, b,* 234, 247–64	226,228,229, 230,231,233, 235–46		
VII			265	280, 282–91	266–79, 281		

HANDLED BEAKERS AND CUPS.   (Pl. xxi, xxii.)

There are about seventeen examples of beakers and cups to which a handle was attached and here they are kept together, though they belong to very different stages of the Bronze Age. Some few belong to the Beaker and Food-vessel periods, others to the time when cremation prevailed.

Fig. 292, height 6 in., from Appleford near Abingdon, Berks., was found standing near the shoulder of an adult skeleton.

Fig. 293, height 7⅛ in., from B. 113 Goodmanham, E.R., belonged to a secondary interment 5 ft. from the centre, and was found with the skeleton of a middle-aged man and a flint flake. *B .B.* 321.

Fig. 294, height 5¾ in., was found in a small cairn near Pickering, North Riding, with a skeleton. A little south of the interment were several calcined instruments of flint. Bateman, *Diggings*, 209.

Another, much like the above, from March, Cambridgeshire, is figured by Thurnam.[1]

Figs. 295, 296 from Brixworth, Northamptonshire, are in the Northampton Museum.

Fig. 295 *bis*, height 4½ in., from B. 116 Aldro, E.R., is contemporary with beakers 119, 120. The bottom is ornamented with a cross on a field which is cross-hatched. Mortimer, pp. 54–6.

Fig. 296 *bis*, height 7 in., from Rothwell, near Kettering, Northampton, contained burnt bones.

[1] *Arch.* xliii. 397, fig. 88.

Fig. 296a, height $5\frac{5}{8}$ in , from B. 264, Huggate and Waterwold, E.R. It lay near the top of a large central grave with the bones of an infant.   Mortimer, p. 317.

Fig. 296b, height $5\frac{1}{2}$ in., from B. 104 Garrowby Wold, E.R., was found 16 ft. from the central grave, and is later than the three beakers figs. 122-4.   Mortimer, pp. 134-6.

In a cist at Balmuick, Comrie, Perthshire, a handled cup, $5\frac{3}{4}$ in. high, was found with probably a cremated interment.[1]

Fig. 297, height 4 in., is from Wereham, Norfolk.

Fig. 298, height $4\frac{3}{8}$ in., from Frome Whitfield or Whitwell, Dorset, was found with three skeletons.

Fig. 299, height $4\frac{1}{2}$ in., from a barrow at Martinstown near Dorchester, was found in a grave in the solid chalk with a female skeleton. At her head were the skeletons of three infants and the food vessel fig. 299a.[2]

Fig. 300, height $2\frac{3}{4}$ in., came from a barrow at Bagber, near Milton Abbas in Dorset, and belongs to Bronze Age IV or later.

Fig. 301, height $3\frac{7}{10}$ in., from Denzell in Cornwall, was found in a shallow hollow in the ground, under a barrow 9 ft. high, with calcined bones. The cup stood mouth upwards and contained some of the calcined bones. Externally the clay is ruddy, but the interior has a coating of yellow. A turf had been placed on its mouth. Borlase, *Naenia Cornub.* 245-6.

Fig. 301 *bis*, height $1\frac{3}{4}$ in., from Darley Dale, Derbyshire, was found with cinerary urns, one of which is represented by fig. 481, of Bronze Age IV or later.   *The Antiquary*, iv. 201-6.

---

[1] Figured by Anderson, fig. 97 ; *P. S. A. S.* xviii. 307.

[2] The information and the photographs were kindly sent me by Mr. St. George Gray.

CHAPTER III

CONTINENTAL AND BRITISH ORNAMENTATION COMPARED [1]

COMPARING British designs on type A with those on bell-beakers on the Continent, much that is similar will be observed, but the former are more complicated and the ornamented zone, covering a larger space, has encroached upon the plain zone which sinks into comparative insignificance. But this greater width of the decorated zone is also characteristic of pottery of Ciempozuelos type, figs. 20*, 21*, and of a similar ceramic from the valley of the Guadalquiver. A chequer surface pattern, though carried out differently in detail, is common to Bohemia and Wilts. The line-saltire is a common motive in Germany, but though this simple form occurs in Kent (F6), in Wilts. it appears as a bar-saltire, which may be a later development. The single bar-chevron motive on a shaded ground is common to Province I and to the continent, but the triple arrangement on a late beaker from Dorset (F15) is not found in Germany, though it occurs in a slightly different manner in the south of Spain on vessels of the same class as figs. 20*, 21*. The decoration of this ceramic is very elaborate, and two vessels found by Mr. Bonsor exhibit double and quadruple rows of bar-chevrons on a shaded ground [2] quite similar to the Dorset example. The line lozenge motive belongs to both sides of the Channel, with the difference that here it shows light on a shaded background, while there it is shaded on a light background. In the older examples of the bell-beaker east of the Rhine the whole pattern is contained between two parallel lines (Rottleben, Smichov, Erfurt), bounded on each side by plain zones. But in those which from their form are to be considered later (Ober Olm, Herrensheim, Horchheim, Andernach, and Urmitz) several parallel lines border the principal design and thus enlarge slightly the depth of the ornamented zone. In South Britain there are not many examples of a design being bounded merely by the plain zones, although it is met with when the motive is very simple and occupies a subordinate position (figs. 1, 5, 7, 14). As a rule the design is bordered by at least two lines, or by an extra band or two, composed of a different motive (F4, 6, 9, 10).

The simple elements that compose the decoration of type B, such as crossed and short vertical lines (figs. 20, 21, 22, 23, 28, 29) are seen on late bell-beakers from Urmitz and Herrensheim. The easy decoration of zones composed of parallel lines, made with a punch or with a pointed tool, alternating with plain bands (figs. 25, 26, 30), is seen on fig. 47* from Holstein; also on two beakers from Ca' di Marco in the district of Brescia, a cemetery belonging to the aeneolithic period. [3] Neither of these are like figs. 15*, 16*, but one of them

---

[1] See Plates iv and xxiii, &c. In references to the Plates of British ornament, instead of fig., I have used F to indicate the beaker to which reference is made.

[2] *Rev. Ar.* xxxv, fig. 121, 133.

[3] *Bull. di Pal. It.* xxiv, tav. xi, figs. 6, 11.

has something of the form of fig. 17*, though with a much more rounded and globular body. Although of a simple nature, the ornamentation of type B is different from that on the oldest specimens from Sicily and Spain, as well as the simply decorated zones found on bell-beakers from Brittany. The severe style of ornament seen on the above specimens from Dorset does not seem to imply that they are of greater antiquity than others more richly decorated, for their form and comparative height (7–8½ in.) tell against such an inference, and similar zones of ornament are seen on the late beaker fig. 42 *bis* of type C.

THE ORNAMENTATION
PROVINCE I

Although the decoration of the beaker, like the form, was traditional in the sense that it remained strictly geometrical and composed of straight lines, the potters were evidently not so tied down as in shaping the vessel. Latitude was given them to display their personal proclivities and to select the motives of ornament that most suited their fancy and their taste. Hence it will be found that no two beakers carry exactly the same ornament, for to each zone of ornament was assigned a different motive or set of motives, and the possible permutations of these are very great. Some of the patterns were evidently imitated or adapted from plaiting, weaving, and basket-work, at any rate in the first instance, and these were operations which were familiar to the women who made and decorated the beakers.

In exhibiting the patterns, I have taken the zone as the unit and not each simple motive that composes the design. In type A we may observe first a chequer pattern and a variety of it made with shaded hanging triangles, both on the same Wiltshire vessel (F2). A lattice-work design with shaded lozenges occurs twice in Wilts. (F4a, 8). A somewhat analogous arrangement is a series of shaded bar-chevrons, placed so as to give the effect of lattice-work, though in a ruder manner, and this also comes from Wilts. (F5). Patterns which include as a motive either the simple or the bar-saltire, sometimes with the adjacent triangles shaded to give it more effect, are found in Kent and twice in Wilts. (F6, 4, 9a). A design composed of a single bar-chevron on a shaded ground is from Somerset (F12); a development of this including three parallel bar-chevrons on a shaded ground belongs to Dorset (F15). Small, shaded, hanging triangles, as on the Continent, sometimes terminate a pattern at the foot of the vessel; such are found in Wilts. and Dorset (F4, 15, 21); the last however belongs to type B.

Type B.

The scheme of ornamentation on type B is on the whole different and less elaborate than that on type A. When the whole surface is not covered with parallel horizontal lines at short intervals (figs. 35, 36), the ornament consists of narrow zones of horizontal lines, separated by plain bands, as we find in Dorset (figs. 25, 26, 30). Sometimes, in the centre of the horizontal lines the monotony is broken by a narrow band of crossed or vertical lines, or by a herring-bone motive.[1] There are only two examples of type B decorated in a manner analogous with type A.

[1] Figs. 23, 26, 27, 28, 29.

In F24 from Wilts. we find an upper row of shaded triangles opposed to another row of shaded triangles and separated by an ornamented band, the general effect being that of a dark lozenge on a light ground traversed by a horizontal bar. The same motive, but effected in quite a different manner is seen on a Berkshire beaker of the variant BC (F41).

PROVINCE II

Without going into tedious descriptions, it will be readily seen by looking at the Plates of Ornament that the decoration applied to beakers of type A in Provinces I and II is very similar. The hanging triangles, the lozenge and chequer motives, the bar-chevron on a shaded ground— all recur with slight modifications. Shading by means of cross-hatching, to give the effect of dark lozenges on a light ground, occurs first in East Staffordshire (F55); later on it was used in Northamptonshire and South Lancashire (F66, 67) for shading the background to enhance the effect of lozenges and semi-hexagons against a dark ground. Another novelty is the hexagon and semi-hexagon motive, which appears during the second phase of type A in Oxfordshire (F64) and in the third phase in South Lancashire (F67).

There is so little ornament on the examples of type B that I have refrained from giving special illustration of it; it is best seen on the beakers themselves.

The ornamentation of type C does not call for special remark, except that the simple motives on fig. 89 are analogous to what is seen on some beakers of Type B in Province I; while the motives on F91 are of the same nature as those we see on type A in both Provinces.

PROVINCE III

The ornamentation applied to beakers in Province III was not essentially different from what was in current use in the provinces lying south of it. The shaded triangles, the bar-chevron, the bar-saltire, and the lozenge in various combinations are all familiar motives in the three provinces. The hexagon as a motive first appeared at a late period in Province II, and another example (F108) from Province III must equally be placed far down in the series of beakers. Nearly all the combinations of motives shown on the plates reproducing the ornamentation are taken from type A, and only F155 belongs to type C. In this type these larger motives are almost unknown, though in Province II they are found twice, and the zones of ornament are composed of narrow bands, each containing a single, simple motive, such as is seen on F136, 155. In this respect it follows the tradition of type B in Province I [1] and a fine example of type C from Suffolk.[2]

Although shading by means of cross-hatching is not unknown on some neolithic pottery of the Continent, it does not seem to have been brought over to Britain in the first instance. It is apparently an afterthought and a later development. We have already found it in the counties of Stafford, Northampton, and Lancaster,[3] but in Yorkshire it recurs more frequently.[4] In this last province we now observe for the first time a certain change of taste which had

---

[1] Figs. 23, 28, 29.　　　[2] Fig. 89.　　　[3] F. 55, 66, 67.　　　[4] F. 95, 107, 108, 110, 111.

become, as time went on, more finicking and fastidious. The straight lines formerly used to give the effect of shading were now broken into zigzags, and narrow bands of ornament were composed of such lines, although this new and meticulous procedure must have required much more trouble and care to produce.[1]

The fringe, as a finish to a zone of ornament, may be noticed on two beakers of type A in Province II (fig. 53, F59). This fancy was quite to the taste of the potters of Province III, who extended its use to other types and variant forms, especially to the later ones. The fringe is now found in nine examples, five of which belong to type C.[2] This feature is seen on some of the early bell-beakers from Spain, where it takes the form of a dentated edging to the ornamented zone. There it reproduces exactly the dentated edges of a narrow plaited band of straw or esparto grass.

PROVINCE IV

In coming north it is quite apparent from the Plate of ornamentation that a change has taken place in the scheme of decoration. The more effective motives of the two southern provinces—the bar-chevron against a shaded ground, the hexagon, bar-saltire, and chequer motives, and the shaded lozenge on a light background—have disappeared. Yet it may happen in the future that some of these motives will come to light. The lozenge motive on a shaded ground appears once on fig. 159, but the execution is so careless that it is not reproduced on the Plate of ornament, and a very rudely scratched design in which a lozenge can be discerned may be seen on fig. 166.

The shaded bar-chevron now assumes two aspects, unknown in the two southern provinces, though both varieties were employed in Yorkshire. (1) The shading consists of several parallel line-chevrons,[3] which have a stringy effect, far less effective than the bolder bar-chevrons of the two southern provinces. (2) The upper and lower indentations of the bar-chevron are small, and the upper and lower angles formed by them are united by lines which serve as shading.[4] The reason for this change in the scheme of ornament is to be sought in the gradual extinction of type A, with which the bolder designs and motives were associated.

PROVINCE V

The scheme of ornament in Province V is not very different from that of Province IV. The bar-chevron standing out upon a shaded ground, the hexagon, the bar-saltire, and the shaded lozenge on a light ground—motives which are missing in the latter province—do not reappear between the Tweed and the Tay. The bar-chevron however, on a shaded ground, though not found on any sepulchral beaker, appears on a fragment discovered in the kitchen-middens of Gullane Bay, fig. 215. The new northern variety of the shaded bar-chevron, in which the shading consists of several parallel line-chevrons, persists.[5] The same principle is also applied to produce a bar-lozenge (F207 from Midlothian), though not for the first time,

---

[1] F101, 116, 122, 132.

[2] A, fig. 103; AB, fig. 149; BC, figs. 135, 156; C, figs. 115, 117, 125, 129, 148.

[3] E. Riding, F152, Northumberland, F160, 183.

[4] E. Riding, F150, 155; Cumberland, F175; Northumberland, F178.

[5] F206, 209, 211.

as it also occurs on a rudely ornamented beaker from near Alnwick in Northumberland.[1] The method of shading by means of broken lines continued and may be seen on two examples from Roxburgh and Mull.[2]

In Province V we find a considerable development of the idea of dividing a horizontal zone into several compartments. It began in Province I,[3] but assumes a different character as it advances northwards into Suffolk and Derbyshire[4]; again it changes in Yorkshire by becoming more minuscule and finicking in appearance, in accordance with the changing taste of the period.[5] It attains its maximum development in this respect in F209 from Lanarkshire, though less elaborate examples are also known from East Lothian, Stirlingshire, and Perthshire.[6] The absence of this scheme of decoration in Province IV is to be ascribed to the small number of beakers that it has furnished hitherto.

A remarkable coincidence of similarity of design may be observed on a beaker from Woodhorn in Northumberland (F160) and on another from near Cockburnspath on the Berwickshire coast (F211), for as many as five similar arrangements of lines are found in the same order upon both vessels.

PROVINCE VI

The ornamentation on beakers of Province VI is homologous with that on similar vessels in Province V. The minute work of the metopic pattern from Lanarkshire (F209) recurs on F227 from Aberdeenshire, as well as the motive consisting of two rows of crossed lines united by longer or shorter verticals. This motive is a special development found only north of the Tweed and occurs in Lanark, Kinross, and Aberdeen.[7] A lozenge pattern from Ellon in Aberdeenshire (figs. 230, 231), of rude, careless work, and not reproduced on the Plates of ornament, is of the same kind as that on F207 from Midlothian.

PROVINCE VII

In Province VII the ornamentation is essentially the same as in the last province.

The peculiar bar-chevron from South Aberdeenshire, F232, is found again in Banffshire, F267. And a motive that first occurs in Northumberland, F178, and twice in Aberdeenshire, F235, 243, recurs in Ross and Caithness, F269, 286. The chequer pattern from Banff, F287, is to be seen on F190 from Fife.

THE TECHNIQUE

The instruments used to produce the ornament were apparently (1) a thin curved[8] slip of wood or bone slightly notched at short intervals, (2) a sharp, and (3) a blunt point, (4) a twisted cord, (5) a tube, and (6) the finger-nail.

---

[1] Bruce, pl. xii.   [2] F188, 217.   [3] F3, 4, 6, 9a.
[4] F45, 46, 49, 50.   [5] F101, 116, 122.
[6] F192, 203, 218.   [7] F186, 214, 233.
[8] Mr. John Ward has remarked that the slip of wood or bone was probably convexly curved and possibly

formed the periphery of a disc, to accommodate it to the varying curves of the vessel and, it may be added, to enable long and short lines to be made at will, which could not be effected by a straight slip. *Archaeol. Cambrensis*, 1902.

The notched slip of wood with a convex curve, when impressed upon the moist clay, left small square depressions separated by a very thin wall or septum. Dr. Tischler attributed these marks to a cogged wheel and this view is accepted in Germany. This technique is frequently found on the Continent on vessels of the bell-beaker class and is the most usual process employed in Britain for decorating beakers. Sometimes the depressions were filled with a white paste, which greatly enhanced the value of the design and introduced the important element of colour, as the white contrasted with the colour of the clay of which the vessel was made. In Britain there are only two or three examples of the use of a white filling, fig. 21 of type B 1 from Wilts., fig. 239 from Aberdeenshire, and perhaps fig. 190 from Fife. The white matter from this last example was analysed by Professor Olshausen and found to be composed of phosphate and carbonate of lime, probably the result of burnt bones.[1] The sharp point seems to have been used when the clay was already dry, and under this circumstance excellent work of high quality could be produced[2]; the blunt point on moist clay was apt to give coarser results.[3]

Impressions made by a twisted cord are never found on beakers of type A, but they occur occasionally on vessels of type B, some of which were intended for domestic use.

Quite exceptional was the use of a reed or the bone of a bird cut across to make a tube by which to produce small circular depressions, for it is only found on two beakers of type A in Wilts. and Berks.[4] Finger-nail impressions are also of rare occurrence.[5]

Sometimes two techniques are employed on the same vessel, such as the finger-nail and the notched slip of wood; the notched slip of wood and the point; the cord and the sharp point, &c. But in addition to these more regular methods any angular piece of wood, the first that came to hand, might be used to form cuneiform impressions at random on the surface of the vessel.[6]

---

[1] *Zeitsch. f. Ethnologie*, 1898, p. 546.   [2] Fig. 29.   [3] Figs. 33, 36.   [4] Figs. 3, 7.   [5] Figs. 3, 91.   [6] Fig. 17.

CHAPTER IV

OBJECTS FOUND WITH BEAKER INTERMENTS[1]

PROVINCE I

TABLE OF FINDS I

Type	No. of Beaker	Place	Stone bracer	Flint				Stone axe-hammer	Buttons with V-shaped perforation	'Pulley' ring	Disc beads	Bronze			Gold	Plate of Objects
				Scraper	Knife	Dagger	Arrowhead					Knife-dagger	Awl	Necklace		
A	1	B. 5 Winterbourn Stoke, Wilts.	..	×	..	..	..	..	×	×						
	3	B. 39 Stonehenge, Wilts.	..	..	..	×	..	..	..	..						O. 1
	4 bis	Winterbourn Monkton	..	..	×	..	..	..	×	×		..	..	..	..	
	4a²	B. near Avebury, Wilts.	..	..	..	..	..	×	..	..	..	×	..	..	..	O. 5
	10	B. at East Kennet, Wilts.	..	..	..	..	..	×	..	..	..	×	..	..	..	O. 6
	11	B. Stogursey, Somerset	..	×	..	..	..	..	..	..	..	×	..	..	..	
	12	B. Stogursey, Somerset	..	..	..	×	..	..	..	..	..	..	..	..	..	O. 2
	13	B. Fernworthy, Devon	..	..	..	..	..	..	×	..	..	×	..	..	..	Fragment
	13 tris	B. Oldbury Hill, Wilts.	..	..	..	..	..	..	..	..	..	×	..	..	..	Fragment
B	19	B. Mere Down, Wilts.	×	..	..	..	..	..	..	..	..	×	..	..	×	O. 8
	21	B. Roundway, Wilts.	×	..	..	..	×	..	..	..	..	×	..	..	..	O. 7
	24	B. Winterslow Hut, Wilts.	×	..	..	..	..	..	..	..	..	×	..	..	..	O. 9
	38	B. Devil's Dyke, Brighton	..	..	..	..	..	..	..	..	×	..	..	×	..	
	lost	B. 164 Normanton, Wilts.	..	..	..	..	..	..	..	..	..	×	..	×	..	O.10(A.W.205)
C	42	B. Wincanton, Somerset	..	×	..	..	..	..	..	..	..	×	..	..	..	

Reference	Place	Skeleton Interments without Beakers														
A.W. 200	B. 144 Normanton, Wilts.	..	..	..	..	..	..	..	..	..	×	..	..	..	lost	
A.W. 239	B. 9 Fovant, Wilts.	..	..	..	..	..	×	×	×	..	×	..	..	..	O. 3, 11a, b	
A.W. ii. 90	B. Overton Hill, Wilts.	..	..	..	..	..	..	..	..	..	×	×	..	..	and small bronze celt	

The *Table of Finds I* shows the number of objects found with beakers and they are not many. The most important are—

  Two flint daggers.

  Two stone axe-hammers.

  Three jet buttons with the V-perforation.

[1] See Plates lix, lx, showing the objects; the reference is given by O. followed by a numeral. [2] Not figured here.

Two or three stone bracers or wrist-guards.

Two 'pulley' rings.

Six flat knife-daggers of bronze or copper and two fragments.

Two gold discs.

The flint daggers found in this country vary in length from $4\frac{1}{2}$ to $7\frac{1}{2}$ in.; the form of the blade is lancet-shaped and the sides taper towards the butt. Examples are O. 1, 2. The first, found with beaker fig. 3 from B. 39 Stonehenge, measures $7\frac{1}{8} \times 2\frac{1}{8}$ in., and the second, found with fig. 12 from Somerset, is $5\frac{3}{8}$ in. long.

Both the hammer-axes that accompanied figs. 4a, 10 from a barrow near Avebury and East Kennet are similar in form. The latter is a very fine specimen measuring $6\frac{1}{4} \times 1\frac{3}{4}$ in. and is figured by Thurnam.[1]

The conical jet buttons with a V-shaped perforation at the base are so well known to archaeologists that it need only be remarked that the one found with figs. 4 *bis, tris*, belonged to a male interment, and other examples of this fact will be noted later on. On the Continent such buttons belong to the end of the neolithic and to the aeneolithic periods; in Britain they lasted into the later period when cinerary interments prevailed.

The so-called jet or shale 'pulley rings'—a designation given them by Hoare—have a diameter of about $1\frac{1}{2}$ in. and a groove on the outer edge with two or three intercommunicating perforations at one side. They are supposed, perhaps erroneously, to have been used for fastening the dress; the example found with the conical jet button above, and beakers 4 *bis, tris*, had been deposited with a male skeleton, and is a finer specimen than O. 3 from Fovant, as the upper surface instead of being plain is ornamented with fine lines in relief radiating from the centre.[2] This sort of ring is associated sometimes with a bronze knife-dagger. For instance, O. 3 was found with O. 11a, which measures 8 in. in length, a bronze pricker, and four well-made flint arrowheads, O. 11b. A ring of the same description from bar. 68, Rudstone, East Riding, was discovered by Canon Greenwell with a bronze knife-dagger and a button with the V-shaped perforation.[3] All these objects had been laid beside a male skeleton.

The wrist-guards or bracers are of fine-grained stone, either flat or curved in section, with two or three holes at each end and from 4 to $4\frac{1}{2}$ in. in length. Both the bracers found with figs. 21, 24 are flat and measure $4\frac{1}{2} \times 1\frac{3}{8}$ in. and $4\frac{3}{4} \times 2$ in. respectively. An example with three holes at each end from Brandon in Suffolk is shown by O. 4. On the Continent, as we have seen above, these bracers are sometimes associated with bell-beakers.

The gold disc (O. 8) found with beaker fig. 19 and the bronze knife (O. 8) has a diameter of $1\frac{1}{8}$ in. and is ornamented with a hatched cross. It was attached by two holes near the centre.

Small, thin, perforated discs of jet or lignite have been found in the north of Scotland with neolithic interments, and necklaces formed of such discs constitute the earliest type of necklace in Britain, one which lasted no doubt for a long time. An example from Yorkshire is shown by O. 31. The idea of making such discs is so elementary that the Bushmen of South Africa still make them out of ostrich shell.

The dimensions and some other particulars regarding the six knife-daggers of bronze or copper that have been preserved are given in tabular form :—

[1] *Arch.* xliii. 410, fig. 96.   [2] *Crania Britan.* ii, pl. 58, 2.   [3] *B.B.* figs. 123, 125.

Plate of Objects	No. of Beaker	Place	Length and Width	Rivets	Description
O. 5	Fig. 4*a*	Avebury, Wilts. . . .	$4 \times 1\frac{3}{8}$	3	Flat, well-rounded head
O. 6	„ 10	East Kennet, Wilts. . .	$5\frac{1}{2} \times 2\frac{3}{8}$	3	„ „ „ „
	„ 13	Fernworthy, Devon . .			A mere fragment
O. 7	„ 21	Roundway, Wilts. . .	10×2	tang	Flat, weighs $5\frac{1}{4}$ oz.
O. 8	„ 19	Mere Down, Wilts. . .	$5 \times 1\frac{3}{8}$	tang	Flat
O. 9	„ 24	Winterslow, Wilts. . .	$5\frac{3}{8} \times 1\frac{3}{4}$	tang	Flat, rather rounded head
O. 10	lost	Normanton, Wilts. . .	$5\frac{3}{4} \times 1\frac{3}{4}$	3	Narrow, three parallel lines
O. 11*a*	No beaker	Fovant 9, Wilts. . . .	$8\frac{7}{8} \times 2\frac{3}{8}$	4	Flat, rounded head

In this country these knives and knife-daggers have always been regarded as of bronze, though none has been analysed. A flat axe from Butterwick, East Riding, which Dr. Much assumed to be copper,[1] when analysed by Prof. Gowland turned out to be of unexceptionable bronze containing 10·74 per cent. of tin.[2] The small knife-dagger of the same type as that from Avebury found with it is presumably of the same material. Nevertheless, judging by the colour of the metal where the patina has been removed, O. 7, 9 appear to be either of copper or of an alloy poor in tin, though certainty on this point can only be gained after an analysis of the metal.[3]

These blades are of two distinct types: (1) the handle is attached to the base of the blade by three rivets; (2) the handle is attached to a tang.

The first type is associated with examples of type A and the second with type B, though whether that circumstance is accidental or not cannot at present be decided. Neither is it certain that one type is earlier than the other. Neither type can be compared with the small lancet-shaped copper blades from Hagia Triada in Crete, as they belong to too early a date, or with the copper daggers from the Lake Dwellings of Switzerland, for these are too pointed.

In Central Europe it is not easy to find small dagger blades with a relatively broad base and a rounded head like those from near Avebury and East Kennet, O. 5, 6. But very similar blades of small dimensions, for the most part of copper, have been found by M. Siret at El Algar and other places in the south-east of Spain, though none of them seems to have a bevelled edge as in O. 6. One from El Algar figured by him, though a little smaller and broader with a rounded head, is much like O. 5 in every respect.[4] We must look perhaps to the Iberian Peninsula as the ultimate source from which issued our earliest bronze, though it would probably arrive not as a direct import but mediately through Gaul. For instance, M. A. Bertrand has figured from Lozère a small bronze dagger, which though rather narrow is not unlike O. 5.[5] That the earliest bronze was imported into Britain can hardly be doubted. For if copper or tin had been known in Cornwall

[1] *Die Kupferzeit in Europa* (1893), p. 180.

[2] *J. Anthrop. Inst.* xxxvi. 26.

[3] Since the above was written, O. 7, 8 have been analysed and found to be of pure copper. Judging from its appearance O. 9 is also of copper.

[4] Siret, *Premiers âges du métal . . . de l'Espagne*, pl. xxxix, from grave 635.

[5] *La Gaule avant les Gaulois*, 219.

or Devon at the beginning of the beaker period, large quantities of blades would no doubt have been found there, just as in Spain where copper ore abounds. With the exception of fragments of one bronze blade from Devon, no metal has been observed with the various beaker interments in Devon and Dorset, nor in any of the inhabited sites of the Bronze Age hitherto explored in Devon and Cornwall.

The knife-dagger (O. 10), found with fragments of a 'richly ornamented drinking cup', differs very considerably from O. 5, 6. The blade is narrow with a stout centre, and is decorated with three parallel lines. It therefore belongs to a later type of blade than the above, and appears to bring the beaker class further down in time than is usually believed, in fact into Bronze Age II. It is not impossible that Sir R. Hoare has here committed the same mistake as when he applied the term 'drinking cup' to a vessel of cinerary urn type,[1] which is figured in the next volume (fig. 1).

The tanged knife-daggers (O. 7, 8, 9) differ from the above mentioned in that the blade is proportionally narrower and longer. Central Europe again fails us in the quest for similar blades, but several are known in Gaul. A copper blade 10 in. long by $1\frac{3}{4}$ in. wide, with a bevelled edge and a short, rather broad tang, from the Grotto Bounias near Arles, is quite comparable with O. 7 from Roundway, Wilts.[2] A blade from Coatjou-glas, Finisterre, though measuring only 4 in. × $\frac{15}{16}$ in. and having the tang perforated by a rivet-hole, is much like O. 9 from Winterslow, Wilts.[3] Yet it must not be inferred that the British blades belong exactly to the same time as those from Gaul, for the grave furniture and the nature of the sepulchre make it clear that the former are of a later date.

In the *Table of Finds I*, I have added three skeleton interments without beakers, but found with objects of the same sort as those in the upper part of the Table. Of the objects enumerated, only one dagger (O. 11*a*), three flint arrowheads (O. 11*b*), and 'pulley' ring (O. 3) seem to have been preserved. The blade, though longer and narrower than O. 5, 6, like them is flat and round-headed, and from being found with a 'pulley' ring and a conical button with the V-shaped perforation may probably be included in the beaker period.

The number of beakers found in Province I, including twenty-nine mentioned by Hoare but now lost, must amount to about ninety and the number of bronze or copper blades to nine, or perhaps eleven. As these interments have to be spread over a space of about 400 years or so, it is evident the percentage of bronze for any one century is very small. But the wealth of the community in the matter of metal can hardly be estimated correctly by what is found deposited with the dead. It is only necessary to think of the very considerable number of axes and axe-hammers of stone, and of flat axes of bronze and copper exhibited in our Museums, and to compare them with the very trifling percentage of such objects that have been found in graves. It must be evident, then, that the grave equipment by no means furnishes a fair criterion of the amount of stone or of metal in use

---

[1] *A. W.*, Normanton bar. 156, p. 202.

[2] *Matériaux*, xi. 544.

[3] Other tanged blades are figured in *Matériaux*, xiv. 491; xxii. 157. Two flat tanged copper blades from Palencia, in form almost identical with the last, are in the Archaeological Museum in Madrid. Two other tanged blades from Brittany and St. Nazaire are preserved in the Musée Dobrée at Nantes, another from St. Pé Dardet (H. Garonne) is at Toulouse.

in the earliest bronze period, or Bronze Age I of Dr. Montelius.[1] The amount of metal was certainly small, but not so small as the percentage of interments with bronze to interments without metal would lead us to believe. A good many daggers would be lost or were never deposited with the dead.

PROVINCE II

TABLE OF FINDS II.

TYPE	NO. OF BEAKER	PLACE	Flint scraper, spear-head	Flint knife	Flint dagger	Flint arrowhead	Buttons, V-shaped perforation	Bone mesh-rule	Stone bracer	Bronze awl	Bronze ear-ring	Bone pin
A	48	Green Low, Derby . . .	×	..	×	×	..	×	..	..	..	×
	49	Smerril Moor, Derby . .	×	..	×	..	..	×				
	51	Haddon Field, Derby . .	..	..	..	×	..	×	..	×		
	52	Bee Low, Derby . . .	..	×								
	54	Hay Top Hill, Derby . .	×									
	56	Stanshope Barrow, Stafford	×									
	60	Mouse Lowe, Stafford . .	×	..	..	×						
	62	Stakor Hill, Derby . . .	×	..	..	..	..	..	..	..	×	
	63	Dowel, Derby	..	..	..	×	×	..	..	..		
	68	Minning Lowe, Derby . .	×	..	..	..	..	..	..	×		
	71	Stanshope Barrow, Stafford	×	..	..	..	..	..	..	..		
B	82	Brandon Fields, Suffolk .	..	..	..	..	..	..	×			
A	lost	Norton, Northampton[2] .	..	..	×							

The *Table of Finds II* shows that three flint daggers, four flint arrowheads, eight flint implements, one jet button with the V-shaped perforation, three 'mesh-rules' of bone and one bone pin were found with examples of type A; but of bronze only two awls or prickers, and a pair of ear-rings of the simplest kind. The flint dagger, three arrowheads, a 'mesh-rule' and bone pin from Green Low, Derbyshire, are figured under O. 12. Both this 'mesh-rule' and the one from Smerril Moor were found with male interments. The bronze ear-rings were described by Bateman as two small pieces of thin bronze, bent in the middle, just sufficiently to clasp the ear.

To type B belongs, as in the Southern Province, a stone bracer (O. 4).

As it happens, no bronze blades have occurred with beakers in this Province, but I add a List of *Bronze celts and knife-daggers with skeleton interments* found in thirteen barrows, from which it appears certain that one if not two small bronze knives—from Parcelly Hay and Stanshope Barrow—belong to the Beaker period.

---

[1] Dr. O. Montelius, in a very valuable paper on the *Chronology of the British Bronze Age* (*Arch.* lxi. 97–162), divides it into five periods, but to Period I he adds the sub-title *Copper Age*. All the knife-daggers of the Beaker period belong to his Bronze Age I.

[2] *P.S. Ant. Lond.*, 2nd ser., xix. 307 (richly ornamented).

BRONZE CELTS AND KNIFE-DAGGERS WITH SKELETON INTERMENTS

References	Place	Celts	Knife-Daggers		Depth of Grave	Interment		Other Objects with the Interment
			Length	No. of rivets		Primary	Secondary	
Bateman (2),² p. 34	*Shuttlestone Barrow, Derby?³	×	4"	2	8'	×	..	Jet bead; circular flint; horn handle
„ „ pp.38-9	*End Low Barrow, Derby	..	6¼"	3	6'	×	..	Flint spear-head
Bateman (1),¹ p. 68, Evans, Bronze fig. 3	*Moot Low,¹ Derby	×	..	..	..	×	..	Lower jaw of a pig
Bateman (2), p. 21	*Kenslow Barrow, Derby	..	3"	3	..	×		
„ „ p. 119	*Thorncliff Barrow, Stafford?	..	5"	3	..	×	..	Neat flint implement
„ „ p. 115	*Deep Dale Barrow, Stafford	..	5½"	3	over 3'	×		
Bateman (1), p. 90	*Wormhill, Derby	..	6⅜"	3	3'	×	..	Wooden sheath; two flint implements
Bateman (2), p. 160	*Stanshope Barrow, Stafford	..	4½"	2	9"	..	×	Flints; in same barrow three beakers were found
Bateman (1), p. 66	*New Inns Barrow, Derby	..	5"	3	..	×	..	Wooden sheath probably
„ „ p. 61	*Brier Low,⁴ Derby	..	5½"	3	..	×		
„ „ p. 64	*Carder Low,⁴ Derby	..	5⅛"	3	..	×	..	Basalt axe-hammer
Bateman (2), p. 24	*Parcelly Hay, Derby	..	4¾"	3	..	..	×	Granite axe-hammer. In grave below were sherds of a beaker
Bateman (1), p. 48	*Borther Low, Derby	×	..	..	..	..	×	Sherds of plain, coarse urn, flint arrowhead, two canine teeth of dog or fox

The asterisk * shows that the bronze celts and knife-daggers are preserved in the Sheffield Public Museum.

The List contains three flat celts and eleven flat knife-daggers of smaller size than some of those in Province I, yet all cannot be included as contemporary with beakers, for some must be left for the food-vessel period, when inhumation was also in vogue. The number of beakers at present known in Province II may be about seventy, so that probably more than one or two of these small knives are contemporary, though we cannot say how many. Bateman mentions four barrows in which he found a skeleton interment with an awl or pricker, but no other article of bronze.⁵ Some or all of these simple instruments may be considered contemporary with the beakers of this province.

Bronze was undoubtedly rare, more so than in Province I, a fact which tends to show that the metal was imported from the south, and that only the smaller pieces found their way north. And so far as the evidence afforded by interments goes, we cannot be sure at present that flat celts of bronze were in use during the beaker period in either of the two southern provinces. Though as they have been found in Province III near a beaker and also with a food vessel it is probable that they were known in Provinces I and II.

¹ Bateman, *Vestiges of the Antiq. of Derbyshire.*
² Bateman, *Ten Years' Diggings.*
³ *Arch.* xliii. 445, figs. 149, 150.
⁴ *Op. cit.* pl. 32, figs. 3, 4.

⁵ Barrow near Gotham. Bateman (1), pp. 104-5.
Bee Low, 2 bronze awls; in same barrow as fig. 52.
Waggon Low, small awl, 1½ in. long.
Elkstone, Barrow 1, bronze awl. Bateman (2), pp. 71-2, 85, 171.

PROVINCE III

TABLE OF FINDS III

No. of Beaker	Place	Flake knives, flakes worked flint	Flint knife	Round flint scraper	Flint dagger	Flint flat axe	Stone axe-hammer	Stone bracer	Jet button, V-perforation	Amber button, V-perforation	Jet 'Pulley ring'	Jet button or bead	Jet disc necklace	Bone pin	Bronze awl or pricker	Bronze knife-dagger	Gold-headed rivets	Stag-horn pick
98	Garton Slack, Barrow 37	..	..	..	×	..	×	..	×									
102	Garton Slack, Barrow 161	..	×	..	..	..	..	..	×									
109	Ferry Fryston, Barrow 161	..	..	..	..	..	..	..	..	..	..	..	..	..	×			
112	Painsthorp Wold, Barrow 4	×	×															
114	Painsthorp Wold, Barrow 4	..	×															
115	Garton Slack, Barrow 163	..	×															
116	Garton Slack, Barrow 163	×	×	..	..	×	..	..	..	..	..	..	..	×				
121	Aldro, Barrow 116	×	..	..	..	..	..	..	..	..	..	..	..	..	×			
126	Hanging Grimston, Barrow 55	×	..	..	..	..	..	..	×									
129	Rudstone, Barrow 66	..	..	×														
130	Ganton, Barrow 21	..	×															
138	Rudstone, Barrow 62	..	×															
139	Rudstone, Barrow 62	×	×	..	..	..	..	..	..	..	..	..	..	..	×			
144	Rudstone, Barrow 61	..	..	..	..	..	..	..	..	..	..	..	..	..	..	..	..	×
147	Huggate, Barrow 254	..	..	..	..	..	..	..	..	..	..	..	..	..	×	..	..	
149	Driffield	..	..	..	..	..	..	×	×	..	..	..	..	..	..	×	×	
153	Middleton on the Wolds	×	..	..	×	..	..	..	×	..	..	..	..	×				
156	Garton Slack, Barrow 81	..	..	..	..	..	..	.:	×									
lost	Thwing, Barrow 60	..	..	..	..	..	..	..	×	..	×							
frag.	Acklam Wold, Barrow 124	..	..	..	..	..	..	..	×	×	×							
Skeleton, no beaker	Garton Slack, Barrow 152	..	..	..	×	..	..	..	×									
,,	Garrowby Wold, Barrow 64	..	..	..	..	..	..	..	..	..	..	×	..	×				
,,	Langton, Barrow 2	..	..	..	..	..	..	..	..	..	×	..	..	×				
,,	Helperthorp, Barrow 49	..	..	..	..	.	..	..	..	..	..	..	..	..	..	×		
,,	Rudstone, Barrow 68	..	..	..	..	..	..	..	×	..	×	..	..	..	×			

The Table of Finds shows that the principal objects deposited with the dead, apart from a beaker, were mainly of flint or other stone.

To the three flint daggers perhaps a fourth may be added, though not found with a beaker; making a total in the three provinces of nine such weapons, of which eight had been placed beside a beaker. An example measuring $6\frac{1}{4}$ in. in length, and found with fig. 98, is shown by O. 13 from the collection of Mr. Mortimer.

The flat axe of black flint found with fig. 116 is beautifully polished, and is $2\frac{7}{8}$ inches long with a cutting-edge $1\frac{1}{8}$ in. wide.[1]

The stone axe-hammer that accompanied a flint dagger and a jet button, perforated at the base, as regards form is not very unlike the two from Province I already mentioned.[2]

[1] Mortimer, fig. 541.   [2] Mortimer, fig. 513.

Nearly all the jet buttons with a V-shaped perforation at the base are plain, but one found by Canon Greenwell at Thwing with a beaker so broken as to be past mending is shown by O. 14. And another similar button (O. 15), from bar. 68, Rudstone, was found with a male skeleton interment. The cruciform ornament of the former is of the same kind as that on the gold disc O. 8, but as it had to be adapted to a conical form it necessarily assumed the aspect of a Greek cross. They may have been used, as Canon Greenwell suggests, to fasten the dress, but the dress of a man not of a woman, for there are five undoubted instances in which these buttons have been found deposited with a male skeleton.[1] And probably two more instances in which the buttons were accompanied by flint daggers may be added,[2] bringing up the total to seven. A man seems only to have needed one button, which might have been sewn on to one corner of a garment, such as a cloak, which was closed by passing the button through a button-hole or a loop sewn on to the opposite corner.

The two 'pulley rings' from Thwing and Acklam Wold, together with buttons with the V-shaped perforation, had been placed beside the bodies of men ; so twice in Wilts., and twice in the East Riding, these articles of dress have been found together. The use of these rings is less obvious than the use of the buttons, but if a string were passed through the holes in the circumference, such a ring could be worn round the neck as an ornament or an amulet.

The small slender awls or prickers of bronze, about $1\frac{1}{4}$ in. long, have sometimes been found inserted into a wooden handle, and generally appertain to female interments. They are adapted for sewing skins together in the same way that a shoemaker uses an awl. Two found with fig. 139 belonged to an interment probably of a woman, and three together with cowrie shells were discovered by Canon Greenwell with the skeleton of a dolichocephalic woman at Langton (B. 2), a burial which probably falls within the beaker period. On the other hand, Canon Greenwell found a bronze knife-dagger, and a bronze drill or pricker $2\frac{3}{8}$ in. long, with a male skeleton at Butterwick (B. 39) ; and Hoare found a knife-dagger, a small celt and a pricker, all of bronze, at Overton Hill (B. 1),[3] where the body may also have been that of a man.

The bronze knife-dagger, the stone bracer with gold-head studs, and an object of bone of unknown use, from Driffield, are shown under O. 16. The blade is imperfect, measuring $3\frac{1}{2} \times 1\frac{3}{4}$ in., and when complete may have had a length of $4\frac{5}{8}$ in. It is thin, flat, with a bevelled edge, and is provided with a tang nearly as wide as the base of the blade. Near the end is a rivet. Mr. Mortimer found another bone object, like the one here figured, with a food vessel at Garton Slack (B. 162).

Taking the number of beakers in Province III at about 70, the percentage of bronze objects laid beside them is very small, even if we include some from the five barrows containing skeleton interments. On the other hand, the interments are also poor in stone axe-hammers, for one only of these typical Stone Age implements has been found, and none with a beaker in Province II. This leads us to suppose that the people were living in a transition period when flint knives and flakes were naturally abundant, as the East Riding is a flint-bearing area, but axe-hammers of stone were rarely made. The little metal they possessed was

---

[1] With beakers 4a, 102: with a lost beaker from Thwing, bar. 60; with beaker fragments from Acklam Wold, bar. 124, and with a skeleton interment from Rudstone, bar. 68.
[2] With beakers 98, 153.   [3] *A. W.* ii. 90.

evidently imported from the south, where bronze was so much prized that as a rule only very insignificant pieces were allowed to percolate northwards.

Three very remarkable chalk cylinders, found in the same barrow as fig. 152, cannot be passed over without comment, for they are probably contemporary with the beaker and deserve notice on account of their suggestiveness with regard to the religion of the period. These box-like articles were found with the skeleton of a child about five years old. The smallest one lay behind, touching the head; the two others were also behind, just touching the hips. As the body lay north and south the objects were to the west of the body. The largest is $4\frac{5}{8}$ in. the smallest $3\frac{3}{8}$ in. high.[1] Each cylinder is divided into four panels, two wider and two narrower, and in the centre of one of the larger panels of each cylinder are carved the eyes, nose, and eyebrows of a human face.[2] On two of the cylinders the ornament is partly in slight relief; on the one of middle size it is incised. The leading motive is the bar-chevron arranged to form a bar-saltire, although the lozenge motive is also employed. The shading is produced by simple lines by cross-hatching, or by broken lines of parallel zigzags. All the motives and the different methods of shading found on these chalk objects are equally to be seen on the Yorkshire beakers, except the human face, the concentric circles and the four-rayed star on the top of one cylinder. But a similar star may be seen on the bottom of food vessels from Ireland (F. V. figs. 285a, 302a, 310a), and incised concentric circles are visible on stones at Dowth on the Boyne.[3]

M. Déchelette maintains that these cylinders are not to be considered indigenous work, but imports from the coast of the Iberian Peninsula.[4] He bases his opinion upon the similarity of the ornamental designs on these cylinders with what is found on certain fictile vessels and slate plaques which abound in the Iberian Peninsula at the beginning of the Bronze Age. That may be so. But it is very difficult to believe that in the early Bronze Age these chalk cylinders of soft material, some of the work on which is very fine and delicate, could have been shipped at the mouth of the Tagus or at any port on the Cantabrian coast, and delivered as intact as they are at Filey Bay or the mouth of the Humber. Whatever Southern influence they may betray reached Britain by a more circuitous route, and possibly at a much earlier date than the cylinders themselves. Their finder, Canon Greenwell, states that they are made from stone of the immediate district, probably from some of the numerous blocks which fell from the sea cliff and were abundant on the shore. This is only some five or six miles from Folkton, and until more evidence is brought forward to prove they were imported it is safer to believe they were made on the spot.

The meaning of these human faces and what they seem to imply will be discussed later on.

---

[1] The tops and one aspect of each are reproduced in the plates with sepulchral objects O. 17. Canon Greenwell has exhibited the ornament unrolled in *Arch.* lii, pl. ii; also shown in *Guide to Bronze Age Antiquities in Brit. Mus.* p. 91.

[2] It has been suggested that one of these faces, which is less well drawn than the others, represents the *antennae* of a 'butterfly', such as those stamped on gold discs from the earliest shaft-graves of Mycenae, and that there- fore these cylinders show connexion with the Aegean culture. But the lozenge that forms the body of the 'butterfly' is precisely the same in form and occupies the same place in the decorative motive as the lozenge on the largest cylinder, although in the former the longer axis of the lozenge, evidently to save room, is placed vertically instead of horizontally.

[3] G. Coffey, *T. R. I. A.* xxx, pl. vi, figs. 1, 2.

[4] Déchelette, *Archéol. Préhist.* i. 595–6.

PROVINCE IV

The finds unfortunately require no Table to set them forth; they are reduced to a flint dagger found near Wooler, Northumberland, with the fragment of a beaker (fig. 159). It may, however, be mentioned that a fragment of flint and a large cobble-stone weighing 4½ lb. was found in a cist at Amble, Northumberland, with fig. 161a, and that seven flints accompanied beaker fig. 173. The skull found with this last interment had a cephalic index of 78 and the skeleton was that of a woman of weak physique who was perhaps knock-kneed. Yet in spite of the infirmity of her body the beaker deposited beside her was very well formed, and the clay of which it is made was well tempered without admixture of sand or crushed stone.

PROVINCE V

TABLE OF FINDS IV

PLATE OF OBJECTS	FIG.	PLACE	Flint arrowhead	Flint scraper	Flint knife	Stone bracer	Bronze knife-dagger	Bronze bangle	Disc beads	Gold	DESCRIPTION
O. 18	190	Dairsie, Fife	×								
	194	Tippermallo, Perth . .	..	×	×						
	204	Collessie, Fife. . . .	..	..	..	..	×	..	..	×	Blade, thin, flat, 6 × 2⅛ in., gold mounting
	205										
	213	Crawford, Lanark . .	..	..			..	×			Solid, diameter 3 in. Anderson, fig. 65
	217	Callachally, Mull . .	..	..	..	×	×				Thin, flat fragments of a blade
	frag.	Stoney Kirk, Wigton .	..	..	..	..	..	..	×		
O. 19		Sketraw, Dunbar	..	..	..	..	×	..	..	×	Blade 5¾ in. long, four rivets and gold mounting. *P. S. A. S.* xxvii 7
O. 20		Letham, near Perth . . .	..	..	..	..	×				Blade 3¼ × 1 7⁄16 in., very thin. *P. S. A. S.* xxxi. 183
O. 21		Drumlanrick, Callender. .	..	..	..	..	×				Blade 4½ in. long, three rivets. Anderson, fig. 9
O. 22		Cleigh, Lochnell, Argyll . .	..	..	..	..	×				Blade 5 × 2¼ in., flat, three large rivets. *P. S. A. S.* xii. 455

The *Table of Finds* shows that three pieces of bronze, two of them of larger size than any from Provinces II and III, have been discovered with beakers. The Collessie dagger was found under the same huge cairn (120 ft. in diameter and 14 ft. high) as the beakers, but in a pit about 25 ft. from the centre, along with a burnt interment. Notwithstanding this circumstance, I have assumed above that they are probably contemporary. The reason why these larger pieces are found so far north is that they belong to a later time. It has been shown that, judging from their appearance, both the beakers from Crawford and the

Isle of Mull are very late. And, as the invaders hardly reached Province V till fully 200 years after their first arrival in Britain, both the armlet from Crawford and the blade from Mull are probably about 300 years later than the date of the invasion, and are likewise later than the small knife-dagger from Yorkshire. The Collessie blade with a gold mount (O. 18) is earlier than that from Mull, but still it belongs to a relatively late section of the beaker period in Province V.

At the foot of the *Table of Finds* is appended a note of four skeleton interments with which a thin, flat bronze blade was discovered (O. 19, 20, 21, 22). It is of course uncertain whether these should be reckoned as belonging to the beaker period, or to the food-vessel period. The two partly overlapped, though the latter lasted a good deal longer.

It will also be observed from the *Table of Finds* that though bronze was extremely rare— for these blades have to be distributed over 200 years or more—only one stone bracer and no stone axe-hammers are recorded. But as axe-hammers survived in North Britain as late as Bronze Age III, or later, their absence from beaker interments must be regarded as accidental.

The disc beads of lignite from Stoneykirk, Wigtonshire, vary in diameter from $\frac{1}{4}$ in. to $\frac{3}{8}$ in., with a thickness of about $\frac{1}{16}$ in. They are therefore quite like those shown by O. 31 from Yorkshire, and both necklaces are provided with a central, triangular pendant of the same material.

PROVINCE VI

TABLE OF FINDS V

FIG.	PLACE	Flint					Stone bracer	Jet beads	Amber unshaped	Bone ring	Horn.spoon	Bronze knife-dagger	DESCRIPTION
		Flakes	Scrapers	Borer	Arrowheads	Axe							
226, 227	Broomend, Kintore	×											
228, 229	Cruden, Aberdeen . .	..	..	..	×	×	×	×	×				
230, 231	Ellon, Aberdeen . .	..	..	..	×								
232, 233	Skene, Aberdeen . .	..	×										
243	Kinellar, Aberdeen . .	..	..	×	..	..	..	..	..	×			
248	Leslie, Aberdeen . .	..	..	..	×								
249	Broomend, Aberdeen .	..	..	..	..	..	..	..	..	..	×		Figured with beaker
262	Linlathen, Forfar . .	..	..	..	..	..	..	..	..	..	..	×	Thin, flat blade, $4\frac{1}{2} \times 2$ in. O. 23
264	Turriff, Aberdeen . .	..	×										
O. 24	Barnhill, Broughty Ferry	..	..	..	..	..	..	..	..	..	..	×	Blade, $3\frac{3}{8} \times 1\frac{1}{8}$ in., thin, flat. Two gold nearly plain discs, $1\frac{1}{4}$ in. diameter

As the *Table of Finds* shows, many of the small objects are of flint. But the flat axe from Cruden, which is a fine specimen of polished flint 6 in. long, may be regarded as a survival; for the jet fusiform beads with a rounded knob at each end found with it (O. 25) must be later than the neolithic period to which the flint axe might belong.   The few pieces of amber that accompanied the find are unworked.

Horn was utilized for making spoons and ladles.   An example of the latter is figured with fig. 249 from Broomend in Aberdeenshire.

Province VI lies so far north that metal was of rare occurrence,   In addition to the small blade from Linlathen may probably be added the still smaller, flat, thin blade, O. 24, from Barnhill, near Dundee, found with a skeleton interment in a cist under a large cairn.

PROVINCE VII

TABLE OF FINDS VI

Fig.	Place	Flint chips	Flint arrowhead	Stone bracer	Disc beads
269	Fyrish, Ross	..	..	×	
277	Forglen, Banff . . .	..	×		
280	Lesmurdie, Banff . .	×			
286	Dunrobin, Sutherland .	..	..	..	×

The grave-equipment, as might be expected in the extreme north of Britain, is of the scantiest.   The polished felstone wrist-guard or bracer from Fyrish is $4\frac{1}{2}$ in. long, and only $\frac{1}{2}$ in. shorter than the example from Driffield in the East Riding (O. 16), which in form it exactly resembles.   The disc-beads, 118 in number, were of shale about the size and thickness of a threepenny bit, and only six of them were perforated.   They accompanied the corpse of a young woman with a brachycephalous skull having a cephalic index of 82·4, and it may be supposed that she was expected to finish the perforation of the discs and make herself a necklace during her leisure moments in the next world.

CHAPTER V

ETHNOGRAPHICAL AND HISTORICAL

§ 1. THE PHYSICAL CHARACTERISTICS OF THE INVADERS. THEIR NUMBERS

THE pottery used by the new invaders of Britain having been examined, classified, and arranged in such a manner as to exhibit the relative chronology of the different sections into which it has been divided, it remains to take a glance at the new comers themselves, to learn what manner of men they were. The neolithic men whom they were to encounter were of comparatively refined appearance, with oval faces, regular features, and the type of skull known as dolichocephalic; all or most of them belonged to the Mediterranean race of Sergi, with an average height of about 5 ft. 5½ in.–5 ft. 6½ in., and a physique not remarkable for its strength. To these men some of the new invaders offered the greatest contrast. The skull was short and square, the general aspect of the face rugged and forbidding owing to the great development of the superciliary ridges and of the eyebrows. The cheekbones were prominent and the nose projected much beyond the prominent eyebrows; the lower jaw was square, massive, often prognathous, and terminated in a prominent chin. Coupled with teeth often of extraordinary size many of these invaders must have presented the appearance of great ferocity and brutality, in a degree which far surpasses our modern conventional representation of the criminal of the type of Bill Sikes. They were rather taller than the old inhabitants and had the advantage of a powerful build, and great muscular development. Their women were less ill-favoured; the superciliary ridges were much less developed and the facial outlines being on finer lines gave them a softer and less repelling appearance.[1]

Dr. Thomas Bryce, M.D., who has paid great attention to the prehistoric craniology of Great Britain, more especially of North Britain, finds that, excluding dolichocephalic specimens, there are three main types of Round Barrow crania.

1. A sub-brachycephalic type that corresponds rather closely with the *Borreby* type of skull, and again with the *Sion* type of His and Ruetimeyer—a type which was held by Davis and Thurnam to be the typical Round Barrow cranium.

2. A type with a higher cephalic index, often markedly platycephalous, that corresponds exactly with the *Dissentis* type of His and Ruetimeyer, and is represented nearly pure in the beaker series of North Britain.

3. A type which has the higher index and other characters of the second type with the longer face and stronger jaws of the first.

[1] A good summary of the literature that bears upon the Neolithic and Bronze Age skulls is given by Dr. Rice Holmes in *Great Britain and the Invasions of Julius Caesar*, pp. 393–409, 424–44.

Many of the individuals of the Scottish group were of low or of moderate stature, and thus the beaker interments of North Britain represents in this respect also the Alpine type of Ripley.   It is specially to be noted, moreover, that this series is not consistent with the generally accepted proposition that the Bronze Age immigrants were uniformly a tall people.[1]

CEPHALIC INDEX OF SKULLS FOUND WITH BEAKERS[2]

Province	No. of Beaker	Place and County	Cephalic Index	Sex	Stature	Length of Femur in Inches
I	27	Rotherly, Wilts.	74–6 ?	M ?	5 ft. 9½ in.	
	20	Stogursey, Somerset	77·6			
	25	Rushmore, Barrow 20, Dorset	brachy	M	5 ft. 6¼ in.	
	9	Winterbourn Stoke, Wilts.	80			
	31	Wor Barrow, Dorset	80·6	..	5 ft. 4·6 in.	
	22	Roundway, Wilts.	83	M		
	39	Culbone, Somerset	brachy			
	30	Dorchester	very brachy			
II	52	Bee Lowe, Derby	73·3			
	94b	Plas Heaton, Denbigh	78			
	60	Mouse Lowe, Stafford	78·7	M	very large	
	54	Haytop Hill, Derby	79	M	..	18·7
	51	Haddon Field, Derby	80	M		
	48	Green Lowe, Derby	81·1	M	..	19·2
	49	Smerrill Moor, Derby	82	M		
	lost	Parsley Hay, Derby	82	M	..	18·3
	62	Staker Hill, Derby	84	F		
	55	Castern, Stafford	85·6	..	..	19·5
	94	St. Fagan's, Glamorgan	83·9	M		
			86·15			
IV	161a	Amble, Northumberland	78	F		
	161	Castle Carrock, Cumberland	80	M		
V	189	Juniper Green, Midlothian	82	M		
VI	243	*Klinterty Kinellar, Aberdeen	84·3	M	5 ft. 1 in.	
	239	Auchendoir, Aberdeen	85	M	5 ft. 6 in.	
	238	Parkhill, Aberdeen	85	M	5 ft. 2 in.	
	247	Persley, Aberdeen	85·1	M		
	{232 / 233	Skene, Aberdeen	86·1	M	5 ft. 4 in.	
	253	Parkhill, Aberdeen	87·4	M	5 ft. 7 in.	
	254	*Stoneywood, Aberdeen	92·3	M	5 ft. 1 in.	
	256	Mains of Leslie, Aberdeen	brachy	..	short	
	248	Leslie, Aberdeen	..	..	very tall	
	249	Broomend, Aberdeen	..	..	tall	
VII	269	Fyrish, Ross	80·2	M		
	286	Dunrobin, Sutherland	82	F		
	280	Lesmurdie, Banff	85	M		
	286a	West Watten, Caithness	85·8	M		

[1] *P. S. A. S.* xxxix. 437–8.

[2] Most of these indices as regards Prov. I–V are taken from *Crania Britannica*. The seven skulls between the asterisks are fully described by Dr. Thomas Bryce, M.D., in *P. S. A. S.* xxxix. 426 &c., and by Dr. Alex. Low Demonstrator of Anatomy in *Proc. Anatom. and Anthrop. Soc. University of Aberdeen*, 1902–4.

The *Table of Cephalic Indices* shows that twenty-eight skulls found with beakers are brachycephalic with an index of 80 and upwards, while seven are below that figure, though none have an index lower than 73. It is a question, for I am not sure that it has been answered, whether these dolichocephalic and mesocephalic crania belong to the Mediterranean or to the Reihengräber race of mankind. To know this would settle the point whether these are the long skulls of men who came over to Britain as part of the invaders, or whether they belonged to persons of the older population. The skull from Rotherly, which may have had an index of 74—it was discovered in a very shattered condition—had strongly marked superciliary ridges, and the walls of the skull were thick, while the skeleton had been that of a tall man of 5 ft. 9½ in. On that account I suppose the man belonged to the Reihengräber type, and that he or his ancestors had migrated from the east of the Rhine and landed in Britain in company with the short-headed invaders. Dr. W. Wright, in reporting on sixty-two skulls in Mr. Mortimer's collection from round barrows of the East Riding,[1] states that the types were very mixed and belonged particularly to the Reihengräber race, and that in all probability intermixture began before their arrival in Yorkshire.[2] There is nothing astonishing in this, for a certain mixture of craniological types took place far back in time, so that by the end of the neolithic period north of the Alps it would not be abnormal for a group of persons in the Rhine valley to contain representatives of the long and the short-headed races both speaking a common language. What keeps people together is reciprocal intelligibility. When certain groups of persons of no matter what type of skull live within easy access of each other, to maintain social intercourse at all, they must have a common medium of communication; if this does not exist at first, in course of time it inevitably arises. Thus the invaders, while still living on the Continent, although they probably contained individuals with different types of skull, nevertheless may be regarded as a single people bound together by the common tie of language.

From what part of Europe did the invaders come? There can be no doubt that it was from somewhere east of the Rhine. As their type of skull was that of the Alpine Race it may be supposed that they originally came from the confines of Helvetia. The skull and bell-beaker from Wahlwies in Baden (p. 15) seem to point to this. It would be quite natural if some of them followed the Rhine valley northwards, and the similarity of the beakers from Mainz, Urmitz, Andernach, and other places near the river, to beakers of type B, speaks in this sense. Although possibly the introduction of this type into Britain was the result of another invasion,[3] it is difficult to suppose that the invaders who introduced type A had come from quite a different part of the country. And the Batavian type at the mouth of the Rhine also points to a close connexion of later beaker forms with the Rhine valley. Although some of the skulls of the invaders belong to the Borreby type, it does not follow that any of them came from Denmark or from the Island of Sjeland in particular, as has been urged, for this type belongs to the Alpine Race, a branch of which, according to Ripley, had moved thither from Central Europe.[4] Besides, the Borreby skulls came from a 'Giant's chamber' of the Neolithic Age and therefore belong to a period

---

[1] It must be remembered that some round barrows in the East Riding belong to the neolithic period, before the arrival of the invaders.   [2] Mortimer, p. lxxx.

[3] The three tanged knife-daggers and the stone bracers found with examples of type B seem to mark it off from type A.   [4] *Races of Europe*, p. 211.

considerably earlier than the date of the invasion of Britain. Until more evidence is brought forward I believe it may be assumed that the invaders started from some point in the valley of the Rhine, although some of them may have reached the point of departure from districts further to the east. But they could not have come from any locality so far north as the Cimbric Peninsula, for there, in the earliest part of the Bronze Age, the custom was to bury the dead at full length, and not in a contracted position as in Great Britain. This is an important distinction which must not be overlooked.

We do not know for certain what the impulse was that propelled the new immigrants from the valley of the Rhine towards the shores of Britain, which from time immemorial has been an asylum for the refugee from the Continent. But it was not a quite isolated movement; it was evidently a second parallel movement to that which before the end of the Neolithic Age had brought the Borreby men to Denmark from the Alpine regions of Central Europe some centuries earlier. And at the beginning of the aeneolithic period, probably somewhat earlier than the migration northwards towards Britain, there had been a southerly migration from the north side of the Alps into Italy. The cause of this is perhaps to be attributed to the advent of dolichocephalic invaders, who about the same time were taking possession of the Lake-dwellings of Helvetia, previously inhabited by a brachycephalic population. Hence it may be supposed that it was the presence of hostile forces that in the first instance caused the ancestors of the future invaders of Britain to turn their faces northwards and to follow the course of the Rhine. But after a time it must have been of their own free will and from a love of adventure that they eventually pushed their way, as may be supposed, to the coast of Gaul, to a point from which the opposite coast was sometimes visible. Their precise course cannot be traced, although we have to suppose that at a considerable distance from the mouth of the river some of the invaders branched off to the north-west, while others remained, and at a later period pressed on to Batavia, where their former presence is testified to, not only by the Batavian type of beaker, but also by a brachycephalic element in the population which still persists. It is to be expected that having reached that part of the coast from which Britain is at times visible, the future invaders did not immediately attempt to explore the opposite coast, but settled down for some time until the restless spirit of adventure again incited them to a further advance in a northerly direction.

To an inland people, even though bold and reckless by nature, the sight of a turbulent sea might be expected to deter them from the idea of attempting to cross it. But while living on the Rhine they had no doubt learnt to make dug-out canoes from trunks of oak, or to make coracles by sewing ox-hides together over a framework of withies, and were accustomed to paddle them from place to place. In those days the Rhine was a much larger stream than at present and was sufficiently rough at times to give them some skill in navigating their fragile craft. Presumably with vessels no better than these they had to cross the Channel, with its strong tides and currents. If they had only to transport themselves, their women, and children, the difficulties of crossing in fine weather would not have been so great. But unless they knew beforehand that Britain was inhabited and that its people owned cattle, they would be obliged at all hazards to carry their domestic animals with them, for a pastoral or semi-pastoral people cannot separate itself from the flocks and herds upon which it subsists.

How they surmounted these difficulties we can only imagine. We may conjecture, however, that taking advantage of some fine summer's day when the days were long, the first party of adventurers, perhaps not more than a hundred in all, launched their canoes and paddled across the Channel, landing at some unknown point on the south coast of Britain. It was certainly a notable achievement, the tradition of which may have been handed down for several generations. It is natural to ask in what numbers did these invaders arrive? No certain answer can be given, but a few actuarial calculations in the note below may afford useful aid in forming an opinion.[1]

If all the figures, except those of the years, in the same horizontal line are multiplied by the same figure an equally reliable result is obtained. For instance, it can be seen at a glance that by multiplying the last line by 10, 100 original settlers composed of 50 men, 40 women and 10 children at the end of 10 generations or 300 years might have increased to 5,590 and that 17,350 would have died. Or taking the line above, 150 emigrants might have increased to 5,660 and 17,350 would have been buried in the space of 9 generations or 270 years. An original body of 300 or 600 souls, half of whom were men and the remainder women and children might increase to 16,770 or 35,540 at the end of 300 years. Taking the total area of England as 50,842 square miles, these two sets of figures would give a density of population equal to 0·3 and 0·7 persons per square mile, or in other words three persons or seven persons to every ten square miles. These figures are at once doubled to 0·6 and 1·4 persons to the square mile if we assume with great probability that half the area of the country was under forest, or so swampy as to be unsuitable for human habitation. Besides, it is necessary to add the neolithic population, which it may be presumed was considerably more numerous than that of the invaders. If we rather more than double the above figures, so as to get round numbers, we obtain a rate of 1·5 persons or three persons to the square mile, for the whole population of South Britain after the invaders had been there for 300 years, and on the supposition that they had arrived 300 or 600 persons all told. If that seems too scanty a population after such a lapse of time, it may be mentioned that at the present day, after more than 3000 years, the density of the population in Sutherland only amounts to twelve persons to the square mile. And the density of the population of Cape Colony, founded in 1652, was only one person to two square miles at the end of 163 years.

[1] ACTUARIAL CALCULATIONS.

Original no. of settlers	Composed of			Total of deaths in			No. of survivors
	men	wom.	ch.				
19	9	6	4	210	years	1041	357
9	5	3	1	270	,,	1041	340
6	3	2	1	300	,,	1041	335
25	13	8	4	210	,,	1388	476
12	6	4	2	270	,,	1388	453
8	4	3	1	300	,,	1388	447
32	16	11	5	210	,,	1735	595
15	8	5	2	270	,,	1735	566
10	5	4	1	300	,,	1735	559

These figures were worked out for me by Mr. R. Hill Stewart, actuary in Edinburgh, on the assumption that there were more adult males than females, that each woman would have on the average 6 children, that the mortality of these was high and the mortality of the settlers would be 50 % higher than that shown by the English Life Table no. 3, based upon the population returns of England and Wales for the years 1841–51. It was also assumed that with respect to births the males and females were equally divided.

From the above figures it may be assumed, I think, that in all probability the maximum number of the invaders did not exceed 600 persons, of whom only about 300 were full-grown men; that probably a small tribe of 300 or 400 persons all told is nearer the mark, and that it is not likely that all came over at one time on account of the difficulty of transporting the domestic animals. The small number of beaker types and the fact that after from ten to twelve generations this pottery was supplanted in the northern half of England and in North Britain by another class of pottery of totally different origin, partly derived from a native neolithic prototype, also seem to indicate that the invaders, though full of enterprise and of the spirit of adventure, were never really a numerous body.

Smallish areas that were suitable for pastoral purposes could be populated to a density of 1·7 persons to a square mile in seven generations, or 210 years, by a very small number of settlers, in fact by a single large family. For instance, the district so well explored by Canon Greenwell and Mr. Mortimer in the East Riding has an area of about 200 square miles and the beakers account for about eighty interments. Supposing that this only represents $\frac{1}{13}$ of the real number of deaths, and that 1,040 deaths have to be spread over 210 years, we see from line 1 of the Actuarial Table that an original settlement of 19 souls, consisting of 9 men, 6 women, and 4 children, would yield that number of deaths and leave about 357 survivors to cover 200 square miles. And if the time is prolonged to 300 years, we see from line 3 of the Table that the same mortality might have happened if the original number of colonists had consisted of only 3 men, 2 women, and 1 child.

§ 2. THE SOCIAL CONDITION OF THE INVADERS

All that can be said under this head is necessarily conjecture, though founded on what seem to be reasonable inferences from observed facts. The funeral furniture is so scanty and betrays such a slight degree of civilization, that these round-headed invaders may be looked on as barbarians of the higher order, who lived chiefly on the produce of their flocks and herds.[1] In a less degree they lived by the cultivation of the soil, for as wheat was known both in the Pile-dwellings of Helvetia and also in Denmark in the Neolithic Age it may be assumed that they brought some of that grain with them; at any rate they knew it a few generations later.[2] They may have been on a par with the warlike and pastoral Zulus and Masai, who also cultivate a little maize and know how to forge iron assagais. Mr. Mortimer believes that the frequent association of broken human bones with those of animals in some of the barrows points to cannibalism. These bones were generally in better preservation than those in the interment below and had a different appearance, as if they had been cooked.[3] It is not impossible that cannibalism was occasionally practised, owing to a belief that the strength and courage of a valiant foe killed in battle would be absorbed by feeding upon his flesh. But we cannot say with certainty that it was habitual, as it is among certain tribes in Central Africa.

[1] The bones of domestic animals found with beaker interments are of *bos longifrons*, another breed of ox, goat or sheep, swine, horse, and the dog; of wild animals, beaver, red deer, roe, and hare.

[2] Mr. James Cree found impressions of wheat, as large as is now grown in Scotland, on a piece of pottery in a kitchen-midden at North Berwick, in close connexion with beaker fragments. *P. S. A. S.* xlii. 289, fig. 20.

[3] Mortimer, p. 24.

HABITATIONS

As regards the habitations of the invaders we have hardly any certain evidence, for only once have beakers been mentioned in connexion with an inhabited site, and the report of their discovery is extremely summary and vague. The small beakers figs. 72–4 from Taplow, Bucks., were recovered in removing 'several [pit-]circles, containing food vessels, drinking cups and cinerary urns, bones of various domestic animals, such as the ox, sheep, pig, etc.' These pit-circles 'were constructed by delving into the ground from 3 to 7 ft., throwing the removed earth round the surface of an opening from 14 to 20 ft. in diameter. On the top of the bank thus raised they would insert stakes leaning towards the centre of the dwelling and forming a hole for the smoke to escape at the top.' [1] The stakes would be roofed with sods of turf or heather and thus form a rude dwelling sufficient for the small needs of the hardy invaders.

THEIR GENERAL LIFE

If all the men led the same sort of life, which was mainly pastoral, and only the fittest children survived, one man would be as good as another and the social body would be essentially democratic, although ruled by a council of elders who were well versed in tribal custom and on emergency by an elected chief. In this rather early stage of civilization the hereditary principle would hardly come into play, especially if the family was of a very primitive type such as suggested below.[2] The chief occupation of the men would be to look after the cattle, the swine, and the domestic animals, and to protect them from the attacks of wolves and other rapacious animals. Others would hunt or trap the deer and the wild boar that frequented the forests and swampy ground. And if the invaders on first arrival were few in numbers they would have to make friends with the natives they found in the country rather than to fight them, although encounters between them must sometimes have taken place. It was the same when the colony at the Cape was first founded; the Dutch settlers made friends with the Hottentots, who at that time were vastly superior in numbers and warlike into the bargain. And as white women were scarce they sometimes took Hottentot wives.

Although the status of women was such that after death they were accorded the same honourable burial as men, during their lifetime they had to work. The manufacture of domestic and sepulchral pottery would be left to them; the little agriculture that was practised would certainly be their business, and they probably dug or helped to dig the graves. Canon Greenwell records the finding of a pick, made from the shed antler of a red deer, near the knees of a skeleton, probably that of a woman.[3] The preparation of skins and sewing them into garments was undoubtedly left to the women, and this accounts for the small bronze prickers or awls occasionally found with female skeletons. Between cooking, looking after their children, and the tasks above mentioned their day was fully occupied.

---

[1] *Maidenhead and Taplow Field Club*, 8th an. report (1890–1), p. 46.

[2] In Volume II some evidence will be produced to make it not improbable that in Period II of the Bronze Age the inhabitants were ruled by queens of royal descent who traced back their origin to a goddess. But this practice may not have been instituted when the invaders first landed.

[3] At Rudstone, with beaker fig. 144.

Although it is to be supposed that the invaders lived chiefly on their flocks and herds, yet they developed a taste for shell-fish. Perhaps in winter when shell-fish are in season, and the rigour of the climate was tempered by the superior temperature of the sea, the new settlers sometimes congregated on the sea-shore to feast on the products of the sea. Mr. A. Curle has recently found the sites of small kitchen-middens at Gullane Bay in East Lothian. They were composed of heaps of shells of whelks, limpets, oysters, and mussels, mixed with crabs' claws and animals' bones, and the sand among which they lay had been blackened by the decomposition of animal matter. Dispersed through the mass lay a few flint scrapers and flakes, a bone pin and fragments of 27 beakers.[1] In two other kitchen-middens at North Berwick, found by Mr. J. Cree, one of which measured about 150 ft. by 36 to 45 ft. wide and from 10 to 12 inches deep and lay 8 ft. below the surface, large numbers of shells and other objects were picked up. These consisted of whelks, limpets, a few oysters, crabs' claws and fish bones, a few well-worked flints, stone pounders, and fragments of beakers. At the bottom of a potsherd—not a beaker—were seen the impressions of grains of wheat, as has already been mentioned.[2] That no such kitchen-middens have been noticed on the East coast of England is to be attributed to the extensive erosion by the sea, which has swept away all trace of such sites.

INFERENCES FROM SEPULCHRAL PHENOMENA

Old men, at least some of them, were respected and held in honour. In Wilts a patriarch of from 70 to 80 years of age had been buried with a bronze dagger—the largest found with any beaker—a stone bracer, and a beaker the ornament of which had been filled with a white substance.[3] As his stature had been about 6 ft., he must have been a man of mark in his day and a chief elected for his size and strength.

Both Canon Greenwell and Mr. Mortimer came to the conclusion which can scarcely be questioned that it was the habit to bury with the dead chief his wives, children, and probably slaves. In arriving at this result, both drew their conclusions from a survey of the interments of the whole Bronze Age, but here I expressly limit my observations to the earliest phase of it, to the time when beakers were in use. I have had moreover to exclude examples, which perhaps illustrate their inference, because no pottery happened to accompany the interments. In the Iron Age, when society was on a large scale and the power of certain individuals had much increased, it was possible and even customary for wives and slaves to be put to death at the funeral of a Scythian king or of a Gaulish or Teutonic chieftain. But it does not follow that such a practice was compatible with society on a small—perhaps very small—scale, many centuries earlier, when the population was scanty and the power of the chiefs, for all we know, was of a limited nature. If the custom existed among the invaders, it was not habitual. For instance, the barrow raised over the grave of the patriarch mentioned above, who was undoubtedly a man of note, contained no other interment.

It was exceptional for a man and woman to be buried together. Only six certain instances seem to have been recorded in which the body of a man and another adult, presumably a woman—for the sex could not always be determined—were found side by side, or one lying on the other in the same grave.[1]   And these examples, it must be remarked, are spread over a space of several generations.

When a mother died her child was sometimes buried with her, either to keep her company or because there was no one left to look after it.   There are four certain instances of this practice.[2]

There are three instances in which a male had been buried with a young child, the sex of which was determined only in one instance, when it was female.   In Yorkshire Canon Greenwell found the body of an old man, in front of whose feet lay the body of a very young child, and in front of his leg another still younger child.[3]   In Derbyshire Bateman observed that the body of an infant had been deposited near the pelvis of a man.[4]

Again, in Aberdeenshire the skeleton of a large, tall man was found in the same cist with a female child.[5]   It is not very obvious why an infant should be put to death—supposing always that its death had been violent—on the demise of a man and buried with him.   But a possible explanation will be given below.

LIST OF BEAKERS FOUND WITH INTERMENTS OF MEN, WOMEN, CHILDREN

MEN		WOMEN	CHILDREN
Fig. 4a	Fig. 247	Fig. 51 awl[6]	Fig. 18
„ 21	„ 248	„ 57	„ 53
„ 25	„ 249	„ 62	„ 56
„ 33	„ 253	„ 68 awl	„ 71
„ 48	„ 254	„ 90 bis	„ 99
„ 49	„ 256	„ 109 awl	„ 108
„ 59	„ 280	„ 111	„ 110
„ 60	„ 286a	„ 113	„ 131
„ 102		„ 117 awl	„ 132
„ 103		„ 121 awl	„ 142
„ 106[7]		„ 128	„ 152
„ 116		„ 130	„ 178
„ 135		„ 133	„ 286
„ 136		„ 138	
„ 137		„ 139 awl	
„ 146		„ 143	
„ 149		„ 144 probably	
„ 155		„ 145	
„ 161		„ 147 awl	
„ 180		„ 173	
„ 238			
„ 239			
„ 243			
Total ..	31 male	20 female	13 children

The rule was to bury each man and woman alone, and judging by the preponderance

[1] In Wilts. with beakers figs. 14, 19; Fovant, bar. 9, beaker lost; in Yorkshire, with beakers 116, 117; Willerby bar. 235.

In a grave at St. Fagan's, Glamorganshire, two skeletons were found together, one of an aged person, the other of an individual of about 20 years of age, but the skulls were so similar that a close relationship probably existed between them.   No certain conclusion can there-fore be drawn from this instance.   The skeletons were accompanied by beaker fig. 94.

[2] With beakers figs. 57, 71, 101, 128.
[3] Bar. 62, beaker fig. 135.
[4] With beaker fig. 48.   [5] With beaker fig. 249.
[6] Awls have been found several times with interments of women, but they are not absolutely confined to such burials.   [7] Large adult.

of male skeletons the men were more numerous than the women.[1] As we have already learnt, the number of instances in which a wife may have been put to death to be buried with her husband are rare. How is this rarity to be explained if, as is probable, the ferocious-looking invaders had no conception of the sanctity of human life? As the women were evidently considerably less numerous than the men, to accommodate this fact to practical life in a relatively barbarous community where nearly all the men were on an equal footing, we may well suppose that polyandry in some form or other existed and that the relations between the sexes were lax. Hence, when a man died, save under special circumstances, he was buried alone, for the others who shared a wife with him would naturally not allow her to be put to death. If this is so, it follows that monogamy was of exceptional occurrence. A system of polyandry explains better than monogamy does why a female infant should be laid in the same grave as a man. This is certain in one only out of the three examples given above of the concurrent inhumation of a man and one or two children in the same grave or cist, but it may be presumed in the two other instances. The explanation of this would be that occasionally, when a man of a certain importance died and it was considered fitting that he should have a wife in the next world, a female infant was given him as a surrogate, who from the point of view of the community, or perhaps after some magic ceremony, would be considered potentially a full-grown woman.

   To return to the subject of slaves. It is difficult to say whether the invaders possessed them or not, though I believe that taking into consideration their very simple mode of life, slaves would have been of little service. Still, prisoners of war might have been kept to be slain at funerals, though I cannot find any evidence to confirm this idea. It is true that sometimes several bodies, which seem to have been buried simultaneously, are found lying close together, but as no pottery is found with them to connect the interments with the beaker period, these instances cannot be used ; and the probability that some infectious disease had carried off several members of the same crowded pit-dwelling at the same time is a consideration that must be taken into account. Mr. Mortimer records two instances in which three persons were found in the same grave with beakers.[2] In the first they consisted of an old woman and two youths, one of whom was from 8 to 12 years of age. In the other they consisted of the mutilated body of a middle-aged person and two others, one of whom was again a youth of from 10 to 12 years of age. From these two examples nothing definite can be concluded. There are several examples of two or three interments being laid in the same grave, but separated by a depth of earth varying from six inches to three and a half feet. But it is impossible to be sure that all the burials were made at the same time. It would seem that a grave sometimes 6 ft. deep was dug, a body was deposited in it and covered up with earth, but leaving room enough for two or three subsequent interments. Until the grave was full no mound was raised over it.

   There are four instances in which a child had been buried with some degree of honour and respect, in two of them with remarkable honour. In Wilts., Hoare found the skeleton of a child of not more than two or three years of age in a shallow grave at the centre of a barrow

---

[1] The *List of beakers found with men, women, and children* shows that the proportion of men to women was as 3 : 2.

[2] Bar. 4, with beakers figs. 112, 113; bar. 116 with beakers figs. 119, 120.

nearly 14 ft. high.[1]   Bateman found in Derbyshire in a barrow with a diameter of 36 ft., and a height of 1 ft., the skeleton of a child of about 10 years of age as the central interment at a depth of 2 ft. below the natural surface.[2]   In a Staffordshire barrow with a diameter of about 120 ft. and a height of 2 ft. he obtained, from a circular grave 3 ft. in diameter and about 2 ft. deep, the skeleton of a child, probably a male, as a flint spearhead had been deposited with it[3] ; in an adjoining grave of the same size a woman and child had been interred and the beaker in each grave seemed to have been made by the same hand.   In Yorkshire, Canon Greenwell found the body of a child scarcely 1 year old as the central interment under a barrow with a diameter of 100 ft. and a height of 9 ft.[4]   It had been placed in a slight hollow lined with wood, and close to it were some bones of apparently a young woman.   The explorer had no doubt that, when the child was buried, certain parts of another body had been placed with it, these bones having been removed from some other place.   He also supposed that the child must have been that of the chief of a powerful tribe.

Fire, no doubt, was considered a purifying agency, one likely to remove noxious influences and generally speaking to produce a beneficial result.   Accordingly, a few examples are found in which the surface whereon the barrow was to be raised was first prepared by fires being lighted over the whole area or over a considerable part of it.   Canon Greenwell observed that this had been done at Rudstone, barrow 61.   Again at Willerby, barrow 235, he noted that at the centre for a space of 12 ft. in diameter the ground was much burnt, and that this had taken place before the central grave was dug.   This had a depth of 8 ft. ; on the floor two bodies had been deposited and the grave filled up to a height of $5\frac{1}{2}$ ft.

Before the secondary interment was made in the same grave, though at a higher level, a fire had been lit in it which reddened the walls to a depth of 3 or 4 in.   Mr. Mortimer also observed that in one instance the central grave showed traces of burning, for the floor was reddened and some of the wood ashes of the fire still remained; in another, the body had been laid on the natural surface and there was a good deal of burnt earth and charcoal below it.[5]   These last three examples show that the fire was not kindled for cooking purposes preparatory to a funeral feast, but for some such reason as suggested above.

Burial Customs.

When life came to an end the body was deposited in a grave or a stone cist, in a flexed position with the knees bent up towards the chin, and the hands were generally placed near the head.   On two or three occasions in Provinces I and III, the skeleton has been found lying on wooden planks but the practice was rather rare.   The corpse, which was probably clothed,[6] was laid either on the right or left side, sometimes on the back, though always in a flexed position, without regard to the sex of the deceased.   The head might be turned towards almost any point of the compass, but the face was always directed to a point lying between north-east and

---

[1] Beaker lost; *A. W.* i. 120.   [2] With beaker fig. 53.

[3] With beaker fig. 56.

[4] Rudstone, bar. 67. No beaker was deposited with this interment, but figs. 142, 143 are from the same barrow.

[5] Mortimer, bar. 7, 254.

[6] Hoare found with a skeleton what appeared to be leather (*A. IV.* i. 153), and Lord Londesborough noted that the body found with fig. 149 had been wrapt in linen from head to foot (*Arch.* xxxiv. 255).

north-west in passing by the south. In other words it always looked towards some point in the sun's course.[1] If, as is probable, the direction of the face gives the time of day when the interments took place, then over 74 per cent. of them occurred between about 9 a.m. and 3 p.m. They never happened very early or very late in summer, and a usual time was midday.

In Provinces I and III, and often in Province II, hardly any attempt was made to protect the body from the pressure of the earth by placing it in a cist or by walling it round with stones. This absence of protection for the body is commonly met with in Germany in connexion with interments containing bell-shaped beakers.[2] In Devonshire, however, where the beakers belong to a late date, the body was sometimes placed in a small cist.

In Wilts. the grave was usually shallow, consisting of an oval excavation in the chalk rock from 1 to 2 or 3 ft. deep. On the Yorkshire Wolds of Province III the depth of the oval grave varied from 2 to 12 ft., although the usual depth was not more than from 3 to 4 ft. In only four instances was the body protected by a cist. The difference of the graves in Province II, as compared with those in Provinces I, III, was caused by the nature of the ground. Instead of excavating a grave out of chalk rock, they had in Derbyshire to cut it out of the limestone or sandstone rock, not of course by chiselling it out, but by breaking the upper bed of weathered rock and thus forming, without much difficulty, an irregularly shaped grave from 2 to 3 ft. deep. Occasionally the sides of these Derbyshire graves were made waterproof by a lining of clay and the corpse was sometimes surrounded by stones arranged so as to form a rude cist, or it was simply laid upon the natural surface. This last practice also occurred in Yorkshire, but very rarely. In Province IV and in those to the north of it, where there was no chalk and where flat stones were easily procurable, the corpse was enclosed in a small rectangular cist of from 3 ft. 3 in. to 4 ft. long, by about 2 ft. 6 in. wide and about 1 ft. 6 in. deep. When slabs of sufficient size could be obtained, each side was formed by a single stone and a much larger one formed the cover or cap-stone. In Argyll the cists were occasionally of larger size, as much as 6 ft. by 3 ft. 9 in. by 2 ft. 4 in. deep. Sometimes the floor of the cist consisted of a slab or a paving of small stones, but more usually the natural soil was sufficient. These cists were constructed either at the bottom of a grave or upon the natural surface.

After the burial of the corpse a circular mound or a cairn was nearly always raised over the spot, though there are exceptions. For instance, several interments in Kent and East Anglia, found while digging for gravel, seem not to have been covered by mounds, and a few more instances might be given. But it is quite true that at present no flat cemeteries containing beaker interments have been found in Britain. Out of thirty-four barrows, containing beakers, opened by Sir R. Hoare in Wilts., ten are qualified as low, small, very low,

---

[1] Direction of the face in 39 beaker interments from the East Riding.

S.	15	both sexes
SE.	3	both sexes
SE. by E.	1	
ESE.	2	6
E.	3	

S. by W.	1	
SSW.	2	8
SW.	5	both sexes
W.	2	
WNW.	1	
On the back	4	both sexes

[2] Reinecke, *Westdeut. Zeitschr. f. Geschichte u. Kunst*, Jahrgang xix. 232.

insignificant; of thirteen no remark is made and only eight were large. Although he rarely states the dimensions of the barrows, he has noted a few :—

Diameter 40 ft.	Height 3 ft. 9 in.
,, 110 ft.	,, 5 ft.
,, 90 ft.	,, 7 ft.
,, 78 ft.	,, 7 ft.
,, 145 ft.	,, 14 ft. 6 in.

These barrows are of two types, bowl-shaped and bell-shaped, the first being by far the commoner. The diameter of the Bowl-barrow usually ranges from 20 to 60 ft. though some exceed 100 ft.; in height it varies from 1 to 10 ft. The Bell-barrow is moulded with much accuracy and symmetry into a form that somewhat resembles a bell. It is surrounded by a ditch and between this and the barrow is a flat circular area. Such barrows have a diameter of 100 ft. or more, and a height of from 5 to 15 ft.

In Derbyshire and Staffordshire the diameter of the tumulus ranged from 27 to 120 ft. and the height from 1 to 8 ft. In Yorkshire the diameter of the barrow was the same as in Derbyshire and the height varied, where the ground had been repeatedly ploughed over, from almost nothing to 9 ft. In Province V, tumuli also assumed large dimensions. A cairn in Fife had a diameter of 120 ft. with a height of 14 ft., and the mound above the Bridge of Allan, from which fig. 203 was taken, had an altitude of no less than 21 ft. with a diameter of 78 ft.

The barrow was rarely surrounded by a stone circle or setting. Two instances occur in Devonshire, on Dartmoor and Broad Down, Honiton[1]; and in Derbyshire Bateman records that a barrow of small dimensions was surrounded by an irregular circle of large stones.[2] In the East Riding one barrow was surrounded by a trench 7 ft. wide at the top and 3 ft. 6 in. deep[3] and this seems to be the only example. Sometimes a circle of stones or a circular trench was found inside the barrow. Mr. Mortimer found a circle of stones with a diameter of 21 ft. 6 in., the stones being about 2 ft. high, within a barrow at Hanging Grimston,[4] and Canon Greenwell found a circular trench 20 ft. in diameter inside B. 235 at Willerby.[5]

§ 3. THEIR RELIGIOUS IDEAS

We are justified in supposing, I presume, that the invaders held animistic views of nature, and gave credence to the idea that the world around them was full of spirits, some kindly, some malevolent, who had to be propitiated; and that spirits could take up their abode, at any rate temporarily, in animals, trees, and stones of striking form. They would certainly believe in sympathetic magic, and many of their customs and practices must have had their origin in such a belief. But in their stage of civilization they may have formed some notion of higher divinities, such as a sky-god who sent rain and storm, thunder and lightning, but also the fine weather so needful for their cattle. Yet as a pastoral people depending upon their flocks and herds it was necessary these should have a good supply of grass. As vegetation, especially in our climate, is more evidently dependent upon the earth from which it grows than upon the sky

---

[1] With beakers figs. 13, 16.   [2] With fig. 49.   [4] With beakers figs. 125–7.
[3] Mortimer, bar. 163 with beakers figs. 115–17.   [5] With fig. 151.

or the sun, their chief divinity would probably take the form of a great Goddess, an Earth-mother, a goddess of fertility and reproduction in general. This seems really to have been the case, and the time has now come to discuss the meaning of the three symbolical faces carved on the three chalk cylinders (Pl. lix, O. 17) already described.

Some twenty years ago Canon Greenwell pointed out the strong resemblance of the visages on the chalk cylinders to the so called 'owl-head' on many of the vases found by Schliemann at Hissarlik, and he also compared them with some rude human figures engraved on stone at Collorgues (Gard) and in sepulchral graves in La Marne and at La Bellehaye à Boury (Oise), but he drew no conclusions.[1] M. Déchelette, however, has taken up the matter, and with the advantage of writing eighteen years later than his predecessor has been able to throw more light upon the subject. He mentions four areas in France where rude representations of the human figure have been noted; the group of the Marne, the group of the Seine and the Oise in the north; the Gard group and the group of the Aveyron, Tarn, and Hérault in the south. The faces from the Marne are carved in relief on the wall of the ante-chamber in front of the artificial grottos containing the skeletons of the dead, as if they were the guardians of the place. In addition to the eyes, nose, and eyebrows, the breasts and a necklace of one or more rows are sometimes added, showing that the sepulchral divinity was thought of as a woman. Even when the sex is not indicated it may be assumed that it was feminine. Sometimes she is provided with an object like a hockey stick, which may be intended for a hafted axe or for the haft alone, for this she would carry in her capacity as guardian of the dead. In one instance an axe-head is clearly attached to a handle. In M. Déchelette's opinion all seems to show that we are really in presence of a feminine idol, a primitive personification of maternity and a prototype of the mother-goddesses so popular in the ancient world. He also compares these faces and images from Gaul with the faces on some of the pottery of the second city of Troy and with the so-called Cycladic idols, representing a goddess, from Amorgos and other islands of the Archipelago, and as these were found in graves they may be called sepulchral.[2]

M. Déchelette has succeeded, I believe, in showing that in the Aegean area, in Gaul, and in Britain, a female divinity—a warden of places of sepulchre and a mother-goddess—was recognized by the inhabitants of these countries in the early Bronze Age in the Aegean and at the end of the Neolithic Age in Gaul. As the short-headed invaders buried their dead in the earth it would be quite natural for them to place the other world, the land of the dead, below ground where the Earth-mother also resided. As a benevolent divinity she might be supposed to nourish and protect the dead from injury. An analogy for this can be found in Egypt in the person of Isis, whose worship in Dr. Budge's opinion may date back to the predynastic period. 'Isis', he says, 'was the great and beneficent goddess and mother whose influence pervaded all heaven and earth and the abode of the dead. She was the personification of the great feminine, creative power which conceived and brought forth every living creature. . . . What she brought forth she protected and cared for, and fed and nourished.'[3]

Judging from the analogy of an infant being sometimes laid in the grave at its mother's back, the position in which a child was usually carried, it may be inferred that, as the three

[1] *Arch.* lii. 27.   [2] Déchelette, *Manuel d'archéologie préhistorique*, i. 584–96.   [3] *The Gods of the Egyptians*, ii. 202, 203.

chalk drums (O. 17) were also placed at the child's back, she was intended to carry them to the next world, not as playthings, but as a costly offering from her mother to the great Mother-goddess, who was also goddess of the Underworld, under whose protection the child was now placed.

These ornamented cylindrical objects with a rounded top represent, perhaps, the domestic *baetyls* in which the divinity was believed to reside. No doubt they stand in some relation to stone-worship, a cult which survived throughout Europe till extinguished by the energy of the early Christian missionaries. In Ireland such stones are mentioned in the Ancient Laws as *ail adrada*, 'stones of worship,'[1] and Bishop Cormac in the ninth century has recorded that the 'altar-stones' of the pagan Irish were ornamented with figures.[2] In 1904 Mr. George Coffey published excellent illustrations of two 'stones of worship', decorated with Late Celtic ornament, which no doubt represent such 'altars' as Bishop Cormac had in mind. Both these stones are somewhat cylindrical, with a rounded top. The Turoe stone (Loughrea), an erratic granite boulder, stands 4 ft. high, and seen from one side is wider at the middle than at the base, as is also the case with two of the Folkton cylinders. The ornament in relief is very distinct. The Castlestrange stone, near Roscommon, is also an erratic block of granite, $2\frac{1}{4}$ ft. high, and here again the diameter at the base is narrower than at a third of the height from the top. The ornament is incised.[3]

Though on a much smaller scale the profile of the two larger chalk cylinders much resembles that of the Castlestrange stone and both were used for a similar purpose. The larger stones were for the use of the public and stood in the open country, but in Bronze Age I the inhabitants of a single dwelling appear sometimes to have had household *baetyls*, to which they prayed for the increase of their herds or whatever else they desired.

The number three no doubt had a significance, but whether it here implies the presence of three different divinities or not remains uncertain.

We have already learnt that the Gaulish female divinity was armed with a stone axe. Perhaps four flat bronze axes found in a Yorkshire barrow without any interment, at a distance of 8 ft. from the centre and 6 in. above the natural surface, may be regarded as a votive offering to some divinity such as the Earth-mother. They seem to have been deposited at the time of the erection of the mound.[4]

It has been shown above that in depositing the corpse in its grave care was taken to turn the face in the direction of the sun at the moment of burial. As in our climate the sun is often hidden the face must often have been directed merely to some point in the sun's course apart from the hour at which the ceremony took place. This testifies to a regard on the part of the relatives that the deceased should enjoy as it were a last look at the sun, but it hardly allows us to infer any great cult of the sun. In a paper on 'Sun-worship in prehistoric times'[5] M. Déchelette has shown that at an early period in the Aegean area the solar disc was often represented by a four-spoked wheel. Among other solar symbols derived from it he includes cruciform figures inscribed within a circle, such as are seen on the gold disc O. 8, the jet

[1] *Anc. Laws of Ireland*, iv. 143.

[2] W. Stokes, *Three Irish Glossaries*, p. 25, *s.v. Hindelba*.

[3] Coffey, *P. R. I. A.* xxiv, Sect. C, no. 14, pp. 257–66, pl. xviii–xxi. A view of each of these stones is repro- duced, after Mr. G. Coffey, on p. 92.

[4] Bar. 235 Willerby, E. R., from which came beaker fig. 151. *Arch.* lii. 2, 3.

[5] *Revue Archéologique*, 4e sér., xiii (1909), p. 305, &c.

buttons O. 14, 15, and concentric circles such as we have on the tops of the chalk cylinders O. 17. No doubt these are solar symbols; but the question arises, Are they evidence of sun-worship in Britain at the dawn of the Bronze Age? The answer depends upon whether we suppose them to have been made intentionally to symbolize the movement of the sun across the face of the sky or not. If these cruciform figures are taken to represent a wheel, it is necessary to suppose that the invaders were acquainted with wheeled carts, a proposition that can hardly be entertained, considering the early time with which we are dealing. Some other explanation is therefore needed to account for these wheel-like motives. Cruciform designs are sometimes found on the bottom of food vessels, especially in Hibernia, and these might be imitated from the bottom of a basket made of osier rods or of bast, where a cruciform shape may sometimes be observed.[1] There is a possibility, however, that the invaders had learnt the motive before reaching Britain and attributed some religious importance to it without recognizing it as a wheel. Nevertheless it would be premature, I believe, to infer on the evidence of these buttons and cylinders that the invaders were to any extent sun-worshippers. For natural reasons, from the much weaker force of the sun in higher latitudes when compared with its strength in lower latitudes, sun-worship does not appear to have been a prominent cult among the more northern peoples of Europe until a relatively late period of the Bronze Age; and then it was imported from the South. There is good evidence to show that Apollo was not originally a Hellenic sun-god before the Hellenes descended into the Aegean area and became acquainted with solar divinities of the prehellenic populations of Crete and of the Cyclades.[2] It would be wrong to assert positively that the invaders paid no attention to the influence of the sun on the growth of vegetation and on the prosperity of themselves and their cattle and therefore did not worship it at all. But its worship was subordinate and overshadowed by the nearer influence of the great Earth-mother. It seems quite probable, too, that the sun was included in the idea they formed of the sky-god and was not regarded as a separate entity, but as an integral part of the vault of heaven—as the eye of the great god. As the sky could not be represented graphically, the sky-god was symbolized by an axe to represent the thunderbolt, or by a circle which stood for the sun. When this circle is double, as is often the case, it appears to represent an eye.[3] From this point of view the sun-symbols may, as often as not, represent the sky-god himself and not merely the sun.[5]

---

[1] Haddon, *Evolution of Art*, pl. ii, fig. 9.

[2] Farnell, *Cults of the Greek States*, iv. 144.

[3] The word for 'sun' in all the Indo-European languages of Europe seems to go back to a form which is explained by the Irish *suil*, an 'eye'.

[5] A circle with a central dot does not of necessity suggest the sun; to a Bushman it indicates a natural hole or cistern in the rocks. Sollas, *Ancient Hunters*, 258.

CHAPTER VI

THE COLONIZATION AND DIFFUSION OF THE INVADERS

Province I. The first party of invaders landed it must be supposed at some unknown point on the south or south-east coast and then spread over the province lying south of the Thames. Their progress and diffusion can be traced to a certain extent by the barrows in which they had deposited their dead, and it is unfortunate that so many beakers, the only means by which they can be identified, have perished like the invaders themselves. No less than twenty-nine of such vessels discovered by Sir R. Hoare no longer exist. But the presence of the invaders in over forty places is well assured and, though without doubt this number will be largely increased in future years, at present we must be content with the material that exists.[1]

Although the new comers landed on the coast, the earliest beakers which seem to herald their arrival in Britain were found within a couple of miles of Stonehenge, and of these three came from barrows well within a mile of that celebrated megalithic monument.[2] Others of the earliest phase of type A have been found near the still greater stone circles at Avebury,[3] at Lambourne Down[4] in Berks., some twenty miles north-east of Avebury, and also at Brendly[5] near Faversham in East Kent. In the earlier part of type B1 we find them at Roundway Hill, near Devizes, at Mere Down on the western side of the county of Wilts., at Winterslow near Salisbury[6] and at Christchurch, Hants (see p. 22 note).

Later on, during Phase II of type A and the later part of type B, some continued to reside near Stonehenge and Avebury[7]; others had pushed westwards and extended their discoveries as far as Stogursey,[8] a few miles north-west of Bridgewater in Somerset and close to the Bristol Channel. Others still more enterprising made their way as far to the south-west as Dartmoor and Broad Down near Honiton in Devon,[9] and occupied parts of Dorset near Blandford and Cranbourne Chase.[10] In Berkshire they were now found at Cholsey, about twenty miles north-east of Lambourne Down and not far from the Thames.

During the later phases of the beaker types, the invaders populated more densely both Wilts. and Dorset, and in Somerset they spread still further westward to Culbone[11] on Exmoor, again coming quite close to the Bristol Channel. Later graves prove that they continued to reside near Lambourn in Berks., Yeovil in Somerset, and on Dartmoor in Devon.[12] The age of four Kentish beakers from near Chislet in North-east Kent and from near Erith[13] on the Thames is uncertain, though I think they belong to a rather late part of the beaker period, when the invaders had also spread southwards to the coast of Sussex near Brighton.[14] The most northerly point occupied by them, certainly at a late date, was Abingdon in Berks.[15]

---

[1] See Map showing beakers found in Province I (p. 19).
[2] Figs. 1–4.   [3] Figs. 4 *bis*, 4 *tris*.   [4] Fig. 7.
[5] Fig. 6.   [6] Figs. 19, 21, 24.   [7] Figs. 9, 10.
[8] Figs. 11, 12, 20.   [9] Figs. 13, 16.
[10] Figs. 15, 23, 25, 27.   [11] Fig. 39.
[12] Figs. 41, 40, 42 *bis*, 42a.   [13] Figs. 34–7.
[14] Fig. 38.   [15] Fig. 43.

So far as I can learn, no beakers have been discovered as yet in the counties of Surrey, Cornwall, and Gloucester.

Province II.[1] Oxfordshire was naturally colonized from the south, as fig. 75 compared with similar beakers from Wilts. and Dorset shows clearly enough. But the number of beakers in the southern and south-eastern parts of the province are so scanty during the first phase of type A, that we cannot trace the route by which the invaders reached East Anglia and Derbyshire. Probably the cause for this is not far to seek. At this early period in the history of Britain, judging from the small number of graves and relics of any part of the Bronze Age that have been discovered in the Midland Counties, it is likely that these counties were scantily inhabited. From their flatness and low level they were covered with marshes, partly natural, partly made by the damming up of streams by the beavers, and with thick scrub or forest where cattle could not feed without being attacked by wolves, and where the conditions for human life were less eligible than in higher and more open parts of the country. Advancing from the south, the new colonists would therefore pass rapidly through the low, damp, thickly forested country, and not make any permanent settlement till they reached the northern half of Derbyshire, the district of the High Peak. Here the elevation is from 1,000 to 1,500 ft. above the sea-level, while the country to the south of it has a general elevation of from 500 to 1,000 ft. The land was mountainous and rocky, but on that account more open and salubrious, while there was excellent pasturage for the flocks and herds. The advantages of this district had already been discovered before the arrival of the invaders, for the earlier neolithic inhabitants have left considerable evidence of their presence in the shape of stone implements and chambered cairns. Whether the invaders of truculent aspect had to fight their way into the new territory is uncertain, but at any rate they made it their own. The dolichocephalic skull, however, found with fig. 52 of the first phase of type A, and the number of mesaticephalic skulls of the Bronze Age found in Derbyshire, seem to show that the older race was not extirpated, but on the contrary amalgamated with the invaders.

During Phase I of type A, though not at the beginning of it, the new settlers had pushed their way northwards to near the centre and north-west of Suffolk, and as far as Castle Acre in Norfolk.[2] During this period they took possession of the Peak district as far north as Grindlow to the north-east of Tideswell,[3] and the country to the south of it, where their presence is testified by six beakers,[4] and before the end of Phase I they had extended westwards into East Staffordshire.[5]

In the second phase of type A we find them at Oxford,[6] at Snailwell in Cambridgeshire,[7] at Kettering in Northamptonshire,[8] at Denton[9] in South Lincolnshire, and at Horncastle[10] in the centre of the county, as well as in other places in the counties of Derby and Stafford.

During Phase III they had progressed as far to the north-west as Woolston[11] on the Mersey in South Lancashire, besides maintaining their ground in other places.

During the time when beakers of type B were in use, which seems to have been later than Phase I of type A, we find a settlement near Taplow on the north bank of the Thames,[12] at three places in Oxfordshire,[13] at Great Clacton on the north-east coast of Essex, at

---

[1] See Map showing beakers found in Province II (p. 24).   [6] Fig. 64.   [7] Fig. 65.   [8] Fig. 66.   [9] Fig. 58.
[2] Figs. 45–7, 44.   [3] Fig. 50.   [10] Fig. 60a.   [11] Fig. 67.   [12] Figs. 81–3.
[4] Figs. 48, 49, 51–4.   [5] Figs. 55, 56, 59, 60, 71.   [13] Figs. 75, 77, 79.

Fingeringhoe in the same county[1]; at Felixstow on the coast of Suffolk, at Ipswich and Brandon in the same county[2]; at Somersham in Huntingdon,[3] at Stalham near the coast of Norfolk and further inland near Methwold.[4]

When type C had come into use, the new settlers remained in their possessions in Cambridgeshire[5] and extended their colonization in Norfolk and Suffolk.[6]

In Wales the invaders did not appear till rather late, for at present there appears to be nothing to show that they occupied any part of the Principality before Phase II of type A. By that time they were in the north and south of Glamorgan[7] and also in Anglesea, where they continued to remain during Phase III.[8] During the existence of type B they occupied two positions in Denbighshire[9]; during that of type C they can be traced in the counties of Montgomery and Carnarvon.[10]

Province III. There is nothing in the appearance of the beakers of this province to suggest that the new settlers had started from the Peak district lying to the south-west. On the contrary, it is evident, as has already been pointed out, that all that is not purely local is related to what is found in East Anglia, so the direction taken by the settlers was nearly due north. As all the examples of Phase I of type A (AC) belong to the groups of barrows explored by Mr. Mortimer, it is clear that the more southerly part of the area was occupied first, and that the settlement of the country was gradual. But having once obtained possession of the land the settlers remained there till the end of the beaker period. When they arrived they must certainly have encountered some of the earlier inhabitants. From the Howe Hill barrow, which contained over fifty interments, several crania were extracted which have been fully described by Dr. J. Garson.[11] Out of eight skulls, five were hyperdolicho, one was dolicho- and two mesaticephalic. In the Hedon Howe barrow, from which fig. 99 was taken, four dolicho crania were obtained, and beaker fig. 153 was found in a sandpit with a large skeleton, the skull of which had a cephalic index of 66·5, and the femur measured 19 inches in length. Finding beakers with dolichocephalic skulls implies either that the invaders made friends with the earlier inhabitants or that the former were already a mixed people. The size of the last skeleton seems to speak in favour of the second view.

Province IV.[12] The gradual spread northwards of the invaders could not have been very rapid, for we have seen that the whole of type A, as it is known in Province I, had time to die out, and only survived in a secondary form in a single instance found at Rothbury in the centre of Northumberland. Although other examples may come to light in the future, it will not alter the inference that the difference of time between the beginning of type A in the south and the earliest beaker in Province IV is considerable, hardly less than five generations, or about 150 years. From the general aspect of the Northumberland beakers compared with those in Yorkshire it is evident, as indeed might be expected, that the new comers had advanced northwards following the coast. The route taken to reach Westmorland and Cumberland cannot be exactly traced, but a fairly early example of type C from each of these counties[13]

---

[1] Figs. 85, 87.   [2] Figs. 86, 84, 82, 83.   [3] Fig. 76.

[4] Figs. 81, 80.   [5] Fig. 89.   [6] Figs. 90-3.

[7] Figs. 93*b*, 94.   [8] Figs. 93*a*, 94*a*.

[9] Figs. 94*b*, 95.   [10] Figs. 96, 97.

[11] Mortimer, *Forty Years*, &c., pp. 30-40.

[12] Vide Map showing the distribution of beakers in Province IV (p. 33).

[13] Fig. 176 from Clifton, Penrith; fig. 175 from Nether Moor, Hunsonby.

is much like another from near Durham. and from the East Riding[1] and a new variety of the bar-chevron motive is common to Yorkshire and Cumberland.[2]   It is probable therefore that a bifurcation took place in Yorkshire, some colonists moving due north, while others inclined to the north-west and entered Westmorland from the east.   For at Crosby Garrett, on the eastern side of the county, Canon Greenwell found a single fragment of a beaker with a primary interment.[3]

Province V.   The invaders would cross the Tweed without difficulty, and one of the earliest witnesses to their presence in Berwickshire is a beaker from Manderston, about one mile east of Duns.[4]   About the same time we find them at Eckford in Roxburgh, and Carluke in Mid Lanarkshire[5]; somewhat later they left traces of their presence near Edinburgh and at Dairsie in Fife.[6]   Later again they had pushed on to Stirlingshire, South Perthshire, and the neighbourhood of the Crinan Canal in Argyll.[7]   But they had really reached this locality a good deal earlier, for a beaker that seems to be the oldest in the whole province[8] came from the parish of Kilmartin.   Perhaps it is not quite so old as it appears[9] and is not earlier than the beaker from Manderston, but at any rate it points to a relatively early invasion of that part of Argyll.   As it is extremely unlikely that the invaders reached that part of the country by going round the head of Loch Fyne, they must have arrived by sea.   Before the advent of the new settlers, Cantire, Arran, Bute, and the country just north of the Crinan Canal were inhabited by the older neolithic inhabitants, who must have been accustomed to cross the Firth of Clyde and to visit Ireland in dug-out canoes or in coracles.   Hence it is quite likely that the invaders followed their example and took to the water.   If this is so, it accounts for their presence on the west coast at a date as early as on the east coast or even earlier.   Galloway may have been colonized from the west coast earlier than Berwickshire, which lies nearly a degree further north, for it has already been observed that the ornamentation on a beaker from Largs in Ayrshire was quite peculiar and only found on another from Denbighshire. Future discoveries may clear up this obscure point.

As time went on, the number of settlements increased, especially in the valley of the Tweed, in the Lothians and in Fife.   But as the map shows, except on the actual west coast and at one point on the south coast, the invaders did not apparently pass the fourth degree of longitude west of Greenwich.

There is no evidence to show from what point beakers first passed over to Ireland, though it is reasonable to suppose they were brought there from Galloway.   Neither can we be sure if the appearance of this new ceramic in Hibernia was due to the brachycephalic invaders, or to the hand of one of their women who had been captured by Hibernian raiders.

During the beaker period in this province, a time which may be estimated at about eight generations, the invaders were evidently living in a period with hardly any knowledge of metal till near the close of it.   As there is no tin in the country the two bronze daggers and the bronze bangle must have been brought from South Britain or from Hibernia.   Whether this

---

[1] Figs. 177, 129.   [2] Ornament F137, 138, 163.
[3] *B. B.* 391.   [4] Fig. 187.   [5] Figs. 188, 186.
[6] Figs. 189, 190.   [7] Figs. 193, 192, 191.
[8] Fig. 185.

[9] The diagonal fringe below the upper zone must be regarded as a late feature, although the beaker belongs to type A.

inflow of bronze was due to trade relations with the south, or was merely the result of plunder gained in raiding excursions, it is impossible to say.   Yet, judging by the enormous size of the cairn under which the Collessie knife-dagger with a gold mount was discovered, it is evident the deceased must have been a great personage and on that account a man who was likely to make expeditions for the sake of reputation and booty.   Again, the Isle of Mull is so remote, so unlikely to be visited by a trader and yet so adapted for a place of refuge for sea-pirates, that we may incline to believe that the three bronze articles of this province were brought thither, not peacefully, but as prizes of war.

Province VI.   So few beakers have been brought to light between the Tay and the Dee that the gradual advance of the new settlers cannot be exactly traced.   But in fairly early examples from Lochee near Dundee, from Kirkbuddo, from near Edzell and Noranside,[1] both in North Forfarshire, they have left their mark.   The bronze dagger from Linlathen in South-east Forfarshire evidently belongs to the later half of the beaker period in this province.

In the southern half of Aberdeenshire, which was occupied before the northern half, the invaders have left traces of themselves near Torphins, at Parkhill and Persley both near Aberdeen, at Auchendoir to the south of Loch Skene, and at Klinterty Kinellar in the valley of the Don.[2]   Pushing up the river we find them at Broomend in the parish of Kintore, and still later at Inveramsay on the Urie, a tributary of the Don.[3]

The beakers from the north-east of the county, from Ellon on the Ythan, from Ardiffrey in the parish of Cruden, from Savock near Peterhead, and from Pitsligo[4] on the north coast, all belong to a time later than the southern specimens mentioned above, showing again that the northward extension of the settlers was gradual.   Although some families moved northwards others remained behind, either staying where they were or spreading more widely over the southern part of the county.   Evidence of this is seen in beakers from Broomend in the parish of Kintore, from the Mains of Leslie in the parish of Premnay, from Pittodrie in the parish of Oyne, from near Aberdeen, from near Peterculter and Banchory,[5] both on the lower course of the Dee.

Province VII.   The counties of Banff, Elgin, and Nairn are so intimately connected with Aberdeenshire from a geographical point of view, that properly speaking they belong to the same area.   The invaders had therefore no difficulty in pushing their colonization westwards, though at a period later than their first arrival in the south of Aberdeenshire, for none of the beakers from the above three counties seems to be so old as some from nearer the Dee.[6]   But while Aberdeenshire was filling up we find the new colonists at Buckie on the coast of Banff, at Deskford, at Lesmurdie, as far up the Spey as Knockando, and at Nairn.[7]   Somewhat later they may have pushed on, following the coast as far as Fyrish in Ross and Dunrobin in Sutherland, reaching their furthest points north at West Watten in Caithness[8] and Bettyhill at the foot of Strath Naver in Sutherland, close to the extreme north coast of Scotland.   At the end of the period we find remains of the invaders at Cawdor in Nairn, at Cullen and

[1] Figs. 250, 236, 242, 240.
[2] Figs. 223*a*, 238, 247, 239, 243.
[3] Figs. 249, 244.
[4] Figs. 230, 231, 228, 229, 246, 260.

[5] Figs. 226, 227, 256, 233*a*, *b*, 261, 259*a*, 245.
[6] Figs. 238, 239, 243, 247.
[7] Figs. 267, 270, 280–2, 268, 273.
[8] Figs. 269, 286, 286*a*.

Abirchirdir in Banff, near Urquhart in Elgin, at Corran Ferry in the south-west of Inverness-shire and at Brahan Castle in Ross.[1]

The beaker period had now come to an end and an interesting episode in the early history of Great Britain was brought to a close. Yet the invaders who by this time mustered several thousands must have remained, for we cannot suppose that they were suddenly annihilated or had migrated elsewhere; though for some reason they now exchanged the beaker for other forms of food vessel. In North Britain their descendants perhaps remain to this day as an integral part of the population. Sir William Turner[2] 'has found a strong brachycephalic admixture in the crania of modern Scots in Fife, the Lothians, Peebles, and as far north as Shetland. In 116 specimens measured, twenty-nine, i.e. one quarter, had a length-breadth index of 80 and upwards, and in five of these the index was more than 85.' Even if all these 116 persons could not claim to be descended from the enterprising and vigorous invaders, certainly a considerable proportion of them may be considered modern representatives of this by-gone people.[3]

TYPE A, AS A TIME-SCALE

The whole object of attempting to arrange the beakers that exist in relative order of time is to subserve the interests of history. If that result can be in some measure attained, we have a scale by which certain historical events can be dated in terms of the pottery itself. Of all the varieties of the beaker, type A is the one best suited for our purpose. No doubt uncertainties in its arrangement exist. For instance, the exact order, necessarily lineal, in which each individual beaker is placed in the series is uncertain; but that type A forms a series with a definite beginning and end is certain. This certainty is assured by the fact that the type gradually disappeared as it travelled northwards and apparently never crossed the Tay. The certainty that Phase I is older than Phase II is derived from the fact that the former in passing north becomes less numerous in proportion to Phase II, although in Province I the two phases exist in nearly equal proportions. Naturally the older phase would die out earlier than the later phase.

In trying to estimate the duration of type A in Province I we have two questions to consider :—

1. What is a reasonable time to allow for forms like fig. 1, 2 to degenerate to forms like figs. 18, 18 *bis*?
2. What is a reasonable time for the invaders to pass from south of the Thames to the Tay? The answer is the same for both.

To make a beginning, I estimate the duration of Phases I, II of type A at five generations each or ten generations in all. As the type never reached Province VI, its duration coincides with the length of time required to advance as far as the Tay. From the South of England to the Tay is about $5\frac{1}{2}$ degrees of longitude or 385 miles, but in reality, as the invaders did not advance as the crow flies, the distance may be reckoned at about 500 miles: the distance by

[1] Figs. 273, 274, 276, 275, 288, 290.

[2] Lecture given at the Roy. Inst. of Great Britain in March, 1897, by Sir William Turner, D.C.L., LL.D., F.R.S.

[3] Since this was written Dr. J. Brownlee has published a paper in which he tries to separate the proportion of the Teutonic, Alpine, and Mediterranean races in the population of 117 districts of Scotland. The proportion of the Alpine race apparently varies from 29 % to 49 %. *Journ. Anthrop. Inst.* xli (1911), pp. 197–9.

railway amounts to 447 miles. Accordingly they moved at the rate of about 50 miles in each generation, or about 5 miles every three years.

The distance from the Thames to the Humber is nearly 200 miles; thence to the Tweed about 150 miles. Allowing for no northerly movement till after the first generation, the invaders would reach Province III by the end of the fifth generation. In the seventh generation they would be in Province IV and in the eighth generation in Province V. Not before the end of the tenth generation would they cross the Tay into Province VI, by which time type A was extinct.

The earlier types of B1, BC may be considered contemporary with Phase I of type A. Probably Phase II was prolonged by the latest examples of Phase III, B1, 2, C for some three generations. So the total duration of the beaker in Province I may be estimated at about thirteen generations, or 400 years.

As beakers appeared first in Province VI about ten generations later than in the south, they probably did not last longer than five or six generations in the northern provinces. Such an estimate assigns to the beaker period in Great Britain a duration of fifteen or sixteen generations, or about 450 years.

Any attempt to fix the approximate date of the invasion must be reserved for the next volume, after all the types of pottery of the Bronze Age have been passed in review.

For the sake of clearness, the life of type A and of the beaker class of ceramic in the different provinces may be shown in a diagram. The thick line represents type A, and the dots the other types and sub-types that survived it. To prevent confusion, the types and sub-types contemporary with type A are omitted.

DIAGRAM OF TYPE A TO SHOW ITS DURATION.

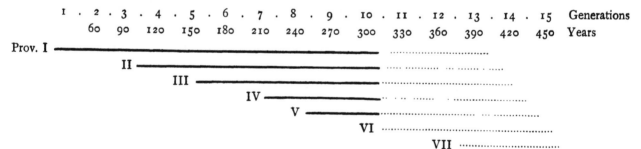

LIST OF CONTINENTAL BEAKERS

1*. Benndorf, Merseburg. 5¼ in. *British.*
2*. Polleben, Mansfeld. 8 in. *Halle.*
3*. Querfurt. 7⅛ in. *Halle.*
4*. Mittelhausen, Weimar. 6½ in. *Halle.*
5*. Aeberode, Salzmünde. 5¾ in. *Halle.*
6*. Eisleben. 3¾ in. *Halle.*
7*. Kaaks, Holstein. 6⅝ in. *Kiel.*
8*. Kaaks, Holstein. 7¼ in. *Kiel.*
9*. Borger, Drenthe, Holland. 4¾ in.
10*. Hademarschen, Holstein. 6¾ in. *Kiel.*
11*. Bordesholm, Holstein. 5¾ in. *Kiel.*
12*. Slaugaard (?) Ribe Amt, Denmark. 8 in. *Copenhagen.*

13*. Jutland. 7½ in. *Copenhagen.*
14*. „ 8¼ in. *Copenhagen.*
15*. Villafrati, Sicily. 3 in. From Montelius, *Chronol. äelt. Br. in N.D.*, fig. 236.
16*. Millares, Valencia, Spain. 4 in. From Montelius, *op. cit.*, fig. 237.
17*. 18*. 19*. La Halliade (H. Pyrénées). From *Matériaux*, xvi, pl. 17, figs. 3, 4, 5.
20*. 21*. Ciempozuelos, Madrid. From *Bol. R. Ac. Historia*, xxv, pl. 6, 7.
22*. Kerallant, Brittany. *Vannes.*
23*. Quelvezin, Carnac. 5¼ in. *British.*
24*. Between Carnac and Plouharnel. 5 in. *British.*

25*. Er-roh, Trinité-sur-Mer. 5$\frac{5}{16}$ in. *Vannes.*
26*. Manébeg-Portivy, Quibéron. 4$\frac{1}{2}$ in. *Vannes.*
27*. Erd, Buda-Pest. 4 in. *British.*
28*. 29*. Rottleben, Rudolstadt. *Berlin.*
30*. Bitterfeld. *Halle.*
31*. Wanzleben, Pr. Saxony. *Halle.*
32*. Ober-Olm, Rhein-Hessen. *Mainz.*
33*. 34*. Horchheim. *Mainz.*
35*. 36*. Loc. unknown. *Mainz.*
37*. 38*. Andernach. *Berlin.*
39*. Urmitz. *Bonn.*
40*. Urmitz. *Berlin.*
41*. Frankenthal. *Mainz.*
42*. Urmitz. *Bonn.*

43*. Herrensheim. *Mainz.*
44*. Andernach. *Berlin.*
45*. Gross-Bornholt, Holstein. 5$\frac{7}{8}$ in. *Kiel.*
46*. Edeberg bei Lensahn, Holstein. 6$\frac{1}{2}$ in. *Kiel.*
47*. Beldorf, Hademarschen, Holstein. 6$\frac{1}{2}$ in. *Kiel.*
48*. Brummen, Holland. 6$\frac{1}{2}$ in. *Leyden.*
49*. Wageningen, Holland. 5$\frac{3}{4}$ in. *Leyden.*
50*. Beekbergen, ,, 5$\frac{3}{4}$ in. *Leyden.*
51*. Epe, Holland. 6$\frac{5}{8}$ in. *Leyden.*
52*. 53*. Epe, Holland. 5$\frac{1}{4}$ in., 2$\frac{3}{4}$ in. *Leyden.*
54*. Keréon en Crozon, Finistère. 7$\frac{1}{4}$ in. P. du Chatel-lier, *Époques préhist. dans le Finistère*, 2nd ed., p. 186. *Kernuz.*

LIST OF BRITISH BEAKERS[1]

Fig. 1. Winterbourne Stoke, B. 5. H. 5$\frac{3}{4}$ in. *A. W.* 118. *Devizes.*
Fig. 2. Stonehenge, B. 36. H. 7$\frac{3}{4}$ in. *A. W.* 163. *Devizes.*
Fig. 3. Stonehenge, B. 39. H. 8$\frac{1}{4}$ in. *A. W.* 164. *Devizes.*
Fig. 4. Durrington, B. 93. H. 7$\frac{1}{2}$ in. *A. W.* 168. *Devizes.*
Fig. 4 *bis, tris.* Winterbourne Monkton, Wilts. *Crania Brit.* ii. 58 (2). *Devizes.*
Fig. 4*a*. Near Avebury, Wilts. H. 7 in. *P. Arch. Instit.* 1849, p. 110, fig. 12.
Fig. 5. Figheldean, Wilts. H. 7$\frac{1}{4}$ in. *Arch.* xlii. 147–8. *British.*
Fig. 6. Brendly, Kent. H. 6$\frac{7}{8}$ in. *Taunton.*
Fig. 7. Seven Barrows, Lambourne Downs, Berks. H. 7$\frac{7}{8}$ in. *Trans. Newbury Distr. Field Club* (1870–1), pp. 178, 197, 207. *British.*
Fig. 8. Wilsford Down, Wilts. H. 8 in.
Fig. 9. Winterbourne Stoke, Wilts. H. 6 in. *P. Soc. Ant.*, ser. 2, ii. 429. *British.*
Fig. 10. East Kennet, Wilts. H. 7$\frac{1}{2}$ in. *Arch. Jour.* xxiv. 28–9.
Figs. 11, 12. Wick Bar., Stogursey, Somerset. H. 7$\frac{1}{4}$ in. 6$\frac{1}{2}$ in. *Report on Wick Barrow* by St. George Gray, p. 20. *Taunton.*
Fig. 13. Fernworthy, Dartmoor, Devon. H. 7$\frac{1}{8}$ in. *Vict. Hist. Devon*, i. 358. *Plymouth.*
Fig. 13 *bis.* Brigmerston or Brigmilston, Wilts. No details known. *Devizes.*
Fig. 13 *tris.* B. on Oldbury Hill. *W. A. M.* xxiii. 215. *Devizes.*
Fig. 14. Winterbourne Stoke, B. 27. H. 7 in. *A. W.* 125. *Devizes.*
Fig. 15. Blandford, Dorset. H. 6 in. Warne, *Celt Tum.* ii. 19.
Fig. 16. Broad Down, Honiton, Devon. *Arch. Jour.* xxv. 307.

Fig. 17. Smaller Clandown Bar., Martinstown, Dorset. H. 5$\frac{1}{2}$ in. *Dorchester.*
Fig. 18. Lake B. 22, Wilts. H. 5$\frac{1}{4}$ in. *A. W.* 211. *Devizes.*
Fig. 18 *bis.* Barrow near Stoke Road to Stonehenge. H. 7$\frac{1}{4}$ in. *Cat. no.* 164. *Devizes.*
Fig. 19. Mere Down, Wilts. H. 6 in. *A. W.* 44. *Devizes.*
Fig. 20. Stogursey. H. 6$\frac{3}{16}$ in. See figs. 11, 12. *Taunton.*
Fig. 21. Roundway, Wilts. *W. A. M.* iii. 185–6. *Arch.* xliii, fig. 120, 154. *Devizes.*
Fig. 22. Cholsey, Berks. H. 6 in. *British.*
Fig. 23. Blackbush Down, Cranborne, Dorset. H. 7$\frac{1}{2}$ in. Pitt-Rivers, iii. 240. *Farnham.*
Figs. 23*a, b.* Boyton, Dean Valley, Wilts. H. 9 in. and 3$\frac{1}{4}$ in. *Arch.* xv, pl. xvii, p. 343.
Fig. 24. Winterslow Hut, Wilts. H. 8$\frac{1}{2}$ in. *Arch. Journ.* i. 156–7. *Ashmolean.*
Fig. 25. Bar. 20, Rushmore Park. H. 8 in. Pitt-Rivers, ii. 26, pl. 77. *Farnham.*
Fig. 26. Stage Lodge, Almer, Dorset. H. 8$\frac{1}{4}$ in. *Farnham.*
Fig. 27. Rotherley, S. Wilts. H. 8$\frac{1}{2}$ in. Pitt-Rivers, ii, pl. 92. *Farnham.*
Fig. 28. Normanton, bar. 161, Wilts. H. 7$\frac{1}{4}$ in. *A. W.* i. 205. *Devizes.*
Fig. 29. Upton Lovel, bar. 3, Wilts. H. 6$\frac{3}{8}$ in. *A. W.* i. 75, pl. ix. *Devizes.*
Fig. 30. Dorchester. H. 7 in. *Private.*
Fig. 31. Wor Barrow, Handley Down, Dorset. Pitt-Rivers, iv. 114, pl. 265. *Farnham.*
Fig. 32. Bloxworth Down, Dorset. H. 4$\frac{3}{4}$ in. *British.*
Fig. 33. B. 13, Wilsford, Wilts. H. 6$\frac{5}{8}$ in. *A. W.* i. 208. *Devizes.*
Figs. 34, 35. Highstead, Chislet, Kent.[2] H. 4 in. *British.*
Figs. 36, 37. Erith, Kent. H. 5$\frac{1}{4}$ in. and 5$\frac{3}{8}$ in. In possession of Mr. Wm. M. Newton, Dartford.

---

[1] The last word in italics is the Museum where the beaker is preserved. B. = Barrow.

[2] In *P. S. A. S.* xxxviii. 336. I put Chislet in Devonshire by a mistake.

Fig. 38. Devil's Dyke, Brighton. H. 5 in. *British.*
Fig. 39. Culbone, Exmoor, Somerset. H. 6¼ in. *Som. Arch. Proc.* xlii (1896), p. 60–5. *Taunton.*
Fig. 40. Chagford Common, Dartmoor. H. 9½ in. *Vict. Hist. Devon*, i. 360. *Plymouth.*
Fig. 41. Lambourne Down, Berks. H. 5¾ in. *British.*
Fig. 42. Wincanton, Somerset. H. 9½ in. *Taunton.*
Fig. 42*a*. Langcombe, Plym valley, Devon. *Trans. Devon. Ass.* xxxii. 50.
Fig. 42 *bis*. Stoford, par. of Barwick, Somerset. H. 6½ in. *Taunton.*
Fig. 43. Abingdon, Berks. H. 4⅞ in. *Ashmolean.*
Fig. 44. Castle Acre, Norfolk. H. 6 in. *Norwich Castle.*
Fig. 45. Curdle Head, Eriswell, Suffolk. H. 7½ in. *Cambridge.*
Fig. 46. Tuddenham, Suffolk. H. 5¾ in. *British.*
Fig. 47. Needham Market, Suffolk. H. 6¾ in. *British.*
Fig. 48. Green Low, Alsop Moor, Derby. H. 7¼ in. Bateman, *Vest.* pp. 59–60. *Sheffield.*
Fig. 49. Smerrill Moor, Derby. H. 9 in. Bateman, *Ten Years*, pp. 102–3. *Sheffield.*
Fig. 50. Grind Low, Derby. H. 4½ in. *Reliquary*, iii. 206.
Fig. 51. Haddon Field, Derby. H. 6½ in. Bateman, *Ten Years*, p. 106. *Sheffield.*
Fig. 52. Bee Low, Derby. H. 6½ in. Bateman, *Vestiges*, p. 35; *Ten Years*, p. 72. *Sheffield.*
Fig. 53. *Sliper* Lowe, Brassington Moor, Derby. H. 7 in. Bateman, *Vestiges*, p. 52. *Sheffield.*
Fig. 54. Hay Top Hill, Monsal Dale, Derby. H. 7¼ in. Bateman, *Ten Years*, p. 76. *Sheffield.*
Fig. 55. Castern, Wetton, Stafford. H. 8 in. Bateman, *Vestiges*, pp. 87–8. *Sheffield.*
Fig. 56. Stanshope, Stafford. H. 6½ in. Bateman, *Ten Years*, pp. 158–9. *Sheffield.*
Fig. 57. Rusden Low, Derby. H. 7¾ in. Bateman, *Ten Years*, pp. 43–4. *Sheffield.*
Fig. 58. Denton, Lincoln. H. 6 in. Canon Greenwell's collection, *Durham.*
Fig. 59. Top Low, Stafford. H. 7 in. Bateman, *Ten Years*, p. 134. *Sheffield.*
Fig. 60. Mouse Low, Deepdale, Stafford. H. 8¼ in. Bateman, *Ten Years*, pp. 115–16. *Sheffield.*
Fig. 60*a*. Horncastle, Lincoln. *Arch. Journ.* xiii. 86.
Fig. 61. Lakenheath, Suffolk. H. 7¼ in. *British.*
Fig. 62. Stakor Hill, Buxton, Derby. H. 7½ in. Bateman, *Ten Years*, pp. 80–1. *Sheffield.*
Fig. 63. Dowel, Sterndale, Derby. H. 6¾ in. Bateman, *Ten Years*, p. 38. *Sheffield.*
Fig. 64. Polstead Rd., Oxford. H. 4½ in. *Ashmolean.*
Fig. 65. Snailwell, Cambridge. H. 5⅓ in. *Cambridge.*
Fig. 66. Loddington, Kettering, Northampton. H. 7½ in. *P. Soc. Ant.*, 2 ser., xix. 307, &c. *Northampton.*
Fig. 67. Woolston (?) Warrington, Lancashire (?). H. 6 in. *York.*
Fig. 68. Minning Low, Derby. H. 8¼ in. Bateman, *Vestiges*, p. 41. *Sheffield.*
Fig. 69. Barnwell, Cambridge. H. 7¼ in. *Cambridge.*
Fig. 70. Worlington, Suffolk. H. 5 in. *British.*
Fig. 71. Stanshope, Stafford. H. 7 in. Bateman, *Ten Years*, pp. 158–9. *Sheffield.*
Figs. 72, 73, 74. Hitcham, Taplow, Bucks. H. 4 in., 3¾ in. 4½ in. *Maidenhead Nat. Field Club, 8th Ann. Report*, 1890–1, p. 46. *British.*
Fig. 75. Summertown, Oxford. H. 7¾ in. *British.*
Fig. 76. Somersham, Hunts. H. 10⅘ in. *Cambridge.*
Fig. 77. Yarnton, Oxford. H. 6$\frac{3}{16}$. *Ashmolean.*
Fig. 78. Felixstow, Suffolk. H. 6 in. *British.*
Fig. 79. Yarnton, Oxford. H. 4½ in. *British.*
Fig. 80. Methwold, Norfolk. H. 5½ in. *British.*
Fig. 81. Devil's Ditch, Stalham, Norfolk. H. 5 in. *Norwich Castle.*
Figs. 82, 83. Brandon Fields, Suffolk. H. 4 in. and 5 in. *P. S. Ant. London*, 2 ser., v. 271–2. *British.*
Fig. 84. Ipswich. H. 5¾ in. *Ipswich.*
Fig. 85. Great Clacton, Essex. H. 5⅝ in. *Colchester.*
Fig. 86. Felixstow, Suffolk. H. 5 in. *British.*
Fig. 87. Fingeringhoe, Essex. H. 4¾ in. *Colchester.*
Fig. 88. Gospel Hillock, Cow Dale, Derby. H. 7 in. *Reliquary*, viii. 85–90.
Fig. 89. Snailwell, Cambridge. H. 7½ in. *Cambridge.*
Fig. 90. Kelling Heath. H. 5 in. *Norwich Castle.*
Fig. 90 *bis*. Blake Low, Derby. H. 7½ in. Bateman, *Ten Years*, p. 41. *Sheffield.*
Fig. 91. East Winch, Norfolk. H. 8¼ in. *Norwich Castle.*
Fig. 92. Rackheath, Norfolk. H. 6¼ in. *Norwich Castle.*
Fig. 93. Barton Hill, Mildenhall, Suffolk. H. 5⅗ in. *Colchester.*
Fig. 93*a*. Banks of the Alau. Anglesea. Fragment. *British.*
Fig. 93*b*. Cwm Car, Dolygaer, Glamorgan. H. 7½ in. *Arch. Cambrens.* (1902), p. 26.
Fig. 94. St. Fagan's, Glamorgan. H. 6½ in. *Arch. Cambrens.* (1902), pp. 28–32.
Fig. 94*a*. Rhosbeirio, Anglesea. H. 8 in. *Arch. Cambrens.* 3 ser., xiv. 271.
Fig. 94*b*. Plas Heaton, Denbigh. H. 8 in. *Arch. Cambrens.* 3 ser., xiv. 273.
Fig. 95. Glan yr Avon, Denbigh. H. 4⅞ in. Taken from *Arch.* xliii. 394.
Fig. 96. Aberbechan, Newton, Montgomery. H. 4 in. Taken from *Arch.* xliii. 394.
Fig. 97. Moel Hebog, Snowdonia, Carnarvon. H. 5⅝ in. *British.*
Fig. 98. Garton Slack, bar. 37. H. 6¼ in. Mortimer, *Forty Years*, pp. 209–11. *Driffield.*
Fig. 99. Hedon Howe, bar. 281. E. Riding. H. 8⅛ in. Mortimer, *Forty Years*, 346–50.
Fig. 100. Middleton Hall, East Riding. Mortimer, *Forty Years*, p. 354.

Fig. 101. Towthorpe, bar. 21. H. 7¾ in. Mortimer, *Forty Years*, p. 12. *Driffield.*

Fig. 102. Garton Slack, bar. 161. H. 8½ in. Mortimer, *Forty Years*, pp. 211–12. *Driffield.*

Fig. 103. Garton Slack, bar. 75. H. 8¾ in. Mortimer, *Forty Years*, pp. 222–4. *Driffield.*

Fig. 104. Hanging Grimston, bar. 56. H. 7½ in. Mortimer, *Forty Years*, pp. 98–9. *Driffield.*

Fig. 105. Heslerton, bar. 5. H. 7 in. Greenwell, *B.B.* 144. *British.*

Fig. 106. Huggate Wold, bar. 216. H. 7¼ in. Mortimer, *Forty Years*, pp. 309–10. *Driffield.*

Fig. 107. Warter Wold, Yorkshire. H. 9⅛ in. *British.*

Fig. 108. Folkton, bar. 242. H. 7¼ in. Greenwell, *Arch.* lii. 11. *British.*

Fig. 109. Ferry Fryston, bar. 161. West Riding. H. 6⅝ in. Greenwell, *B.B.* 373. *British.*

Fig. 110. Rudstone, bar. 63. H. 5⅞ in. Greenwell, *B.B.* 247. *British.*

Fig. 110 *bis.* Acklam Wold, bar. 204. H. 5⅞ in. Mortimer, *Forty Years*, pp. 86, 87.

Fig. 111. Goodmanham, bar. 116. H. 5⅜ in. *B.B.* 325–6. *British.*

Figs. 112, 113, 114. Painsthorpe Wold, E.R. H. 5⅞ in., 6 in., and 5⅝ in. Mortimer, *Forty Years*, pp. 113–17. *Driffield.*

Figs. 115, 116, 117. Garton Slack, bar. 163. H. 8¼ in., 7 in., 7¾ in. Mortimer, *Forty Years*, pp. 214–15. *Driffield.*

Figs. 118, 119, 120, 121. Aldro, bar. 116. H. 5 in., 4⅝ in., 2½ in., 7½ in. Mortimer, *Forty Years*, pp. 54–6. *Driffield.*

Figs. 122, 123, 124. Garrowby Wold, bar. 104. H. 9 in., 9¼ in., 6¼ in. Mortimer, *Forty Years*, pp. 134–6. *Driffield.*

Figs. 125, 126, 127. Hanging Grimston, bar. 55. H. 8½ in., 5 in., 6½ in. Mortimer, *Forty Years*, pp. 100–2. *Driffield.*

Figs. 128, 129. Rudstone, bar. 66. H. 8½ in., 7¼ in. Greenwell, *B.B.* 253–5. *British.*

Figs. 130, 131. Ganton, bar. 21. H. 6¾ in., 7¾ in. Greenwell, *B.B.* 162–3, 165–6. *British.*

Figs. 132, 133, 134. Goodmanham, bar. 99. H. 8 in., 5¾ in., 6⅞ in. Greenwell, *B.B.* 308–9. *British.*

Figs. 135, 136, 137, 138, 139. Rudstone, bar. 62. H. 7¾ in., 8½ in., 7¾ in., 6 in., 6¾ in. Greenwell, *B.B.* 235–44. *British.*

Figs. 140, 141. Aldro, bar. 54. H. 7 in., 5½ in. Mortimer, *Forty Years*, pp. 63–6. *Driffield.*

Figs. 142, 143. Rudstone, bar. 67. H. 4⅞ in., 4¼ in. Greenwell, *B.B.* 259, 261. *British.*

Fig. 144. Rudstone, bar. 61. H. 7⅞ in. Greenwell, *B.B.* 231. *British.*

Fig. 145. Towthorpe, bar. 211½. H. 5⅘ in. Mortimer, *Forty Years*, p. 19. *Driffield.*

Fig. 146. Garton Slack, bar. 80. H. 9 in. Mortimer, *Forty Years*, pp. 235–7. *Driffield.*

Fig. 147. Huggate and Warterwold, bar. 254. H. 8½ in. Mortimer, *Forty Years*, pp. 320–1. *Driffield.*

Fig. 148. York. H. 7 in. *York.*

Fig. 149. Driffield. H. 7 in. *Arch.* xxxiv, pl. xx, fig. 6, pp. 251–5. *British.*

Fig. 150. Thwing, bar. 60. H. 9 in. Greenwell, *B.B.* 226–8. *British.*

Fig. 151. Willerby, bar. 235. H. 4½ in. Greenwell, *Arch.* lii. 2–4. *British.*

Fig. 152. Folkton, bar. 245. H. 8⅛ in. Taken from *Arch.* lii. 16.

Fig. 153. Middleton on the Wolds. H. 7½ in. Mortimer, *Forty Years*, pp. 230–1. *Driffield.*

Fig. 154. Sherburn, bar. 7. H. 8½ in. Greenwell, *B.B.* p. 146. *British.*

Fig. 155. Weaverthorpe, bar. 42. H. 7¾ in. Greenwell, *B.B.* 193. *British.*

Fig. 156. Garton Slack, bar. 81. H. 7½ in. Mortimer, *Forty Years*, pp. 238–41. *Driffield.*

Fig. 157. Pickering, N.R. H. 7½ in. Bateman, *Ten Years*, p. 231. *Sheffield.*

Fig. 158. Rothbury, Northumberland. H. 6⅝ in. *British.*

Fig. 159. Lillburnsteds, Wooler, Northumberland. *Kelvingrove.*

Fig. 159a. Beanly Moor, Northumberland. H. 6⅝ in. Bruce, *Cat. Alnwick Castle Mus.* pl. xii. *Alnwick Castle.*

Fig. 160. Woodhorn, Northumberland. H. 6½ in. *British.*

Fig. 161. Castle Carrock, Cumberland. H. 7½ in. Greenwell, *B.B.* 379. *British.*

Fig. 161a. Amble, Northumberland. H. 8 in. *Arch. Jour.* xiv. 282. *Alnwick Castle.*

Fig. 162. Alwinton, Northumberland. H. 7⅛ in. *British.*

Fig. 163. Clifton, Penrith, Westmorland. H. 7 in. *Carlisle.*

Fig. 164. Ford, Northumberland. H. 6 in. *British.*

Fig. 165. Clifton, Penrith, Westmorland. *Ashmolean.*

Fig. 166. Loc. unknown. *Newcastle.*

Fig. 166a. Brougham, Westmorland. H. 3¾ in. *Arch.* xlv. 414.

Figs. 167, 168, 169, 170, 171. Dilston Park, Hexham, Northumberland. H. 5¾ in., 5¼ in., 5½ in., 5 in. Gibson, *Arch. Aeliana*, 3 ser., ii, pp. 136–46.

Fig. 172. Hawkfield, Lesbury, Northumberland. H. 9¾ in. *Newcastle.*

Fig. 172a. Lesbury, Northumberland. H. 5 in. Bruce, *Cat. Alnwick Castle Mus.* pl. xii. *Alnwick Castle.*

Fig. 173. Tarret Burn, Northumberland. H. 7¼ in. *Arch. Aeliana*, 3 ser., ii. 131; *Arch. Aeliana*, xv. 49–51. *Newcastle.*

Fig. 173a. Whitehouse, Alnwick. H. 9 in. Bruce, *Cat. Alnwick Castle Mus.* pl. xi. *Alnwick Castle.*

Fig. 174. Bellingham, Northumberland. H. 6⅞ in. *British.*

Fig. 174a. Loc. unknown. H. 8½ in. Bruce, *Cat. Alnwick Castle Mus.* pl. xiii. *Alnwick Castle.*

Fig. 175. Nether Moor, Hunsonby, Cumberland. H. 8½ in. *Carlisle.*

Fig. 176. Clifton, Penrith. H. 7¾ in. *Carlisle.*

Fig. 177. Sacriston, Durham. H. 6¾ in. Canon Greenwell's coll. *Durham.*

Figs. 178, 179. Blue Bull Inn, North Sunderland. H.8 in., 5 in. *Berwickshire Nat. Club Trans.* iv, pl. xiii, 4. Greenwell coll. *Durham.*

Fig. 180. Cursed Field, Ancroft, Northumberland. H. 6¾ in. Greenwell coll. *Durham.*

Fig. 181. Bamborough, bar. 197. H. 5½ in. Greenwell, *B. B.* 415–16. *British.*

Fig. 182. Morton coll., Carlisle. H. 6 in. *Carlisle.*

Fig. 183. Norham, Northumberland. H. 7 in. *British.*

Fig. 184. Gryndan, Norham, Northumberland. *Edinburgh.*

Fig. 185. Kilmartin, Argyll. H. 7 in. *P. S. A. S.* vi. 348–9. *British.*

Fig. 186. Mossplat, Carluke, Lanark. H. 7½ in. *P. S. A. S.* iv. 165. Edinburgh.

Fig. 187. Manderston, Berwickshire. Taken from *Berwickshire Naturalist's Club* (1882–4), p. 305, pl. i.

Fig. 188. Eckford, Roxburgh. H. 8¼ in. *P. S. A. S.* xxv. 29. *Edinburgh.*

Fig. 189. Juniper Green, Midlothian. H. 6½ in. *Edinburgh.*

Fig. 190. Dairsie, Fife. H. 7⅝ in. *P. S. A. S.* xxi. 132, *Edinburgh.*

Fig. 191. Loc. unknown. H. 6¼ in. *Poltalloch coll*

Fig. 192. Tippermallo, Methven, Perth. *Stirling.*

Fig. 193. Loc. unknown. *Stirling.*

Fig. 194. Tippermallo, Methven, Perth. H. 5¾ in.

Fig. 195. Bathgate, Linlithgow. H. 5⅝ in. L. Mann, *P. S. A. S.* xl. 369–71. *Edinburgh.*

Fig. 196. Park Law, St. Andrews, Fife. *P. S. A. S.* xli. pp. 401–6. *Edinburgh.*

Fig. 197. East Barns, E. Lothian. H. 7¾ in. *Edinburgh.*

Fig. 198. Lairgie, Poltalloch, Argyll. H. 9 in. *P.S.A.S.* vi. 344–5. *British.*

Fig. 199. Court Hill, Dalry, Ayrshire. H. 9 in. *Edinburgh.*

Fig. 200. Ballielands, Auchterarder, Perth. H. 5¾ in. *P. S. A. S.* xxxii. 314. *Edinburgh.*

Fig. 201. Tents Moor, Leuchars, Fife. H. 5 in. *P. S. A. S.* xvii. 384–5.

Fig. 202. Tartraven, Linlithgow, H. 5½ in. *P. S. A. S.* xxi. 199. *Edinburgh.*

Fig. 203. Fairy's Know, Pendreich, Bridge of Allan. *P. S. A. S.* vii. 519–21.

Figs. 204, 205. Collessie, Fife. H. 7 in., 9 in. Anderson, *Bronze and Stone Ages*, figs. 4, 5. *Edinburgh.*

Figs. 206, 207. Caickmuir Hill, Borthwick, Midlothian. H. 6¾ in., 7½ in. *P. S. A. S.* ii. 482. *Edinburgh.*

Figs. 208, 209. Lanark Moor, Lanark. H. 7½ in., 6¾ in. *Edinburgh.*

Figs. 210, 211. Hoprig, Cockburnspath, Berwick. Taken from James Hardy, *British Urns found at Hoprig*, in 1887.

Fig. 212a. Macksmill, Gordon, Berwick. H. 9 in. *Berwick. Naturalist's Club* (1885–6), p. 194.

Fig. 213. Crawford, Lanarkshire. H. 6 in. Anderson, *Bronze and Stone Ages*, figs. 64, 65. *Edinburgh.*

Fig. 214. Tillyochie, Kinross. H. 5¾ in. *Edinburgh.*

Fig. 215. Kincardine Castle, Perth. H. 5 in. *Edinburgh.*

Fig. 216. Windy Mains, Humbie, Haddington. H. 6½ in. *P. S. A. S.* iii. 51. *Edinburgh.*

Fig. 217. Callachally, Glenforsa, Mull. H. 6½ in *Edinburgh.*

Fig. 218. West Links, North Berwick. *P. S. A. S.* xxxiv. 123. *Edinburgh.*

Fig. 219, 220, 221. Gullane Bay, E. Lothian. *P. S. A. S.* xlii. 308–19. *Edinburgh.*

Fig. 222. North Berwick, E. Lothian. *P. S. A. S.* xlii. 270. *Edinburgh.*

Fig. 223. Mount Stewart, Co. Down. Taken from *Dublin Penny Journal*, 1838.

Fig. 224. Fragments from Moytura, Sligo. *Dublin.*

Fig. 225. Aberdeenshire. H. 4¾ in. *Edinburgh.*

Fig. 225a. Sundayswells Hill, Torphins, Aberdeen. H. 5¾ in. *P. S. A. S.* xl. 312–13.

Figs. 226, 227. Broomend, Inverurie, Aberdeen. H. 6 in., 7 in. *P. S. A. S.* vii. 110–13. *Edinburgh.*

Figs. 228, 229. Ardiffrey, Cruden, Aberdeen. H. 7⅜ in., 5¾ in. Wilson's *Prehist. Annals*, 75. *Peterhead.*

Figs. 230, 231. Ellon, Aberdeen. H. 5⅛ in., 4½ in. *P. S. A. S.* xxvi. 262. *Edinburgh.*

Figs. 232, 233. Skene, Aberdeen. H. 6½ in., 8 in. *P. S. A. S.* xl. 28–30. *Aberdeen University.*[1]

Figs. 233a, b. Pittodrie, Oyne, Aberdeen. H. 7 in., 8½ in. *P. S. A. S.* xl. 23–8.

Figs. 234, 235. Balbridie, Durris, Kincardine. H. 6 in. *P. S. A. S.* xl. 304–6. *Aberdeen University.*[1]

Fig. 236. Kirkbuddo, Forfar. Taken from Thurnam, *Arch.* xliii, pl. 31, fig. 6.

Fig. 237. Cruden, Aberdeen. H. 6½ in. *P. S. A. S.* xi. 408.

Fig. 238. Parkhill, Aberdeen. H. 7½ in. *Aberdeen University.*

Fig. 239. Ord, Auchendoir, Aberdeen. H. 7⅞ in. *Property of Prof. Reid.*

Fig. 240. Noranside, Fern, Forfar. H. 8¼ in. *P. S. A. S.* xxvii, 66.

---

[1] For the photos. of these beakers I am indebted to Prof. R. Reid of Aberdeen University.

Fig. 241. Freefield, Aberdeen. H. 7 in. *P. S. A.* xv. 193.

Fig. 242. Priest-town, Edzell, Forfar. *Edinburgh.*

Fig. 243. Clinterty Kinellar, Aberdeen. H. 7⅞ in. *Aberdeen University.*

Fig. 244. Inveramsay, Ch. of Garioch, Aberdeen. H. 7¼ in. *P. S. A. S.* iv. 165. *Edinburgh.*

Fig. 245. Clashfarquhar, Banchory, Aberdeen. H. 6¼ in. *Free Ch. coll. Aberdeen.*

Fig. 246. Savoch, Longside, H. 5⁷⁄₁₆ in. *Peterhead.*

Fig. 247. Persley Quarry, Aberdeen. H. 6⅛ in. *Aberdeen University.*[1]

Fig. 248. Leslie, Aberdeen. H. 8 in. *The Reliquary,* new ser., iii. 49. Coll. of Mr. Young of Tortola.

Fig. 249. Broomend, Inverurie, Aberdeen. H. 6½ in. *P. S. A. S.* vii. 115–17.

Fig. 250. Wellgrove, Lochee, Forfar. H. 6½ in. *P. S. A. S.* xl. 40–2. *Edinburgh.*

Fig. 251. Aberdeenshire. *British.*

Fig. 252. King St. Road, Aberdeen. H. 8 in. *P. S. A. S.* xxiv. 446. *Edinburgh.*

Fig. 253. Parkhill, Aberdeen. H. 5½ in. *P. S. A. S.* xvi. 70.

Fig. 254. Stoneywood, Aberdeen. H. 5¼ in. *Aberdeen University.*[1]

Fig. 255. Cairnie, Huntly, Aberdeen. H. 5 in. *Elgin.*

Fig. 256. Mains of Leslie, Premnay, Aberdeen. H. 6¾ in. *Aberdeen University.*[1]

Fig. 257. Fyvie, Aberdeen. *Aberdeen University.*[1]

Fig. 258. Aberdeenshire. H. 6½ in. *Edinburgh.*

Fig. 259. Fallows, Monikie, Forfar. H. 8 in. *Edinburgh.*

Fig. 259*a*. Glasterberry, Peterculter, Aberdeen. H. 8½ in. *P. S. A. S.* xxxvi. 627–8.

Fig. 260. Bankhead, Pitsligo, Aberdeen. H. 4¾ in. *Peterhead.*

Fig. 261. Near Aberdeen. H. 8 in. In coll. of Mr. Young of Tortola, Nairn, who gave me the photo.

Fig. 262. Linlathen, Forfar. H. 7 in. Taken from *P. S. A. S.* xii. 449.

Fig. 263. Aberdeenshire. H. 4⅜ in. *British.*

Fig. 264. Slap, Turriff, Aberdeen. H. 6 in. *P. S. A. S.* x. 740. *Edinburgh.*

Fig. 265. Cambusmore, Dornoch, Sutherland. H. 5½ in. For the photo. I am indebted to the Rev. I. M. Joass, Golspie. *Dunrobin.*

Fig. 266. Nairn. H. 7 in. For the photo. I am indebted to Mr. Young of Tortola, Nairn.

Fig. 267. Buckie, Banff. H. 7½ in. *Reliquary,* new ser., i. 249. I owe the photo. to Mr. Young of Tortola.

Fig. 268. Acres, Knockando. H. 5½ in. *Elgin.*

Fig. 269. Fyrish, Evanton, Ross. H. 6 in. *P. S. A. S.* vi. 233. *Edinburgh.*

Fig. 270. Carestown, Deskford, Banff. H. 8 in. *Banff.*

Fig. 271. Near Elgin. H. 6¾ in. *Edinburgh.*

Fig. 272. Achroisk, Boharm, Banff. H. 6 in. *P. S. A. S.* viii. 381. *Edinburgh.*

Fig. 273. Cawdor Castle, Nairn. H. 6½ in. *British.*

Fig. 274. Cullen. H. 5 in. *Banff.*

Fig. 275. Sleepies Hill, Urquhart, Elgin. H. 5¾ in. *Elgin.*

Fig. 276. Burnside of Whitefield, Aberchirdir, Banff. H. 4⅝ in. *P. S. A. S.* xl. 306–10. *Forglen House.*[2]

Figs. 277, 278, 279. Forglen, Banff. H. 6½ in., 6⅞ in., 7¾ in. *P. S. A. S.* xl. 279–90. *Forglen House.*[2]

Figs. 280, 281, 282. Lesmurdie, Banff. H. 7¾ in., 5¾ in., 7½ in. *P. S. A. S.* i. 205–8. *Edinburgh.*

Fig. 283. Gardenstown, Banff. H. 6¾ in. *The Reliquary,* new ser., ii. 178. For this photo. I am indebted to Mr. Young, Tortola, Nairn.

Fig. 284. Gordonstone, Elgin. H. 6¼ in. *Elgin.*

Fig. 285. Loc. unknown. *Elgin.*

Fig. 286. Dunrobin, Sutherland. H. 7 in. For this photo. and information I am indebted to the Rev. I. M. Joass, curator of the *Dunrobin Museum.*

Fig. 286 *bis.* Acharole, West Watten, Caithness. *Edinburgh,* 7¾ in. *P. S. A. S.* xxxix. 418–19.

Fig. 287. Buckie, Banff. H. 7 in. Taken from *P. S. A. S.* xvi. 415.

Fig. 288. Corran Ferry. Inverness. H. 5½ in. Taken from *P. S. A. S.* xxiv. 437.

Fig. 289. Eddertoun, Ross. H. 5 in. *P. S. A. S.* vii. 268.

Fig. 290. Probably Ross-shire. H. 5¼ in. *Edinburgh.*

Fig. 291. Auchmore, Portsoy. *Banff.*

Fig. 292. Appleford, Abingdon, Berks. H. 6 in. *British.*

Fig. 293. Goodmanham, bar. 113, E. Riding. H. 7¼ in. Greenwell, *B. B.* 321–2. *British.*

Fig. 294. Pickering, N. Riding. H. 5¾ in. Bateman, *Ten Years,* p. 209. *Sheffield.*

Figs. 295, 296. Brixworth, Northampton. H. 5 in. *Northampton.*

Fig. 295 *bis.* Aldro, B. 116, E. Riding. H. 4½ in. *Driffield.*

Fig. 296 *bis.* Rothwell, near Kettering, Northampton. H. 7 in. *Northampton.*

Fig. 296*a.* B. 264, Huggate and Warterwold, E. Riding. H. 5¼ in. *Driffield.*

Fig. 296*b.* Garrowby Wold, B. 104, E. Riding. H. 5½ in. *Driffield.*

Fig. 297. Wereham, Norfolk. H. 4 in. *Cambridge.*

Fig. 298. Frome Whitfield, Dorset. H. 4½ in. *Dorchester.*

Fig. 299. Martinstown, Dorset. H. 4½ in. *Dorchester.*

[1] For the photos. of these beakers I am indebted to Prof. R. Reid of Aberdeen University.

[2] For these photos. I am indebted to Captain Douglas Abercromby.

Fig. 300. Barrow at Bagber, Milton Abbas, Dorset. H. $2\frac{7}{8}$ in. *Dorchester.*

Fig. 301. Denzell, Cornwall. H. $3\frac{7}{10}$ in. *British.*

Fig. 301*a.* Darley Dale, Derbyshire. H. $1\frac{3}{4}$ in. From *Arch.* xliii. 358, fig. 37.

Fig. 10 taken from Thurnam, *Arch.* xliii. fig. 83.

Fig. 15 „ „ Warne, *Celtic Tum.* pl. 7, fig. 1.

Fig. 16 „ „ Jewitt, *Ceram. Orn.* fig. 43.

Fig. 50 „ „ Thurnam, *op. cit.* fig. 81.

Fig. 88 „ „ Jewitt, *op. cit.* fig. 44.

Fig. 90 *bis* „ Thurnam, *op. cit.* pl. 31, fig. 3.

Figs. 99, 101 taken from Mortimer, *Forty Years*, figs. 1014, 27.

Fig. 194 taken from *P. S. A. S.* xxxiii. 145.

Fig. 201 „ „ „ xvii. 384.

Fig. 215 „ „ „ xii. 682.

Fig. 218 „ „ „ xxxiv. 123.

Fig. 240 „ „ „ xxvii. 66.

Fig. 241 „ „ „ xv. 193.

Fig. 249 „ „ Anderson, *Stone and Bronze Ages*, fig. 89.

Fig. 253 „ „ Anderson, *Stone and Bronze Ages*, fig. 94.

Fig. 289 „ „ Anderson, *Stone and Bronze Ages*, fig. 111.

THE CASTLESTRANGE STONE. HEIGHT 2¼ FT.

THE TUROE STONE. HEIGHT 4 FT.

CHAPTER VII

THE FOOD-VESSEL CLASS

THE class of vessels with which we are now concerned served the same purpose as the beakers, and were evidently placed in the grave for the use of the deceased; in some of them bones of small animals or the remains of decayed animal and vegetable matter have been observed. Compared with beakers the walls of the vessels are thicker, more solid, and though generally of small size (from 4 to 6 inches in height), are heavier than a beaker of greater height. The forms are quite different and none can be derived from it; the ornamentation is far simpler, and no longer arranged in alternate zones; the technique of the ornament is also often different. The food vessels of Britain south of the Tweed may be arranged under six main types, with several by-forms or sub-types.

TYPE 1 (*grooved shoulder with stops*).

The lower part consists of a low, truncated, and inverted cone; above this is a grooved shoulder with several ears or stops, sometimes perforated horizontally, but more often imperforate; the neck, which rises above the groove, curves slightly inwards and terminates at the lip. (Fig. 125.)

1*a*.

In this sub-type or variant, the lip is bevelled and ornamented on the inside surface. Generally there is a raised moulding round the rim on the outside; sometimes there is a raised moulding above the groove and this forms the base of the neck. (Figs. 126, 142.)

1*b*.

This sub-type is like the last, but has two rows of stops, each in its own groove. (Figs. 39, 99, 134.)

TYPE 2 (*grooved shoulder*).

The lower part of this type is the same as in type 1, and both often resemble each other, but type 2 has no stops in the shoulder groove. Sometimes the groove is bounded above and below by two raised mouldings. As in 1 *a*, the lip is bevelled and ornamented on the inside and generally there is a raised moulding round the rim on the outside. (Figs. 169, 171, 174.)

2*a*.

A third moulding is sometimes found below the grooved shoulder. (Fig. 89.)

Type 3 (*concave neck*).

The lower part is the same as in the previous types. The shoulder is the angle formed by the lower part of the neck, which describes a cavetto curve and terminates at the lip. Generally the lip is bevelled on the inside and shows a moulding at the rim, as in 1*a*, 2. Sometimes there is a raised moulding at the shoulder. (Figs. 196, 197, 200, 201.)

Type 4 (*biconical*).

The vessel is composed of two truncated cones united at the base to form a shoulder; the upper part is much shorter than the lower. The lip is sometimes bevelled on the inside and sometimes there is a raised moulding at the shoulder. (Figs. 206, 208.)

4*a*.

In this by-form there is a raised moulding round the rim or lip. (Figs. 209, 210.)

4*b*.

In this by-form there are two grooves at the shoulder. (Fig. 244.)

Type 5 (*truncated cone*).

This type has the form of a truncated cone or a flower-pot, though sometimes the walls swell out like an old fashioned beehive. (Fig. 215.)

5*a*.

This only differs from the above by having a moulding, sometimes very slight, round the lip. (Fig. 217.)

Type 6 (*cylindrical*).

The type is a simple cylinder, sometimes barrel-shaped and generally of very rude work. (Figs. 218, 230.)

Some of these types are very difficult to classify; for instance, type 3, when the rim is moulded, is hardly to be distinguished in some examples from type 4*a*, and I may have gone wrong sometimes in assigning a food vessel to type 3 instead of 4*a* and *vice versa*.

Besides these types and by-forms there are isolated examples of handled cups, already described, cup-like vessels, small bowls, vessels with feet, &c., which are too rare to be considered typical of the food-vessel class.

The better to show the gradual passage of the beaker from south to north, Great Britain was divided into seven provinces. But as these are no longer applicable, the United Kingdom is now divided into three 'regions', using a different word to prevent confusion.

Region I includes the counties lying south of Derbyshire and Staffordshire.

Region II includes these two counties and the rest of the north of England.

Region III consists of Scotland and Ireland.

REGION I

Region I is very poor in food vessels so far as is known at present, though skeleton interments are common enough. Of the interments mentioned by Warne as occurring in Dorset 63·6 % were by cremation and 36·4 % by inhumation. But in the latter are included many skeletons of a much latter age than the period with which we are now concerned, for some were fully extended, and with one such interment two pieces of Samian ware were observed.

1. In Bradbury barrow, five miles from Wimborne, Dorset, Mr. Austin found two food vessels, perhaps of type 3, a small cup-like vessel 1½ in. high, and another small vessel 2½ in. high, of type 5, but with two projecting perforated ears. Two cinerary urns and a round piece of thin bronze 1⅝ in. in diameter, with two minute holes near the circumference, were also found in the barrow.[1]

2. Barrow 1, three miles west of Dorchester, Mr. Sydenham found in a large grave cut into the chalk, and lying at the bottom, two contracted skeletons and a burnt interment. Among the flints of the cairn overlying the grave was the skeleton of a child, and a small plain vessel of type 5.

3. In Barrow 2, the grave in the chalk was 4 ft. deep and contained a skeleton at full length with a broken vessel lying at the left side and an antler at the right. Above the nucleus of flint overlying the grave lay a child's skeleton and a food vessel of type 2, 6 in. high. A few inches above was a large inverted urn of very coarse material.

4. In Barrow 3, the primary interment consisted of three skeletons, all the secondary interments were unburnt, but no pottery had been deposited with them.

5. In Barrow 7, contiguous to the outer vallum of the great earthwork Maiden Castle, near Dorchester, there was no grave, but three interments by inhumation lay on the floor of the barrow. Near its summit lay a small food vessel, ornamented all over, of type 6.

6. Barrow 12. At the centre was a grave 6 ft. long, lined with flat stones set on end and covered with a large flat stone. In this lay a skeleton, an antler, and several large teeth of a boar. At the foot of the skeleton was a vessel, perhaps of type 2, containing burnt bones of an animal, probably of a fox or badger. It also contained a triangular spearhead of stone, a flint arrowhead, and a perforated boar's tusk.

7. Barrow 18 was about 8 ft. high. There was a depression of 18 in. at the centre. Below it was a cist, 4 ft. × 2 ft. wide and 18 in. deep, composed of large, unhewn flat stones. Within the cist lay food vessel fig. 1, of rude work, of type 2.[2]

Fig. 2 of type 1a is in the Farnham Museum, Dorset, though where it was found is unknown. But I conjecture that, as General Pitt-Rivers was also a Yorkshire landlord, it was found in that county and given to him, or that he bought it at an auction in a composite lot. A good example of this type and the only certain one I know of in Region I was found at Tenby in South Wales with another vessel of type 2.[3]

Fig. 3 of type 2 was found at Park Town, Oxford, in 1864, but no details seem to be known with regard to its discovery.

Fig. 4 of type 2 was found in Somerset and is now in the Taunton Museum.

Fig. 5 of type 2, but with a double groove, is in the Devizes Museum, though where found is unknown.

Fig. 6 of type 3 is from Standlake, Oxon., but nothing more seems to be known about it.

Fig. 7 of type 4a is from Yarnton, Oxon.

Fig. 8 of type 4 was found in a barrow near Came, Dorset. The grave was covered by a huge stone weighing nearly three tons, and contained a skeleton and six beautifully made, barbed and stemmed arrowheads of flint, very thin and weighing only from 16 to 18 grains (*Label attached to the vessel*).

Fig. 8 *bis* is only 3¼ in. high and came from Drayton, near Abingdon, Berks.

Fig. 9 is a by-form of type 4a and was found in 1824, between Addington and Charlton, Oxon.

[1] Badly figured in Warne, *Celt. tum.*, pl. vii. 5, 6, 3, 2 ; *Arch. Journ.* iii. 348–52.

[2] *Arch.* xxx. 327–37, pl. 17 ; Warne, *Celtic Tum*, pl. 8.

[3] *Arch. Cambr.* 3rd ser., xiv. 266.

Fig. 10 of type 4 was found at Great Oakley Hall Farm, Essex.

Fig. 11 of type 4 came from a long barrow on Warminster Down, Wilts. Near the centre was a grave, cut into the subsoil, containing a skeleton. Over it near the surface was this vessel. (*A.W.* 74.)

Fig. 12 of type 4 from B. 25, Winterbourne Stoke, Wilts., is only 1½ in. high, and was found under a large barrow on the natural surface with a skeleton. Another found with it was very neatly ornamented but is now lost. Both vessels were placed on the right side of the head of the skeleton.[1]

Fig. 13 of type 5 is only 2 in. high, and was found by Pitt-Rivers in the Black Burgh tumulus, Sussex, near a bronze knife-dagger and about 2 ft. from a Bronze Age skeleton, slightly contracted.

Fig. 13 *bis* is from Brixworth, Northampton, but I do not know if it was found with an unburnt interment or not.

Figs. 14, 15, both of type 6, though one is provided with a handle, were discovered while digging for stone at Wynford Eagle, Dorset. At a depth of about 3½ ft. the workmen came upon a circular grave about 3 ft. in diameter and 4 ft. deep. It contained a skeleton and these two vessels.[2]

Fig. 16, H. 3¾ in., from Upper Swell, Gloucestershire. It was found as a later interment over the facing of the northern 'horn' of a long barrow, near its eastern extremity. It is ornamented all over with lines forming no distinct pattern, partly made with a pointed tool, partly with a notched strip of wood or bone. Perhaps it is derived from a neolithic vessel like fig. 214*a*, by flattening the bottom.

Fig. 17, H. 3¾ in. is from the Thames, London, and is marked on the British Museum label as 'perhaps neolithic'.

Fig. 18, of the same height as the last, was found at Dummer, Hants, and is also marked 'perhaps neolithic'.

Figs. 19, 20 were found, while making a drain in Colchester, with another vessel which has disappeared.

Fig. 21, 2¾ in. high, came from the Thames at Kew.

It will be seen in the next volume that small urns of type 6, with knobs or bosses below the lip, are not uncommon south of the Thames during the period when cremation prevailed. Hitherto they have not been found with any objects by which they could be dated, but as on the whole the custom of cremation is later than that of inhumation it is probable that these vessels belonged to the Bronze Age. They were most likely domestic vessels, the form of which varied but slightly from age to age. In one instance we have sure proof that knobs or bosses were applied to vessels in the later part of the Bronze Age. Mr. Austen found in a barrow on the Isle of Purbeck the skeleton, probably of a woman, beside which lay a green glass bead, in form merely a drop of glass perforated. On the breast of the skeleton had been placed a food vessel about 6 in. high, with a row of knobs a little below the lip. The illustration shows a vessel of type 3 with a row of 10 or 12 knobs or bosses below the lip.[3] The presence of a glass bead proves that knobs were still applied to vessels at a latish period of the Bronze Age.

In North Italy small vessels of type 6 with knobs below the lip are found both in the aeneolithic and the early Bronze Ages. Colini figures such a vessel, not quite 4 in. high and quite like figs. 19, 20, from the necropolis of Fontanella (Brescia) of the aeneolithic period[4] and another quite similar from the pile-dwelling of Cataragna (Brescia), 2 in. high, which belongs to the earlier Bronze Age.[5]

Fig. 21 *bis* is a handled cup 3¾ in. high, with four feet, from Woodyates (B. 4). In a large bell-barrow at a depth of 10½ ft. were two skeletons, and near them a small vessel with four feet, a black bead, and a brass spearhead (bronze knife-dagger).[6] Both these are now lost. Other cups with feet are figs. 113, 222–3 *bis*.

In Barrow 26, Winterbourne Stoke, Wilts., with a height of 9½ ft., was found as the sole interment a skeleton lying in a shallow wooden case of boat-like form. Round the neck were a great variety of amber and jet beads, a 'lance-head' (knife-dagger) of brass and a small vessel broken in pieces.[7] In the catalogue of the Devizes Museum [8] the latter is described as 'fragment of a small cup with a height of 1¾ in. with vertical sides (type 6) with vandyke pattern (line-chevrons) in impressed dots', just as we find on a Dorset vessel in the Plates of ornament.

[1] *A. W.* 124.

[2] Warne, *Celt. Tum.* pt. iii. p. 36, 37.

[3] *Arch. Journ.* vii. 384–5.

[4] *Bul. Pal. It.* xxv, tav. ii. 10.

[5] Colini, *op. cit.* xxix, tav. v, fig. 2.

[6] *A. W.* 237.   [7] *A. W.* 124–5.   [8] No. 334.

REGION II

(*Northern half of England.*)

On entering this region we find ourselves on ground where the food-vessel class is much more diffused than in the south, and its best examples, such as types 1, 1*a*, 1*b*, are, with one exception from Wales, not represented at all. As the study of single interments leads to no result, when attempting to ascertain the sequence of the different types of pottery, I begin with fifty-four paragraphs giving a brief notice of as many barrows with multiple interments or containing objects of bronze.

BARROWS WITH MULTIPLE INTERMENTS

1. B. 75, *Garton Slack*, East Riding. Diameter 90 ft., height 3¼ ft. At the bottom of the central grave, 6 ft. deep, lay a male skeleton and a beaker (fig. 103). In the same grave, but 3⅓ ft. higher, lay a female skeleton, a jet necklace composed of discs and one triangular plate,[1] a small bronze pricker, and fig. 22 of type 2. At the feet of this skeleton was a heap of burnt human bones. Still higher, at 16 in. from the top of the grave, was a long heap of burnt bones and fig. 23 of type 1*a*. To the south of the centre, near the brink of the grave, lay a female interment, with a flint knife, a bronze pricker, and fig. 24 of type 3. All these interments were made before the raising of the barrow. *Mortimer*, pp. 222-4.

2. B. 21, *Towthorpe*, East Riding. Diameter 45 ft., height 1½ ft. A few feet west of the centre was a small grave with no relics in it. Under this and 1½ ft. below the natural surface was a skeleton, a chipped flint, and fig. 25 of type 5. At the bottom of the grave, which was 4 ft. 10 in. deep, lay another skeleton, probably of a woman, and beaker fig. 101. *Mortimer*, pp. 11, 12.

3. B. 4, *Painsthorpe Wold*, East Riding. The dimensions of the barrow are not stated. At the centre, and 2 ft. 10 in. from the top of the mound, was the skeleton of a child and fig. 26 of type 2. The floor of the grave below this was 7 ft. from the top of the mound, and here lay the remains of a youth and of an old woman of small stature, a flint knife, two flake knives, and beakers figs. 112, 113. In a grave 4 ft. below the natural level and somewhat to the east of the last, were the remains of a child, a flint knife, and beaker fig. 114. All these interments seemed to be anterior to the erection of the mound, as the clay capping did not appear to have been broken through. *Mortimer*, pp. 113-17.

4. B. 104, *Garrowby Wold*, East Riding. Diameter about 45 ft., height 3½ ft. On the floor of the central grave, 6¼ ft. deep, lay two beakers (figs. 122, 123), without trace of a skeleton. Three feet higher in the same grave was an adult skeleton and beaker fig. 124. Close by the edge of the grave, but on the natural surface, were the remains of a child, a flint knife, and the handled cup of type 3, fig. 27. This was a secondary interment made after the erection of the mound. *Mortimer*, pp. 134-6.

5. B. 21, *Ganton*, East Riding. Diameter 60 ft., height 3 ft. At the centre was a grave 3 ft. deep, containing two skeleton interments, each at a different end of the grave, a barbed flint arrowhead, and fig. 28 of type 4. About 9 ft. south-east of the centre, in a grave sunk 3½ ft. into the chalk, was a skeleton and beaker fig. 130. At 7 ft. from the centre and 2 ft. above the natural surface were the remains of a child and fig. 29 of type 3. At 8 ft. from the centre and 2 ft. below the natural level lay the skeleton, probably of a woman, and fig. 30 of type 3. At 12 ft. from the centre was the skeleton of a young child and beaker fig. 131. The depth at which this interment lay is not stated. At 15 ft. from the centre on the natural surface lay a male and female skeleton facing each other. The man's right hand lay on the hips of the woman and between them were two small vessels of type 2, each with a cover (fig. 31). *B. B.* pp. 161-6.

---

[1] A necklace formed of lignite discs was found in a chambered cairn of the neolithic period in Caithness (*Anderson*, p. 240) and another with beaker fig. 286 from Sutherland. But in neither of these instances was there the usual triangular plate of the same material.

6. *B. 36, The Riggs*, East Riding. Diameter 60 ft., height 1 ft. At a depth of nearly 2 ft. below the natural level and south of the centre were the remains of an adult and fig. 32 of type 1*a*. Under this was a red-deer's antler, and a little lower the remains of a young person with fig. 33 of type 2. A few feet north of the centre and only a few inches below the mound was a skeleton and fig. 34 of type 1*a*. *Mortimer*, pp. 173–4.

7. *B. 253, Bempton*, East Riding. Diameter 90 ft., height 2 ft. In the central grave, 2 ft. 9 in. deep, lay a child interment and fig. 35 of type 2. At 25 ft. from the centre was found fig. 36 of type 1*a*, without any interment. *Arch.* lii. 28, 29.

8. *B. 45, Weaverthorpe*, East Riding. Diameter 54 ft., height 2 ft. In the central grave, 1¾ ft. deep, was a decayed body, a red-deer's antler and fig. 37 of type 2. At 9 ft. from the centre the remains of a child lay in a shallow grave, and 1 ft. from it was fig. 38 of type 1*a*. *B. B.* p. 199.

9. *B. on Seamer Moor*, North Riding. In a central cist, the floor of which was 7½ ft. below the top of the barrow, lay ashes, a piece of flint and fig. 39 of type 1*b*. At 9 ft. from the central grave was a large stone, embedded in the natural soil, at one corner of which lay fig. 40 of type 2. *J. B. A. A.* iv. 101–3.

10. *Blake Low*, Derbyshire. The dimensions of the cairn are not given. At the centre was an irregular rock-grave about 3 ft. deep, lined with flat stones and covered with four or five slabs. It contained a deposit of calcined bones of an adult; in one corner lay the skeleton of a child, in the opposite corner figs. 41, 42 of types 1*a*, 2. *Ten Years*, pp. 41–2.

11. *B. near Cawthorn Camps*, North Riding. Diameter 38 ft. About 6 ft. east of the centre was a 4-ft. deep grave, at the bottom of which lay two skeletons, three flint implements, and figs. 43, 44 of types 1*a*, 2. *Ten Years*, pp. 207–8.

12. *B. 41, The Riggs*, East Riding. Diameter 90 ft., height 7½ ft. About the centre of the barrow was a grave 3½ ft. deep, on the floor of which lay a skeleton, a flint knife, and fig. 45 of type 1*b*. At an earlier date, fig. 46 of type 3 had been found near the base of the barrow. *Mortimer*, pp. 180–3.

13. *B. 87, Aldro*, East Riding. Diameter 64 ft., height 3 ft. 7 in. About the centre of the mound was a grave, the floor of which was about 10 in. below the natural surface. It contained an adult skeleton, a spear-point of flint, and fig. 47 of type 1*a*, and another vessel of 5*a*. *Mortimer*, p. 67.

14. *B. 255, Bishop Burton*, East Riding. Diameter 98 ft., height 9 ft. At 2 ft. north of the present centre, but probably the old centre, and 2 ft. 9 in. below the surface of the barrow, lay fig. 48 of type 1*a* without any interment. Nearly 5 ft. below this were the remains of an adult, a beautiful flint knife with serrated edges, and fig. 49 of type 1*a*. *Arch.* lii. 31.

15. *B. 169, Garrowby Wold*, East Riding. Diameter 60 ft., height 7½ ft. About the centre, but 1 ft. above the natural level, lay three bodies of different ages and with one of them fig. 50 of type 1*a*. On the natural level there lay, close together, one cremated and thirteen skeleton interments, with one of which lay fig. 51 of type 1*a*. *Mortimer*, pp. 138–40.

16. *B. 101, Garrowby Wold*, East Riding. Diameter 48 ft., height 16 in. At the centre was a grave, 2 ft. 8 in. deep, containing the remains of a young person, and fig. 52 of approximately type 1*a*. In another grave, 3 ft. deep, and close to the last, lay the skeleton of a woman, a bronze pricker, and fig. 53 of type 4. *Mortimer*, pp. 136–7.

17. *B. 111, Goodmanham*, East Riding. Diameter 50 ft., height 1¼ ft. At 3 ft. south-south-west of the present centre, but probably the original centre, the body of a young woman lay in a hollow a little below the natural surface, with a round flint scraper and fig. 54 of type 1*a*. At 8 ft. south-south-east of the centre, on the natural surface, lay the body of a child, and a small bowl (fig. 55). *B. B.* pp. 319–20.

18. *B. 280, Marton Hall*, East Riding. Diameter 45 ft., height 2½ ft. At the centre was a grave, 4 ft. deep, on the floor of which lay a large male skeleton. About 2¾ ft. higher in the grave were three child-interments, one of them by cremation, and with them lay side by side figs. 56, 57, 58 of types 1*a*, 3. The last of these accompanied the cremated child. *Mortimer*, pp. 344–6.

19. *B. 153, Garton Slack*, East Riding. Diameter 60 ft., the height was hardly noticeable. At the centre was a 3-ft. deep grave at the bottom of which lay a large skeleton, and under its legs the skeleton of a young person. On each side of the skull was a slightly ornamented bronze ring with a diameter of 1½ in., an article of jet, and in front of the face fig. 59 of type 1*a* with perforated stops. *Mortimer*, p. 218.

20. *B. 141, Garton Slack*, East Riding. The rise of the barrow was scarcely distinguishable. At the centre was a grave, 6 ft. deep, on the floor of which lay the skeleton of a strong man, and some bones of a slender person. A foot and a half higher lay a female skeleton, a handled cup, and a small bowl (figs. 60, 61). *Mortimer*, p. 259.

21. B. 140, *Garton Slack*, East Riding. Height from 10 to 12 in. Near the centre was a grave, 3 ft. deep, on the floor of which lay a male skeleton—ceph. index, about 72·, length of femur, 19½ in.—and fig. 62 of type 3. About 4 ft. east of this grave was another about 4 ft. deep, on the floor of which lay an adult skeleton, with a ceph. index of 84·5, a femur of 17 in., and fig. 63 of type 3. The same or a similar tool was used for ornamenting both vessels. *Mortimer*, p. 244.

22. B. 33, *The Riggs*, East Riding. Diameter 40 ft., height 20 in. Near the centre, a little below the base of the barrow, was a hole 1 ft. deep, containing a few burnt bones, and a small, nearly globular pot, fig. 64. The texture of this is unusual, the colour black, the walls only ⅜ in. thick, and the exterior has a glazed appearance. Fragments of similar ware are often found scattered in barrows and probably represent domestic pottery. In a small hollow near the last interment lay a pot of type 5. It is of the same quality of pottery as the other, but the surface is dull. *Mortimer*, p. 175.

23. *Cross Low, Parwich*, Derbyshire. Height of B. about 5 ft. Near the centre was a rude cist resting on the solid rock which formed the floor. On this lay a large skeleton, with a ceph. index of 82·4 and fig. 65 of type 3. At the feet of the skeleton were the calcined bones of two children, and fig. 66 of type 2. Outside the cist and nearer the centre lay a skeleton, with fig. 67 of type 5 at its head. On the north side of the barrow about 1½ ft. below the surface of the mound was a skeleton interment with a bone pin, and fig. 68 of approximately type 1a. *Vestiges*, p. 49.

24. B. 13, *Sherburn*, East Riding. Diameter 90 ft., height 2½ ft. About the centre was a 4-ft. deep grave, on the floor of which was the body of a woman, and fig. 69 of type 5a. At 2 ft. from this grave was another, nearly as deep, at the bottom of which lay the body of a young man, and fig. 70 of type 2. In the opinion of Canon Greenwell these two interments are contemporary. *B. B.* pp. 152–4.

25. B. 94, *Goodmanham*, East Riding. Diameter 68 ft., height 4½ ft. At the centre, in a hollow a little below the natural level, was the body of a strong man lying at full length, two small round scrapers of flint, and fig. 71 of type 4a (?). At 15 ft. from the centre, and 1 ft. above the natural surface, lay fig. 72 of type 3, without any interment. *B.B.* pp. 302–3.

26. B. 205, *Acklam Wold*, East Riding. Diameter about 56 ft., height about 3 ft. At the bottom of the central grave, 4 ft. deep, lay a male skeleton and a flat bronze dagger blade, 6 in. long with three stout rivets. At some little distance to the east was a secondary interment in a grave 1½ ft. below the natural level, containing a skeleton, a small flint knife, and fig. 73, with perforated ears, but of no special type. *Mortimer*, pp. 87–8.

27. B. 294, *Life Hill*, East Riding. Diameter 65 ft., height 2 ft. At the centre was a grave 4 ft. deep, on the floor of which were the remains of an old man, a flint knife, and a small bronze dagger blade, 3 by 1¼ inches, with two rivets. (Pl. lxi, O. 33.) About 6 in. higher in the same grave lay a heap of cremated bones, a fine flint knife, a small bronze pricker, and, a few inches off, a vessel of type 3.[1] All these interments had been made before the barrow was raised, as the chalk rubble taken from them had not been put back. *Mortimer*, pp. 203–5.

28. B. 116, *Aldro*, East Riding. The centre and a large part of the east side of the barrow had been removed. Near the centre was a grave 3½ ft. deep, on the floor of which lay a skeleton, and a bronze knife-dagger 4½ in. long, with three stout rivets. At the edge of the grave, but on the natural level, lay beaker fig. 118. About 18 in. from the north-west side of this last grave was another only 6 in. deep, at the bottom of which lay three bodies, beaker fig. 120, the handled cup fig. 74, and beaker fig. 119. About 26 ft. south-east of the centre was a grave, 4 ft. deep, on the floor of which lay the remains of a youth, a flint flake, a bronze pricker, and beaker fig. 121. At 20 ft. west of the centre, and 1 ft. above the natural surface, lay a vessel with a cover (fig. 75 of type 1a), without any interment. *Mortimer*, pp. 54–6.

29. B. *ten miles north-east of Pickering*, North Riding. Diameter 61 ft., height 8 ft. Mr. Bateman's record of the opening of this barrow is wanting in precision, but fig. 76 of type 1a seems to have been found 5 ft. below the natural surface without any interment, while fig. 77 of type 2, was inverted on the

---

[1] I have no photograph of this vessel as it is not in the Driffield Museum.

natural level over a neat flint lance-head and three calcined flint implements. At a short distance from it were fragments of human bone lying in charcoal. *Ten Years*, pp. 218–19.

30. *B.* 257, *Bishop Burton*, East Riding. Diameter 70 ft., height 5½ ft. At 4 ft. west of the present centre was a 2-ft. deep grave, containing a flint knife, and fig. 78 of type 5. Nearly 8 ft. from the centre, and 3 ft. 10 in. above the natural surface, lay fig. 79 of type 1*a*, without any trace of a body. *Ar.* lii. 33–4.

31. *B.* 159, *Aldro*, East Riding. Diameter 90 ft., height 7 ft. About the centre, and 4 ft. from the top were the remains of an infant, and fig. 80 of type 3. Close to this were traces of another child, and fig. 81 of type 1*a* inverted. About 1 ft. below these was a quantity of calcined bones, which must be considered the primary interment. About 13 ft. north of the centre the remains of a child were found in a shallow hollow in the old turf-line with fig. 82 of type 3. All these interments were made before spreading a layer of chalk grit underlying the outer coating of the mound. *Mortimer*, pp. 69–71.

32. *B.* 233, *Towthorpe*, East Riding. Diameter 68 ft., height 7¾ ft. Near the centre, at a depth of 1 ft. from the top of the mound, lay fig. 83 of type 1*a*, without any interment. About 8 or 9 ft. from the supposed centre was a grave, 4 ft. 7 in. deep, on the floor of which lay a tall skeleton and a fine bronze dagger 6 in. long, with a midrib, rudimentary tang, and six small rivets (O. 30). A large piece of a very similar dagger, from Hutton Buscel (*v.* para. 62) is figured by Canon Greenwell in *B. B.*, p. 359. *Mortimer*, pp. 6, 7.

33. *B.* 237, *Blanch Group*, East Riding. Diameter 60 ft., height 2½ ft. Near the centre in a shallow hole reaching into the subsoil, lay an adult skeleton, a flint scraper, and fig. 84 of type 1*a*. A little south of the centre, a few inches above the natural surface, were the skeleton of a child and fig. 85 of type 1*a*. About 5 ft. north-east of the first-mentioned grave, and about 6 in. above the base of the barrow stood fig. 86 of type 3. *Mortimer*, pp. 325–6.

34. *B.* 71, *Folkton*, East Riding. Diameter 36 ft., height 5 ft. At 8 ft. north-west of the present centre was a 4-ft. deep grave at the bottom of which lay a male body, a small conical bone button with the V-shaped perforation, and fig. 87 of type 5*a*. At 9 ft. south-south-west of the present centre, was a 5-ft. deep grave, on the floor of which lay the skeleton of a powerful old man. This interment seemed to have disturbed two earlier ones of an adult and child. One foot above the male skeleton, was the body of a young woman, a round flint scraper, three bone beads with patterns (*B. B.* fig. 50), a bronze awl, and fig. 88 of type 1*a* perhaps, but abnormal with six pierced ears. *B. B.* pp. 274–9.

35. *B.* 32, *Garrowby Wold*, East Riding. Diameter 46 ft., height 1 ft. Near the centre of the mound was a pavement of flints; below this a second pavement, close under which lay a skeleton, and fig. 89 of type 2*a*. A little south of this interment, in a rather deeper grave, was a skeleton, and a bronze dagger 5 in. long by 2⅝ in. wide and very thin. Part of the bone pommel of the handle, which had been attached by three large rivets, was found with it. *Mortimer*, pp. 145–6.

36. *B.* 62, *Garrowby Wold*, East Riding. Area of barrow uncertain, and less than 1 ft. in height. Somewhat north of the centre, and 8 in. from the surface, were a few human bones and fig. 90 of type 3. On the north side of the mound, about 5 ft. from the centre, was a grave 3½ ft. deep, at the bottom of which lay fig. 91 of type 2. *Mortimer*, pp. 141–2.

37. *B.* 98, *Painsthorpe*, East Riding. Diameter 48 ft., height 3 ft. Near the centre was a grave 3¼ ft. deep, at the bottom of which lay a strong male skeleton and fig. 92 of type 3. At 2 ft. from the centre, and 9 in. above the natural level, lay the unique vessel fig. 93, by the side of a heap of decayed matter. At 5½ ft. from the centre, and about 2 ft. above the natural level, was fig. 94 of no definite type, but resembling a cinerary urn. *Mortimer*, pp. 130–2.

38. *B.* 225, *Huggate Wold*, East Riding. Height 2½ ft. Near the centre was a grave 4½ ft. deep, on the floor of which lay the skeleton of a young person. At various depths in this grave were parts of a brachycephalic skull and bones of a large person. Over the grave, but on the natural level, lay the vessel fig. 95 of type 2, inverted over burnt bones. It is 10 in. high and an excellent example of the transition of a vessel of food-vessel type into a cinerary urn by merely increasing its size. On the same level as this urn, but at a little distance to the south-east, lay fig. 96 of type 5. Also on the natural surface, but to the west of the first-mentioned vessel, lay fig. 97 of type 2, with remains of an infant. *Mortimer*, pp. 301–2.

39. *B.* 187, *Ford*, Northumberland. Diameter 16 ft., height 3 ft. At the centre on the natural surface, was a small stone cist, containing the skull of an infant, and fig. 98 of type 2 (?). Round the cist were six burnt bodies in as many cinerary urns, only one of which could be preserved (cinerary urn fig. 119). Canon Greenwell was quite sure that all the interments were deposited at the same time. *B. B.* pp. 408–9.

40. *B.* 281, *Hedon Howe*, Langton, East Riding. Diameter 50 ft., height about 8 ft. On the floor of the barrow there were five large cists of stone slabs; one at the centre, and the others symmetrically arranged to the north, south, east, and west of it. The central cist contained the skeletons, more or less complete, of three persons. Near the south side of it, but a little higher in the mound, lay a vessel of type 2. Close above the north side of the southern cist were the decayed bones of a child, and a well formed beaker (fig. 99). In the northern cist lay the disturbed bones of an adult, and a leaf-shaped arrowhead of flint. Four of the skulls taken from the cists were dolichocephalous, and all the cists had been constructed before the mound was thrown up. *Mortimer*, pp. 346–50.

41. *B.* 37, *Garton Slack*, East Riding. Diameter 110 ft., height 1 ft. At the centre, on the natural level, lay fig. 99 of type 1*b*, with a skeleton interment. A little to the north-west of the centre, and 1 ft. below the natural level, lay beaker fig. 98 of type A, Phase I, with a fine flint dagger 6¼ in. long, a perforated stone hammer, and a jet button with the V-shaped perforation. A little west of the centre, probably on the natural surface, stood fig. 100 of type 2*b*, together with a deposit of burnt bones and a bone pin. *Mortimer*, pp. 209–11.

42. *Hay Top barrow*, *Monsal Dale*, Derbyshire. Diameter 60 ft., height 4 ft. There was no central interment, but according to the plan there were five graves sunk into the rock round the central part of the barrow. The southern grave, sunk 1 ft. into the rock and lined with a few flat stones, contained a male skeleton with a cephalic index of 79·2, a perforated bone pin, and fig. 101 of type 1*a*. The grave on the north side, excavated to a depth of 2 ft., was of larger dimensions than the others. About the centre of it lay two skulls, near them beaker fig. 54, and at a little distance the skeleton of a child and a cylindrical jet bead. On the west side of the barrow, about 3 ft. below the natural surface of the rock, was a small cist of four slabs, containing the skeleton of a child, and fig. 102 of type 1*a*. *Ten Years*, pp. 75–6.

43. *B.* 138, *Driffield*, East Riding. Height about 4 ft. At the centre was a stone cist containing a large skeleton, beaker fig. 149, part of a bronze dagger, and a stone bracer with gold-headed rivets. Just outside the north side of the cist were two skeletons, laid one upon the other. Above the head of one of them was fig. 103 of type 2, and a well-chipped flint spearhead. Among the bones of the hand of one skeleton was a piece of bone 1½ in. long, with a projection in the middle of which was a hole through which had been fastened, it is said, a small hollow iron ball, the size of a marble.[1] A similar bone object, together with food vessel fig. 137, was found by Mr. Mortimer in B. 162, Garton Slack, fig. 531. The iron ball, now lost, must have belonged to a much later interment. *Arch.* xxxiv. 252–4; *Mortimer*, pp. 272–5.

44. *B.* 161, *Ferry Fryston*, West Riding. Diameter 54 ft., height 7 ft. At the centre was a grave, sunk 2¾ ft. into the limestone rock, on the floor of which a body, beaker fig. 109, and small bronze awl had been deposited. Evidence seemed to show that it was a secondary interment. At 6 ft. from the centre, and just above the natural surface, lay a skeleton and a cremated interment, accompanied by fig. 104 of type 1*a*, with four perforated stops. *B. B.* pp. 371–3.

45. *B.* 63, *Rudstone*, East Riding. Diameter 78 ft., height 6½ ft. In the central grave, the bottom of which was 6 in. above the natural surface, lay, as a secondary interment, a male skeleton, a beautiful barbed arrowhead, and fig. 105 of type 1*a*. At 16 ft. from the centre, in a hollow 4 in. below the natural surface, was the body of a very young child, and a small, rudely made beaker (fig. 110). *B. B.* pp. 245–51.

46. *B.* 67, *Rudstone*, East Riding. Diameter 100 ft., height 9 ft. The primary interment of an infant had been laid in a small hollow in the natural surface, 7 ft. north-north-east from the present centre. Half a foot further in the same direction, but 7½ ft. above the natural surface, was a female skeleton and fig. 106 of type 1*a*. About 6 ft. from the primary interment, and 6½ ft. above the natural level, a child had been interred with fig. 107 of type 4*a*. At 1½ ft. east of this was the body of another child, and beaker fig. 142, probably on the same level as the last. About 21 ft. south-west of the original centre, and 6 ft. above the natural surface, was a male skeleton, a flint scraper, and fig. 108 of type 1*a*, with a shallow groove and stops. About 26 ft. from the original centre, and 6 ft. above the natural level, was a female skeleton, with beaker fig. 143. Not far off, at the same distance from the centre, and at the same level, was the skeleton of another woman, and fig. 109 of type 5*a*. *B. B.* pp. 257–62.

---

[1] See Pl. lix, O. 16. 1, 2, 3.

47. *B. 62, Rudstone*, East Riding. Diameter 66 ft., height 4½ ft. At the centre was a large grave 10 ft. deep, at the bottom of which were two cists. One of these contained the bodies of an old man, two children, and beaker fig. 135. In the other cist lay a deposit of burnt bones and beaker fig. 136. Between the first cist and the side of the grave was the burnt body of a strong male and beaker fig. 137. These interments seemed to have disturbed a previous one also interred with a beaker. At 4 ft. from the centre, and 4 ft. above the natural level, lay the body of a woman, a bronze awl, and fig. 110 of type 2. At some distance from the centre, and 3 ft. above the natural surface, lay the body of a woman, a flint knife, a bronze awl, and beaker fig. 139. At some distance from the centre, and just above the natural level, was the body of a young woman resting on a bed of charcoal, a bronze awl, and beaker fig. 138. *B. B.* pp. 234–45.

48. *B. 204, Acklam Wold*, East Riding. Diameter 56 ft., height 3 ft. On the natural surface, and 10 ft. from the centre, were the remains of a child and beaker fig. 110 *bis*. At 8 ft. from the centre, and also on the natural surface, lay a heap of burnt adult bones, a well-made flint knife, and fig. 111 of type 1*a*, with eleven perforated stops. *Mortimer*, pp. 86–7.

49. *B. 43, Weaverthorpe*, East Riding. Diameter 54 ft., height 4 ft. The central interment consisted of a skeleton. At 5 ft. from the centre, and 2 ft. above the natural level, lay the body of an adult, a well-chipped flint implement, and fig. 112 of type 2. At 15 ft. from the centre, and about 1 ft. above the natural level, lay a body, probably of a young man, and the four-footed vessel fig. 113. At 19 ft. from the centre on the natural surface, and not near any interment, lay fig. 114 of type 1*a*, with a narrow groove. *B. B.* pp. 193–7.

50. *B. 118, Painsthorpe Wold*, East Riding. Diameter 62 ft., height 3½ ft. The central grave, 2¼ ft. deep, contained a skeleton, and a jet link. About 3 ft. from the centre, and close to the surface of the barrow, was an infant interment, and an example of type 5. This vessel resembles in texture the dark-coloured, dish-shaped vessels found scattered in barrows, usually on the old surface-line. About 3 ft. from the centre, and near the surface, were the remains of a child, and close to it fig. 115 of type 2. At 3 ft. south of the first-mentioned vessel, and 6 in. below the surface, was another skeleton of a child, and fig. 116 of type 1*a*. In a hole 1½ ft. deep, and 6 ft. from the centre, lay fig. 117 of type 2*a*. *Mortimer*, pp. 125–8.

51. *B. 70, Folkton*, East Riding. Diameter 28 ft., height 3½ ft. Close to the present centre was a grave 3½ ft. deep, at the bottom of which lay the body of a young man and a curved pin, made from a boar's tusk. In the same grave, but 3 ft. higher, lay fig. 118 of type 4*a*, and a little higher the burnt bones of a child. At 7 ft. from the centre, on the natural surface, lay a body, probably of a woman, and fig. 119 of unique form, though it may be compared with fig. 93. At 9 ft. from the centre, and 1½ ft. above the natural surface, was the body of a young child, and fig. 120 of type 4*a*. At 9½ ft. from the centre in the opposite direction, and just above the surface-level, was the body of a child and fig. 121 of type 4*a*. At 13 ft. south of the centre, on the natural surface, lay fig. 122, probably an ill-made example of type 4*a*. *B. B.* pp. 272–4.

52. *B. 152, Hutton Buscel*, North Riding. Diameter 98 ft., height 11 ft. At 2 ft. from the centre, and 7 ft. above the natural surface, was a stout bronze dagger, like that mentioned in par. 32 from Towthorpe, and a large beautifully flaked flint knife. The primary interment of an unburnt body lay on the natural surface 3 ft. below the dagger. At 24 ft. from the centre, and 3 ft. above the natural surface, was a small stone cist, containing fig. 123 of type 3, but with an unusually deep neck. *B. B.* pp. 357–61.

53. *B. 200, Eglingham*, Northumberland. The base of the demolished cairn was surrounded by a circle of stones with a diameter of 36 ft. At 9½ ft. from the centre was a stone cist containing fig. 124 of type 4*a*. At a distance of 3 ft. west of this was a rather smaller cist, without a cover stone, containing a necklace composed of ten fusiform and nearly a hundred disc beads of jet, as well as a flint knife. *B. B.* pp. 418–21.

54. *B. 242, Folkton*, East Riding. The primary interment of an adult had been laid on wood at the centre. At 13 ft. east by south of the centre was an oval grave 1½ ft. deep, containing beaker fig. 108 of type A, Phase II. At 13 ft. east of the centre, and 2 ft. above the natural level, lay food vessel fig. 196, with the remains of a child. *Arch.* lii. 10–12.

These fifty-four paragraphs, which take notice of twenty-seven beakers and 103 food vessels, contain nearly all the material on which to found a chronological arrangement of the food vessels of Region II, and from which their relation to the beaker class of ceramic can be inferred. They are not however of equal value; some afford indubitable evidence on certain points, others offer probabilities of greater or less certainty, and a residuum is of no practical use at all. Twenty-eight paragraphs can be used to prove beyond doubt which of several vessels was deposited first in a particular barrow. This of course is a very important point, especially when dealing with the question of the relative position in time of beakers and food vessels. But it leaves quite unsettled how great was the interval of time between the first and second interment. Whether this amounted to one day or one hundred years must be deduced from other considerations. An examination of the above paragraphs leads to the following certain conclusions with regard to the primary interment, and these can be best displayed in tabular form.

I. TABLE OF UNDOUBTED PRIMARY INTERMENTS

PARAGRAPH	BRONZE	TYPE DEPOSITED		
		EARLIER	LATER	AT SAME TIME
1, 2, 3, 4	..	eight beakers	1a, 2, 3, 5	
5	..	Type 4	two beakers, type 3	
1, 6	..	Type 2	1a	
7, 8	..	Type 2	1a	
9	..	Type 1b	2	
12	..	Type 1b	3	
10, 11	..	..	..	1a, 2
13	..	..	..	1a, 5a
14, 15	..	Type 1a	1a	
17	..	Type 1a	small bowl	
16	..	..	..	1a, 4
18	..	..	..	1a, 3
19	ear-rings	..	..	1a
20	..	..	..	handled cup and bowl
21	..	..	..	3, 3
22	..	..	..	5, globose pot
23	..	..	..	2, 3
24	..	..	..	2, 5a
25	..	Type 4a (?)	3	
26	dagger, three rivets	..	vessel of no type	
27	dagger, two rivets	..	..	3
28	dagger, three rivets	..	abnormal 1a, four beakers	

From the above Table I it will be seen that eight beakers, all of good form, were certainly placed in the barrows before examples of types 1a, 2, 3, 5. Of these beakers, three belong to Phase I of type A (figs. 101, 103, 114), one to Phase II (fig. 113), two to AB (figs. 112, 124), and two to C (figs. 122, 123). But two beakers of the later part of Phase II (figs. 130, 131) were deposited later than a food vessel which seems to belong to type 4. And four beakers—two of Phase II (figs. 121, 118, the latter a late specimen), one of B1 (fig. 120) and one of C (fig. 119)—together with a handled cup were deposited later than a flat bronze knife $4\frac{1}{2}$ in. long with three stout rivets.

All the types of food vessel are broadly contemporary, for examples of types 1a, 2, 3, 4, 5, 5a, have been laid in graves at the same time.

A pair of bronze ear-rings and a bronze knife with two rivets are of the same age as an example of types 1a and 3. But a bronze knife with three rivets was deposited before a food vessel of no regular type.

II. TABLE OF PROBABLE PRIMARY INTERMENTS

PARAGRAPH	BRONZE	TYPE DEPOSITED PROBABLY		
		EARLIER	LATER	AT SAME TIME
29	..	1a	2	
30	..	5	1a	
31	..	..	..	1a, 3
32	dagger, six rivets	..	1a	
33	..	1a	3	
34	..	5a	1a with six ears	
35	dagger, three rivets	..	2a	
36	..	2	3	
37	..	3	two vessels, no type	
38	..	..	..	2 (cinerary, 10 in. high), small 2
39	..	..	..	2 (?) and cinerary urns

From Table II several important facts may be learnt. The bronze dagger of paragraph 32, with a midrib and six rivets, of a stouter kind than is found with beakers and belonging to Bronze Age II, had been probably deposited before a good example of type 1a (fig. 83), showing that as a class food vessels came down later in time than the beaker class.

In paragraphs 38, 39 we come across four vessels which must belong to the end of the food-vessel period. An example of type 2 (fig. 95) with a height of 10 in., double the usual height of a food vessel, had been used as a cinerary urn inverted over burnt bones, while a smaller one of the same type had been placed beside an uncremated infant. In the last paragraph we find an example of type 2 (?) (fig. 98), surrounded by several cinerary urns of the 'overhanging rim' type, which appeared to have been placed there at the same time as the food vessel. These two instances tend to show that no hiatus existed between the end of the food-vessel period and the beginning of the period when cremation prevailed.

It remains now to consider and discuss the last sixteen paragraphs, as the evidence they afford is in various degrees and on various points uncertain.

P. 40. The cists, judging from the leaf-shaped arrowhead, and the dolichocephalous skulls, belong to, or are not far removed from, the neolithic period. The beaker of excellent form, and the food vessel of type 2 are evidently later. Judging from the plan given by Mr. Mortimer, they must have lain rather near to each other, and from the description they must have been nearly on the same level—a little higher than the cists. So perhaps they should be considered as broadly contemporary.

P. 41. The doubt that exists here is, that if we accept the record as it stands, an unusually elaborate and fine specimen of type 1b (fig. 99), must be placed earlier than a well formed beaker of type A, Phase I, and a flint dagger. The necessary corollary to this assumption is that type 1a, of which it is a variety, developed in some other area than South Britain, since there are no simple forms of an earlier date to lead up to it. It appears possible that the primary interment was the skeleton with the beaker, which lay in a shallow grave, and not on the natural surface, like the food vessel, and that the original centre had become slightly displaced, as is not uncommon, by the enlargement of the barrow, which contained thirteen interments. But I believe it is better to consider both vessels as contemporary.

P. 42. The plan of the graves given by Mr. Bateman leads one to suppose that all the interments were made before the cairn was heaped up, and therefore that all are contemporary. As the cairn was only 2 ft. high, and therefore might have been easily reopened, it is easy to imagine that interments were made at intervals. But, as at any rate fig. 102 seems to belong to an early form of type 1*a*, I am inclined to believe that beaker 54 of type A, Phase I, is contemporary with it. Fig. 101 appears to be a little later than the other food vessel, but, on the whole, all three vessels may provisionally be accepted as broadly contemporary.

P. 1. Mr. R. Mortimer points out that all the interments were made before the erection of the barrow, and there was no trace of later infraction. He therefore concludes that beaker fig. 103 of Phase I, type A, is contemporary with examples of types 2, 1*a*, 3, though all were found at different levels in the same grave. It is not impossible that when the head man of a pit-dwelling died, he was buried in a deep grave, which was not entirely filled up at the time, and room was left for the interment of other members of the dwelling, as they died in succession. Not until the grave was full was the grave sealed, by raising a barrow over it. As the type of necklace, found with fig. 22 of type 2, is an early one, the interval between the deposition of the beaker and food vessel need not have been long. So on the whole we may conclude that, if all the interments in this barrow were not made exactly at the same time, they are broadly contemporary.

P. 43. Lord Londesborough, who explored this barrow, believed that the skeleton with the food vessel was in all probability deposited before the interment in the cist, containing a beaker of type AB (fig. 149). But from his description I can only understand that both burials were, or might be, contemporary, and Mr. Mortimer is of the same opinion.

P. 44. As both interments were secondary, a doubt must exist as to which was deposited first, but I believe preference should be given to the beaker of type A, Phase II, in the central grave below the natural surface.

P. 45. Both interments are again secondary, but as the food vessel is a fine example with five perforated stops, and lay in the central grave, it seems quite likely that it was deposited before the beaker, which is a poor and late specimen of type A, Phase III.

P. 46. Here we may probably assume that an example of type 1*a* (fig. 106) was placed earlier than fig. 108, a unique example of type 1*a*, with a very narrow groove and stops, and that the former is older than two late beakers of type B 1, and an example of 4*a*.

P. 47. Although the three beakers of type BC found in the deep central grave were secondary, they had disturbed an older beaker interment, and are probably older than the example of type 2 (fig. 110) which lay 4 ft. above the natural level. This vessel again, on account of its higher position, is probably later than beaker fig. 139 of type B 1.

P. 48. It may probably be assumed that there is no great difference in time between the food vessel of type 1*a*, and the late beaker of type A, Phase III, the former being perhaps the older of the two.

P. 49. Though all the interments were secondary, it seems probable that the example of type 2 was deposited earlier than the four-footed vessel, and the example of 1*a* with a narrow groove.

P. 50. All the interments are secondary, and all so near the surface of the ground that nothing even fairly probable can be deduced, except that they all seem to be late.

P. 51. There seem to have been four examples of type 4*a*, though only one is well formed, in this tumulus, and the unique vessel fig. 119 is evidently contemporary.

P. 52. The bronze dagger, like that mentioned in P. 31 is probably older than the example of type 3, of unusual profile.

P. 53. An example of type 4*a* is probably contemporary, with a jet necklace, composed of discs, and fusiform beads.

P. 54. As the beaker of type A, Phase II, was in a grave, and food vessel fig. 196 of type 3 lay at a higher level, it is probably a little the later of the two vessels.

These results are tabulated in Table III.

III. TABLE OF LEAST CERTAIN RESULTS

PARAGRAPH	BRONZE	TYPE PROBABLY (1) OR PERHAPS (2) DEPOSITED		
		EARLIER	LATER	AT SAME TIME
40	..	..	..	(2) beaker, type 2
41	..	(2) beaker	1b, 2b	
42	..	(2) beaker	1a, 1a	contemporary (?)
1	..	..	..	(2) beaker, 2, 1a, 3
43	..	..	..	(2) beaker, 2
44	..	(1) beaker	1a	
45	..	(1) 1a	beaker	
46	..	(1) 1a	1a, two beakers, 4a	
47	..	(1) four beakers	2	
48	..	..	..	(1) beaker, 1a
49	..	(1) 2	1a, four-footed vessel	
51	..	..	..	unique vessel, 4a
52	(1) dagger, six rivets	..	3	
53	..	..	..	(1) 4a, jet necklace
54	..	(1) beaker	3	

In attempting to arrange our Bronze Age ceramic in relative order of time, it is important to have a clear idea of the extent to which the beaker and food-vessel classes are contemporary. In Phases II and III of type A there is no doubt whatever of their contemporaneity. Although it cannot be demonstrated with the same certainty that this holds true for Phase I, yet the records of the finds under consideration make it difficult to avoid the conclusion that quite at the beginning of the beaker period in Region II the two classes were coeval. If this is so, we must infer that food vessels of types 1, 1a, which do not occur in Region I south of the Thames, were already in use among the native inhabitants, and afterwards adopted by the invaders. The other forms of food vessel, all very simple and also found in Region I, may have developed partly among the invaders themselves.

Although these two classes of pottery may be considered contemporary in Region II, there are differences, which call for attention, in the grave-goods that accompanied each. In the fifty-four paragraphs we observe that no flint daggers, stone bracers, or bronze knives with one exception actually accompanied interments with food vessels, though they belong to the same time. This points to a probability that there was some difference of status between persons buried with beakers and those buried with food vessels. The former would belong to the ruling caste of invaders, the latter to descendants of the original inhabitants or to persons of lower degree though descended from the intruders. Bronze knives and flint daggers were insignia of rank and dignity in the social body which could not be given to persons of servile origin or of little importance among the conquerors. A difference of status will also explain why an invader accompanied by a beaker was interred first and those of lower degree were buried with food vessels afterwards in the same deep grave at a higher level. This inferiority is perhaps exhibited in a marked manner by Paragraph 43, which shows that a bronze dagger and a stone bracer with gold-headed rivets were deposited in a stone cist with the body of a large man of undoubted estimation and dignity, while a flint implement and a food vessel were sufficient for the underling whose body was laid outside the cist. Of course it is not certain that both persons were buried at the same time, though both the beaker and the food vessel may be assigned to the period of Phase II, type A.

In Region II the skulls found with food vessels appear to belong to a more mixed type than those with beaker interments. Mr. R. Mortimer tells me that the cephalic indices of twenty-three adult skulls, disinterred by him in the East Riding with food vessels, were :—

8 Dolichocephalic, index 71·15

8 Brachycephalic, index 85·96

7 Mesocephalic, index 77·7.

Here the long skulls of the older neolithic inhabitants are as numerous as those of the short-headed invaders, while the intermediate skulls point to inter-marriage. These facts also afford some ground for supposing that a social difference existed between those interred with food vessels and those interred with beakers.[1]

By way of recapitulation, and to give a conspectus of the relation between the beakers and food vessels mentioned in the fifty-four paragraphs, the most important of them are arranged in a tabular form (Table IV), with their numbers attached. As the beakers, relatively

TABLE IV. CONTEMPORANEITY OF BEAKERS AND FOOD VESSELS IN REGION II

PARA-GRAPH	BEAKERS	TYPE 1a	1b	2	2b	3	4	
41	98 A i	126, 127c	99		100	214c		
42	54 A i	102, 101						
1	103 A i	23		22		24		
		127–9		195c, 168–73, 194c, 33, 174, 175				
44	109 A ii	104						
		105, 131–3	45			30		
43	149 AB	137*		103				*A similar bone article found with 137 and 103
5	130, 131 A ii			31		29	28	
			39	37, 176 *bis*, 177				
3	113 A ii			26				
		138–40, 59, 38, 49, 141–6, 152, 114, 76		183–5, 192c, 42, 179–81, 35, 40, 77, 70		46, 196, 197, 200	124, 206	
46	142, 143 B 1	106, 108						
47	135–7 BC			110				
						201, 90		
48	110 *bis* A iii	111						
		153, 154, 157		187, 188				
	(16 A iii							458c, Vol. II) Region I
		54, 151 [160–7c]		95c, 97				
				BRONZE AGE II.				*cinerary urn, type 1*
32		83						
52						123		
39				98			119	

---

[1] Canon Greenwell, in a letter to me, will not allow any social distinction between those interred with beakers and with food vessels. I do not insist upon the point though it has to be considered.

speaking, offer definable points in time, their numbers and those of the food vessels from the same barrow are given in larger and thicker type. The intervals between food vessels, relatively dated by beakers, are filled in with others not mentioned in the paragraphs for the most part, and these are in smaller and thinner type. Even if there had been space, I have not ventured to assign a place to all the food vessels figured, only to a selection. The records given in the paragraphs show that the beakers are sometimes earlier, sometimes later than the food vessels in the same barrow, though to keep them together they have to be set on the same line. Occasional cremation—indicated by a 'c' placed after the number—appears sporadically as early as Phase I of type A, and from its form I have given to fig. 214c a place earlier than any beaker, though it is quite uncertain.

Further, the Table shows that food vessels survived beakers and descended into Bronze Age II. One late beaker from Region I is here inserted at the end of Bronze Age I, as it was deposited later than a burnt interment with an urn of food-vessel type (cin. urn, fig. 458, Vol. II).

CHAPTER VIII

Type I (Grooved Shoulder with Stops).

There is, so far as I know, only one example of this type in Region II, viz. that from Colewell on the north Tyne (fig. 125). It has perforated stops and the chevron pattern round the upper part is executed in false relief, a technique the importance of which will appear later on. The whole surface is decorated and the lower part is well rounded, as if derived from a round-bottomed prototype. Nothing was found with the vessel to throw any light upon its age.

Sub-type 1a.

As the stops or ears, generally four to six in number, placed in the shoulder groove are sometimes perforated to receive a string and sometimes not, we must assume that, at any rate typically, vessels with perforated stops are older than others where they are imperforate. This is confirmed by P. 6, where fig. 32, in which the stops are perforated, lay at a lower level than fig. 34, where they are not perforated. Again in P. 15, figs. 50, 51 are probably contemporary and in both the stops are perforated; in P. 42, figs. 101, 102 have imperforate stops, and both vessels are probably contemporary.

Figs. 126 to 136 illustrate small vessels belonging to 1a, varying in height from 3¼ to 4½ inches, though fig. 129 is under 2 inches. The ears or stops are perforated and the whole surface is covered with ornament. Fig. 128 was found with a stone axe.[1] Fig. 134 formed part of a central interment and is distinguished from others of the type by an extra groove below the shoulder, as if the intention had been to make an example of 1b. On the upper part of the vessel is a row of chevrons in false relief and three rows on the lower part, better seen on Mr. Mortimer's illustration (fig. 380). In figs. 137 to 139 the ornamentation only partly covers the lower half of the vessel or not at all. With fig. 137 was found a bone object like that mentioned in P. 43 as having been deposited with fig. 103. All these fourteen examples, except fig. 127, so far as is known, accompanied skeleton interments.

Figs. 140 to 146 are examples of 1a in which the ears are unpierced, but the whole vessel is still covered with ornament. These vessels vary in height from 3 to 5 inches. A cross formed by the intersection of two bands of lines has been detected on the bottom of fig. 141 from the North Riding and of fig. 145 from Northumberland.

In figs. 147–52, besides having imperforate stops, the lower part of the vessels is no longer entirely covered with ornament. These vessels range in height from 4¼ to 6¼ inches. Fig. 148 had been laid beside a brachycephalic man of middle age, but what gives the vessel

---

[1] The axe was probably perforated, though the label in the York Museum only states that it had fine curves.

a special interest are the three grains of a small kind of wheat which Mr. Mortimer discovered in its walls. In fig. 152, though the stops in the shoulder groove are imperforate, the handle under the lip has a hole through it. The ornamentation is beautifully made with the greatest care, and here again a chevron in false relief can be observed. All these thirteen vessels accompanied unburnt interments.

Figs. 153–9 exhibit certain by-forms and variations of the original type which are not without interest. The specimens vary in height from $3\frac{1}{2}$ to 6 inches. Figs. 153, 154 show the same enlarged groove with multiplication of stops as fig. 111 and all belong to the East Riding. Fig. 111 has eleven stops, and the two others ten and nine respectively. It also formed part of a non-central interment with the body of a child; fig. 153 had been deposited at the centre beside a dolichocephalic person, and fig. 154 had been given to a middle-aged man with a cephalic index of eighty, whose grave lay at the centre of another barrow. These three food vessels have perforate stops, but the ornament does not quite cover the whole surface. Fig. 155 again shows the false relief technique more elaborately displayed than in previous examples. Fig. 158 formed part of a central interment and was accompanied by a perforated whin-stone axe, $4\frac{1}{10}$ in. long. Fig. 159, in which the shoulder groove has developed into a wide flat surface, is from Jesmond in Northumberland.

Figs. 160–7 are examples of 1a that accompanied burials with cremation. With the exception of the first, all have the stops imperforate, and on the last three the surface decoration is incomplete. In height these vessels vary between 4 in. and $5\frac{1}{2}$ in. Where the record of the finding of these food vessels can be depended upon, it will be found that they were placed on or by the side of the burnt deposit, and did not themselves contain cremated bones. In other words, they were not cinerary urns, but probably served the same purpose as similar vessels deposited beside uncremated bodies.

TYPE 2 (GROOVED SHOULDER).

Figs. 168–81 range in height from 4 to $5\frac{3}{4}$ inches; in some the ornament covers the whole surface, in others it is less complete and one is quite plain. So far as is known, all were found with uncremated burials. Figs. 169, 170 were both found in the same Derbyshire barrow, one on each side of the central cist, which contained a brachycephalic skull. Fig. 176, like fig. 22 of the same type (P. 1), was accompanied by a jet necklace of disc-shaped beads with a triangular pendant at the centre. Fig. 181 contained two ribs of a small animal, which shows the use to which these vessels were put.

Figs. 182–8, except fig. 187, which is only 5 in. high, range in height from $5\frac{3}{4}$ to $6\frac{3}{4}$ inches, and all belong to uncremated interments. With fig. 184 lay a large wild boar's tusk 7 in. long, and two very neat flint arrowheads. The form of fig. 187 is abnormal, but when compared with fig. 186, also from Staffordshire, it appears to belong to type 2, though the space between the lip and the upper moulding of the groove has been absorbed by the groove. It is probably a late by-form, for it was found as a secondary interment only 2 ft. from the surface. The central interment, placed in a stone cist 4 ft. below the surface, contained at the bottom a skeleton, at a higher level a deposit of burnt bones and a small bronze knife, $3\frac{1}{4}$ in. long with two rivet-holes. Fig. 188 presents the same abnormal appearance as the last, and it too is most likely a later by-form, for in the material of the barrow was picked up a fusiform jet bead, a style which in this country is generally later than the disc-shaped beads found with figs. 22, 176.

Figs. 189, 190 are 7 in. and 7¾ in. high respectively. The latter is one of the largest of the type,[1] and had been deposited with a body apparently of a middle-aged woman. The walls of the vessel are very thick and the paste is full of broken stone.

Figs. 191–5 vary in height from 5⅛ to 6¾ inches, and were found with cremated interments. In three of them the whole surface is ornamented. Although fig. 194 is said to have contained calcined bones, in the other instances the food vessel stood beside or near the pile of burnt bones.

Hitherto it has not been possible to determine the direction taken by the development of types 1a, 2, but by more closely examining the instances in which they have occurred in the same barrow, something definite may be learnt regarding this important point.

Fig. 22 of type 2 (P. 1), with the shoulder groove placed low, decorated all over, and accompanied by a necklace of disc-shaped beads and a bronze pricker, was deposited before fig. 23 of 1a, with imperforate ears, and the lower part of the body only partly ornamented.

Fig. 33 of type 2 (P. 6), with a rather wide groove, placed rather low, and decorated all over, was deposited before figs. 32, 34 of 1a. The first is a rude example, though with perforated stops, set in a high-placed groove, and the body is only partly ornamented. In the second the groove is narrow, and placed rather low, but there is an extra moulding just below the lip.

Fig. 35 of type 2 (P. 7), in which the space between the upper moulding of the groove and that of the lip is very much restricted, is earlier than fig. 36 of 1a, with a narrow groove placed high, so that the interval between it and the lip moulding is short, with imperforate ears, and the lower part of the body nearly plain.

Fig. 37 of type 2 (P. 8), in which the groove is relatively low, moderately wide, and the surface of the vessel nearly plain, is older than fig. 38 of 1a, in which the groove is moderately wide, relatively low, with imperforate stops, and the lower part of the body plain.

Fig. 42 of type 2 (P. 10), in which the groove is wide and placed high, so that the lip-moulding rises immediately above it, as in fig. 35, is exactly contemporary with fig. 41 of 1a, with imperforate stops, set in a groove, placed rather high, so that the space between it and the lip is restricted, and with the lower part of the body partly ornamented.

Fig. 44 of type 2 (P. 11), with a moderately high-placed groove and almost plain, is exactly contemporary with fig. 43 of 1a, with a moderately high-placed groove, containing four perforated stops, and the lower part perhaps entirely ornamented.

Probably fig. 77 of type 2 (P. 29) with a high-placed groove, the upper moulding of which is close up to the lip-moulding, and hardly decorated on the lower part of the vessel, is later than fig. 76 of 1a, with perforated stops in a narrow groove placed moderately high, so that a considerable space exists between the groove and the lip-moulding, and with the lower part of the vessel plain.

Fig. 83 of 1a, with a high-placed shoulder, imperforate (?) ears, and the lower part of the vessel plain, is later than a very fine bronze dagger, 6 in. long, with midrib, rudimentary tang, and six smallish rivets.

From the above it may be inferred that examples of type 2 in which a moderately wide groove is placed a little above the centre of the vertical height of the vessel, the whole surface of which is covered with ornament, belong to the older specimens. Those in which the groove is placed so high that there is little or no space between the upper moulding of the groove and the lip or the lip-moulding are considerably later.

It is much the same as regards 1a. Vessels with a moderately high-placed groove with

---

[1] The largest, 10 in. high (fig. 95), as has been mentioned above, was used as a cinerary urn.

imperforate stops, only partly ornamented, sometimes very well made specimens, or with a high-placed groove with or without perforated stops and the lower part of the body plain or nearly so, belong to the later part of the series. So it must be assumed that vessels with a low-placed groove, in which the stops are perforated and the whole surface of the body decorated, form the earlier part of the series (p. 130). Among the earlier vessels may be placed fig. 59 of 1a with a rather low-placed groove, perforated stops, and the lower half partially ornamented. It is contemporary with a pair of ornamented bronze ear-rings. Examples of 1a with many ears, like figs. 111, 153, 154, are perhaps contemporary with late beakers like fig. 110 bis, vide P. 48.

On applying the above test to fig. 127 and to the group figs. 160-7, all found with cinerary interments, it will be observed that the first has all the characteristics of a very early example; figs. 162, 163, though with imperforate ears, are also apparently fairly early examples; the others seem to belong to the later part of the series.

2a (with extra groove and moulding).

Fig. 89 is probably somewhat later than a flat bronze knife-dagger, 5 in. × 2$\frac{5}{8}$ in., very thin, and with three strong, round-headed rivets.

TYPE 3 (CONCAVE NECK).

Fig. 65 is contemporary with fig. 66, one of the early examples of type 2. As a rule, however, these vessels appear rather late. For instance, fig. 24 is later than fig. 23, a latish example of 1a; fig. 46 is later than fig. 45 of 1b; fig. 86 is probably later than figs. 84, 85, two late examples of 1a; fig. 90 is probably later than fig. 91, a late specimen of type 2; fig. 196 is probably later than a latish beaker, fig. 108[1]; fig. 123 is probably later than a dagger with a stout midrib, similar to that found with fig. 83 of 1a.

Fig. 58 is contemporary with figs. 56, 57, two rather late examples of 1a; an example of type 3 is probably contemporary with a bronze knife-dagger measuring 3 in. × 1$\frac{1}{4}$ in. with two rivets (P. 27); figs. 80, 82 are probably contemporary with fig. 81, a late specimen of 1a.

Figs. 196-205 vary in height from 3$\frac{3}{4}$ to 7$\frac{3}{4}$ inches. Fig. 197 was found at a depth of 4 ft. with a skeleton, the skull of which had a cephalic index of 75. Fig. 202 was a secondary interment; fig. 203 lay at the centre of another barrow on the natural surface. Fig. 204 from Derbyshire perhaps does not belong to type 3 at all, as both in form and ornamentation it differs somewhat from other examples. The bottom is ornamented with a cross inscribed in an irregular rhomboidal frame which is surrounded by cord marks.

TYPE 4 (BICONICAL).

From the multiple interments we learn that fig. 28 is older, though perhaps not much older, than the latish beakers figs. 130, 131; fig. 53 is probably of the same age as fig. 52, a late example of 1a.

---

[1] These two vessels ought to have been included among the paragraphs concerning multiple interments. They came from B. 242, Folkton. The central interment was a skeleton accompanied by a flint knife and several flakes. At 13 ft. east by south of the centre was an oval grave 1$\frac{1}{2}$ ft. deep, containing beaker fig. 108. At 13 ft. east of the centre, and 2 ft. above the natural surface, lay food vessel fig. 196. *Arch.* lii. 10-12.

Figs. 206–8 in height lie between 5 in. and $6\frac{1}{4}$ in. The first was found with a burnt interment in a small cist at Amble, Northumberland, as a secondary interment. The primary unburnt burial was in a larger cist, which contained an example of 1a with three perforated ears and part of a small bronze knife with three rivets. Figs. 207, 208 are both abnormal in form, for in the first the lip is bevelled so as to form an angle with the neck, and in the second a shallow groove occurs just below the shoulder. It was found without any sign of an interment.

4a (with moulded lip).

Fig. 71 is older than fig. 72 of type 3; fig. 124 is perhaps contemporary with a necklace of disc-shaped and fusiform beads of jet.

Figs. 209–14 vary in height from $4\frac{1}{2}$ in. to $6\frac{1}{4}$ in. The first is an ambiguous example from the North Riding and perhaps belongs to type 2. In the next two and in the last example a raised moulding runs round the shoulder as a later development. Fig. 212 came from the same cairn as fig. 206, but accompanied an unburnt interment. Fig. 213 (H. $6\frac{1}{4}$ in.) lay on its side in contact with the burnt remains of a child. Fig. 214, which is $4\frac{1}{2}$ in. high differs from the others from having a sharply bevelled lip and from its relative breadth. It ought to have been included under the heading below, 'Vessels that cannot be included in the above types.' It was found in a barrow about 12 ft. high at the south entrance to the well-known stone-circle at Arbor Low, Derbyshire. On the natural level about the centre of the barrow was a six-sided stone cist containing a quantity of calcined human bones, a bone pin, a piece of spherical iron pyrites, this vessel, and fig. 215 of type 5. Except that it is flat-bottomed, this vessel in form and proportion much resembles a round-bottomed plain vessel, found by Mr. Mortimer in barrow 110, which I believe is neolithic or subneolithic, and another from a chambered cairn at Auchnacree, Loch Etive, Argyll (fig. 214a), which is 4 in. high and belongs to the neolithic period.

TYPE 5 (TRUNCATED CONE).

Fig. 25 is not a good example, as it has a slight angle at the shoulder, and moreover is provided with a button-shaped knob by way of a handle. It is later than beaker fig. 101. An example of type 5 (P. 22) is contemporary with fig. 64, a nearly globular pot of black colour, with thin walls only $\frac{3}{8}$ in. thick, and the outside surface of which has a glazed appearance. The other vessel is of the same black ware but the surface is dull. Fragments of similar ware were often found scattered in barrows by Mr. Mortimer and probably represent domestic pottery. Fig. 67 is probably later than figs. 65, 66 of types 2, 3. Fig. 78 is probably earlier than fig. 79, a fairly early example of 1a with perforated ears. Fig. 215 was found with a burnt interment in the same cist at Arbor Low as fig. 214.

5a (with moulded lip).

An example of 5a (P. 13) is contemporary with fig. 47, a moderately early example of 1a. Fig. 69 is contemporary with fig. 70, a rather late example of type 2. Fig. 87 is probably earlier than fig. 88, a quite abnormal variety of 1a.

Additional examples are fig. 216, perhaps from Derbyshire, and fig. 217 from near Alnwick, Northumberland.

TYPE 6 (CYLINDRICAL).

This does not appear to be a common type in Region II, and I do not know if the following three examples (figs. 218–20) were found with unburnt interments or not, although as the first came from Stanhow Moor, North Riding, in all probability it accompanied a cinerary interment. In height they range between 4 in. and 4½ in.

VESSELS THAT CANNOT BE INCLUDED UNDER THE ABOVE TYPES.

Fig. 221, with a height of 3¼ in., is perhaps an example of type 2a. It was found with a skeleton.

(P. 49) Fig. 113 is 5½ in. high, has the form of 2a, but with four small feet. It is probably later than a moderately late type 2 (fig. 112). Fig. 222 is 3⅞ in. high and was the primary interment. Each of the four feet is perforated with a hole large enough for the passage of a thong. In front of the skeleton lay a beautiful saw of black flint 2½ in. long, serrated on both edges. A bowl very similar in the form of the body, but with three longer, imperforate legs and 3¾ in. high, from Male Čičovice, in Bohemia, is figured by Dr. Pič.[1] It belongs probably to the end of the neolithic or the beginning of the Bronze Age. Another three-legged vessel with a relatively wider bowl than fig. 222 and 5¾ in. high, from near Cagliari (Sardinia), is figured by Colini. It was found with a fragment of a bell-beaker and belongs to the aeneolithic period.[2] Fig. 223 from Corbridge, Northumberland, is 3¼ in. high and very remarkable from its ornamentation of curved lines. Its four feet are also perforated.

(P. 4) Fig. 223 bis comes from the North Riding and is 2½ in. high. It is much repaired. Fig. 27 is a handled cup, in form like a type 3, and is 5½ in. high. It is later than the beakers figs. 122, 123.

(P. 20) The handled cup (fig. 60) 6½ in. high, and the small bowl (fig. 61), 2¼ in. high, are contemporary.

(P. 28) The handled cup (fig. 74), 4¼ in. high, is ornamented on the bottom with a cruciform pattern inscribed in a circle and is contemporary with beakers figs. 119, 120.

Fig. 224 is a handled cup 5 in. high, and differs from the others by standing on a base which has almost the form of a cross. It was found with a skeleton as the primary interment. A very similar vessel from Heighington, Lincoln, is figured by Thurnam.[3]

(P. 17) The small bowl (fig. 55) is only 2¼ in. high, and is later than fig. 54, a rather late example of 1a.

(P. 26) Fig. 73 with perforated ears is 3 in. high, and is later than a flat bronze knife-dagger 6 in. long, with three rivets.

Fig. 225 with four small ears was found in a Staffordshire cairn with a brachycephalic skeleton, a tine of a stag's horn, and several pieces of flint. Punctures similar to those on the inside of the lip are also to be seen in the same position on figs. 140, 142, 210.

Fig. 226 with four handles is 6¾ in. high, and was found in a cist with a male interment. The belt of ornament at the centre of the vessel does not pass entirely round. The vessel comes from Northumberland.

---

[1] *Čechy před.* i, Tab. xxxv. 14.   [2] *Bull. Pal. It.* xxiv, Tav. xviii. 1, 3.   [3] *Arch.* xliii. 380, figs. 71, 72.

(P. 37) Fig. 93, 8 in. high, is of very unusual form and is probably later than an example of type 3.

(P. 51) Fig. 119, however, is not unlike it and has nearly the same height, $8\frac{1}{2}$ in. It is probably contemporary with sub-type 4a.

Fig. 227 from Jesmond in Northumberland is remarkable from the nearly globular form of the base, and from the use of a technique not indigenous to the country.

Fig. 228 is also a remarkable vessel of quite a different kind from the usual food-vessel ware. It is of a palish brown colour and the paste is remarkably fine, without any admixture of broken stone; in point of density it is so light that Canon Greenwell compares it in that respect with the best Greek pottery. It was found in a trench 16 ft. long, sunk into the chalk rock, with one end lying 25 ft. east of the centre of the barrow. Though the trench was full of burnt earth, chalk, and charcoal, there was no sign of burning on the sides of the trench itself, throughout which were scattered many sherds of pottery, principally of dark ware, certainly fragments of domestic utensils. Amongst these were the broken portions of fig. 228. It is 5 in. high with a diameter of 10 in. Mr. Mortimer figures another vessel much like this, $5\frac{1}{8}$ in. high, and also round-bottomed.[1] It was found in a pit-dwelling under a barrow. Another round-bottomed, plain vessel of the same ware was found by him in a barrow with objects which belong to the neolithic or subneolithic period.[2]

Fig. 229, though found with a cremated interment, may be reckoned perhaps among the food vessels. Without the cover it is 2 in. high. At the centre of the barrow was a $3\frac{1}{2}$-ft. deep grave, at the bottom of which the body of a man had been laid. On the natural surface at the west side of the grave was a deposit of burnt bones of an adult woman and in contact with it this vessel. At the north-west edge of the grave, also on the natural surface, lay food vessel fig. 230, $3\frac{1}{2}$ in. high. These two pieces of pottery were the best manufactured and most delicately ornamented of any that Canon Greenwell had met in his excavations in Yorkshire. The clay was well tempered and without any admixture of broken stone. Both seem to have been made by the same hand. The 'chain-loop' technique with which they are decorated is frequently found on cinerary urns.

As nothing definite can be learnt from the food vessels of Region I, partly owing to the scantiness or complete absence of any record of the finds, it is well to compare the vessels of the two Regions to see how far they correspond. Of those compared, figs. 4, 6, 7, 8, 13, may be assigned to Bronze Age I.

Type 1, 1a is apparently entirely wanting.[3]

Fig. 1 of type 3, cf. figs. 187, 188, from Staffordshire and the East Riding, for the high position of the upper moulding—a late feature—and for the puncture technique cf. figs. 28, 171, 181, 192 from Yorkshire.

Fig. 3, cf. fig. 98, of Bronze Age II, from the East Riding.

Fig. 4, cf. fig. 193, from the East Riding.

Fig. 6 of type 3, cf. figs. 24, 46, of period Phase II type A, with the same cord technique, and fig. 72.

Fig. 7 of type 4a, cf. figs. 71, 212.

Fig. 8 of type 4, cf. fig. 53.

Fig. 13 bis of type 5, cf. figs. 78, 215, for form.

Fig. 14, handled cup, cf. fig. 74, for form and set-on of the handle.

Vessels of type 6 with knobs do not seem to be known in Region II.

---

[1] Mortimer, fig. 238.　　[2] Op. cit. p. 29, fig. 65.

[3] The example from near Tenby is so much like

Hibernian examples that it may well have come from the Emerald Isle.

CHAPTER IX

REGION III

THIS region includes Hibernia and North Britain. On entering it we find ourselves in a different artistic atmosphere from that of Region II and are confronted with vessels which have no representatives in Regions I, II, and yet with others which have forms common to both these parts of Britain. The ornamentation on the whole is very different and far more elaborate, disclosing a greater feeling for art, and is often executed with a boldness which is scarcely to be seen in the other regions. It seems to indicate that the makers of these vessels belonged to a different stock of people, endowed with a more lively fancy than the brachycephalic invaders.

The new forms may be classified as follows :—

Type A.

This is a small bowl-shaped vessel, like an Indian *lota*, with a nearly round bottom, which is frequently ornamented. By degrees the bottom flattens and various modifications take place in the profile of the vessel; secondary grooves appear below the neck or above the base; a thickened belt develops round the centre and so forth (figs. 281, 288, 291, 301).

Another modification is seen in A1 (fig. 240).

Type B.

This is apparently a development of type A and structurally is so nearly the same as type 2 that, to prevent confusion, I have cited examples of it as type 2 (figs. 238, 245).

Type C.

This is a bowl-shaped, flat-bottomed vessel with three or more deep grooves round the body (figs. 234, 254).

Type D.

This has an ornamented, globular body with short everted lip and a flat bottom (fig. 258).

Type E.

The lower part is biconical, and above the shoulder rises an everted neck (fig. 256).

Again we begin with a short description of thirty-two multiple interments or instances, numbered 54 *bis* to 85, in which a vessel has been discovered with some object that helps in the smallest degree to date it. Our object is to ascertain, so far as the limited material permits, the relative age of the different forms that occur, either common to both regions or confined to the third. It is very important to know whether type 1*a* appeared first in the west and from there passed over into Region II, for if so, we understand why this special form of food vessel appears there as a fully developed type and never reached the southern half of Britain.

MULTIPLE INTERMENTS OR WITH OBJECTS

54 *bis*. Cairn at *Loughloughan*, Broughshane, Co. Antrim. Diameter 52 ft. from east to west and 39 ft. from north to south, height from 3 ft. to 4 ft. On the floor of the cairn were three stone cists. That lying west of the centre, rather larger than the others, contained fig. 231 of type 1*a*, 4¾ in. high, with three ears. The cist to the east of the centre contained fig. 232 of type A, 3 in. high, decorated with a bold chevron in false relief. The third cist lay near the south-west edge of the cairn and had been rifled, but on removing the stones of which it was constructed a disc bead of jet or lignite, evidently part of a necklace, was fortunately recovered. Though fig. 231 is in every way better made and better burnt than the other, they are probably contemporary within a few years. *J. R. S. A. I.* xxxii (1902), p. 163, and letter from Mr. Knowles.

55. *Oldbridge House*, Co. Meath. Diameter of the mound 60 ft., height 6 ft. While preparing to plant a tree on the mound a double cist covered by a large cap-stone was unearthed. In the east corner of the north chamber was a fine vessel of type A with an ornamented bottom. The floors of both cists were covered with particles of decomposed bone among which were the crowns of several human teeth. There seemed to have been two males interred in the north cist and a woman in the southern one. With the latter was a fine lignite necklace of fusiform and disc beads, besides one small triangular plate. *P. R. I. A.*, 3 ser., iii. 747–50.

56. Cairn at *Mount Stewart*, Co. Down. Diameter 30 ft., height about 5 ft. While removing the cairn in 1786 some sixty or seventy cists[1] were uncovered on the south side of it. The bottom of each cist was strewn with fragments of charred bones and charcoal, and contained an urn in the north-west corner. At the centre of the cairn was a cist four times the size of the others but it contained nothing. No cists were found north of the centre. Eleven or twelve vessels were apparently saved at the time, but only four perfect specimens came subsequently into the hands of Dr. R. Stephenson who figured them in *U. J. A.* ix. 111–12. It has already been mentioned that in the *Dublin Penny Journal* (1832–33), p. 108, three vessels from this find are engraved (beaker fig. 223). This last is like a beaker of type B and unlike any of four figured by Dr. Stephenson; the other two are fig. 233 of type A and fig. 334 of type C. These are now in possession of Col. McChance, who inherited them from Dr. Stephenson, and kindly gave me permission to have them photographed. Fig. 235 of type A is also in his possession and he believes it came from the Mount Stewart cairn, but it is not among the four reproduced in Dr. Stephenson's paper.

57. Cairn at *Duncragaig*, Poltalloch, Argyll. Diameter about 100 ft., height uncertain. At the centre was a cist of four slabs with cap-stone, on the top of which lay a decayed body. The cist contained clay mixed with sand, gravel, and calcined bones, and fig. 236, 3¾ in. high, of type A. Below this mixture was a pavement of stones and under it a skeleton in a flexed position. About 22 ft. east of this was another cist of small dimensions partly filled with gravel and burnt bones. On the surface of the gravel lay fig. 237, 3¾ in. high, of type A. *P. S. A. S.* vi. 347.

58. Cairn at *Kilmartin*, Argyll. Diameter 110 ft., height 13½ ft. At the centre was a hollow, lined with rounded boulders, forming a cist 7½ ft. long and 3 ft. deep, covered by a large slab 9 ft. long by 4½ ft. wide. It contained fig. 238, 5 in. high, of type 2, a quantity of dark unctuous matter but no trace of bone. About 30 ft. from the centre was another cist, half the size of the other and surrounded by a double circular setting of stones. It contained fig. 239, 5 in. high, of type A, but with four ears or perforated stops and a jet necklace of twenty-eight beads, two of them oblong plates 1½ in. by ½ in. with six holes drilled through them lengthways, three cylindrical, and twenty-three thin discs. *P. S. A. S.* vi. 339–41.

59. Cairn at *Moylethid* on Belmore Mountain, Fermanagh. Diameter about 40 ft., height 10 ft. On the floor of the cairn was a cruciform passage of large limestone slabs, the principal axis of which was 13 ft. long, lying in the direction north-west and south-east. The transverse axis measured 7⅓ ft. There were no cover-stones on the passage or on the head and side chambers, with the exception of the left chamber. The contents of the passage and of the head and right-arm chambers consisted of a mass of burnt bones, on the top of which the stones of the cairn had been thrown without any structural arrangement. Among the bones were found three beads and seven pendants (O. fig. 46). One of the beads is a small carnelian pebble, rubbed down to make it rudely globular. The other beads and pendants, except one of the latter, which is a perforated tooth, are of soft siliceous stone resembling serpentine. The pendants are highly polished, well made, and very similar to those obtained from the Lough Crew cairns.

[1] The plan in *U. J. A.* ix, p. 111 only shews 46 cists containing urns.

The left-arm chamber, which had two stories, was covered by a slab. The lower compartment contained a human skull and other unburnt human bones, also bones of deer, pig, rabbit, and birds, several large boars' tusks and a few sea-shells. The upper compartment contained fig. 240, about 4 in. high, of type A1, and burnt bones, though none were in the vessel itself. It has lost the bottom, but was very little deeper than the illustration shows; though much less decorated, it has the same form as one of the vessels from Mount Stewart. In a secondary cist near the top of the cairn were found burnt bones and fig. 241 of type A, 3½ in. high. *P.R.I.A.*, 3 ser., iv. 659–66.

60. Mound at *Letterbrick*, Cloghan, Donegal. Figs. 242, 243 of type A were found with human bones in two cavities in the mound. Other details seem to be wanting. *Dublin Mus. Cat.* nos. 159, 160.

61. *Cnoc maraidhe, Phoenix Park*, Dublin. Diameter 120 ft., height 15 ft. Within the tumulus, but several yards from the centre, were discovered four vessels containing ashes of burnt bones. They were enclosed in small stone cists and were broken, except one (fig. 244). Subsequently, a large cist was unearthed at the centre, the cap-stone of which measured 6½ ft. × 3½ ft. and 14 inches thick. It rested on five stones and contained two skeletons, under each head of which was a considerable quantity of small shells (*Nerita littoralis*). They had been rubbed down to form a second hole, evidently with the intention of being strung as a necklace, also a small bone pin with a head at each end, and a flint knife. *P.R.I.A.* i. 187–9.

The cephalic index of these two skulls was 76·8 and 78·, and according to Prof. Haddon they appear to belong to a mixed race. One is probably a modification of the dolichocephalic group and might be classed among them, while the latter seems to belong to the brachycephalic group. *P.R.I.A.*, 3 ser., iv. 578, 581.

62. *Ardna*, Keel, Co. Meath. Fig. 245 of type 2 and fig. 246 of type 5 were found at opposite ends of the same cist. *Dublin Mus. new cat.* p. 3.

63. *Corky*. Antrim. In a cist with a skeleton interment was found fig. 247, nearly 4 in. high, of type 2, and a small bronze knife-dagger 3¾ in. long with two rivets (O. 47). *J.R.H.A.A.I.*, 4 ser., ix. 108.

64. *Lug na curran*, Queen's County. Three cists lying east and west and parallel to each other were unearthed from a bed of sand in a dry field. The cap-stones lay about 7 in. below the surface and the cists contained skeleton interments. Two of the cists contained each a food vessel lying in the south-east corner. In one of the vessels, fig. 248 of type 2, lay two bronze rings with a diameter of 3 in., of circular section, the ends of which overlap by 2¼ in. and taper towards the extremities (O. 48). In the same, or in the other vessel, were 'what appeared to be two little links of [1] beads of some mineral substance of bluish colour and highly polished'. *J.R.H.A.A.I.*, 4 ser., v. 446–7.

65. *Brownhead cairn*, Arran. Diameter 26 ft.; only the base of the cairn was left, the stones having formerly been removed. A little south of the centre was a cist lying east and west, filled with dark mould, but no bones, burnt or unburnt, were observed. Near the bottom was food vessel fig. 249, 5 in. high, of type 2, a flint flake, and fourteen discs of lignite. The bottom of the vessel was ornamented with a design forming three arms of a cross. *P.S.A.S.* xxxvi. 120–2.

66. *Mount Stuart*, Bute. About 18 in. below the surface of a hillock, the cap-stone of a cist lying north and south was exposed. It contained a skeleton, a small fragment of bronze, a food vessel (fig. 250), 7 in. high, of type 2, and a jet necklace composed of seven plates and one hundred fusiform beads. Dr. Beddoe was of opinion that the owner had been a young woman, and was not sure whether the skull was brachy- or dolichocephalic, though he inclined to think it was the former. Dr. Bryce has no doubt that the skull belongs to the same class as the Auchantirie skull, also from Bute, the cephalic index of which he estimated at 81. *P.S.A.S.* xxxviii. 63–8.

67. *Mauchrie Moor stone circle*, Arran. At the centre of the circle and 3½ ft. below the surface, was the cap-stone of a cist 3 ft. long by 2 ft. deep. It contained a bronze pin or awl about 2½ in. long, some fragments of bone, 3 arrowheads or implements of flint of the rudest form, and fig. 251, 5 in. high, of type 2. In another circle close by, also in a central cist, was found a better-formed vessel 7½ in. high, of the same type (fig. 252). *P.S.A.S.* iv. 506, &c.

---

[1] The phrase is difficult to understand, perhaps it should read links *or* beads.

68. *Kinneff*, Kincardine.   In trenching ground an unburnt burial was found, two bronze rings, 3 in. in diameter, of nearly circular section, and fig. 253 of type 2.   *Anderson*, pp. 59, 60.

69. *Rathbarran*, Coolaney, Sligo.   Fig. 254, 4¾ in. high, of type C, was found in an ancient Rath, in a cist containing calcined bones, a small disc of mica slate, and a shale celt 3½ in. long (O. 49).   *J.R.H.A.A.I.*, 4 ser., viii. 271–2.

70. *Killicarney*, Co. Cavan.   The mound, with a diameter of about 24 ft. and height 15½ ft., was of natural formation, but the surface had been heaped over with from 2 ft. to 4½ ft. of earth and then covered with stones.   On removing some of the loose stones from the top, a cist was discovered at a depth of 3 ft. from the surface.   It was divided into two compartments in each of which was a vessel.   Only one, fig. 255, 6 in. high, of type C, was preserved.   Both vessels are said to have been full of bones.   In one of the compartments was a small stone celt 2⅞ in. long by 1³⁄₁₀ at the cutting edge, and a piece of worked bone 1⅖ in. × 1½ in. of quadrangular form, with two hasps or hooks on one face (O. 50a, b).   *J.R.H.A.A.I.*, 4 ser., v. 189–93.

71. Cairn on *Toppet Mountain*, Enniskillen, Fermanagh.   Diameter about 90 ft. at the base and 50 ft. at the top, height about 12 ft.   A cist, measuring 4 ft. × 2½ ft. × 2 ft. deep, covered by a cap-stone, was discovered about 10 ft. from the east margin of the cairn ; the level at which it was found is not precisely stated but it seems to have been near the top of the cairn.   The cist contained fragments of a skull, a bronze dagger, 5⅜ in. × 1⅖ in., ornamented with 2 lines parallel to the cutting edge, broken at the butt end, but with two rivet-holes remaining, and half of a small gold band that probably encircled the handle, as a mounting to the dagger (O. 51) ; also fig. 256, 5½ in. high, of type E.   At the north end of the cist lay a cremated interment between two flagstones.   *P.R.I.A.*, 3 ser., iv. 651–5.

72. *Succoth Place, Edinburgh.*   In making a new road, two stone cists in contact were unearthed about 4 ft. below the natural surface.   In one of these lay fig. 257, 4¾ in. high, of type 4 ; in the other, fig. 258, 3½ in. high, of type D.   *P.S.A.S.* xxxvi. 670–4.

73. *Ballywillan*, Portrush, Co. Antrim.   While preparing a field for crop a small cist was unearthed containing fig. 259, 4½ in. high, of type 1a, and fig. 260, 3½ in. high, a variety perhaps of type 5a, lying on the top of it.   *P.R.S.A.I.*, 5 ser., i. 438.

74. *Hamilton* (near), Lanarkshire.   Fig. 261, 4¾ in. high, of type 1, and fig. 262, 5½ in. high, of type 5, were found, together with human bones.   *Label, Hunterian Mus., Glasgow.*

75. *Glenhead Farm*, Doune, Perthshire.   Fig. 263 of type 1a was found with a burial under a cairn. Along with it was a small perforated hammer of veined quartzite, 2½ in. long × 1½ in. in diameter, finely polished and rounded at both ends (O. 52).   *P.S.A.S.* xvii. 452–3.

76. *Kingsbarns Law*, Crail, Fife.   A retaining-wall giving way, two cists were discovered in a sandy hillock.   The lower and smaller cist lay at a depth of 4½ ft. and contained fig. 264, 5 in. high, of type 1a, as well as the bones of a skeleton.   At a rather higher level was a somewhat larger cist containing fig. 265, 5¾ in. high, of type 2.   *P.S.A.S.* x. 244 ; *Anderson*, p. 82.

77. Cairn at *Skalpsie Bay*, Bute.   Diameter 45 ft. × 43 ft., height 4–5 ft.   On the floor of the cairn was placed a cist, covered by a large cap-stone, which contained fragments of burnt human bones, a bit of a bronze pin, a jet fusiform bead, and fig. 266, 5½ in. high, of type 1a, the bottom of which is decorated with a cruciform design.   *P.S.A.S.* xxxviii. 52–6.

78. *Battle Law*, Naughton, Fife.   In an irregularly-shaped cist, 10 in. below the surface, two vessels, fig. 267, 4 in. high, of type 1a, and fig. 268, 5 in. high, of type 2, were found with incinerated remains. *P.S.A.S.* xxxv. 301–9.

79. *Balcalk*, Tealing, Forfarshire.   Close to the surface of the ground two cists were discovered, one of which merely contained pieces of a broken urn and fragments of unburnt bones.   The other cist contained the remains of a skeleton (fig. 269), 4½ in. high, of type 4, a flint knife, the end of a bronze pin, and a jet or lignite necklace composed of seven plates and 142 fusiform beads, much resembling that from Mount Stuart in Bute (P. 66), but of more delicate workmanship than the latter.   *P.S.A.S.* xiv. 260–1.

80. *Lunanhead*, Forfar.   In excavating for gravel, the cap-stone of a cist, weighing a ton or more, was encountered about 2 ft. below the surface.   The cist contained the remains of a skeleton interment and a very fine jet or lignite necklace consisting of six plates and seventy-two fusiform beads of the same type as those from Mount Stuart and Balcalk.   From 6½ ft. to 7 ft. east of this was another cist, the bottom of which was 9 ft. below the natural surface; it contained a flint flake and fig. 270, 5 in. high, of type 4. *P. S. A. S.* xii. 288, &c.

81. *Ratho*, Midlothian. The portion of a bronze ring said to have been found with fig. 271, 4¾ in. high, of type 1*a* is apparently of the same character as that from Kinneff (P. 68). *Anderson*, p. 60.

82. *Kellas*, Murroes, Forfarshire. Fig. 272, 6½ in. high, of type 2, was found with a cylindrical bead and small plate of jet forming part of a necklace. *P. S. A. S.* xxiv. 9, 10.

83. *Duncra Hill Farm*, Pencaitland, E. Lothian. In ploughing a sandy knoll the cap-stone of a cist was struck at 11 in. below the surface. It contained a few bones of a skeleton and three vessels, figs. 273, 274, perhaps of type 3, measuring 4¾ in. and 4¼ in. respectively, and fig. 275, 5½ in. high, a variety perhaps of type 4. *P. S. A. S.* xxxiv. 131-4.

84. *Doune Station* (near), Perthshire. In making a new road a cist was discovered at a depth of over 6 ft. from the surface. On the floor lay ashes and burnt bones, and near the opposite ends of the cist were figs. 276, 277, respectively 4¾ in. and 5 in. high, of type 2 (?). *P. S. A. S.* xxxvi. 685-7.

85. *Duff House*, Banffshire. Inside the vessel fig. 277 *bis*, which was inverted over a flat stone, were two large plain penannular rings, and three smaller ones of gold, and fragments of a thin blade of bronze. The larger rings or armlets had a diameter of 2¼ in., the smaller ones vary in their longest diameter from ⅞ in. to ½ in. The interment was probably after cremation. Anderson, *Bronze and Stone Ages*, p. 61, figs. 68-72.

V. TABLE OF RESULTS

Country	Paragraph	Objects Found	Type certainly (1) or probably (2) deposited		
			Earlier	Later	At same time
Hib.	54	Disc bead	..	..	(2) A, 1*a*
H.	55	Disc and fusiform beads	..	..	(1) A
H.	56		..	..	(2) A, C
NB.	57		A	A	
NB.	58	Necklace, two plates, disc, and fusiform beads (with A)	2	A	
H.	59	[1]Rude beads and pendants	A i	A	
H.	60		..	..	(2) A, A
H.	61	Shell necklace, two mesocephalic skulls	..	..	(2) 4 *b*
H.	62		..	..	(1) 2, 5
H.	63	[1]Bronze blade 3¼ in. long, two rivets	..	..	(1) 2
H.	64	[1]Two bronze rings	..	..	(1) 2
NB.	65	Disc beads	..	..	(1) 2
NB.	66	Bronze fragment necklace, plate and fusiform, brachy. skull	..	..	(1) 2
NB.	67	Bronze pin, rude flint implement	..	..	(1) 2
NB.	68	Two bronze rings	..	..	(1) 2
H.	69	[1]Shale celt	..	..	(1) C
H.	70	[1]Stone celt	..	..	(1) C
H.	71	[1]Bronze blade, two lines, gold mount	..	..	(1) E
NB.	72		..	..	(1) D, type 4 (?)
H.	73		..	..	(1) 1*a*, no type
NB.	74		..	..	(1) 1, 5
NB.	75	[1]Perforated stone hammer	..	..	(1) 1*a*
NB.	76		1 *a*	2	
NB.	77	Bronze pin, fusiform bead	..	..	(1) 1*a*
NB.	78		..	..	(1) 1*a*, 2
NB.	79	Necklace, seven plates and fusiform beads, bronze pin	..	..	(1) 4*a*
NB.	80	Necklace, six plates and fusiform beads	..	..	(2) 4
NB.	81	Fragment of bronze ring	..	..	(2) 1*a*
NB.	82	Necklace, plate, and fusiform bead	..	..	(1) 2
NB.	83		..	..	(1) 3, 4 modified
NB.	84		..	..	(1) 2, 2 (?)
NB.	85	Five gold rings, fragment of bronze blade	..	..	(1) 5

[1] *Vide* Pl. lxi, O. 46, 47, 48, 49, 50*a*, *b*, 51, 52.

CHAPTER X

TYPE A IN HIBERNIA

In the earlier half of this type (figs. 279–89) the vessels assume at the beginning the form of a round-bottomed bowl. On this account it seems legitimate to suppose that the type is derived from a plain, nearly hemispherical bowl, such as fig. 278 from near Larne, Co. Antrim. Although nothing is known concerning the discovery of this vessel, it so much resembles a certainly neolithic bowl discovered by Dr. Bryce in Bute,[1] that I believe it must be ascribed to that particular period. There is unfortunately only one reliable and good account of the finding of any of the vessels of type A; for the most part there is no record at all. Some are said to have accompanied burials with cremation, though they have the appearance of food vessels. Although we shall find that these vessels must belong to an early period, certainly as early as Phase I of the beaker class, the fact of cremation in Hibernia at such a period is not astonishing. Canon Greenwell observed burnt human bones in a chambered cairn at Largie in Argyll, and at Kilchoan in the same county Mr. Mapleton found deposits of burnt bones in another chambered cairn. Both these places of burial date from before the arrival of the brachycephalic invaders. The similarity of the ceramic between the north of Ireland and Argyll at the time when type A was coming into being is so great that we may be certain the inhabitants of both were identical in stock and civilization, with similar ideas regarding their disposal of the dead.

From fig. 279 to fig. 289 we have a series of small vessels from $3\frac{1}{4}$ in. to 4 in. in height, beginning with a nearly round bottom, which gradually becomes flatter. At first the walls form a fine unbroken curve, but towards the end of the series the curve becomes modified. The bottom of the vessels was often ornamented, which probably implies that when not in use the bowls were inverted. The small native women, sometimes under 5 ft. high, who made these little vessels had certainly a fine sense of form and a delicate perception of the beauty of curved forms. The care and precision with which the ornament was effected and the richness of the effect produced by simple means may excite our admiration. We cannot be sure how far back in time the earlier half of type A is to be dated, but fig. 281 from Co. Tyrone is said to have been found with a nearly rhomb-shaped arrowhead of black stone, thin and finely chipped (fig. 281a). If this was really the case the vessel may be considered as belonging to the neolithic period. Fig. 280 is said to have been discovered in a 'subterraneous cavern, approached by a narrow passage' at Dunagore Moat, near Antrim. Moreover, flint arrowheads and a stone celt are said to have been found in the vessel. The 'subterraneous cavern' was probably a

---

[1] *P. S. A. S.* xxxviii. 26, fig. 5.

chambered cairn approached by a passage,[1] a kind of sepulchre which preceded the Bronze Age. Another indication of the age of the first half of type A is afforded by the bowl from Co. Meath (P. 55). It was found in a double cist, each chamber of which measured 4 in. × 2 in. × $2\frac{3}{4}$ in. deep, or rather larger than is usual in the Bronze Age. The female skeleton was accompanied by a lignite necklace of disc-shaped and fusiform beads together with a small triangular pendant of the same mineral. Both forms of bead are ancient and can be earlier than the true Bronze Age.

In the second half of the type from fig. 290 to fig. 302 we have a series which begins with a slight horizontal indentation round the middle of the vessel and ends in a groove so well marked that shortly afterwards type A passes into type 2. In fact, the last three examples might be placed in the latter category, but for the rather deep raised belt immediately above the groove, a feature which has evidently developed from a more rounded profile like that of fig. 299; and this, like fig. 300, was found in the county of Dublin. Some few of these vessels are over 4 inches in height, but none touches 5 inches. We may observe in the decoration of the later vessels new motives of ornament, such as the bar-hexagon, the lozenge formed by two rows of bar-chevrons and two rows of bar-chevrons united by short vertical lines,[2] precisely as we have seen upon some beakers. Yet here borrowing can hardly be thought of; these motives may have suggested themselves spontaneously on both sides of the Channel. At any rate the rows of square fields shaded with vertical lines[3] are peculiar to Hibernia. All the vessels here figured that belong to type A and were found on Hibernian soil came from the Provinces of Ulster and Leinster with the exception of figs. 293, 297, which came from Co. Sligo in the Province of Connaught.

A rare by-form apparently of type A, which I have termed A 1, is to be seen in fig. 240 from Belmore Mountain, Co. Fermanagh (P. 59). It was found in a cruciform chamber which though on a diminutive scale is comparable as regards its plan with some of the megalithic chambers of Lough Crew, and the beads of perforated pebbles from another part of the chamber are characteristic of the neolithic period. Several feet higher in the tumulus was found fig. 241, which may be placed in the second half of type A, and is evidently later than the above. Both interments were after cremation of the body. As mentioned above, a vessel of the same form as fig. 240, but ornamented with the false-relief technique, was found among the vessels from Mt. Stewart, Co. Down, but is now only known by a woodcut.

An interesting by-form of type A is seen in fig. 302 *bis*, probably from Ulster; it may be compared with fig. 302*b*, $3\frac{1}{2}$ in. high, found in a megalithic cist in the south of Kintyre, Argyll, and, doubtless, belonging to the neolithic period. The only difference in form lies in the flat bottom of the former vessel.

TYPE A IN NORTH BRITAIN

With the exception of three examples from Argyll[4] this type is sparsely represented in North Britain. Perhaps a vessel older than type A is to be seen in fig. 303*a* from Inveresk, Midlothian. In form, height, and ornamentation it closely resembles a vessel found 20 ft. below

---

[1] Native Irish writers used *uaimh*, 'a cave or cavern,' when referring to the chambered tumuli near New Grange.

[2] Figs. 296, 298, 299, 300.

[3] Fig. 297.

[4] Figs. 236, 237, 239.

the surface of a bog near Clones, Co. Monaghan. It was accompanied by two fine greenstone celts, and Mr. G. Coffey attributes the find to the neolithic period.[1] Fig. 303, 4½ in. high, seems to be an early example of the type. It is from Wartle in Aberdeenshire, and it will be observed that the motive of the ornament, though here executed with the finger-nail, is precisely the same as on fig. 282 from Co. Antrim, where use was made of a notched instrument. Fig. 304 from Methlick, Aberdeenshire, is a fine specimen, corresponding closely with fig. 291 from Co. Tyrone. Fig. 305, 5¼ in. high, from near Lamlash in Arran, probably belongs to the type. Fig. 306, 4½ in. high, from Barsleisnach in Argyll, is a very fine example of the second half of type A.

TYPE 2 IN HIBERNIA

As in Hibernia this type is a direct development of type A, I take it before 1a. Three illustrations of it have already been given among the multiple interments[2] and now twenty-eight additional examples are appended, figs. 307–34. It cannot be said that they form a continuous series for there are evident gaps, and certain by-forms, the exact place of which in the sequence is uncertain, must be inserted somewhere. Hardly anything is known as regards the discovery of these specimens. As the type is derived from a bowl-shaped prototype, the vessels in which the lower part below the groove is more or less rounded are evidently earlier than those in which the sides are quite flat. The lip is sometimes everted, sometimes moulded like those in Region II, but this feature does not seem to constitute a certain criterion of the age of the vessel, for in some examples with a straight or upright neck the lower part of the vase is flat-sided.[3] So too, although a wide but flattish groove is a sign of later date, it does not follow that a narrow groove is necessarily a certain mark of earlier date, for some specimens with such a groove have their lower portion flat-sided or nearly so.[4] All these vessels are small, ranging in height from 3¾ to 5¾ inches, the larger ones being found towards the end of the series. Although the exact locality where many of these vessels were found is unknown, it is almost certain that those of the Bell collection in the National Museum of Antiquities, Edinburgh, and those in the British Museum were found in Ulster.[5] When the locality is known the vessels were brought to light in the Provinces of Ulster and Leinster.

We find a useful synchronism with Region II, in fig. 247, from Corky, Co. Antrim (P. 63), which was found with a small triangular flat bronze knife 3¼ in. long, with 2 rivets. As regards size and the number of rivets it resembles one found in the East Riding by Mr. Mortimer (P. 27) with a skeleton interment (pl. lxi, O. 33, 47), and 6 in. higher a specimen of type 3, much like fig. 72, but somewhat broader. The Corky example seems to be earlier than fig. 328 from Dromore, Co. Tyrone, but later than fig. 310 from the Gap of Gorteen in the same county.

I have placed quite at the end of type 2 three examples in which the groove is filled up and quite flat, a circumstance which shows that the old tradition was on its last legs. This view is supported, I believe, by fig. 248 from Lug na Curran, Queen's County (P. 64), which was

---

[1] *J. R. Soc. Ant. Ireland*, xxxiv (1904), 271–2.
[2] P. 62, 63, 64, figs. 245, 247, 248.
[3] Figs. 329, 330. [4] Figs. 325–7. [5] Figs. 308, 309, 323–7.

found with two bronze spiral bracelets of circular section, the ends of which overlap by $2\frac{1}{4}$ inches and taper towards the extremities (O. 48). Bracelets of this type belong on the Continent to Bronze Age I,[1] but these may be placed somewhat later than the small thin blade from Corky.

TYPE 2 IN NORTH BRITAIN

Seven certain and two uncertain examples of this type have already been figured among the multiple interments and sixteen more are now added to the number. As in Hibernia, hardly any particulars are known with regard to the finding of these vessels, though the locality in which they were discovered is generally certain. Though they have a certain individuality of their own, their form and ornamentation is more reminiscent of Hibernia than of Region II. In height they vary from 4 to $6\frac{1}{2}$ inches, and the last three have a height of 6 inches or more.

From the low position of the groove, coupled with a lower half that is slightly rounded, fig. 335 from Musselburgh seems to belong to a rather early part of the type and to be earlier than the Kilmartin example. Owing to its general form it may be compared with fig. 125 of type 1*a* from Colwell, North Tyne, though the latter is the older of the two. If the comparison holds good and its relative age is correctly estimated, it follows that the Northumberland example was there before the invasion of Northumberland by the brachycephals took place. And this is not an isolated example in that part of the country. The small cup, fig. 223, from Corbridge, Northumberland, with four perforated feet, showing four sets of triple semi-circular lines round the body and ornamented besides with the early square-notch technique, may be compared with fig. 307, an early example of type 2 from Co. Fermanagh, where a zone of curved lines appears on the neck and the surface is covered with ornament made with the square-notch technique.[2] The third vessel is fig. 227 from Jesmond, Northumberland, with Hibernian decoration. Certainly it is more probable that these vessels, two of them so evidently Hibernian in appearance, should be the handiwork of natives of Hibernian stock who occupied that part of the country before the arrival of the invaders in Northumberland, than after that event. The alternative is that they were made by women captured by the invaders, though against that must be set the considerations, stated above, tending to the great probability that the vessels are too early for such a hypothesis.

Where the well-made fig. 336 was found is unknown, though in all probability it came from the west coast. Both it and fig. 337 from Biggar in Lanark, fig. 339 from Dunbar, fig. 340 from the I. of Cumbrae (which last—judging from the size of the cist—must have accompanied a cremated burial), are all under 5 in. in height and are apparently somewhat anterior to the invasion of the short-headed men; perhaps to these may be added fig. 341 from Galloway and fig. 342 from Argyll. Besides the tests for development posterior to the invasion afforded by figs. 249–52, above mentioned, we have another in fig. 253 from Kinneff, Kincardine (P. 68), which was found with a pair of solid bronze rings precisely like a bronze ring that accompanied beaker fig. 213 from Crawford in Lanark, so that the food vessel and

---

[1] Cf. Montelius, *Chronologie*, figs. 124, 128; Splieth, *Inventar d. Bronzalt. aus Schleswig-Holstein*, pl. ii. fig. 16.

[2] Similar curved lines and technique are also to be seen on a food vessel from Co. Carlow, *Arch.* xliii. 382, fig. 75.

the beaker are nearly contemporary. In the Kinneff example the groove is filled up and nearly flat, as in some of the latest Hibernian specimens, such as fig. 248 from Queen's County, found with two spiral bronze bracelets of Bronze Age I (O. 48).

Fig. 347 from near Stonehaven, fig. 348 from East Lothian, fig. 349 from the I. of Skye, and fig. 350 from near Arbroath, all of inferior workmanship, are evidently of later date, and the last three have a height of from 6 to $6\frac{1}{2}$ in.

Fig. 350 *bis* from Over Dalserf in Lanark has a height of $4\frac{1}{2}$ in., and is perhaps a variety of this type with two grooves at the shoulder.

TYPE 1a IN HIBERNIA

Not many examples of this type have come down to us, but they are none the less interesting. Like type 2 it is evidently descended from a bowl-shaped prototype. This is seen very clearly by comparing fig. 351 of 1a with fig. 308 of type 2, both of them from Ulster. Both have the same height of $3\frac{3}{4}$ in., and the only difference, apart from the ornamentation, consists in the ears or stops placed in the groove of the former vessel. Most of the examples are of small size. The first three, figs. 351-3, all probably from Ulster, have a height of $3\frac{3}{4}$ in.; the next two, figs. 354, 355, have a height of $4\frac{1}{2}$ in. and less. Fig. 259 from Ballywillan, Co. Antrim, is only $4\frac{1}{2}$ in. high, but in general appearance resembles fig. 357 from Croghan, Co. Tyrone, which has a height of $6\frac{3}{4}$ in., and is, moreover, a by-form, having developed a second groove below the shoulder. Figs. 356, 358, both small vessels, are later forms which seem to descend from 1a. A very fine example of 1a, 5 inches high, from Co. Tyrone, with flat sides in the lower part of the vessel, with five perforated stops set in a narrow groove, and with a well-moulded lip, looks quite like a specimen from Region II.[1] In form and height it closely resembles fig. 137 from the East Riding, while the ornament, which covers entirely the lower part of the vessel, is much like that on fig. 141 from the North Riding. It follows from this that it is the later Hibernian examples of 1a that most resemble those from Region II.

TYPE 1a IN NORTH BRITAIN

Altogether two dozen examples of this type are reproduced and some of them must be passed briefly in review. The series is irregular and, no doubt, covers a considerable space of time. With few exceptions, both in form and especially in ornamentation, these examples differ considerably from the older Hibernian specimens and stand nearer to those of Region II.

In three examples from Lanarkshire, Ayrshire, and Arran[2] the lip is not moulded, in which respect they tally better with Hibernian examples. The first two are small with a height of $3\frac{3}{4}$ and $4\frac{3}{4}$ inches, but the third from Arran is 6 in. high, and is ornamented on the bottom with a double row of triangular impressions. Fig. 362 from Ardrossan, Ayrshire, was found with a cremated interment. In an adjoining cist lay fig. 362 *bis* of type 2. Fig. 363, with a height of 5 in., is a fine example with two perforated ears, from Netherdale in Banffshire, and is the most northerly of the twenty-four specimens here figured. Fig. 364 of the same height as the last, with four large perforated ears, is from Forfarshire, and differs very considerably from the others; here again the lip is not moulded. Fig. 365, found in East Lothian, measures only $3\frac{3}{4}$ in. in height, and greatly resembles examples from Region II. Fig. 366, with a height of $4\frac{1}{4}$ in., was found in a cist with a cremated interment under a cairn on the Isle of Cumbrae, close to the cairn which contained fig. 340 of

---

[1] *J. R. Hist. Arch. Ass. Ireland*, 4 ser., vol. i. 9.　　　　[2] Figs. 261, 359, 360.

type 2, and perhaps in age the vessels are not very far apart. Fig. 367, of about the same size as the last, came from North Ayrshire, and fig. 368 with a height of 5 in., now in the Hunterian Museum, Glasgow, was probably found in the vicinity of that city. All three examples are much alike. Figs. 370, 371, with a height of 5¼ in. and 4¾ in., from near Stirling and near Borthwick, Midlothian, like the first three mentioned, have a straight unmoulded lip, and the form of the latter reminds us of fig. 358 from Co. Londonderry. In fig. 372, with a height of 5 in., from near Dunfermline, Fife, the ears are external from not being protected by the groove, which has become a flat surface. Both figs. 374, 376, which appear to be late examples, are from Forfarshire.

Fig. 263 from near Doune, Perthshire, was found with a small mallet-shaped hammer of veined quartzite, 2½ in. long, that could hardly have been meant for use. The vessel itself is not unlike fig. 264 from near Crail in Fife, which was found with fig. 265, 5¾ in. high, an example of type 2, in which the space between the moulded lip and the upper moulding of the groove is reduced to a minimum. These three vessels may therefore be considered as later than the invasion. Fig. 266, 5½ in. high, from Bute, was found with a burnt interment, and is ornamented on the bottom with a cruciform motive. It was accompanied by a fusiform jet bead and a bronze awl or pricker. In all probability it is later than the invasion. Figs. 267, 268 from Fife are undoubtedly late examples. Fig. 271 from Midlothian is said to have been found with a portion of a bronze ring like that with fig. 253 from Kinneff, though this statement is not quite certain.

TYPE C IN HIBERNIA

This is a type derived from a bowl-shaped vessel on the sides of which two or more grooves have developed. Being few in number—only nine examples are figured—they do not form a con-secutive series, though all show some evidence of their origin and descent.

Fig. 234, 4⅜ in. high (P. 56), was found under the same cairn at Mt. Stewart, Co. Down, as the lost beaker fig. 223. Fig. 254, 4¾ in. high (P. 69), from Co. Sligo, was found with a cremated interment, and a small but thick stone celt, 3½ in. long, the butt-end of which terminates in a point (O. 49). Fig. 255, 6 in. in height (P. 70), from Co. Cavan, was also found with a small stone celt, measuring 3¾ × 1⅜ in., and a bone hasp (O. 50a, b). The type has a wide range from Co. Londonderry in the north to Co. Wexford in the south, with three western examples from Co. Sligo and Mayo. On figs. 379, 380 from Co. Kilkenny and Co. Sligo we may observe a double row of bar-chevrons arranged so as to form a bar-lozenge motive, but more perfectly executed than on fig. 299 of the later half of type A. The square-notch technique is perhaps visible on fig. 379, but not on other examples, so that it has evidently fallen into disuse. Fig. 382 from Moytura, Co. Mayo, so celebrated in the mythical traditions of Hibernia, is evidently a good deal later than the others and, moreover, is provided with four imperforate stops.

TYPE D IN HIBERNIA AND NORTH BRITAIN

This extremely rare type is evidently derived from a bowl-shaped vessel which has developed an everted neck. Each example differs so much from the others that there can be no genetic relation between them, but to avoid too much splitting and subdivision I have grouped them together.

Fig. 383 was found in a cist under a cairn near Tuam, Co. Galway, and is probably an early example. Where fig. 384 was discovered is unknown, and its ornamentation is so unique that it is impossible even to guess where it was brought to light. The only observation to be made is that it belongs to a time prior to the final extinction of the false-relief technique. Fig. 385 from Co. Waterford is evidently later; we find new linear motives of ornament no longer executed with a notched instrument. In both these examples it will be noticed that the ornament is directed rather vertically than horizontally, especially in the former.

The North British example, fig. 258, 3½ in. high (P. 72), from Murrayfield, Edinburgh, shows Hibernian influence very clearly in the ornamentation, which is beautifully executed. The well-formed bar-lozenge motive forming a zone a little below the centre may be compared with that on fig. 379 from Co. Kilkenny.

In this type may be included fig. 227 from Jesmond, Northumberland. The central zone of bar-lozenges in false relief is the same as that on the lower zone on fig. 258 from Edinburgh, a fact which strengthens the belief that the vessels of Hibernian appearance in Northumberland were due to the presence of some natives of North Britain.

Perhaps fig. 386, 5 in. high, from Greenford, Forfarshire, belongs to this type. It is a fine and apparently early vessel, as the lower part is so well rounded and the ornament so carefully executed.

TYPE 3 IN NORTH BRITAIN

In Hibernia this form of vessel does not seem to be known. It is sometimes impossible to say whether a vessel ought to range under type 3 or type 4, especially when the rim is moulded and the vessel has been subjected to posthumous deformation.

Fig. 387 from Forfarshire is 5⅜ in. high, and was found with a semicircular knife of agate. Fig. 388, 3¾ in. high, is from Yetholm, Roxburgh. Fig. 389 from Rudle, Argyll, is 6 in. high, and came from a small cist without any remains of a body. The next two, figs. 390, 391 from Alness in Ross, were from the same grave. Figs. 273, 274 from East Lothian were found in the same cist as fig. 275, which perhaps is an example of type 4. All these examples seem to belong to the last half of the food vessel-period.

TYPES 4, 4a, 4b, E, IN HIBERNIA

In its most simple form the biconical vessel is very rare in Hibernia, and only one example is figured, fig. 403. In spite of its simple form I have placed it later than the examples of type 4a with everted lip, as it is certainly later than some of them. In type E, of which there seems to be but a single example, the neck is unusually long, and may be regarded as a variant of type 4a.

Fig. 392 from Headfort, Co. Galway, is 5¼ in. high, and seems to be derived from a vessel like fig. 383 of type D from the same county by flattening the rounded curves of the body. The localities where figs. 393, 398, 400, all in the Dublin Museum, were discovered is unknown. Figs. 396, 397 are probably from Ulster. Fig. 394, with a height of 5½ in., was found in a small chamber (a cist?) at the Moat of Sionon, Co. Westmeath. Fig. 395 is 5 in. high, and was found in a cist with another vessel in the Townland of Ballyare, Co. Donegal. Fig. 256 (P. 71) of type E from Co. Fermanagh was found with a flat bronze dagger, 5⅜ in. long, with two engraved lines parallel to the edges, and originally with four rivets, of which two remain (O. 51). Fig. 399, 3¼ in. high, from Kilbride, Co. Wicklow, was found inverted in a cist so as to cover two small human bones, the joints of a finger and toe. Fig. 401 from near Fermoy, Co. Cork, has begun to develop a moulding at the shoulder, and the ornament shows that the false-relief technique is not quite extinct, although in Volume II it will be found that this technique extended into the Cinerary Period of Bronze Age II, or later. Fig. 402 is 5¼ in. high, and came from near Talbotstown, Co. Wicklow. Fig. 403 is a good example of type 4, and probably was found somewhere in Ulster. Fig. 404 has a height of 5½ in., and probably came from Ulster. It differs much from other examples, has a groove round the middle, and perhaps does not belong to the type at all.

Fig. 244, with a height of 6 in., is an example of type 4b (P. 61). Though not a central interment the rounded form of the lower half of the vessels shows that it is fairly early, and the bar-chevrons in false relief may be compared with those on figs. 313, 353. It was found in a large mound in the Phoenix Park, Dublin, with two others which were broken. Another vessel much like it in form came from a cairn on Forth Mountain, near Wexford.[1] For a very similar variety of the biconical type see fig. 362 *bis* from near Ardrossan in Ayrshire, a vessel which is probably contemporary or nearly so with fig. 362.

[1] *P. R. S. A. Ir.*, 5 ser., v. 384.

TYPES 4, 4a IN NORTH BRITAIN

Here again it is not easy to be certain that all the examples illustrated belong to these types or to 3a. But as the types must have been largely contemporary this difficulty and uncertainty is of less moment. The examples form anything but a connected series, and no details are known with regard to the discovery of figs. 405–11.

Fig. 405 from a cist near Loch Awe, Argyll, has a height of 6½ in. Fig. 406 from Cramond, Midlothian, was found beside a row of cists and has a height of 5 in. Fig. 407, with a height of 4 in., was found in a gravel pit near Old Luce in Wigtonshire. Fig. 408, with a height of 4¾ in., came from Cawdor in Nairnshire. Fig. 410, with a height of 5½ in., was found in a cist at Quinish in the I. of Mull. Fig. 411 from Gullane, East Lothian, has a height of 4¾ in., and came to light while excavating for a quarry.

Examples that resemble fig. 269, which has a height of 5½ in., can be dated to a certain extent. This one was found at Balcalk, Forfarshire, with an unburnt body in a cist, together with a lignite or jet necklace composed of fusiform beads, six very neatly ornamented plates of the same material, and one small triangular pendant. Fig. 270, 5 in. high, from near Forfar, was found in a rather large cist while excavating for gravel. In an adjoining cist, about 7 ft. from the above, but at a higher level, had been deposited a lignite necklace similar to the other one. Clearly fig. 270 belonged to the earlier interment, and it has all the appearance of being an older specimen than fig. 269. These necklaces are certainly later than those composed of disc-shaped beads with a small triangular pendant (P. 79, 80).

TYPE 5 (TRUNCATED CONE) IN HIBERNIA AND NORTH BRITAIN

In neither quarter of Region III is this a common type. A fairly early example of it is seen in fig. 246 from Ardna, Co. Meath. It is contemporary with fig. 245 of type 2 (P. 62).

Fig. 412, 4½ in. high, was found in a small cist near Ardrossan, Ayrshire, and contained burnt bones and charcoal.

Fig. 277 bis from Banffshire was found with gold rings and fragments of a bronze blade (P. 85).

Fig. 262 from near Hamilton, Lanarkshire, is contemporary with fig. 261 of type 1 (P. 74).

TYPE 6 IN HIBERNIA AND NORTH BRITAIN

The cylindrical form was not much used in Region III, though a few good specimens are known.

Fig. 413 is a Hibernian example, but the place where it was disinterred is unknown. It belongs to a period during which the notched technique was in use.

Fig. 414 is 5½ in. high, and was found at Darnhall, Peeblesshire. It seems to belong to about the same time as fig. 371 from near Borthwick, Midlothian.

Fig. 415 is 3½ in. high, and was found near Urquhart, Elginshire, in a rather large cist with abundance of charcoal and ashes, but no trace of bone.

Fig. 416 has a height of 4⅜ in., and comes from Tyrie in Aberdeenshire. The cist was of no great volume, and was paved with rounded pebbles of uniform size and appearance. It contained the skeleton of an aged man with a cephalic index of 83·6, and with a height of about 5 ft. 4 inches. No doubt this old man was descended from the brachycephalic invaders. The slight constriction round the middle is seen on fig. 338 from Inverness-shire.

VESSELS OF NO TYPE IN HIBERNIA AND NORTH BRITAIN

There are a few vessels of anomalous form which cannot easily be enrolled under any of the above types and are therefore taken separately at the end.

Fig. 417 was brought to light at some unknown place in Ireland. Perhaps it is a variant of type 4 a, such as fig. 392.

Figs. 418, 419, 420 came from near Stirling. The first of these is 5½ in. high and resembles type C in Hibernia, though this vessel seems to be later than those figured above. The second was found in a sand quarry, about 1 ft. from the surface, and is ornamented with the cord technique.

Fig. 421, from Urquhart in Elginshire, appears to be derived from a bowl-shaped prototype, and belongs to a time when the square-notch technique was still in current use.

Fig. 422 is 5½ in. high and came from a cist at Kirkmabreck, Kirkcudbrightshire.

THE TIME RELATION BETWEEN REGIONS II AND III

After describing the various types of pottery in Region III on both sides of the Irish Channel, it remains to correlate them with types in Region II. To obtain a relatively fixed point of departure, we begin with the beaker said to have been found in the cairn at Mt. Stewart, Co. Down, within sight of the coast of Galloway. It is apparently contemporary with examples of types A and C. But before going further one observation must be made. Although all the variations of type A and its derivative type 2 are derived from a similar round bowl, yet the original form seems to have persisted without much change of form while the developments were taking place, just as the stem of a tree continues its upward growth, though throwing out lateral branches from time to time. For instance, in Par. 54 *bis* we have to assume that fig. 231 of type 1 a is contemporary with fig. 232 of type A, and that both are derived from a similar bowl-like vessel. The first assumption may be erroneous, but at present there is no escape from it.

According to the Time-scale of beakers, such a vessel may have reached Galloway and immediately have passed over to Hibernia about six generations after the invasion of Britain by the brachycephals. The same date must be assumed for fig. 233 of type A from Mt. Stewart, Co. Down. The examples of type A from Duncragaig in Argyll (figs. 236, 237) may be a little earlier. As the base of the example of type A, fig. 239, from Kilmartin, also in Argyll, is considerably smaller than that of the Mt. Stewart specimen, it is the earlier of the two. The example of type 2 (fig. 238) from Kilmartin is again earlier, as it belonged to the central interment.

It can hardly be doubted that the example of type A, fig. 232, and of type 1 a from Broughshane, Co. Antrim, are earlier than any of the preceding vessels. The ornament on the last-named food vessel is partly produced by a notched slip of wood, a process seldom seen on food vessels in Region II. A fine specimen of type 2 (fig. 310), from the Gap of Gorteen, Co. Tyrone, may be nearly contemporary with the vessels from Broughshane.

Beginning from the end of the 6th generation, the above observations may be tabulated as follows :

YEARS	GENERAT.	PLACE	BEAKER	TYPE A	TYPE 1a	TYPE 2
180	6	Mt. Stewart	223	233		
		Duncragaig		236, 237		
150	5	Kilmartin		239		
120	4	Kilmartin				238
		Gap of Gorteen				310
90	3	Broughshane		232	231	

As the earliest food vessels of type 1a that can be dated by beakers in Yorkshire are not earlier than the end of the 5th generation, and the earliest Derbyshire example is hardly earlier, it is evident that the type was known in Hibernia at a period anterior to these, and may have been introduced into Region II before the arrival of the invaders. For instance, fig. 125 of type 1 from Colewell, Northumberland, has much the form of fig. 310 from the Gap of Gorteen, and may with certainty be considered earlier than the invasion of Region II. Further north the great cairn at Kilmartin (P. 58), from which came a beautiful specimen of type 2 (fig. 238), was there before the invaders entered Argyll, and therefore before the beaker (fig. 185) from the same parish of Kilmartin was fabricated. On the other hand, the examples of type 2 (figs. 249, 250) from the islands of Arran and Bute are later than the Kilmartin specimen, are posterior to the invasion of Region III, and might be assigned to the 7th or 8th generation of the invaders. A still later example of type 2 (fig. 253), from Kinneff, Kincardine, and perhaps fig. 271, an example of type 1a from Ratho, Midlothian, may be equated with beaker fig. 213 of type C, from Crawford, Lanarkshire, by reason of similar bronze rings, 3 in. in diameter, found with each, though the Ratho example is uncertain. The age of beakers of type C in Province V is difficult to determine, but it might fall perhaps in the 9th or 10th generation, and this would suit the development of type 2, comparing fig. 253 with figs. 249, 250.

An example of type 2 (fig. 247), from Corky, Co. Antrim (P. 65), is later than that from the Gap of Gorteen (fig. 310), and may be equated with an example of type 3 like fig. 72 from the East Riding, owing to a similar bronze knife found with each. They may belong to about the 5th generation, corresponding with Phase I of beaker type A in Region II.

In trying to ascertain the direction taken by the sequences of types 2 and 1a in Region II, we arrived at the conclusion that vessels with a low-placed groove are older than those in which it is placed high. This conclusion is supported by observing the development of these types in Hibernia. In the series figs. 307–11 of type 2 the groove is very low, and fig. 310 from the Gap of Gorteen we have seen to be older than any example in Region II. Fig. 351 of type 1a from Ulster, with low-placed groove and well-developed moulding above it and large ears, may be compared with figs. 126, 127 of the same type, from Yorkshire and Derbyshire, which seem to be the oldest examples in Region II. Another early example from Derbyshire, fig. 102, has considerable analogy with fig. 310 from the Gap of Gorteen. In both the mouldings of the groove are angular, and in both these mouldings are ornamented with vertical markings. But the latter is the older of the two, as its lower part is more rounded and bowl-shaped.

The difference in form between vessels of type 1 in Hibernia and 1*a* in Region II is that in the latter the lip is always moulded, while that feature is exceptional in the former country. But we find fairly early specimens of type 1*a*, such as figs. 362, 363, in North Britain, and it is probably from there that this type permeated into Region II. The moulded lip served a useful purpose and so came early into use in Region II, in fact it is seen on neolithic vessels from Yorkshire and Argyll. So, if type 1 rather than type 1*a* was first introduced, it would at once be modified into type 1*a*.

In conclusion, Table VI has been drawn up to show some of the food vessels of Region III arranged in what appears to be roughly their chronological sequence. It stops at about the 10th generation, which is approximately determined by the beaker fig. 213 of type C. Later than that it is impossible at present to fix any relative dates. Fortunately, a bronze knife-dagger of Bronze Age II allows us to bring down with certainty one vessel (fig. 256, P. 71) at any rate to that period. The vessel is characterized by a rather high neck, and is ornamented with shaded triangles. Shaded triangles such as are seen on figs. 392, 393, 402 are found on several Hibernian urns of the cinerary period. So possibly these vessels, and perhaps others like them in form, also belong to the Bronze Age II.

There is a difficulty in synchronizing vessels of type A owing to its persistence, as has been mentioned above, and so the generations to which I have assigned various vessels of types 1, 1*a*, 2 must not be taken too strictly. They are only approximations, and are partly meant to show that certain vessels in North Britain are anterior to its invasion by the brachycephals.

TABLE VI. RELATIVE AGE OF FOOD VESSELS IN REGION III

Years	Generations	Beakers	Type A	1, 1a	2	E	C	D	3	4a	6
90	3		232 306	231	308, 299 310, 309						
120	4		293–7	351	238						
150	5		239 236, 237	352, 353 355	311, 339 340–2, 336			258			244
180	6	223	233, 304	362, 363 365, 366	245, 337 247		234 379				
210	7			369, 370	249, 250		254, 255				
240	8			264	265 316, 317		380	383			
270	9				252						
300	10	213		271	253		382				
				273 266	346					387–91	269–70 405–12
				376							
								384 385			392–403
	BRONZE AGE II					256					

CHAPTER XI

ORNAMENTATION

(*Vide* Plates lvi, lvii, lviii) [1]

REGION I

THE ornamented food vessels of this region are so few in number that all that need be said is that the motives, though geometrical and simple, are not necessarily derived from those occurring upon beakers of Province I. Five examples are given on pl. lvi.

REGION II

By far the most usual ornament upon food vessels is a surface pattern, consisting of parallel line chevrons, which covers the whole vessel without any intervening plain band. Sometimes in the later examples the lower part of the vessel is left plain. Occasionally, however, we find motives that are used to decorate beakers. For instance, the bar-chevron formed by several parallel line chevrons from Derbyshire (F173) is found on beakers from the East Riding, Westmorland, and Northumberland.[2] The hanging triangles with diagonal shading from Yorkshire and Northumberland (F23, 144) are also to be seen on a North-umberland beaker (fig. 168). The rudely scratched bar-chevron motive from Derbyshire (F170) recurs on two Derbyshire beakers (figs. 52, 54). An irregular chequer pattern from Northumberland (F217) may be compared with a more regular one on a Yorkshire beaker (fig. 128), and with another which is more like it on a beaker from Fife (fig. 190). It is possible that in some instances the ornamental motives found upon a food vessel have been suggested by those seen on a beaker, but on the whole the ornamentation of the food vessel and beaker classes of ceramic is quite different, and is based upon a different tradition. A new motive, foreign to the beaker class, is found in three examples from Derbyshire and the East Riding.[3] It consists in horizontal lines of horse-shoe shaped marks, probably made by pressing on the moist clay with a piece of cord inserted under the thumb nail. The motives on two Northumberland food vessels (F223, 227) are quite strange, and we have already found reason to attribute the vessels to a Hibernian influence that had penetrated into the country from Region III, before Northumberland was reached by the short-headed invaders.

REGION III

Although in this region some of the ornamental motives on food vessels are similar to those that occur on beakers, the absence of plain bands proves that the original tradition of these two classes of ceramic was different. Even when the motive is the same, we may some-times be sure that no borrowing had taken place. For instance, the chequer pattern from

---

[1] References to the Plates of Ornament are made by F followed by a numeral.

[2] Figs. 137, 152, 160, 163, 183.

[3] F119, 195, 204, 213.

Antrim and Londonderry (F231, 377), one made with short strokes the other with the finger-nail, need not be compared with a similar motive on a beaker from Fife (F190), as the technique in each case is different. Nor can the bar-chevrons from Antrim and Aberdeenshire (F232, 304) be compared with others from the East Riding,[1] for here again the technique is different; the two former are executed in false relief, the two latter are flat. The motive formed by two bar-chevrons, placed so as to form an incomplete lozenge, from Co. Dublin (F299), is found upon a vessel belonging to the second part of type A, one sufficiently early to hinder us from believing that any influence attributable to the beaker ceramic could have reached so far south when the food vessel was made, though the same motive is to be seen on a Yorkshire beaker (F107). The bar-lozenge motive occurs on several beakers from the counties of Derby, Lancaster, and York,[2] but on none of them is the motive in all its details the same as that on a food vessel from Sligo (F380) and on another from Edinburgh (F258), and on none of the beakers is the design executed in false relief as is the case with the two food vessels. Apart from the probability that both these vessels are earlier than the invasion of the brachycephals into North Britain, it is hardly credible that this simple motive was a foreign importation. The hexagon motive on Hibernian vessels of type A (F296, 298) is also executed in false relief, and in that respect differs materially from the incised hexagons on beakers from Oxford and the East Riding (F64, 108). The idea must have suggested itself independently to the brachycephalic women who made beakers in South Britain and to the potters of Hibernia. Certainly for the square panels in false relief on a vessel of type A from Co. Sligo (F297), and for a later development of the motive on an example of type 1 from Ulster (F351), and for the four-rayed star pattern from West Meath (F394) there is no sort of analogy upon any beaker. The conception of these motives is purely Hibernian; another new design is to be seen in F325.

In Region III we can observe on later vessels a change in the style of ornamentation. The false-relief technique and the motives of ornament for which it is specially adapted fell into disuse and were replaced by combinations of incised straight lines, thus bringing the ornamentation into line with the simple decoration of food vessels in Region II. It is difficult to say whether this development on Hibernian soil was entirely spontaneous or the result of influence from the east—the result of an inflow of brachycephalic strangers after their occupation of Province V. For instance, a fine example of type 1a from Co. Tyrone, both in form and ornamentation,[3] as has already been said, is quite like examples from Region II, and the rather elongated line chevrons of F332 from Co. Down on a late example of type 2 are to be seen on vessels from Arran and Bute[4] that belong to a time subsequent to the invasion of the brachycephals. The elements that compose the incised decoration of F348 from East Lothian, a late example of type 2 and also later than the invasion, are common on the beakers of North Britain. The same may be said for the chequer pattern from Forfarshire (F387) executed with the cord technique and for the motives that compose the ornamentation of F421 from Elginshire. These three North British specimens were probably ornamented by persons who had inherited a knowledge of the ornament used for beakers, and if that is true for North Britain it may also be true for Co. Down (fig. 332). And this does not stand alone, for

[1] F112, 130.
[2] F54, 67, 98, 104, 124, 152.
[3] The ornament is shown on Plate lviii next after F352. Figs. 249, 250.

in another example from the same county (F329) the elements of the motive can be recognized as those of the beakers of North Britain.

Beaker fragments from Sligo and the lost beaker from Co. Down are not in themselves sufficient to make it certain that the brachycephalic invaders of Britain passed over into Hibernia in any numbers. It may be that these vessels were made by the foreign women captured in war, or by natives who had learnt the art in Britain. Nothing but craniological evidence, which at present is not forthcoming, can throw any light upon this important problem. If in the future there should be discovered in Hibernia brachycephalic or mesocephalic skulls associated with pottery of the end of the beaker period or somewhat later, the point would be settled. As the matter stands at present, when once the beaker fell into disuse, there is no means of tracking the movements of the brachycephals except by their skulls, when these happen to be found with other kinds of pottery. It would be rather remarkable that a people, so pushing and so venturesome as the short-headed invaders of Britain undoubtedly were, should refrain from crossing the narrow sea that separates Galloway from the coast of Hibernia. So it cannot be thought unlikely that some of these hardy and enterprising people did penetrate into the north-eastern part of Hibernia, and perhaps their presence there may be witnessed by the two food vessels from Co. Down cited above.

THE TECHNIQUE

Ornamentation was effected partly in the same way as with beakers, partly by newer processes. The instruments employed by the makers of beakers and still in use were—(1) the square-notch stamp, (2) the twisted cord or thong, (3) the sharp or blunt point used both for incising and for making dots, (4) the finger-nail. To these three more must now be added—(5) the false-relief, (6) the whipped cord or thong, (7) the 'chain-looped' cord[1] techniques.

Although, as we have learnt, the square-notch stamp was the most usual technique employed in the ornamentation of beakers, it is extremely rare on food vessels of Region II.[2] It is very common, however, in Region III, though with the difference that the square impressions are often larger than those found on beakers, and the notched slip of wood was usually straight and not curved. As this technique was known and used in Hibernia and in the Isle of Arran as far back as the neolithic period, it could not have been borrowed from the beaker-using invaders of Britain.[3]

The twisted cord or thong technique was known in Region I, and was very commonly used in Region II for the ornamentation of food vessels, but it does not appear to have been used in Hibernia; in North Britain it is rare, and only seen on vessels which seem to be later than the invasion.[4] On this account it may be assumed that this technique was taken over from the invaders.

---

[1] A single cord looped rather tightly into what is known as the 'chain-loop' or 'chain-stitch' gives impressions on wet clay quite similar to those seen on some food vessels and cinerary urns. A cord is very easily and rapidly looped in this way. Mr. L. Mann maintains that such impressions were made with a four-plaited cord (*P. S. A. S.* xxxix. 537), but my experiments with such a plait do not bear out this contention, and the four-plait cord is much more difficult to make.

[2] Figs. 129, 137 of type 1*a* with perforated ears, fig. 102 of type 1*a* with imperforate ears, and fig. 194 of type 2. In Region I, fig. 4.

[3] *J. R. S. Ant. Ir.* xxxiv (1904), p. 271, fig. 3; *P. S. A. S.* xxxvii. 52, figs. 14, 16.

Figs. 374, 387, 388, 411, 412.

The false-relief technique was produced by pressing with a triangular-headed slip of wood or bone in such a way as to produce a bar-chevron in false relief, as the clay surrounding the motive had been pressed down. The deepest part of the impression was always at the point. In some instances the triangular head is very much rounded as if the thumb-nail had been used instead of a slip of wood. But the principle is always the same—the motive had to stand out in apparent, though not real, relief. This technique was common in Region III, especially in Hibernia, where no doubt it originated. There it was often used in a bold and effective manner which is very striking. On the other hand, it was hardly known in Region II,[1] where it was only once used in a way that recalls the tradition of Region III. It has already been shown that the false-relief technique began early and made a good start, but gradually sank into insignificance, till finally it faded away.

The whipped cord or thong technique seems to have been effected by whipping fine twine or a slight thong round a thin pin or needle, sometimes round a stouter thong, and pressing it upon the moist clay, thus leaving a row of short parallel strokes like those that would be made by a fine-tooth comb.

This technique, judging from a woodcut, was known on the Isle of Arran in the neolithic period.[2] In Hibernia it appears on three early examples of type A from Ulster,[3] and on an early specimen of type 1a[4] from Co. Antrim. All these vessels are earlier than any food vessels ornamented with the same technique from North Britain or from Region II. It is also to be seen on an example of type 2 from Co. Tyrone,[5] and on a vessel of uncertain type from Ulster.[6]

In North Britain we find this technique employed on vessels of type 2, some of them late and none very early[7]; also upon vessels of types 3, 4a, 5, 6, and of no particular type.[8]

In Region II the whipped-cord technique is found on twelve examples of type 2[9]; twice on examples of type 1a,[10] four times on specimens of type 3,[11] and once on a four-footed vessel.[12] Figs. 22, 33 are early specimens, the first being contemporary with a necklace of disc-shaped beads. The others are later in various degrees.

As this technique was evidently indigenous in Hibernia and North Britain, it may have penetrated from the latter country into Region II, or, perhaps more likely, it was known to the natives of that region who were of the same stock as the Hibernians but had amalgamated with the invaders.

The 'chain-looped'-cord technique was effected by impressing such a cord upon the moist clay. It is very rare on food vessels, but is common on cinerary urns, especially in Cornwall, and only occurs twice in Region II on figs. 71, 229, both from the East Riding. The first is perhaps an example of type 4a, is 6½ in. high, and was found with a skeleton extended at full length, a very rare occurrence at this period. Food vessels of this form and height are therefore very late—nearly at the close of the food-vessel class of ceramic. The other vessel, in shape like a round box with a lid, is quite unique and recalls the three round box-like objects of chalk found with beaker fig. 152.

[1] Figs. 152, 155, both of type 1a, fig. 188.
[2] *P. S. A. S.* xxxvi. 90, fig. 12.
[3] Figs. 283, 287, 291.　　[4] Fig. 231.　　[5] Fig. 328.
[6] Fig. 404.　　[7] Figs. 253, 265, 268, 346, 349.
[8] Figs. 386, 408, 262, 415, 275, 277, 420.

[9] Figs. 22, 33, 42, 66, 100, 110, 169, 173, 175, 184, 189, 190.
[10] Figs. 136, 150.　　[11] Figs. 24, 196, 202, 214.
[12] Fig. 223 *bis*.

CHAPTER XII

OBJECTS FOUND WITH FOOD VESSELS

PLATES LIX TO LXI

REGION I

THE objects found with food vessels in this region are necessarily scanty in number, as so few vessels have been registered, but they include three knife-daggers of bronze, though all of these are unfortunately missing. To render the picture of the civilization of the inhabitants of South Britain more complete during the food-vessel period, I have added to the Table below some half-dozen bronze finds that occurred with skeleton interments, though here again in two or three instances the knife-daggers are lost. A tracing of a vessel, unique in this country, but which finds a good many close analogies in Armorica is also given, and finally I have included a cinerary interment accompanied by a remarkable knife-dagger which finds an exact parallel in two other similar instruments from the counties of Derby and York, discovered with skeleton interments.

VII. TABLE OF FINDS. REGION I

PLACE	Antlers	Boar's tusk	Spear-head	Axe-hammer	Flint arrow	Bone rings	Jet beads	Amber beads	V-buttons	'Pulley' ring	Awl	Dagger	Celt	Ornaments	Gold	REMARKS
			STONE									BRONZE				
B. 2 near Dorchester	×															
B. 12 near Dorchester	×	×	×	×												
Fig. 8 Came, Dorset					6											
„ 13 Black Burg, Sussex												×				Lost
Four-footed cup, Woodyates 4												×				Lost
Type 6 B. 26 Winterbourne							×	×			×	×				All lost
SKELETON INTERMENTS WITHOUT POTTERY																
B. 144 Normanton, Wilts.												×				Lost
Bush Barrow, Normanton, Wilts.				×		×						× ×	×		×	O. 26 a–f
Overton Hill, Wilts.											×	×	×			Lost
B. 18 Wilsford, Wilts.				×									×	×		O. 27 a–c
B. 16 Winterbourne Stoke, Wilts.												× ×				O. 28 a–c
B. 24 Brigmilston, Wilts.												×		×		Cremated, O. 29a, b
Upton, Wilts.												×				Lost

In a large barrow at Upton, Wilts., 13 ft. high, at a depth of 5 ft. from the top was discovered a skeleton lying in a wooden box or trunk of a tree, and a small brass dagger too corroded to bear removal.[1]

B. 144 Normanton, Wilts., contained a decayed skeleton and a small lance-head (knife-dagger) of brass,[2] (lost).

Bush Barrow, Normanton. On the floor of the barrow lay the skeleton of a tall, stout man. About 18 in. from the head were several bronze rivets (28 small and one large are in the Devizes Museum[3]) and thin bits of bronze mixed with wood. Near the shoulders was a bronze celt 6⅜ in. long (O. 26c) that had originally been inserted in a wooden handle. Near the right arm lay two large knife-daggers, measuring 10⅝ in. × 3⅛ in. and 13 in. respectively; one flat, the other with a stout midrib (O. 26a, b). The handle of the smaller one was ornamented with a pattern of bar-chevrons formed of thousands of minute gold pins ₁⁄₁₈ in. long.[4] This was accompanied by a thin plate of gold, 3 × 2¾ in., with incised lines on its surface and a hook in the centre. ' Possibly this was the gold covering of the end of the sheath and the hook by which it was attached to the belt ' (O. 26f). On the breast of the skeleton lay a lozenge-shaped plate of gold, 7¼ in. × 6⅛ in., with two holes at the top and bottom; the edge lapped over a plate of wood (O. 26e). The extreme accuracy and perfection of the engraved lines could not be surpassed by a modern engraver. On the right side of the body was a perforated stone hammer of oolitic stone 4⅜ in. long (O. 26d). The handle was apparently fixed by a bronze fastening, signs of which remain. Many small rings of bone and a small lozenge-shaped ornament of thin gold slightly ornamented were also found with this interment.[5]

Both this long dagger with a rudimentary tang, which M. S. Reinach derives, if I remember rightly, from tanged arrowheads of flint, and the ornamentation of the handle by means of thousands of tiny gold nails are unique, I believe, in Britain, but have many analogies in Armorica. Five types of dagger with rudimentary tang, with 2, 6, and 8 rivets, from the Côtes-du-Nord and Finistère are figured by M. Micault[6] and four examples from Finistère are figured by Lindenschmit.[7] In the Côtes-du-Nord and in Morbihan six interments have been recorded in which the flat, triangular bronze daggers have had their handles ornamented with minute gold nails about 1 mm. in length. And at Port-ar-Soaz four daggers were found, the leather scabbards of which were similarly decorated.[8]

The interesting find from the Bush Barrow, Normanton, seems to point to direct or indirect communication at an early period with Armorica, and we shall soon see that this is not an only instance.

Overton Hill, bar. 1, Wilts. At a depth of 10 ft. was discovered a skeleton lying in the trunk of a tree, and with it a lance-head (knife-dagger), a small celt, and a long pin, all of brass.[9] These objects appear to be lost.

Wilsford, bar. 18, Wilts. This was a large bell-barrow with a diameter of 121 ft. and a height of 11 ft. On the floor of the barrow lay the skeleton of a very tall, stout man. At his feet was a perforated hammer-axe of diorite 4⅛ in. long (O. 27b), a slightly flanged bronze celt 3¾ × 1⅜ in. (O. 27c), a tube made from the leg bone of an animal, the bone handle of some implement, a grooved whetstone, several articles of bone, and a fork-shaped object of twisted bronze, with three links of a chain suspending from the centre (O. 27a).[10]

Winterbourne Stoke, bar. 16, Wilts. This was a large barrow with a diameter of 112 ft. and a height of 15 ft. The central interment consisted of a skeleton placed in the hollowed trunk of elm, with a vessel of fine red colour having five small handles (O. 28c). Near the breast was a bronze dagger 8½ × 2½ in. 'This is a broad-bladed, straight-sided, and pointed dagger, with a groove and 2 lines following the edge. It had 4 rivets' (O. 28a). With it was a bronze awl with a well-made bone handle.[11] Near the thigh lay another bronze dagger. 'It is narrow bladed, with bevelled edge and 2 parallel lines following the contour, 4 rivets originally (?). Dimensions, 8½ × 2 in.' (O. 28b). [12]

The vessel found with this interment is unique in Britain, but it belongs to the same type as fig. 54* (pl. iii), from Keréon-en-Crozon, Finistère, from the collection of M. du Chatellier, who very

[1] A. W. 52.   [2] A. W. 200.
[3] No. 162.   [4] Evans, Anc. Br. Imp., fig. 289.
[5] A. W. 203, and Devizes Mus. Cat.
[6] Invent. des épées et poign. de bronze trouvés aan ia Bretagne. St. Brieuc, 1883–84.
[7] Alt. uns. heid. Vorzeit i, Heft 11, Taf. ii, figs. 1, 2, 9, 10.
[8] L'Anthropologie x (1899), p. 578.
[9] A. W. ii. 90.   [10] A. W. 209.
[11] Evans, Br. Age, fig. 227.   [12] A. W. 123.

kindly allowed me to photograph several others of the same type in his possession. This one has a height of 7¼ in. and others vary in this respect from 6½ to 9½ in. It was accompanied by a triangular bronze dagger 6 in. long by 1½ in. wide at the base and much thickened at the centre. It is ornamented with a hollow line parallel to the edge.[1] The type belongs to the true Bronze Age and often, if not always, accompanies cinerary interment. This vessel is another proof, in addition to that afforded by the dagger from the Bush Barrow, Normanton, that some intercourse was maintained between the south of Britain and Armorica in the early Bronze Age.

With a cremated interment in bar. 24, Brigmilston or Brigmerston, Wilts., was found a thin, broad, flat bronze dagger measuring 8½ × 2⅜ in. The wooden handle is held together by 30 bronze rivets, and the bone pommel is attached by 2 pegs (O. 29a). With it was a large, stout bronze pin with 2 rings at the head, and a smaller one hanging from each of these (O. 29b).[2] Another bronze pin, crutch-headed, with a spiral twist of the stem and the head pierced lengthways, is believed to have been found in this or in an adjoining barrow (O. 29c). A similar dagger with 30 rivets, and 2 pins of bronze were found beside a skeleton in a barrow at Net Lowe Hill, Derbyshire, together with 2 shale buttons with the V-shaped perforation.[3] Another with 37 rivets was found by Mr. Mortimer in a barrow at Garton Slack (O. 40) with a skeleton.[4]

Assuming that the seven interments without pottery in the Table of Finds belong to the time when food vessels were in use—for only one (B. 9 Fovant) could well be included in the period of beakers—there are 13 finds to compare with 16 beaker finds (v. Table of Finds for Province I, p. 52).

	Flint dagger	Stone axe-hammer	Flint arrowhead	BRONZE				Gold
				Knife-dagger	Awl	Celt	Pin	
Beaker Period . . .	2	2	2	9	o	o	o	1
Food vessel Period . .	o	3	1	11	2	3	2	1

From this abridged Table we observe that flint knife-daggers are not represented among the food vessels, just as we have found above, in Region II, perhaps for the reason there suggested. As regards stone axe-hammers and flint arrowheads the difference between the two classes is trifling. On the other hand, the food-vessel period is richer in bronze, 11 knife-daggers to 9 ; 3 celts, 2 awls, and 2 pins to none. If this represents the true state of affairs it confirms a conclusion already reached that the food-vessel class outlived the beaker class, though both were partly contemporary.

Out of these eleven knife-daggers only five have been preserved, so far as I know. Their dimensions are as follows :

[1] P. du Chatellier, *Les Époques préhist. dans le Finistère*, 2nd ed., p. 186. [2] *Cat. Dev. Mus.*, p. 30

[3] Bateman, *Vestiges*, pp. 68, 69. [4] *Forty years*, pp. 231-2.

PLATE OF OBJECTS (PL. LX)	PLACE	LENGTH	BREADTH IN INCHES	No. OF RIVETS	DESCRIPTION
O. 26a	Bush Barrow, Normanton . .	$10\frac{5}{8}$	$3\frac{1}{8}$	6	Flat, straight sides, embryo tang
O. 26b	Bush Barrow, Normanton . .	13		6	Stout midrib, heavy
O. 28a	B. 16 Winterbourne Stoke . .	$8\frac{1}{2}$	$2\frac{1}{2}$	4	Straight sides, pointed, ornamented
O. 28b	B. 16 Winterbourne Stoke . .	$8\frac{1}{2}$	2	4 ?	,, ,, ,, ,,
O. 29a	B. 24 Brigmilston (cremated) .	$8\frac{1}{2}$	$2\frac{5}{8}$	9	Flat, round-headed ,, ,,

None of these knife-daggers has a regular tang, so they can only be compared with O. 5, 6, 11a of Province I, the last of which was not found with a beaker and perhaps ought not to have been included, although found with a 'pulley-ring'. The only blade comparable with these is O. 29a, contemporary with a bronze pin with a double ring at the head, and found with a cremated interment. O. 10 of Bronze Age II, though smaller than O. 28a, b, approximates them in type, and is later than we should expect with a beaker interment,[1] so we may be quite sure that these last two blades, and also O. 26a, b, are later than any knife-daggers deposited with beakers. Although not found with food vessels they were found with skeleton interments, and are close to the time when cinerary interments were becoming the prevailing fashion.

The bronze celt O. 26c measures $6\frac{3}{8} \times 2\frac{3}{8}$ in., and tapers each way from the central ridge without forming a true stop-ridge.

The bronze celt O. 27c measures $3\frac{1}{4} \times 1\frac{3}{8}$ in. and shows side flanges.

The two bronze pins O. 29b, c measure $6\frac{1}{2}$ in. and $6\frac{1}{4}$ in. respectively. A bone pin with a perforated crutch-head, from a skeleton grave at Male Čičovice in Bohemia, is figured by Dr. Pič.[2] It is a rare type. Prof. Lissauer cites single examples in silver from Remedello, in copper from the pile-dwellings of L. Bienne and from Mecklenburg. The pins with one, two, or three rings at the head are more diffused than the above, but still are rare. He places all these pins in Bronze Age I of Montelius and therefore earlier than the true Bronze Age.[3]

The use of the bronze forked object, O. 27a, which measures $6\frac{1}{8} \times 4\frac{1}{2}$ in., is unknown.

[1] The beaker is lost, and a doubt may be entertained whether the vessel really belonged to that class.

[2] Pič, op. cit. i, Tab. viii. 9.

[3] Lissauer, Z. E. (1907), p. 796, figs. 28–30, p. 793.

FIG.	PLACE	Worked flint, knife or spearhead	Flint scraper	Flint arrowheads	Boar's tusk	Tine of stag	Bone pin	Bone beads	Worked bone	Buttons, V-shaped perforation	Jet necklace	Jet ornament	Bronze awl or pricker	Bronze knife	Bronze ear-rings	REMARKS
22	B. 75 Garton Slack, E. R.	..	..	..	..	..	..	..	..	..	×	..	×			
24	B. 75 Garton Slack, E. R.	×	..	..	..	..	..	..	..	..	..	..	×			
28	B. 21 Ganton, E. R.	..	..	×												
31	B. 21 Ganton, E. R.	..	..	..	×											
43	Cawthorn Camp, N. R.	×														
45	B. 41 The Riggs, E. R.	×														
47	B. 87 Aldro, E. R.	×														
49	B. 255 Bishop Burton, E. R.	×														
53	B. 101 Garrowby Wold, E. R.	..	..							..	..	..	×	..	..	Female interment
54	B. 111 Goodmanham, E. R.	..	×													
59	B. 153 Garton Slack, E. R.	..	..		..	..	..		..	..	..	×	..	..	×	
68	Cross Lowe, Derby.	..	..		..	..	×									
71	B. 94 Goodmanham.	..	×													
73	B. 205 Acklam Wold, E. R.	×														
Like 72	B. 294 Life Hill, E. R.	×	..	..	..	..	..	..	..	..	..	..	×	×	..	Male interment
77	Pickering, N. R.	×														
78	B. 257 Bishop Burton, E. R.	×														
84	B. 237 Blanch Group, E. R.	..	×													
87	B. 71 Folkton, E. R.	..	..	..	..	..	..	..	..	×	..	..	..	..	..	Male interment
88	B. 71 Folkton, E. R.	..	×	..	..	..	..	×	..	..	..	..	×	..	..	Female interment
100	B. 37 Garton Slack, E. R.	..	..	..	..	..	×									
101	Monsal Dale, Derby.	..	..	..	..	..	×									
103	Driffield, E. R.	×	..	..	..	..	..	..	×							
105	B. 63 Rudstone, E. R.	..	..	×												
110	B. 62 Rudstone	..	..	..	..	..	..	..	..	..	..	..	×	..	..	Female interment
111	B. 204 Acklam Wold, E. R.	×														
130	B. 102 Goodmanham, E. R.	×														
133	B. 35 Willerby, E. R.	×														
134	B. 197 Garrowby Wold, E. R.	×														
136	B. 250 Hunmanby, E. R.	×	..	..	..	..	×									
137	B. 162 Garton Slack, E. R.	..	..	..	..	..	..	..	×							
139	B. 233 Gilling, E. R.	×														
141	Newton on Rawcliffe, N. R.	×	..	×												
143	B. 9 Hanging Grimston, E. R.	..	..	×												
149	Kingthorpe, Yorks.	×														
151	B. 69 Rudstone, E. R.	×														
152	B. 243 Folkton, E. R.	×	×													
158	B. 53 Calais Wold, E. R.	..	..	..	..	..	..	..	..	..	..	..	..	..	..	Axe-hammer 4$\frac{1}{10}$ in. long
162	B. 241 Folkton	×	..	..	..	..	×									
168	Broad Lowe, Ash, Derby.	×														
173	Eldon Hill, Derby.	×														
175	Far Lowe, Derby	×														
176	B. 44 Weaverthorpe, E. R.	..	..	..	..	..	..	..	..	..	×					
176bis	B. 42 Garrowby Wold, E. R.	×														
181	B. 74 Garton Slack, E. R.	×														
182	Bostorn, Derby.	..	..	..	..	×										
184	Rolley Lowe, Derby.	..	..	×	×											
192	B. 140 Slingsby, N. R.	..	×													
193	B. 47 Wharram Percy, E. R.	×	..	..	..	..	..	..	×	..	..	..	..	..	..	Flint saw
214 } 215 }	Arbour Lowe, Derby.	..	..	..	..	..	..	×								Piece of pyrites
222	B. 208 Acklam Wold, E. R.	..	..	..	..	..	..	..	..	..	..	..	..	..	..	Flint saw
225	Wetton Hill, Stafford.	×	..	..	..	×										
Lost	B. 39 Butterwick, E. R.	..	..	..	..	..	..	..	..	×	..	..	×	×	..	Bronze flat axe and 5 jet buttons O. 32a, b

OBJECTS FOUND WITH FOOD VESSELS. REGION II

The Table of Finds for this Region, which is confined to the counties of Derby, Stafford, and York, shows that the people were apparently not rich in bronze, for the objects consist for the most part of worked flint, such as knives, spearheads, scrapers, arrowheads, and one stone axe-hammer. Relics of the chase only occur twice in the shape of boars' tusks, and twice as the tines of red deer. There are 6 bone pins of the simplest construction, 4 bone beads, 3 pieces of worked bone, and 7 buttons with the V-shaped perforation. As ornaments, there are 2 jet necklaces (O. 31) and 1 jet ornament. Of bronze we find 7 small awls or prickers, 3 of them found with female interments and 1 with a male skeleton; 2 small knives and 1 pair of ear-rings.

Comparing these results with the finds associated with beakers from the counties of Derby and Stafford in Province II, from the East Riding in Province III, and from Northumberland in Province IV, we find that the civilization of the people who made use of beakers and of those who used food vessels was not quite the same.

| | BRONZE | | | | | | | | | |
	Awl or pricker	Knife	Ear-rings	Flat axe	Axe-hammer	Button, V-perforation	Flint dagger	Jet 'Pulley' ring	Stone bracer	Gold
With beakers	6	1	1	0	1	10	8	2	2	1
With food vessels . .	7	2	1	1	1	7	0	0	0	0

The abridged Table above shows that the latter people had a little more bronze in the shape of 1 knife extra and 1 celt or flat axe, but that exactly as in Region I they seem to have had no flint daggers, stone bracers, or 'pulley' rings. Yet we can hardly suppose that the flint dagger had fallen into disuse. As in Region I, there are several bronze daggers and celts found with skeleton interments which cannot with certainty be assigned to either class of pottery, though there is a probability that 1 or 2 of the small knives might be assigned to the beaker period. However, it is better to keep these extra knife-daggers apart and consider them all together. This addition of wealth consists in 21 knife-daggers, 3 celts, and 2 awls or prickers, and is very considerable when contrasted with the small quantity of bronze actually found with vessels of this class. But we know (P. 32) a food vessel of type 1a (fig. 83) was probably deposited later than a bronze dagger measuring 6 in. × $2\frac{1}{8}$ in. with a well-developed midrib, 3 engraved lines parallel to the cutting edges, and 6 rivets (O. 30), a type of blade which belongs to Bronze Age II. And food vessels are so frequently encountered with the interments of infants and children, that possibly such pottery was held in small estimation and its absence from a grave had no special significance.

Although a list of some of these daggers and celts has already been given, I reproduce it, but now more conveniently arranged according to the size of the blades, with the addition of six knife-daggers.

IX. BRONZE KNIFE-DAGGERS AND CELTS WITH SKELETON INTERMENTS
REGION II

PLACE	KNIFE DAGGERS			CELTS	REMARKS	FIGURED (PL. LXI)
	Length	Width	No. of Rivets			
Life Hill, B. 294, E. R. . .	3	1¼	2	..	. . . .	O. 33
Kenslow Barrow, Derby. .	3½	..	3	..	Flat, lancet-shaped, bevelled edge	
Shuttlestone, Derby. . . .	4	..	2	×	Flat, end broken off	O. 34
Helperthorpe, B. 49, E. R. .	4⅛	2	2	..	Flat	O. 35
Aldro, B. 116, E. R. . . .	4½	2	3	..	Much worn	Mortimer, Pl. xii
Stanshope Barrow, Stafford. .	4½	..	2	..	Rather narrow, flat	
Parcelly Hay, Derby. . .	4¾	..	3	..	Flat, rivets rather large	
Rudstone, B. 68, E. R. . .	4⅞	1⅜	3	..	. . . .	O. 36
Garrowby Wold, B. 32, E. R.	5	2⅝	3	..	Very thin	O. 37
Thorncliff, Stafford. . . .	5	..	3			
New Inns, Derby.	5	..	3	..	Rivets rather small	
Carder Low, Derby. . . .	5⅛	2⅜	3	..	Large rivets, sharp-pointed . . .	O. 38
Brier Low, Derby.	5½	2¼	3	..	Sharp-pointed	O. 39
Garton Slack, B. 107, E. R. .	5⅝	2⅝	4	..	Round-headed	O. 40
Deep Dale, Stafford. . . .	5½	..	3			
Towthorpe, B. 233, E. R. .	6	2⅛	6	..	. . . .	O. 30
End Low, Derby.	6¼	2¼	3	..	. . . .	O. 41
Acklam Wold, B. 205, E. R. .	6	2⅝	3	..	Round-headed	O. 42
Worm Hill Barrow, Derby. .	6⅜	..	3	..	Blunt point.	O. 43
Lett Low, Stafford. . . .	7½	2¼	3	..	. . . .	O. 44
Moot Low, Derby. . . .	..	..	..	×		
Borther Low, Derby. . . .	..	..	..	×		
Dow Low, Derby.	4⅞	..	..	×	Flat, round-headed, 3 engraved lines	O. 45

About a half of the knife-daggers mentioned in the above Table are not larger than others, also with rivets, that have been found with beaker interments, though the rivets are frequently larger than those in Province I. Dr. O. Montelius has placed O. 41, from End Low, Derbyshire, in Bronze Age II. Out of the 13 knife-daggers from Derby and Stafford, perhaps the two small ones from Stanshope and Parcelly Hay might be included in the beaker period; and from the East Riding the small example from Rudstone, B. 68 (O. 36), which was found with a 'pulley' ring and a button with the V-shaped perforation, also the still smaller blade from Life Hill (O. 33).

The additional 25 pieces of bronze mentioned in the Table, added to the 10 pieces actually found with food vessels, make a total of 35 pieces of bronze, and of these the 7 awls or prickers hardly count. Though metal is still very rare it is more abundant than in the beaker period, and so skeleton interments must come down later in time.

The latest of the daggers seems to be O. 30, from Towthorpe, as it has a well-developed midrib, six rivets, and a rudimentary tang. It belongs to the same general type as O. 26a from the Bush barrow, Wilts., but is probably later.

It will be observed that the blade O. 45 is unsymmetrical and has a rounded head like a halberd, but it has the semi-lunar mark at the base of the blade, and Sir John Evans has classed it as a knife-dagger.[1] Montelius has assigned it to Bronze Age II.

OBJECTS FOUND WITH FOOD VESSELS. REGION III

X. TABLE OF FINDS

Fig.	Place	Flint, worked	Arrowheads	Flint knife	Stone celt	Perforated hammer	Stone beads and pendants	Lignite disc beads	Jet necklace	Jet bead (fusiform)	Bone, worked	Bronze pin	Bronze knife-dagger	Bronze spiral armlet	Bronze bangles	Gold	Gold rings	Figured
231–2	Broughshane, Antrim	..	..	..	..	..	..	×										
Type A	Oldbridge, Meath	×	..	..	..	..	..	×										
237	Duncragaig, Argyll	..	..	..	..	..	..	..	×									
240	Belmore Mount, Fermanagh	..	..	..	..	..	×	..	..	..	..	..	..	..	..	..	..	O. 46
247	Corky, Antrim	..	..	..	..	..	..	..	..	..	..	..	×	..	..	..	..	O. 47
248	Lug na Curran, Queen's Co.	..	..	..	..	..	..	..	..	..	..	..	..	×	..	..	..	O. 48
249	Brownhead, Arran	×	..	..	..	..	..	×										
250	Mount Stuart, Bute	..	..	..	..	..	..	..	×									
251	Mauchrie Moor, Arran	×	..	..	..	..	..	..	..	..	..	×	·					
253	Kinneff, Kincardine	..	..	..	..	..	..	..	..	..	..	×	..	..	×			
254	Rathbarran, Sligo	..	..	..	×	..	..	..	..	..	..	..	..	..	..	..	..	O. 49
255	Killicarney, Cavan	..	..	..	×	..	..	..	..	..	×	..	..	..	..	..	..	O. 50a, b
256	Toppet Mount, Fermanagh	..	..	..	..	..	..	..	..	..	..	..	×	..	..	×	..	O. 51
263	Doune, Perth	..	..	..	..	×	..	..	..	..	..	..	..	..	..	..	..	O. 52
266	Scalpsie Bay, Bute	..	..	..	..	..	..	..	..	×	..	×						
269	Balcalk, Forfar	..	..	..	..	..	..	..	×									
270	Lunanhead, Forfar	..	..	..	..	..	..	..	×									
271	Ratho, Mid-Lothian	..	..	..	..	..	..	..	..	..	..	..	..	..	×			
277 bis	Duff House, Banff	..	..	..	..	..	..	..	..	..	..	..	×	..	..	..	×	
280	Dunagore, Antrim	..	×	..	×													
281	Omagh, Tyrone	..	×															
387	Inverarity, Forfar	..	..	×'														
389	Rudle, Argyll	×																
409	North Britain	..	..	×														
420	Birkhill, Stirling	..	..	×														

The comparative absence of flint in this region is to be explained partly by the fact that nearly all the finds were casually made by persons who would take no notice of flint flakes or small knives, and partly by the fact that flint is not found everywhere in Ireland and in no part of North Britain *in situ*, though small pebbles of flint are plentiful enough in the till or boulder clay. Arrowheads of flint or stone are recorded twice, and flat celts of stone three times, in Hibernia, though the latter do not appear to occur in Britain during this period. Of flint or agate knives there are three, and one perforated hammer of veined quartzite (O. 52) from North

---

[1] Evans, *Br. Impl.*, fig. 297.

Britain. The single disc-shaped bead of lignite from Broughshane was probably part of a necklace, so that we have three necklaces of disc-shaped beads like those found in Region II, and four necklaces that include fusiform beads and ornamented plates of lignite, making altogether seven ornaments for the neck to be worn by women.

The ten beads (O. 46) found with fig. 240 are worthy of remark as they are unlike any that have been discovered hitherto in Britain, but resemble others from the cairns of Lough Crew. One of them is a small perforated carnelian pebble rubbed down in places to give it a rudely globular form, one is a tooth, and the others are of soft stone apparently allied to serpentine. Beads of jasper and of schist that resemble these in form have been found in the dolmens of Kercado, Tumiac, and Mont St. Michel, all in Morbihan, and have been published by the *Société polymathique du Morbihan*. These ten beads, taken in conjunction with the cruciform chamber in which they were found, are good evidence that some vessels of type A must be placed in the fringe of time that elapsed between the neolithic and bronze periods.

Bronze was not plentiful, for only two fragmentary pins or awls, three knife-daggers, one of which is represented by a few fragments, and three armlets have been recorded. The small knife, $3\frac{1}{4}$ in. long with two rivets (O. 47), was found inside fig. 247 by Mr. Knowles, and both are now in his possession. The blade is flat, perhaps has been worn down by repeated sharpening, and may be compared with the example from Life Hill (O. 33) in Region II. The dagger from Toppet Mountain (O. 51) is flat, but ornamented with two parallel lines, and is a little over $5\frac{1}{2}$ in. long. As it is a good deal broken away at the base only two rivet-holes now remain. It belongs to Bronze Age II, and may be compared with O. 28*b* from Winterbourne Stoke, which is 3 in. longer. The remains of a fillet of gold, which no doubt ornamented the haft of the dagger, is similar to that found with the Collessie dagger (O. 18).

The two bronze armlets of spiral wire from Lug na Curran (O. 48) have already been described, and references given for foreign analogues (p. 124).

The two bronze bangles from Kinneff have a diameter of 3 in., and are made of stout bronze bar of nearly circular section but slightly flattened on the inside.[1] They are quite like the bronze armlet found with beaker fig. 213 from Lanarkshire.

The penannular gold rings found with fig. 277*bis* were five in number. Two are bracelets with a diameter of $2\frac{3}{4}$ in., the three others are much smaller.[2]

---

[1] Anderson, *Br. and St. Ages*, fig. 67.   [2] *Op. cit.*, figs. 69–72.

CHAPTER XIII

ETHNOGRAPHICAL SECTION

REGION II

As the pottery of the food-vessel class differs entirely from that of the beaker class in Region II and cannot be derived from it, we have to investigate what differences, if any, existed between the people that fabricated each class. Mr. R. Mortimer has kindly informed me that in the East Riding he has unearthed 133 food vessels. They occurred as follows:

with adults	54	40·5 %
with children	20	15·0 %
with burnt bodies	27	20·25 %
alone	23	17·25 %
doubtful	9	6·75 %

Of the 54 skulls of adults only 23 could be measured, with the following result, which I repeat:

8 long skulls	ceph. ind.		71·15
7 mesoceph.	„	„	77·7
8 short skulls	„	„	85·95

This does not agree with the cephalic index taken from a larger area in the annexed Table XI, in which 2 long and 2 short skulls are included from Mr. Mortimer's list. If these are subtracted from the Table and the remainder added to his list the result is:

Long skulls 9. Short skulls 14. Intermediate 8.

Hence the proportion of short-headed persons appears to overbalance considerably that of the long-headed. But this disproportion does not of itself disprove, though it may make less

XI. CEPHALIC INDEX OF SKULLS FOUND WITH FOOD VESSELS. REGION II

Fig.	Place	Cephalic Index	Sex	Length of Femur
62 ⎱	B. 140 Garton Slack, E. R.	72·	M	19½ in.
63 ⎰	B. 140 Garton Slack, E. R.	84·5		
65	Cross Low, Derby.	82·4		
101	Hay Top, Monsal Dale, Derby.	79·2		
148	B. 27 Hanging Grimston, E. R.	Brachy.	M	
153 ⎱	B. 151 Garton Slack, E. R.	Dolicho.		
154 ⎰	B. 151 Garton Slack, E. R.	Brachy.		
155	B. 5 Heslerton, E. R.	80·	M	
170	Hitter Hill, Derby.	86·		
184	Rolley Low, Derby.	82·		
197	B. 1 Acklam Wold, E. R.	75·		
225	Wetton Hill, Stafford.	83·2	M	

Total .. Long skulls 3. Short skulls 8. Mesoceph. 1

Fig. 170. The food vessels were found in another cist a little to the east of the other.

likely, the possibility of a difference of social status between persons buried with beakers and with food vessels.

Although the people who used food vessels seem not to have made flint daggers or bracers of stone, in other respects they do not appear to have differed much from the people who used beakers, though their condition may have been slightly inferior. There is no essential difference in the size of the burial mounds or of the graves and cists between the two peoples, though cremation was now more common. The footnote below[1] shows 29 instances in which a food vessel had been deposited with a cremated interment, 41·3 % with examples of 1a and 31 % with examples of type 2. In another particular a difference may be noted. With the beaker-using people the face of the deceased at the time of burial was always turned, so far as is known, to some point of the compass in the path of the sun's diurnal course. But the Table below[2] shows that in 63 instances of food-vessel interments 8 persons had their face turned to the north and 4 to within a few points of it. This shows that the direction of the face does not indicate the time of day at which the corpse was interred, as it did or seemed to do with beaker interments. It may be that the increasing use of cremation, which nullified the possibility of turning the face in any direction whatever, had a reciprocal influence on burials with inhumation, and thus tended to make the orientation of the face a matter of indifference, at any rate of less importance. Nevertheless, in 58·7 % of the interments the face had been turned to a point lying between east and west, passing by the south.

There is still a preponderance of male interments over those of women, but the number of burials of young persons and children is more than both put together.[3]

[1] REGION II. BURNT INTERMENTS WITH FOOD VESSELS.

FIG.	TYPE	FIG.	TYPE	FIG.	TYPE	FIG.	TYPE	FIG.	TYPE	FIG.	TYPE
23	1a	40	2	41	1a	55	3	64	domestic	65	2
77	2	111	1a	118	3	127	1a	160	1a	161	1a
162	1a	163	1a	164	1a	165	1a	166	1a	167	1a
182	2	192	2	193	2	194	2	195	2	206	4
213	3?	214	2	215	4	229		230			

[2] TABLE 2.

South	17 both sexes		S. by W.	3		
SSE.	1		SSW.	5	13 both sexes	
SE. by S.	1	5	SW.	5	both sexes	
SE.	3		SW. by W.	1		
SE. by E.	1		WSW.	1	5	
ESE.	2	7	West	3	both sexes	
East	4	both sexes	NW.	1		
NE. by E.	1		NW. by N.	1	3	
NE.	1	10	WNW.	1		
North	8		On the back	3 :	Total 63.	

Of those facing North there were: males 3, sex not stated 2, adult 1, young 1, child 1.

[3] Food vessels with adult male interments. Figs. 28, 31, 70, 71, 87, 92, 101, 108, 130, 142, 148, 151, 154, 157, 158, 179 = 16.

With women, Figs. 22, 53, (60 : 61), 69, 88, 106, 109, 119, 176, 229 = 10.

With youths, children, and infants, Figs. 26, 27, 35, 38, 74, 80, 81, 82, 85, 97, 98, 102, 107, 115, 116, 118, 120, 121, 134, 136, 137, 147, 173, 175, 181, 186, 187, 189, 191, 210 = 30.

All the domestic animals being known, the people lived mainly on the produce of their herds and cultivated a little grain, as the grains of wheat found inside the walls of food vessel fig. 148 prove. But there were also hunters among them. Pieces of stags' horn, the tine of a stag, a wild-boar's tusk from three barrows in Derbyshire,[1] the antlers of a red deer and the head of a badger from the East Riding[2] had, it may be supposed, been laid with the bodies of men who had followed the chase during their lifetime. Generally the food offerings made to the deceased were parts of a domestic animal. In a Derbyshire barrow the skeleton of a young person had been laid on the ribs of an ox or other large animal,[3] and bones of a young pig, of a sheep or goat have sometimes been found at the foot of a skeleton. Occasionally the remains of food have been detected inside a food vessel. One contained black carbonaceous-looking matter which analysis proved to contain a large amount of nitrogen; another contained the rib of a small animal the size of a rabbit; in a third was a dark-coloured deposit of vegetable origin; two ribs of a small animal were found in a fourth; and a fifth contained decayed matter.[4] One food vessel (fig. 137) contained a much smaller one, only $1\frac{3}{4}$ in. high, of a kind not infrequently found in cinerary urns, and termed very inexactly an 'incense cup'. This instance helps to prove or make it extremely probable that 'incense cups' really represented small food vessels in an atrophied form.

Two or more skeletons in the same grave.

It is possible to suppose that occasionally when a man died his wife was put to death and buried with him. This event may have taken place in the following four instances :

Section 1. In a grave under B. 21 Ganton the bodies of a young man and woman faced each other, the man's body partly overlay that of the woman and his right hand rested on her hip. With them was the food vessel fig. 31.

2. In B. 153 Garton Slack at the bottom of the central grave lay a large male (?) skeleton, and close beneath the legs was the skeleton of a young person of from 8 to 12 years of age. The bronze earrings on each side of the head show that the body was that of a girl. With them was food vessel fig. 59.

3. In B. 141 Garton Slack at the bottom of the central grave lay the skeleton of a strong man. Close above the hip were two bones of the forearm of a slender person and a piece of a skull. Eighteen inches higher was the skeleton of a middle-aged woman and food vessels figs. 60, 61.

4. In B. 142½ Riggs, in a nearly central grave, the remains of a large man were found at the bottom, and 1 ft. higher the decayed body of a slender person, probably a woman.

There are a couple of instances in which two men were found together, and two more in which the sex was not determined.

5. In B. 21 Ganton at the bottom of the central grave and on the east side of it was found the body of a young man, probably under 20 years of age, and fig. 28. At the west end of the grave lay the body of another young man of about 20 years of age.

6. In B. 56 Cowlam, in the central grave, the bodies of two men were found with their heads nearly in contact and food vessel fig. 179 lying between them.

7. In a grave at Cawthorn Camps, Yorkshire, two skeletons with figs. 43, 44 had been deposited in the same grave.

---

[1] With figs. 182, 184.   [2] With fig. 37.   [3] With fig. 175.   [4] With figs. 71, 99, 142, 181, 203.

8. Again in B. 151 Garton Slack, in the central grave, two interments were found, one close upon the other. The uppermost was the dolichocephalic skeleton of a middle-aged person, together with food vessel fig. 152. On the floor of the grave lay a brachycephalic skeleton, the skull of which had been severed from the body.

There are two instances in which a woman and child were interred together. No doubt this took place on other occasions, but I have limited myself to the cases in which a food vessel was found with the interment.

9. In B. 159 Aldro, at 4 ft. below the top, were the remains of an infant and food vessel fig. 80. Close to it were the remains of another child and fig. 81. Four inches lower lay the remains of a small person, apparently of a woman of from 20 to 22 years of age. One foot lower were calcined human bones that probably formed the primary interment.

10. In B. 140 Garton Slack, in a non-central grave, were the remains of a child, and close beneath it on the floor of the grave lay an adult skeleton with a cephalic index of 84·5 and food vessel fig. 63.

There are a couple of instances in which as many as five persons seem to have been buried at the same time.

11. In Cross Lowe, Derbyshire, the skeleton of a young person and fig. 67 were found in a cist. Just outside it and on the same level were four other skeletons, to all appearance deposited at the same time as the body within the cist.

12. In B. 162 Garton Slack the central grave was 6 ft. deep. At the depth of 2 ft. 3 in. were the remains of a child of from 5 to 7 years of age, and fig. 137. At lower levels were the remains of four other bodies, one of them that of an old woman.

BURNT AND UNBURNT INTERMENTS FOUND TOGETHER

There are two instances in which a male skeleton had been deposited with the cremated remains of a man, and one in which a male skeleton was found beside a deposit of burnt bones the sex of which could not be ascertained.

13. In B. 161 Ferry Fryston, a non-central interment, just above the natural surface, consisted of a male skeleton with fig. 104. Extending under the bones of this was a deposit of the burnt bones of a strong adult man. Both bodies were certainly placed in the mound at the same time.

14. In B. 69 Rudstone, in the shallow central grave, the body of a young man of 25 years of age lay on his back at full length, with food vessel fig. 151. At his left side and in contact with the body lay the burnt bones of an adult man.

15. In B. 140 Garton Slack, at the bottom of the central grave lay a male skeleton with a cephalic index of 72· and food vessel fig. 62. On the opposite side of the grave, about 1½ ft. higher, was a small deposit of burnt bones.

There are two instances in which a female skeleton was found with the cremated body of an adult.

16. In B. 75 Garton Slack, the skeleton of a woman together with fig. 22, a jet necklace, and a bronze pricker were found at the height of 3½ ft. above the bottom of the central grave and a beaker interment. Close to her feet was a heap of burnt bones of an adult.

17. In B. 13 Sherburn, at the bottom of a nearly central grave, were the burnt bones of a nearly, if not quite, full-grown person. Partly lying upon these was the skeleton of a young woman and food vessel fig. 69. On the floor of an adjoining grave lay the body of a young man, between 20 and 25 years of age, with fig. 70. In Canon Greenwell's opinion all three bodies seemed to have been buried together.

Finally, there are four instances in which the skeleton of a child was placed alongside a cremated interment; one instance in which two uncremated children and one cremated were together; and one instance in which the adult was uncremated and the children cremated.

18. In B. 4 Painsthorpe, at a depth of nearly 3 ft. from the top, a child's body was found with food vessel fig. 26, and close by it was a cremated interment.

19. At Blake Lowe, Derbyshire, the skeleton of a child and the cremated bones of an adult were found with figs. 41, 42.

20. At Eldon Hill, Derbyshire, was found, about 18 in. above the natural surface, a deposit of calcined human bones and the skeleton of a child with food vessel fig. 173.

21. In B. 187 Ford, Northumberland, at the centre of a small barrow with a diameter of 16 ft., was a cist containing the skull of a child of about 2 years of age and food vessel fig. 98. Round the cist there were six bodies in as many cinerary urns. One of these cremated persons was about 17 years old.

22. In B. 280 Marton Hall, figs. 55 *bis*, 56, 57 seem to have accompanied the interments of two children by inhumation and one by cremation. These lay 16 inches below the top of a grave, and at the bottom, nearly 3 ft. lower, reposed the remains of a large male skeleton.

23. At Cross Lowe, Derbyshire, there lay in the same cist a large skeleton, with a cephalic index of 82·4 and food vessel fig. 65; at the foot of the skeleton were the calcined remains of two children and food vessel fig. 66.

The light thrown by these first twelve sections on the practice of putting a wife to death at the demise of her husband is not very great, and is clouded with uncertainty. The first four instances of a man and woman being buried together may be accepted as evidence, although it cannot be quite certain that, in a time when pestilence raged and deadly fevers were prevalent, both persons had not been snatched from life at the same moment.

But with regard to sec. 5, 6, where the bodies of two men were buried together, it is very difficult to be sure that one man had been put to death at the demise of the other. In those wild days, when fighting was no unusual occurrence, it must sometimes have happened that two men of the same family or clan were killed at the same time.

That an infant or a young child should be strangled and buried with its mother was a practice quite consonant with the civilization of the period, and was what might be expected almost as a matter of course. Yet we have only two nearly certain examples of such a custom in sec. 9, 10, and four less certain in sec. 18, 19, 20, 23—less certain because the adult had been cremated; and when dealing with the beakers we found an instance or two in which a child had been buried with a full-grown man.

The most remarkable child-burial, and the most difficult to explain, is undoubtedly that noticed in sec. 21, where the grave of a mere infant of 2 years' old was surrounded by six cremated interments. On this case Canon Greenwell writes: ' It may reasonably be inferred that this was the burial-place of the much-beloved child of a man of high standing amongst his people; and it is not improbable that the burnt bodies were those of dependants slain at the funeral and possibly with the view that they might in another world continue to render those services they had before been accustomed to perform.'

Although cremation was a novelty for the invaders, it was not so for the original inhabi-tants of Region II, at least not entirely. The practice of cremation was established in the neolithic period, at any rate in North Britain, before the invasion of South Britain by the brachycephals. In five horned and chambered cairns of Caithness, and in other chambered cairns of circular form from the same district, Dr. Joseph Anderson found the floors of the chambers composed of a compacted mass of clay, ashes, and burnt bones, both human and animal. In a large cairn at Largie in Argyll, Canon Greenwell found the floor composed of dark earth and burnt human and animal bones. At Kilchoan, also in Argyll, Mr. Mapleton found a deposit of burnt bones in a chambered cairn.[1]

This practice continued in Argyll down to the time when the invasion of Britain had taken place, though the invaders had not yet pushed so far north. In Table VI, I have placed the vessel from Duncragaig (fig. 236) in the 5th generation, which coincides with the time when the invaders had reached Yorkshire, but considerably before they entered Argyll.

As cremation was still practised in Region III at a period so near the time of the invasion of Region II, we may suppose that the original inhabitants of this region also used it occasion-ally. For instance, the Derbyshire examples (figs. 127, 214), especially the latter, both seem to be earlier than the invasion of Region II by the brachycephals, and both were found with cremated interments. Hence it would seem that cremation in Regions II and III was due to the influence of the pre-existing inhabitants, who had inherited the custom from their neolithic ancestors. But no special type of cinerary urn came into use; a food vessel was simply deposited by the side of the cremated body.

How cremation first came into use in North Britain, and what ideas were entertained by the natives concerning this rite, it is impossible to say. But once it must have been an innova-tion, and such a great change in the burial rites could hardly have taken place unless it had been imposed from above by persons of rank in the tribe, just as a new religion, to become popular and to prevail, has first to be adopted by the King or the natural leaders of the com-munity. In these matters tribesmen follow the lead of their chiefs.

According to the Homeric doctrine, after the corpse had been cremated the soul left the body and went to Hades, or to the realms of the dead in the far West. In Scandinavia the soul of the deceased after cremation of the body went to Valhalla with his horse, his men and women servants, and whatever else had been burnt with him on the funeral pile.[2] But the spirits of those who had been inhumed were supposed to remain near the place of burial, where they were fed from time to time with offerings, and feasts made in their memory.

It may be supposed that the purifying effect of fire, an idea which is almost universal, had something to do with the inception of cremation. When a king or a great chief died, it may be that he lay in state for some days to allow time for the tribesmen to assemble and for funeral games. To prevent decomposition under these circumstances, or to remove its bad effects had it set in, it would be very natural to burn the body merely in order to purify it, without forming any definite idea of what became of the spirit afterwards. But when this act was repeated and as soon as people began to speculate and wonder what became of a spirit, the body of which had been consumed by fire, from seeing the smoke of the pyre rise and then drift away in some

---

[1] Anderson, pp. 235-73.

[2] Ridgeway, *Early Age of Greece*, i. 513-16.

direction before disappearing in the air, they would naturally imagine that the spirits of the great dead had flitted to some distant and unseen place to which eventually they would give a general name.

We cannot know exactly what passed through the minds of the natives when attending a funeral with cremation or with inhumation. But still we may suppose that they believed in a vague way that, when a body was inhumed under a tumulus, its spirit remained with it in the grave; when the body was burnt, that the spirit fled away to some distant and unseen country where it continued to lead a life not very different from that lived on earth. If this was really the belief of the inhabitants of Region II, it follows that when two persons were interred at the same time, one by inhumation, the other by cremation, they were eternally separated, for one remained in the barrow, while the other journeyed to the Unknown Land whence there was no return. We may now apply this belief to the instances afforded by sec. 13–23, to learn what the result would be and also to see if any social difference between the cremated and the uncremated can be detected.

It may be assumed, I think, that when the interments of two persons were made together, the one deposited first implies that in life he or she was superior in some way to the other who was deposited last. Further, that the placing of a food vessel beside an uncremated burial, while none was given to the cremated person, is of no significance, partly because so many bronze daggers of this period have been found without pottery and partly because a food vessel was not often laid alongside a cremated deposit.

Judging by the food vessel the earliest example of such a double interment is found in sec. 16. Here the feet of the woman, to whom a food vessel, a jet necklace, and a bronze pricker had been given, lay close to the top of a heap of burnt human bones, a circumstance which leads us to suppose that these were deposited first. If, judging by the ornaments, &c., priority of rank is given to the woman, it might be supposed that some one was put to death at her funeral. Women in those days no doubt had a good deal to say for themselves, could make their influence felt, and went to battle with the men, but it is hardly likely that a man would be put to death at the funeral of his wife or even another woman, though perhaps this might happen with a child. But if the two were to be separated in after life, and thus be of no use to each other, we must assume that two persons of different social position happened to be interred at the same time, but nothing more. It may be, however, that the woman and the cremated person were put to death when the man was deposited at the bottom of the grave with a beaker (P. 1). Yet I hesitate to accept this explanation, because the man and woman were separated by $3\frac{1}{2}$ ft. of earth.

In an instance of later date (sec. 13) the burnt bones of a strong adult man lay just below a male skeleton, and in a still later interment (sec. 17) the body of a young woman was found lying on the top of the cremated remains of a person nearly or quite adult, which must have been deposited first. Here again, at any rate for the present, we must assume that the two cremated persons were of superior status to the two uncremated and that they merely happened to be buried at the same time.

Sec. 14 is less decisive in the matter of priority of deposition, for here a young man of 25 years of age had been laid at full length on his back—the food vessel shows that the interment belongs to a late time—and touching his left side were the burnt bones of an adult man.

Although we cannot be sure of the point, it is not unlikely that the senior of the two, the cremated body, was deposited first.

From the other sections nearly all that can be learnt is that children were sometimes cremated while the adult was inhumed, and *vice versa*. In sec. 15 a large skeleton lay at the south end of a grave, and near the opposite side of it and about $1\frac{1}{2}$ ft. higher was a small deposit of human bones. Possibly these were quite independent interments, though in the same grave. In sec. 18 we find one uncremated child close to a cremated interment; in sec. 23 a large skeleton at the foot of which were the calcined remains of two children. If this was the mother, why was she to be separated from her two children by an impassable barrier? It may be that after all she was not the mother, and the connexion between them is purely casual.

In sec. 19, at the centre of a rock-grave about 3 ft. deep lay the calcined bones of an adult and in one corner the decayed skeleton of an infant. Here the cremated body was no doubt the first to be deposited, though that might be expected when the other was an infant. In sec. 20, again, a deposit of calcined human bones was close to the skeleton of a child with its food vessel.

From the above instances it may now be concluded that, taking first deposition in the grave as a criterion, some difference of social position did exist between the cremated and the uncremated in favour of the former. Further that, if the result of cremation was to remove the spirit of the deceased to an infinite distance from its home when in life, we are prevented from supposing that, when a cremated person is found with an inhumed body in the same grave, one was put to death for the sake of the other.

Reverting to sec. 21 we now see the matter in a different light. Cremation had by this time become so general that probably it was no longer a mark of superior social status, and the six cremated persons may not have been superior in rank to the uncremated child, as otherwise we should have had to assume. But the difficulty now occurs that the spirit of the child would remain in the barrow and could not be served by the spirits of the cremated, for these, like birds, would fly away, never to return. And until more is known of the beliefs of these people this difficulty cannot easily be removed.

In treating of the customs of the beaker-using people I came to the conclusion, judging from the apparently greater number of men than women, and from the few instances in which it was certain that a man and woman had been buried together, that a state of polyandry existed, or something like it. For the same reason the custom seems to have held during the food-vessel period. If Caesar's information was correct, polyandry existed in Britain in his time, and so primitive a usage could hardly have been introduced from the Continent or have arisen spontaneously between the end of the food-vessel period and the end of the 1st century B.C. We have seen above that the mortality of children and infants was great, although, as their sex is unknown, we cannot be certain that the larger proportion of it consisted of female infants prematurely put to death. Yet infanticide is so common that it may readily be supposed that this practice was not unknown in Britain at the time when food vessels were in use.

CHAPTER XIV

ETHNOGRAPHICAL

REGION III

In Hibernia there is hardly any evidence from sepulchral mounds to show what type of skull existed at the end of the Neolithic and the beginning of the Bronze Age, although it is believed to have been dolichocephalic, like that of the long-barrow type in Britain. In the Table of Cephalic Indices below none of the food vessels figured in this volume were actually found with any of the skulls. The two skulls from Knockmaraidh in the Phoenix Park, Dublin, came from the central cist, and fig. 244 from a non-central cist in the same tumulus. The vessel from Trillick, Co. Tyrone, is badly figured but seems to belong to type 2. The example of type A from Oldbridge, Co. Meath, is a very fine specimen, in form much like fig. 232 from Broughshane, Co. Antrim. The vessel from Co. Wicklow resembles fig. 382 from Moytura,

XII. TABLE OF CEPHALIC INDICES. REGION III

PLACE	TYPE	CEPHALIC INDEX	SEX	HEIGHT	REFERENCE
Trillick, Co. Tyrone . . .	2 (?)	circa 70·	M	5 ft. 10 in.	*J. R. H. A. A. I.*, 4 ser., i. 582
Oldbridge, Co. Meath . .	A	75·5	M	5 ft. 10 in.	*P. R. I. A.*, 3 ser., iii. 748
Newcastle, Wicklow . . .	like 382	79·4	M	5 ft. 11½ in.	*op. cit.* iv. 62
Ballynahatty, Down . . .	3 cin. urns	74·	F	..	Borlase, iii. 986
Ballynahatty, Down . . .	..	75·	F	..	Borlase, iii. 986
Knockmaraidh, Dublin . .	fig. 244	73·3	M	..	*op. cit.* iii. 978
Knockmaraidh, Dublin . .	..	78·5	M		

Co. Mayo. Perhaps the two skulls from Ballynahatty, Co. Down, should not have been included as they were found in a circular enclosure 7 ft. in diameter, which contained several other interments, including three cinerary urns about 12 in. high, which must therefore belong to a later time than that which we are now considering.

Although the grave mounds are circular, as in Region II, there is sometimes a great difference in their internal structure, which shows that these are modified survivals from the neolithic period.

The cairn on Belmore Mt., Co. Fermanagh, with a diameter of 40 ft. and a height of 10 ft., covered a chamber in form of a Latin cross, the long arm of which measured 13 ft. in length and the short arm 7 ft. 4 in., internal measurement. The internal width of these was 2 ft. 4 in. The sides were built of slabs from 2 to 3 ft. high, and there were no covering stones on the passage or the side chambers except the left-hand chamber. The passage, or long arm, in its total length was divided into five compartments, and this as well as the right-arm chamber consisted of a mass of burnt bones, on the top of which the stones of the cairn had apparently been filled in without structural arrangement. The beads (O. 46) were picked up from among the bones, but it is impossible to say from which compartment they were taken.

The left-arm chamber had two stories, a second chamber being built over the flag covering the lower one. This lower chamber contained a skull and some other unburnt human bones. With these were bones of the deer, pig, rabbit, and some kind of bird, several large boars' tusks and a few sea-shells.

The upper chamber contained fig. 240 and burnt bones, though none were in the vessel itself.

Outside the left arm, in the angle between it and the head of the passage, a rude secondary chamber was found, constructed as a lean-to against the side of the left-arm chamber and closed at the top by a small stone. It contained another human skull, and human as well as animal bones.

At a higher level was found a small cist measuring 2 ft. 4 in. by 1 ft. 8 in., which contained fig. 241.

In Region II the central grave and the secondary graves below the barrow were sunk into the ground, and a primary interment laid on the natural surface is hardly to be found. But in Hibernia we may find a large number of small cists with cinerary interments placed on the natural surface, and then covered with heaps of stones.

The cairn at Mount Stewart on the north-east shore of Strangford Lough, Co. Down, is an example. It had a diameter of 30 ft. and a height of 5 ft. At the centre, and on the natural surface, was a large central cist like a small dolmen, which perhaps still exists.[1] On the south side of it were some 60 or 70 small cists, the bottoms of which were strewn with fragments of charred bones and bits of charcoal. The cists lay east and west, each contained an urn in the north-west corner, and all lay on the south side of the central cist. This was four times the size of the others, lay east and west, and contained neither bones nor urn. Among the food vessels preserved are figs. 233, 234, perhaps 235, and beaker fig. 223.

Both these places of sepulchre show that cremation had begun early in Region III.

In Region II the Hedon Howe barrow, which seems to belong to the neolithic period and to be anterior to the arrival of the beaker-using people,[2] shows two points of agreement with the Mount Stewart cairn. For here there was a central cist round which four others were symmetrically arranged, and all were placed on the natural surface, after which a mound 8 ft. high had been raised over them.

So too in the Broughshane cairn, from which came figs. 231, 232, all three cists had been built up on the natural surface.

The large cairn at Kilmartin, Argyll (Par. 58, p. 117), with a diameter of 110 ft. and a height of 13½ ft., covered two concentric stone circles with diameters of 27 ft. and 37 ft. respectively. The stones were about 3 ft. high by 2 ft. broad and stood from 3 ft. to 5 ft. apart. The central cist was of large dimensions, measuring 7½ ft. by 3 ft. by 3 ft. deep, and was directed NE.

---

[1] It is figured by Borlase, *Dolmens of Ireland*, i, p. 281.
[2] The skulls found in the cists were all dolicho- cephalic, and a leaf-shaped arrowhead of flint was picked up from one of the cists.

and SW. The cap-stone measured 9 ft. × 4 ft. 7 in. The other cist was much smaller, was orientated in the same direction as the other, and lay 30 ft. from the centre. In both instances the skeleton had disappeared. This immense cairn was presumably erected before the arrival of the invaders in Argyll.

In later times, posterior to the invasion of the short-headed people, the cairns and the cists they contain became smaller, like those which, under the name of 'short cists', our archaeologists are accustomed to connect with the Bronze Age. This was the case both in North Britain and Hibernia. For instance, the cairn in Arran from which came fig. 249 had a diameter of 26 ft., and the cist measured 3 ft. 2 in. × 1 ft. 8 in. and 1 ft. 8 in. in depth. The tumulus in Bute from which fig. 266 was taken had a diameter of 45 ft. and a height of from 4 to 5 ft., and the cist measured 2 ft. 10 in. long × 1 ft. 8 in. wide, the interment being with cremation. The cist at Kinneff in which fig. 253 and two bronze bangles were found measured 3 ft. 9 in. × 2 ft. and 2 ft. 4 in. in depth. Fig. 302 from near Ballymena, Co. Antrim, was found in a cist the dimensions of which were 3 ft. 1½ in. in length × 1 ft. 2 in. deep. Yet sometimes there is an exception, for the Forfarshire cist from which came fig. 270, and a lignite necklace of later type, measured 4 ft. 8 in. × 2 ft. 4 in. × 2½ ft. deep.

The records that relate to the finding of sepulchral pottery in Region III are so very scanty and unprecise that from them very little can be gleaned that casts any side-light upon the customs and beliefs of the people. Yet a belief in the purificatory action of fire preparatory to interment in some special instances might be inferred from the fact that the soil round two cists with skeleton interments found near Crail in Fife showed abundant traces of burning; and in Co. Cavan the place about the interment bore evident marks of fire.[1]

In a couple of instances the sepulchral vessel seems to have contained food. A food vessel from Belmore Mountain, Co. Fermanagh, contained traces of some black greasy stuff, though found with a cremated interment; and another from near Arbroath in Forfarshire contained unctuous earth.[2]

In two instances it is recorded that the vessel contained burnt bones. Fig. 286 from Kilmurry, Co. Kilkenny, was nearly filled with small fragments of calcined bones, apparently human, and a few pebbles; fig. 295 from Co. Cavan was found full of ashes.

It is not particularly remarkable that a decapitated man, 6 ft. 2 in. in height, should have been buried in a cist without his head at Kinneff in Kincardine, but it is certainly unusual to find a food vessel inverted over the joints of a finger and a toe, as happened once in Co. Wicklow.[3]

In Region II we found some reason to suppose that when two persons were interred together, one by cremation and one by inhumation, the former had held in his lifetime a higher social status than the latter. This view seems to hold good for Region III, for in the Duncragaig cairn, Argyll, fig. 236 was found in a large central cist with a cremated body, while a decayed skeleton lay upon the cap-stone of the cist.

The appended list of food vessels found with cremated interments is necessarily very incomplete for the reason given above, from the dearth of information respecting the discovery of so many of the vessels.

---

[1] With figs. 264, 265, 295.   [2] With figs. 241, 350.   [3] With figs. 253, 399.

REGION III

Food Vessels with Cremated Interments.

Fig. 223 Hib.	Fig. 276 N. Brit.
„ 234 „	„ 277 „
„ 235? „	„ 277 *bis* N. Brit.
„ 237 N. Brit.	„ 286 Hib.
„ 241 Hib.	„ 295 „
„ 254 „	„ 307 „
„ 266 N. Brit.	„ 333 „
„ 267 „	„ 366 N. Brit.
„ 268 „	„ 412 „

LIST OF FOOD VESSELS

1. Ridgeway Hill, Dorset. $6\frac{1}{10}$ in. *Arch.* xxx. 334. Hall loan coll. *Dorchester.*

2. Locality unknown. 8 in. *Farnham.*

3. Park Town, Oxford. $5\frac{1}{4}$ in. *Ashmolean.*

4. Somerset. $4\frac{3}{4}$ in. *Taunton.*

5. Unknown loc. $3\frac{3}{4}$ in. *Devizes.*

6. Standlake, Oxon. $6\frac{6}{10}$ in. *British.*

7. Yarnton, Oxon. $4\frac{1}{4}$ in. *Ashmolean.*

8. Came, B. 2, Dorset. 6 in. *Dorchester.*

8 *bis.* Drayton, Berks. $3\frac{1}{2}$ in. *British.*

9. Between Addington and Charlton, Oxon. $5\frac{3}{4}$ in. *Ashmolean.*

10. Great Oakley Hall Farm, Essex. $4\frac{1}{2}$ in. *Colchester.*

11. Upton Lovel, Bar. 1, Wilts. $3\frac{7}{8}$ in. *A. W.* 74. *Devizes.*

12. Winterbourne Stoke, B. 25, Wilts. $1\frac{1}{2}$ in. *A. W.* 124. *Devizes.*

13. Black Burgh Tum., Sussex. 2 in. *Farnham.*

13 *bis.* Brixworth, Northampton. $5\frac{3}{4}$ in. *Northampton.*

14. Wynford Eagle, Dorset. 6 in. Warne, *Celt. Tum.,* p. 36. *Dorchester.*

15. Wynford Eagle, Dorset. 4 in. Warne, *loc. cit.,* p. 36. *Dorchester.*

16. Upper Swell, Gloucestershire. $3\frac{3}{4}$ in. *B. B.* 523. *British.*

17. From the Thames, London. $3\frac{3}{4}$ in. *British.*

18. Dummer, Hants. $3\frac{3}{4}$ in. *British.*

19, 20. Colchester, town of, Essex. 4 in. and $2\frac{3}{4}$ in. *Colchester.*

21. Thames at Kew. $2\frac{3}{4}$ in. *British.*

21 *bis.* Woodyates, B. 4, Wilts. $3\frac{1}{2}$ in. *A. W.* 237. *Devizes.*

21a. Tenby, Pembroke. 4 in. *Arch. Cambr.,* 3 ser., xiv. 266.

22, 23, 24. Garton Slack, B. 75, E. Riding. 4 in., 5 in., $5\frac{5}{8}$ in. Mortimer, *Forty Years,* pp. 222–4. *Driffield.*

25. Towthorpe, B. 21, E. R. 6 in. Mortimer, *Forty Years,* pp. 11–12. *Driffield.*

26. Painsthorpe Wold, B. 4, E. R. 4 in. Mortimer, *Forty Years,* pp. 113–17. *Driffield.*

27. Garrowby Wold, B. 104, E. R. $5\frac{1}{2}$ in. Mortimer, *Forty Years,* pp. 134–6. *Driffield.*

28, 29, 30, 31. Ganton, B. 21, E. R. $6\frac{1}{2}$ in., $3\frac{3}{4}$ in., $4\frac{3}{8}$ in., $2\frac{1}{4}$ in. *B. B.,* pp. 161–6. *British.*

32, 33, 34. The Riggs, B. 36, E. R. $4\frac{1}{2}$ in., $5\frac{1}{2}$ in., $3\frac{5}{8}$ in. Mortimer, *Forty Years,* pp. 173–4. *Driffield.*

35, 36. Bempton, B. 253, E. R. $3\frac{3}{4}$ in., $4\frac{1}{2}$ in. Greenwell, *Arch.* lii. 28, 29. *British.*

37, 38. Weaverthorpe, B. 45. $5\frac{1}{4}$ in., 4 in. *B. B.,* p. 199. *British.*

39, 40. Seamer Moor, Scarborough, Yorks. 4 in., 5 in. *J. Brit. Ar. Ass.* iv. 101–3. *British.*

41, 42. Blake Low, Longstone Edge, Derby. 6 in., 6 in., Bateman, *Ten Years' Diggings,* pp. 41–2. *Sheffield.*

43, 44. Near Cawthorn Camps, Yorks. $5\frac{1}{2}$ in., $4\frac{1}{4}$ in. Bateman, *Ten Years' Diggings,* pp. 207–8. *Sheeld.*

45, 46. The Riggs, B. 41, E. R. $6\frac{1}{2}$ in., $5\frac{1}{2}$ in. Mortimer, *Forty Years,* pp. 180–3. *Driffield* and *York.*

47. Aldro, B. 78, E. R. $4\frac{1}{2}$ in. Mortimer, *Forty Years,* p. 67. *Driffield.*

48, 49. Bishop Burton, B. 255. 5 in., $4\frac{1}{8}$ in. Greenwell, *Arch.* lii. 31. *British.*

50, 51. Garrowby Wold, B. 169, E. R. $4\frac{1}{2}$ in., 5 in. Mortimer, *Forty Years,* pp. 138–40. *Driffield.*

52, 53. Garrowby Wold, B. 101. $4\frac{4}{5}$ in. $6\frac{1}{10}$ in. Mortimer, *Forty Years,* pp. 136–7. *Driffield.*

54, 55. Goodmanham, B. 111, E. R. $5\frac{1}{2}$ in., $2\frac{1}{4}$ in. Greenwell, *B. B.,* pp. 319–20. *British.*

---

[1] The height in inches follows the place-name and county, or Riding of Yorkshire.

56, 57, 58. Marton Hall, E. R. 6 in. Mortimer, *Forty Years*, pp. 344–6.

59. Garton Slack, B. 153, E. R. 5½ in. Mortimer, *Forty Years*, p. 218. *Driffield*.

60, 61. Garton Slack, B. 141, E. R. 6½ in., 2½ in. Mortimer, *Forty Years*, p. 259. *Driffield*.

62, 63. Garton Slack, B. 140, E. R. 4¾ in., 5 in. Mortimer, *Forty Years*, p. 244. *Driffield*.

64. The Riggs, B. 33, E. R. 2¾ in. Mortimer, *Forty Years*, p. 175. *Driffield*.

65, 66, 67, 68. Cross Low, Parwich, Derby. 6 in., 6 in., 3½ in., 4¼ in. Bateman, *Vestiges*, p. 49. *Sheffield*.

69, 70. Sherburn, B. 13, E. R. 6½ in., 6¼ in. Greenwell, *B. B.*, pp. 152–4. *British*.

71, 72. Goodmanham, B. 94, E. R. 6½ in., 5½ in. Greenwell, *B. B.*, pp. 302–3. *British*.

73. Acklam Wold, B. 205, E. R. 2$\frac{4}{10}$ in. Mortimer, *Forty Years*, pp. 87, 88. *Driffield*.

74, 75. Aldro, B. 116, E. R. 4⅔ in., 3 in., without the lid. Mortimer, *Forty Years*, pp. 54–6. *Driffield*.

76, 77. Bar. 13 miles north-east of Pickering, N. R. 5¾ in., 5 in. Bateman, *Diggings*, pp. 218–19. *Sheffield*.

78, 79. Bishop Burton, B. 257, E. R. 5¼ in., 4¾ in. Greenwell, *Arch.* lii. 33, 34. *British*.

80, 81, 82. Aldro, B. 159, E. R. 4 in., 4½ in., 5 in. Mortimer, *Forty Years*, pp. 69–71. *Driffield*.

83. Towthorpe, B. 233, E. R. 4⅘ in. Mortimer, *Forty Years*, pp. 6, 7. *Driffield*.

84, 85, 86. Blanch Group, B. 237, E. R. 6½ in., 4$\frac{3}{10}$ in., 3¾ in. Mortimer, *Forty Years*, pp. 325–6. *Driffield*.

87, 88. Folkton, B. 71, E. R. 6½ in., 4⅞ in. Greenwell, *B. B.*, pp. 274–9. *British*.

89. Garrowby Wold, B. 32, E. R. 6⅝ in. Mortimer, *Forty Years*, pp. 145–6. *Driffield*.

90, 91. Garrowby Wold, B. 62, E. R. 4⅞ in., 5½ in. Mortimer, *Forty Years*, pp. 141–2. *Driffield*.

92, 93, 94. Painsthorpe Wold, B. 98, E. R. 7 in., 8 in., 5 in. Mortimer, *Forty Years*, pp. 130–2. *Driffield*.

95, 96, 97. Huggate Wold, B. 225, E. R. 10 in., 2⅖ in. Mortimer, *Forty Years*, pp. 301–2. *Driffield*.

98. Ford, B. 187, Northumberland. 3¾ in. Greenwell, *B. B.*, pp. 408–9. *British*.

99, 100. Garton Slack, B. 37, E. R. 5½ in., 5 in. Mortimer, *Forty Years*, pp. 209–11. *Driffield*.

101, 102. Hay Top Barrow, Monsal Dale, Derby. 5¼ in., 4½ in. Bateman, *Diggings*, pp. 75, 76. *Sheffield*.

103. Driffield, E. R. 5½ in. *Arch.* xxxiv. 252–4. *British*.

104. Ferry Fryston, B. 161, W. R. 4¼ in. Greenwell, *B. B.*, pp. 371–3. *British*.

105. Rudstone, B. 63, E. R. 4¾ in. Greenwell, *B. B.*, pp. 245–51. *British*.

106, 107, 108, 109. Rudstone, B. 67, E. R. 5⅛ in. 3⅜ in., 5⅛ in., 4¼ in. Greenwell, *B. B.*, pp. 257–62. *British*.

110. Rudstone, B. 62, E. R. 5⅛ in. Greenwell, *B. B.*, pp. 234–45. *British*.

111. Acklam Wold, B. 204, E. R. 4$\frac{1}{10}$ in. Mortimer, *Forty Years*, pp. 86–7. *Driffield*.

112, 113, 114. Weaverthorpe, B. 43, E. R. 4¼ in., 5 in., 4¾ in. Greenwell, *B. B.*, pp. 193–7. *British*.

115, 116, 117. Painsthorpe Wold, B. 118, E. R. 5½ in., 4¼ in., 5 in. Mortimer, *Forty Years*, pp. 125–8. *Driffield*.

118, 119, 120, 121, 122. Folkton, B. 70, E. R. 3⅝ in., 8½ in., 3¾ in., 4½ in., 4 in. Greenwell, *B. B.*, pp. 272–4. *British*.

123. Hutton Buscel, B. 152, N. R. 4⅛ in. Greenwell, *B. B.*, pp. 357–61. *British*.

124. Eglingham, B. 200, Northumberland. 6¼ in. Greenwell, *B. B.*, pp. 418–21. *British*.

125. Colewell, N. Tyne, Northumberland. 3¼ in. *Arch. Aeli.* xiii. 351. *Newcastle*.

126. Blanch Farm, Huggate, E. R. *British*.

127. Cold Eaton, Derbyshire. 4 in. *British*.

128. Welham, Malton, Yorks. 3¼ in. *York*.

129. Acklam Wold, B. 209, E. R. 1⅘ in. Mortimer, *Forty Years*, p. 90. *Driffield*.

130. Goodmanham, B. 102, E. R. 4 in. Greenwell, *B. B.*, p. 312. *British*.

131. Bishop Burton, B. 258, E. R. 4¾ in. Greenwell, *Arch.* lii. p. 34–5. *British*.

132. Loc. unknown. 4½ in. *Newcastle*.

133. Willerby, B. 35, E. R. 4⅝ in. Greenwell, *B. B.*, pp. 184–5. *British*.

134. Garrowby Wold, B. 197, E. R. 3⅘ in. Mortimer, *Forty Years*, p. 143. *Driffield*.

135. Thorpe, Bridlington, Yorks. 3½ in. *York*.

136. Hunmanby, B. 250, E. R. 4½ in. Greenwell, *Arch.* lii. pp. 18–21. *British*.

137. Garton Slack, B. 162, E. R. 4½ in. Mortimer, *Forty Years*, pp. 212–13. *Driffield*.

138. Blanch Huggate, E. R. 4⅞ in. *British*.

139. Gilling, B. 233, N. R. 5½ in. Greenwell, *B. B.*, pp. 550–3. *British*.

140. Loc. unknown. 5 in. *Sheffield*.

141. Newton on Rawcliffe, N. R. 4 in. Bateman, *Diggings*, p. 212. *Sheffield*.

142. Goodmanham, B. 103, E. R. 4¼ in. Greenwell, *B. B.*, pp. 312–14. *British*.

143. Hanging Grimston, E. R. 3 in. Mortimer, *Forty Years*, pp. 106–7 *Driffield*.

144. Amotherby, Malton, N. R. 5 in. *British*.

145, 146. Alwinton, B. 202, Northumberland. 4⅞ in., 4¾ in. *British*.

147. Towthorpe, B. 6, E. R. 4¾ in. Mortimer, *Forty Years*, p. 8. *Driffield*.

148. Hanging Grimston, B. 27, E. R. 6 in. Mortimer, *Forty Years*, pp. 110–12. *Driffield.*
149. Kingthorpe, Yorks. $6\frac{1}{4}$ in. Bateman, *Diggings*, 234–5. *Sheffield.*
150. Marton, Bridlington, Yorks. 6 in. *York.*
151. Rudstone, B. 69, E. R. $4\frac{1}{4}$ in. Greenwell, *B. B.*, pp. 269–70. *British.*
152. Folkton, B. 243, E. R. $4\frac{3}{4}$ in. Greenwell, *Arch.* lii. 12. *British.*
153. Garton Slack, B. 151, E. R. $3\frac{1}{2}$ in. Mortimer, *Forty Years*, p. 216. *Driffield.*
154. Heslerton, B. 5, E. R. $4\frac{3}{4}$ in. Greenwell, *B. B.*, pp. 141–2. *British.*
155. Fimber, B. 133, E. R. $5\frac{1}{2}$ in. Mortimer, *Forty Years*, pp. 190–1. *Driffield.*
156. Marton, Bridlington, Yorks. $5\frac{1}{4}$ in. *York.*
157. Goodmanham, B. 97, E. R. $5\frac{3}{4}$ in. Greenwell, *B. B.*, pp. 304–5. *British.*
158. Calais Wold, B. 23, E. R. 6 in. Mortimer, *Forty Years*, pp. 153–6. *Driffield.*
159. Jesmond, Northumberland. *British.*
160. Ashford, Derby. 5 in. *Sheffield.*
161. Goodmanham, E. R. $4\frac{1}{2}$ in. *Arch.* xxxiv, pl. xx, fig. 10. *British.*
162. Folkton, B. 241. E. R. 4 in. Greenwell, *Arch.* lii. 9, 10. *British.*
163. Alwinton, Northumberland. 4 in. Greenwell, *B. B.*, p. 426. *British.*
164. Askham, B. 183, Cumberland. $5\frac{1}{2}$ in. Greenwell, *B. B.*, pp. 400–1. *British.*
165. Gibb Hill, Derby. $4\frac{1}{4}$ in. Bateman, *Diggings*, pp. 18–19. *Sheffield.*
166. Gilling, B. 137, N. R. $4\frac{1}{2}$ in. Greenwell, *B. B.*, pp. 346–7. *British.*
167. Blanch Group, B. 266, E. R. $4\frac{3}{4}$ in. Mortimer, *Forty Years*, p. 331. *Driffield.*
168. Broad Low Ash, Ashbourne, Derby. $5\frac{1}{2}$ in. Bateman, *Diggings*, pp. 174–5. *Sheffield.*
169, 170. Hitter Hill, Earl Sterndale, Derby. $4\frac{3}{4}$ in. *Reliquary*, iii. 163–8. *British.*
171. Ilderton, Northumberl. $4\frac{1}{2}$ in. *British.*
172. Goodmanham, B. 90, E. R. $5\frac{1}{4}$ in. Greenwell, *B. B.*, p. 300. *British.*
173. Eldon Hill, Peak Forest, Derby. $4\frac{3}{4}$ in. Bateman, *Diggings*, p. 98. *Sheffield.*
174. From near Pickering, N. R. $4\frac{1}{2}$ in. *Sheffield.*
175. Far Low, Cauldron, Derby. $4\frac{3}{4}$ in. Bateman, *Ten Years*, pp. 132–3. *Sheffield.*
176. Weaverthorpe, B. 44, E. R. 5 in. Greenwell, *B. B.*, pp. 197–8. *British.*
176 *bis.* Garrowby Wold, B. 42, E. R. $5\frac{3}{4}$ in. Mortimer, *Forty Years*, pp. 143–4. *Driffield.*
177. Cawthorn Camps, Yorks. $4\frac{1}{4}$ in. Bateman, *Diggings*, p. 207. *Sheffield.*
178. Moneyash Moor, Derby. 4 in. *British.*
179. Cowlam, B. 56, E. R. 5 in. Greenwell, *B. B.*, p. 214. *British.*
180. Wark, Northumberland. $4\frac{7}{8}$ in. *British.*
181. Garton Slack, B. 74, E. R. $5\frac{1}{2}$ in. Mortimer, *Forty Years*, p. 221. *Driffield.*
182. Bostorn, Dovedale, Derby. $5\frac{3}{4}$ in. Bateman, *Diggings*, p. 27. *Sheffield.*
183. Folkton, B. 238 (?), E. R. $6\frac{1}{4}$ in. Greenwell, *Arch.* lii. 6, 7. *British.*
184. Rolley Low Bar., Wardlow Common, Derby. $6\frac{1}{4}$ in. Bateman, *Vestiges*, 55–6. *Sheffield.*
185. Ganton, B. 17, E. R. $6\frac{5}{8}$ in. Greenwell, *B. B.* 157. *British.*
186. Bitchin Hill, Stafford. 6 in. Bateman, *Diggings*, 185–6. *Sheffield.*
187. Mare Hill, Throwley Hall, Stafford. 5 in. Bateman, *Diggings*, 113–14. *Sheffield.*
188. Goldsborough, Lythe, N. R. $6\frac{1}{4}$ in. Greenwell, *Arch.* lii. 43–5. *British.*
189. Goodmanham, B. 118, E. R. 7 in. Greenwell, *B. B.*, pp. 327–8. *British.*
190. Folkton, B. 237, E. R. $7\frac{3}{4}$ in. Greenwell, *Arch.* lii. 5, 6. *British.*
191. Lean Low Bar. Derby. $6\frac{3}{4}$ in. Bateman, *Vestiges*, 102. *Sheffield.*
192. Slingsby, B. 140, N. R. $5\frac{1}{8}$ in. Greenwell, *B. B.*, pp. 349–50. *British.*
193. Wharram Percy, B. 47, E. R. $5\frac{1}{2}$ in. Mortimer, *Forty Years*, p. 45. *Driffield.*
194. Narrowdale Hill, Alstonefield, Stafford. $5\frac{1}{2}$ in. Bateman, *Vestiges*, 97–8. *Sheffield.*
195. Towthorpe, B. 73, E. R. $5\frac{5}{8}$ in. Mortimer, *Forty Years*, p. 16. *Driffield.*
196. Folkton, B. 242, E. R. $6\frac{1}{4}$ in. Greenwell, *Arch.* lii. 10–12. *British.*
197. Acklam Wold, B. 1, E. R. 6 in. Mortimer, *Forty Years*, p. 83. *York.*
198. Huggate Warter Wold, B. 247, E. R. $5\frac{1}{2}$ in. Mortimer, *Forty Years*, p. 314. *Driffield.*
199. Brigg, Lincolnshire. $3\frac{3}{4}$ in. *British.*
200. Alwinton, B. 202, Northumberl. 6 in. Greenwell, *B. B.*, pp. 422–24. *British.*
201. Marton, Bridlington, Yorks. $5\frac{3}{4}$ in. *York.*
202. Garrowby Wold, B. 120, E. R. 6in. Mortimer, *Forty Years*, pp. 146–7. *Driffield.*
203. Garrowby Wold, B. 39, E. R. $4\frac{3}{4}$ in. Mortimer, *Forty Years*, pp. 140–1. *Driffield.*
204. Elk Low, Derby. $4\frac{3}{4}$ in. Ll. Jewitt, *Ceram. Art of Gt. Brit.* i, figs. 47, 48. *British.*
205. Ashington, Northumberland. 6 in. *Newcastle.*
206. Cairn, Amble, Northumberland. $5\frac{5}{8}$ in. *Arch.* lii. 67, 68. *British.*
207. The Riggs, B. $142\frac{1}{2}$, E. R. $6\frac{1}{4}$ in. Mortimer, *Forty Years*, pp. 174–5. *Driffield.*

208. Calais Wold, B. 96, E. R. 5 in. Mortimer, *Forty Years*, p. 168. *Driffield*.

209. From 1 mile north of Pickering, N. R. 5½ in. Bateman, *Diggings*, pp. 210–11. *Sheffield*.

210. Goodmanham, B. 119, E. R. 5¼ in. Greenwell, *B. B.*, p. 328. *British*.

211. Ganton, B. 23, E. R. 4½ in. Greenwell, *B. B.*, pp. 167–8. *British*.

212. Amble, Northumberland. 5⅜ in. *Arch.* lii. 69. *British*.

213. Sherburn, B. 11, E. R. 6¼ in. Greenwell, *B. B.*, 149. *British*.

214. Arbour Low Barrow, Derby. 4½ in. Bateman, *Vestiges*, pp. 64–6. *Sheffield*.

214*a*. Auchnacree, Argyll. 4 in. *P. S. A. S.* x. 459. *Edinburgh*.

215. Arbour Low, Derby. 4¾ in. Bateman, *Vestiges*, p. 65. *Sheffield*.

216. Loc. unknown. 4 in. *York*.

217. Windy Edge, Alnwick, Northumberland. *British*.

218. Stanhow Moor, Skelton, N. R. 4½ in. *British*.

219. Beverley, Yorks. 4 in. *York*.

220. Loc. unknown. 4⅛ in. *York*.

221. Acklam Wold, B. 4, E. R. 3¼ in. Mortimer, *Forty Years*, p. 84. *York*.

222. Acklam Wold, B. 208, E. R. 3⅞ in. Mortimer, *Forty Years*, pp. 89–90. *Driffield*.

223. Corbridge, Northumberland. 3¼ in. *Newcastle*.

223 *bis*. Appleton-le-street, N. R. 2½ in. *British*.

224. Blanch Group, B. 265, E. R. 5 in. Mortimer, *Forty Years*, p. 330. *Driffield*.

225. Wetton Hill Bar., Stafford. 4¼ in. Bateman, *Diggings*, p. 139. *Sheffield*.

226. Doddington, B. 189, Northumberland. 6¾ in. Greenwell, *B. B.*, p. 411. *British*.

227. Villa Real, Jesmond, Northumberland. 5¼ in. *Arch. Aeliana*, ii. 315. *Newcastle*.

228. Heslerton, B. 6, E. R. 5 in. Greenwell, *B. B.*, 142–4. *British*.

229, 230. Goodmanham, B. 98, E. R. 2 in. without the lid, 3½ in. Greenwell, *B. B.*, p. 305. *British*.

231, 232. Loughloughan, Broughshane, Antrim. 4¾ in., 3 in. *J. R. S. A. I.* xxxii (1902), p. 163, &c. *Mr. Knowles' coll.*

232*a*. Old Bridge, Co. Meath, 3¾ in. *P. R. I. A.*, 3 ser., pp. 747–50.

233, 234, 235 (?). Mount Stewart Cairn, Grey Abbey, Co. Down. *Ulster Journ. Arch.* ix. 112. *In private hands*.

236, 236*a*, 237, 237*a*. Duncragaig, Argyll. 3¾ in., 3¼ in. *P. S. A. S.* vi. 347. *Poltalloch coll.*

238, 239, 239*a*. Kilmartin, Poltalloch, Argyll. 5 in., 5 in. *P. S. A. S.* vi. 340. *British* and *Poltalloch coll.*

240, 241, 241*a*. Moylethid, Belmore Mt., Co. Fermanagh. 3⅞ in., 3⅞ in. *P. R. I. A.*, 3 ser., iv. 663. *Dublin*.

242, 243. Letterbrick, Donegal. 4 in., 4 in. *Dublin*.

244. Phoenix Park, Dublin. 6 in. *Trans. Kilkenny Arch. Soc.* ii. 43–4. *Dublin*.

245, 245*a*, 246. Ardna, Keel, Co. Meath. 4 in., 4⅝ in. *Dublin*.

247. Loughquile, Corky, Co. Antrim. 4 in. *J. R. H. A. A. I.* (1889). *Mr. Knowles' coll.*

248. Lug na Curran, Queen's County. 4⅜ in. *J. R. H. A. A. I.*, 4 ser., v. 446–7. *Dublin*.

249. Brownhead Cairn, Arran. 5 in. *P. S. A. S.* xxxvi. 120–22, figs. 43–44. *Edinburgh*.

250. Mountstuart, Bute. 7 in. *P. S. A. S.* xxxviii. 63–9. *Edinburgh*.

251. Mauchrie Moor, Arran. 5 in. *P. S. A. S.* iv. 506, &c. *Edinburgh*.

252. Mauchrie Moor, Circle 2, Arran. 7½ in. *P. S. A. S.* iv. 506, &c. *Edinburgh*.

253. Kinneff, Kincardine. Anderson, *Br. and St. Age*, 59, 60. *Edinburgh*.

254. Rathbarran, Coolaney, Sligo. 4¾ in. *J. R. H. A. A. I.*, 4 ser., viii. 271–2. *Dublin*.

255. Killicarney, Co. Cavan. 6 in. *J. R. H. A. A. I.*, 4 ser., v. 191–2. *Dublin*.

256. Toppet Mountain, Enniskillen. 5⅝ in. *P. R. I. A.*, 3 ser., iv, p. 657. *Dublin*.

257, 258. Succoth Place, Edinburgh. 4¾ in., 3½ in. *P. S. A. S.* xxxvi. 670–4. *Edinburgh*.

259, 260. Ballywillan, Port Rush, Co. Antrim. 4½ in., 3¾ in. *P. R. S. A. I.*, 5 ser., i. 438. *Belfast*.

261, 262. Hamilton, Lanark. 4¾ in., 5½ in. *Hunterian*.

263. Glenhead, Doune, Perth. 4½ in. *P. S. A. S.* xvii. 452–3. *Edinburgh*.

264, 265, Kingsbarns Law, Crail, Fife. 5 in., 5¾ in. *P. S. A. S.* x. 244. *Edinburgh*.

266. Scalpsie Bay, Bute. 5½ in. Bryce, *P. S. A. S.* xxxviii. 52–6. *Edinburgh*.

267, 268. Battle Law, Naughton, Fife. 4 in., 5 in. *P. S. A. S.* xxxv. 301–9. *Edinburgh*.

269. Balcalk, Tealing, Forfar. 5½ in. *P. S. A. S.* xiv. 260–1. *Edinburgh*.

270. Lunanhead, Forfar. 5 in. *P. S. A. S.* xii. 288, &c. *Edinburgh*.

271. Ratho, Midlothian. 4¾ in. Anderson, *op. cit.*, p. 60. *Edinburgh*.

272. Kellas, Murroes, Forfar. 6¼ in. *Edinburgh*.

273, 274, 275. Duncra Hill Farm, Pencaitland, E. Lothian. 4¾ in., 4¼ in., 5½ in. *P. S. A. S.* xxxiv, pp. 131–4, *Edinburgh*.

276, 277. Near Doune Stat., Perth. 4¾ in., 5 in. *P. S. A. S.* xxxvi. 687. *Edinburgh*.

277 *bis*. Duff House, Banff. 6 in. Anderson, *op. cit.*, p. 61, figs. 68–72. *Edinburgh*.

278. Drumalis Abbey, Larne, Antrim. 3¼ in. *Belfast*.

279. Kilmurry, Kilkenny. 4¼ in. *Dublin*.

280. Dunagore Moat, Antrim. 3⅜ in. *Dublin*.

281. Mountfield, Omagh, Tyrone. 3¼ in. *Dublin*.

282. Bishop's Cairn, Glenwherry, Antrim. 4 in. *Belfast.*
283. Probably Ulster. 3½ in. Bell coll., *Edinburgh.*
284, 284*a*. Probably Ulster. 3½ in. Bell coll., *Edinburgh.*
285, 285*a*. Knockmunion, Farganstown, Co. Meath. 3⅞ in. *Dublin.*
286. Kilmurry, Kilkenny. 4¼ in. *Dublin.*
287, 287*a*. Probably Ulster. 4 in. Bell coll., *Edinburgh.*
288, 288*a*. Probably Ulster. *British.*
289. Annalong, Dring, Co. Down. 4 in. *Dublin.*
290. Near Newry, Co. Down. *Belfast.*
291, 291*a*. Donaghanie, Tyrone. 4¼ in. *Dublin.*
292. Loc. unknown. 3⅞ in. *Dublin.*
293. Ballysadare (?), Sligo. 3⅞ in. *Dublin.*
294. Kilmurry, Thomastown, Kilkenny. 4¼ in. *Dublin.*
295. Killinagh, Cavan. 3¾ in. *Dublin.*
296. Probably Ulster. 3½ in. Bell coll., *Edinburgh.*
297. Carrig Banagher, Ballysadare, Sligo. 3⅝ in. *Dublin.*
298. Loc. unknown. *Dublin.*
299. Greenhill, Kill, Co. Dublin. 4½ in. *Dublin.*
300. Hill of Tallaght, Kiltatown, Co. Dublin. 3⅝ in. *Dublin.*
301. Killyglan, Larne, Antrim. 4⅜ in. *British.*
302, 302*a*. Between Ballymena and Clough, Killyree, Antrim. *J. R. H. A. A. I.*, 4 ser., ix. 107. *Belfast.*
302 *bis*. Probably Ulster. *British.*
302*b*. Beacharra, Kintyre. 3½ in. *Campbeltown.*
303. Wartle, Aberdeen. 4½ in. *P. S. A. S.* xxiv. 10. *Edinburgh.*
303*a*. Inveresk, Midlothian. 3$\frac{9}{10}$ in. *Cambridge.*
304. Methlick, Aberdeen. *P. S. A. S.* i. 137. *Edinburgh.*
305. Whitehouse, Lamlash, Arran. 5¼ in. *P. S. A. S.* v. 185. *Edinburgh.*
306. Barsleisnach, Argyll. 4½ in. *Poltalloch.*
307. Between Lisbellow and Enniskillen, Fermanagh. 3⅞ in. *Dublin.*
308. Probably Ulster. 3¾ in. Bell coll., *Edinburgh.*
309. Probably Ulster. 4½ in. Bell coll., *Edinburgh.*
310, 310*a*. Gap of Gorteen, Tyrone. 4 in. *Dublin.*
311. Lamanstown, Dunlavin, Wicklow. 3½ in. *Dublin.*
312. Loc. unknown. 4$\frac{1}{16}$ in. *Dublin.*
313, 313*a*. Dunamase, Queen's Co. 4⅜ in., 3½ in. *Dublin.*
314. Tibradden Mt., Co. Dublin. 4 in. *Dublin.*
315, 316, 317. Ballon Hill, Co. Carlow. Height of the last, 4½ in. *Trans. Kilkenny Ar. Soc.* ii. 300. *Private.*
318. Loc. unknown. 4¼ in. *Dublin.*
319. " " 3¾ in. *Dublin.*
320. " " 3⅞ in. *Dublin.*
321. Probably Kilcattan, Londonderry. 4⅝ in. *Dublin.*
322. Nurney, Co. Kildare. 5¾ in. *Dublin.*
323. Probably Ulster. *British.*
324. " " 4½ in. Bell coll., *Edinburgh.*
325. " " *British.*
326. " " *British.*
327. " " *British.*
327 *bis*. Loc. Unknown. 4¼ in. *Dublin.*
328. Dromore, Stewartstown, Tyrone. 4¾ in. *Belfast.*
329. Glenville, Newry, Co. Down. 4⅜ in. *Belfast.*
330. Loc. unknown. 3⅝ in. *Dublin.*
331. " " 3⅝ in. *Dublin.*
332, 332*a*. Loughbrickland, Co. Down. *Belfast.*
333. Leck, Leckpatrick, Tyrone. 4 in. *Dublin.*
334. Woodburn Waterworks, Carrickfergus, Antrim. 4$\frac{5}{16}$ in. *Dublin.*
335. Bellfield, Musselburgh, Midlothian. 4½ inche *P. S. A. S.* xxxii. 8. *Edinburgh.*
336. Loc. unknown. 4½ in. *Edinburgh.*
337. Rachan, Biggar, Lanark. 4⅝ in. *Edinburgh.*
338. Ardochy, Invergarry, Inverness. 5¼ in. *Edinburgh.*
339. Knockenbaid, Dunbar, East Lothian. *Private.*
340. Tomont End, Gt. Cumbrae. 5 in. *Kelvingrove.*
341. Lochinch, Galloway. 4½ in. *Edinburgh.*
342. Loc. unknown. 5¾ in. *Poltalloch.*
343. Glenarm, Urr, Kirkcudbright. 5¾ in. *Edinburgh.*
344. Glenalmond, Perth. 4 in. *British.*
345. Keir, Dunblane, Perth. 5¼ in. *Stirling.*
346. Loc. unknown. 4¾ in. *Edinburgh.*
347. Stonehaven, Kincardine. 5 in. *Private.*
348. Humbie Mill, East Lothian. 6 in. *P. S. A. S.* vii. 198. *Edinburgh.*
349. Isle of Skye. 6¼ in. *Hunterian.*
350. Howyards farm, Letham Grange, Arbroath, Forfar. 6½ in. *P. S. A. S.* v. 100. *Edinburgh.*
350 *bis*. Over Dalserf, Hamilton, Lanark. 4½ in. *Edinburgh.*
351. Probably Ulster. 3¾ in. Bell coll., *Edinburgh.*
352. " " 3¾ in. " " *Edinburgh.*
353. " " 3¾ in. " " *Edinburgh.*
354. Ireland. 4½ in. *British.*
355. Probably Ulster. 4½ in. Bell coll., *Edinburgh.*
356. " " 4½ in. " " *Edinburgh.*
357. Croghan, Strabane, Tyrone. 6¾ in. *Belfast.*
358, 358*a*. Kilcattan, Londonderry. 4¾ in. *Edinburgh.*
358*x*. Mackrackens, Leckpatrick, Tyrone. *J.R.H.A.A.I.*, 4 ser., i. 29.
359. Wallace Town, Ayr. 3¾ in. *P. S. A. S.* xxvi. 58. *Edinburgh,*
360. Shiskin, Arran. 6 in. *P. S. A. S.* xxi. 161. *Edinburgh.*
361. Moulin, Perth. *Edinburgh.*
362, 362 *bis*. Ardrossan Waterworks, Ayr. *Cran. Brit.* ii, pl. 25. *British.*
363. Netherdale, Banff. 5 in. *Edinburgh.*
364. Deerpark, Kinnaird Castle, Forfar. 5 in. *P.S.A.S.* xxx. 201. *Edinburgh.*
365. East Lothian. 3¾ in. *Edinburgh.*
366. Tomont End, cairn 1, Cumbrae. 4¼ in. *Tr. Glasgow Ar. Soc.* ii. 116. *Kelvingrove.*
367. Probably North Ayrshire. 4⅝ in. *Hunterian.*
368. Loc. unknown. 5 in. *Hunterian.*

369. Beechwood Mains, Corstorphine, Midlothian. 5 in. *P. S. A. S.* iv. 379. *Edinburgh.*
370. Cambusbarron, Stirling. 5¼ in. *Stirling.*
371. Shiel Loch, Torcraik, Midlothian. 4¾ in. *Edinburgh.*
372. Calais Muir, Dunfermline, Fife. 5 in. *P. S. A. S.* xx. 247–8. *Edinburgh.*
373. Mill of Queich, Alyth, Perth. 4½ in. *Edinburgh.*
374. Murley Well, Glamis, Forfar. 4¾ in. *P. S. A. S.* v. 81. *Edinburgh.*
375. Loc. unknown. 5¼ in. *Edinburgh.*
376. Zabothy Hill, Inverarity, Forfar. 5½ in. *P. S. A. S.* xxiv. 9. *Edinburgh.*
377. Probably Kilcattan, Londonderry. 5½ in. *Dublin.*
378. Ballyhague, Meath. 4¾ in. *Dublin.*
379. Cooen, Fassidinin, Kilkenny. 4½ in. *Dublin.*
380. Ballymote, Sligo. 5⅝ in. *J. R. H. A. A. I.*, 4 ser., viii. 267. *Dublin.*
381. Ballyhale, Gorey, Wexford. 3⅞ in. *J. R. H. A. A. I.*, 4 ser., v. 744. *Dublin.*
382. Moytura, Cong, Co. Mayo. 5½ in. Ferguson, *Rude Stone Monum.*, p. 179. *Dublin.*
383. Castlehackett, Tuam, Galway.
384. Loc. unknown. 6⅝ in. *Dublin.*
385. Carballybeg, Waterford. 7⅝ in. *Dublin.*
386. Greenford, Guynd, Forfar. 5 in. *P. S. A. S.* i. 86. *Edinburgh.*
387. Hatton Cairn, Inverarity, Forfar. 5⅜ in. *P. S. A. S.* xxiv. 12, fig. 9. *Edinburgh.*
388. Yetholm, Roxburgh. 3¾ in. *P. S. A. S.* xvii. 381. *Edinburgh.*
389. Rudle, Argyll. 6 in. *P. S. A. S.* vi. 350. *Poltalloch.*
390, 391. Alness, Rosshire. *P. S. A. S.* xiii. 257. *Edinburgh.*
392. Headfort, Galway. 5¼ in. *Dublin.*
393. Loc. unknown. 5½ in. *Dublin.*
394. Sionan, Horseleap, Westmeath. 5½ in. *Dublin.*
395. Ballyare, Donegal. 5 in. *Dublin.*
396. Probably Ulster. 4½ in. Bell coll., *Edinburgh.*
397. „ „ *British.*
398. Loc. unknown. 6⅜ in. *Dublin.*
399. Kilbride, Wicklow. 3¼ in. *Dublin.*
400. Loc. unknown. 4½ in. *Dublin.*
401. Castle Hyde, Fermoy, Co. Cork. 4⅜ in *Dublin.*
402. Lug na groach, Talbotstown, Wicklow. 5¼ in. *Dublin.*
403. Drumcaw, Co. Down. *Antiquary*, xx. 134. *Belfast.*
404. Probably Ulster. 5½ in. Bell coll., *Edinburgh.*
405. Loch Awe, Argyll. 6½ in. *P. S. A. S.* xx. 74. *Edinburgh.*
406. Cramond, Midlothian. 5 in. *Edinburgh.*
407. Craigenhollie, Old Luce, Wigton. 4 in. *P. S. A. S.* xiv. 142; xxi. 189. *Edinburgh.*
408. Cawdor, Nairn. 4¾ in. *Edinburgh.*
409. Loc. unknown. *Edinburgh.*
410. Quinish, I. of Mull. 5½ in. *P. S. A. S.* xxvii. 369. *Edinburgh.*
411. Gullane Links, East Lothian. 4¾ in. *Proc. Berwick Nat. Hist. Club*, x. 306. *Edinburgh.*
412. Kirkhill, Ardrossan, Ayr. 4½ in. *P. S. A. S.* v. 110. *Edinburgh.*
413. Loc. unknown. 5 in. *Dublin.*
414. Darnhall, Peebles. 5½ in. *P. S. A. S.* x. 43. *Edinburgh.*
415. Kenny's Hillock, Urquhart, Elgin. *P. S. A. S.* xiv. 109. *Edinburgh.*
416. Blackhills, Tyrie, Aberdeen. *Proc. Anat. and Anthrop. Soc. Univ. Aberdeen* (1904–6), p. 138–41.
417. Loc. unknown. *Dublin.*
418. Birkhill, near Stirling. 5½ in. *P. S. A. S.* iii. 245. *Edinburgh.*
419. Cambusbarron, Stirling. *Stirling.*
420. Birkhill, Stirling. 5¼ in. *P. S. A. S.* xxi. 265. *Edinburgh.*
421. Sleepies Hill, Urquhart. *Elgin.*
422. Kirkmabreck, Kirkcudbright. 5½ in. *British.*

ILLUSTRATIONS OF OBJECTS

O. 1. Flint dagger. Stonehenge, B. 39. 7⅛ × 1⅛. *A. W.* 163, pl. 18. *Devizes.*
O. 2. Flint dagger. Wick Bar., Stogursey, Somerset. 5⅜ in. long. St. George Gray. *Report on Excav. at Wick Bar.*, pl. viii. *Taunton.*
O. 3. 'Pulley' ring. Fovant, B. 9. Diam. 1½ in. *A. W.* 239, pl. xxxiv. *Devizes.*
O. 4. Stone bracer. Brandon, Suffolk. 4⅝ × 1½. *P. S. A.*, 2 ser., v. 272. *British.*
O. 5. Bronze knife, Avebury, Wilts. 4 in. *P. A. Inst.* 1849, p. 110, figs. 12, 13.
O. 6. Bronze knife. East Kennet, Wilts. 5½ × 2⅜. *Ar. Jour.* xxiv. 28–9; *Ar.* xliii, p. 452.

O. 5, 6, 9 taken from *Arch.* xliii, pl. xxxii, xxxiii.

O. 7. Copper dagger. Roundway, Wilts. 10×2. *Wilts. Ar. Mag.* iii. 185–6. *Devizes.*

O. 8. Copper knife. Mere Down, Wilts. $5 \times 1\frac{3}{8}$. *A. W.* 44, pl. ii. *Devizes.*

O. 9. Copper (?) knife. Winterslow, Wilts. $5\frac{3}{8} \times 1\frac{3}{4}$. *Ar. Jour.* i. 156–7. *Ashmolean.*

O. 10. Bronze knife. Normanton, B. 164, Wilts. $5\frac{3}{4} \times 1\frac{1}{4}$. *A. W.* 205. *Devizes.*

O. 11*a*. Bronze dagger. Fovant, B. 9, Wilts. $8\frac{7}{8} \times 2\frac{3}{8}$. *A. W.* 239, pl. xxxiv. *Devizes.*

O. 11*b*. 3 Arrowheads of flint. $1\frac{3}{4}$, $1\frac{5}{16}$, $1\frac{1}{4}$ long, with the above. *Devizes.*

O. 12. Flint dagger, 3 flint arrowheads, a bone 'mesh-rule' and a bone pin. Green Low, Alsop Moor, Derby. Bateman, *Vestiges*, pp. 52–60. *Sheffield.*

O. 13. Flint dagger. Garton Slack, E. R. $6\frac{1}{4}$ long. Mortimer, 209–11. *Driffield.*

O. 14. Jet button. Thwing, E. R. Greenwell, *B. B.*, fig. 3. *British.*

O. 15. Jet button. Rudstone, E. R. Greenwell, *B. B.*, fig. 124. *British.*

O. 16. Bronze dagger, stone bracer, bone object. Driffield, E. R. $3\frac{1}{2} \times 1\frac{3}{4}$; $5\frac{1}{4} \times 1\frac{3}{8}$; $2\frac{1}{4}$ long. *Arch.* xxxiv. 251–5. *British.*

O. 17. Three chalk cylindrical objects. Folkton, E. R. *Ar.* lii. 14–16. *British.*

O. 18. Bronze knife-dagger. Collessie, Fife. $6 \times 2\frac{1}{8}$. Anderson, fig. 4. *Edinburgh.*

O. 19. Bronze knife-dagger. Sketraw, Dunbar. $5\frac{3}{4}$ in. long. *P. S. A. S.* xxvii. 7. *Edinburgh.*

O. 20. Bronze knife. Letham, near Perth. $3\frac{1}{8} \times 1\frac{7}{16}$. *P. S. A. S.* xxxi. 183. *Edinburgh.*

O. 21. Bronze knife. Drumlanrick, Callender. $4\frac{1}{2}$ long. Anderson, fig. 9. *Edinburgh.*

O. 22. Bronze knife-dagger. Cleigh, Lochnell, Argyll. $5 \times 2\frac{1}{4}$. *P. S. A. S.* xii. 455.

O. 23. Bronze knife. Linlathen, Forfarshire. $4\frac{1}{2} \times 2$. Anderson, fig. 7. *Edinburgh.*

O. 24. Bronze knife. Barnhill, Broughty Ferry. $3\frac{3}{8} \times 1\frac{1}{8}$. *P. S. A. S.* xxi. 321, fig. 3. *Edinburgh.*

O. 25. Jet beads. Cruden, Aberdeenshire. *Cat. Arch. Exhib. Edinb.* 1858, pl. iii. Wilson, *Prehist. Annals*, 75. *Peterhead.*

O. 26*a*, *b*, *c*, *d*, *e*, *f*. Two bronze daggers, bronze celt, perforated oolite hammer, a gold plaque, gold plaque with a hook. Bush Bar., Normanton, Wilts. *A. W.* 203–4. *Devizes.*

O. 27*a*, *b*, *c*. Forked object of bronze, stone hammer, bronze celt, Wilsford, B. 18, Wilts. *A. W.* 209. *Devizes.*

O. 28*a*, *b*, *c*. Two bronze daggers, tracing of an urn. Winterbourne Stoke, B. 16, Wilts. *A. W.* 123, pl. xv. *Devizes.*

O. 29*a*, *b*, *c*. Bronze dagger, 2 bronze pins. Brigmilston or Brigmerston, B. 24. *A. W.* 185, pl. 23; 194, pl. 22. *Devizes.*

O. 30. Bronze dagger with midrib and 6 rivets, 6 in. long. Towthorpe, B. 233, E. R. Mortimer, p. 6, pl. ii, fig. 12. *Driffield.*

O. 31. Jet necklace, $11\frac{1}{4}$ in. long. Weaverthorpe, B. 49. E. R. Greenwell, *B. B.*, p. 205. *British.*

O. 32*a*, *b*. Bronze knife, $4\frac{1}{2} \times 2$; bronze celt, $4 \times 2\frac{3}{8}$. Butterwick, B. 39, E. R. Greenwell, *B. B.* 186, figs. 37, 38. *British.*

O. 33. Bronze knife. $3 \times 1\frac{1}{4}$. Life Hill, B. 294, E. R. Mortimer, p. 203, pl. lxvi, fig. 500*b*. *Driffield.*

O. 34*a*, *b*. Bronze knife and flat bronze celt. Shuttleston Bar., Derbyshire. Bateman, *Arch. Ass. Journ.* vii. 217. *Sheffield.*

O. 35. Bronze knife. Helperthorpe, B. 49, E. R. Greenwell, *B. B.* 206, fig. 108. *British.*

O. 36. Bronze knife. Rudstone, B. 68, E. R. Greenwell, *B. B.* 264, fig. 125. *British.*

O. 37. Bronze knife. Garrowby Wold, B. 32, E. R. Mortimer, fig. 391. *Driffield.*

O. 38. Bronze knife. Carder Low, Hartington, Derby. Bateman, *Vestiges*, 64. *Arch.* xliii, pl. 33. *Sheffield.*

O. 39. Bronze knife-dagger. Brier Low, Buxton, Derby. *Arch.* xliii, pl. 33, fig. 3. Bateman, *Vestiges*, 61. *Sheffield.*

O. 40. Bronze knife-dagger. Garton Slack, B. 107, E. R. Mortimer, 231; *Arch.* xliii, pl. 34. *Driffield.*

O. 41. Bronze knife-dagger. End Low, Hartington, Derby. Bateman, *Forty years*, p. 39. *Sheffield.*

O. 42. Bronze knife-dagger. Acklam Wold, B. 205, E. R. Mortimer, fig. 203. *Driffield.*

O. 43. Bronze blade. Worm Hill, Derby. *Cat. Sheffield Mus. J.* 93–439, p. 66. *Sheffield.*

O. 44. Bronze knife-dagger. Lett (or Lid) Low, Warslow, Stafford. Bateman, *Ten Years*, 245. *Arch.* xliii, pl. 33, fig. 5. *Sheffield.*

O. 12 from Bateman, *Vestiges*, 59.
O. 14, 15 from Greenwell, *B. B.*, figs. 3, 124.
O. 19 from *P. S. A. S.* xxvii. 7, fig 1.
O. 18, 21, 22, 23 from Anderson, *St. and Br. Ages*, figs. 4, 9, 8, 7.
O. 24 from *P. S. A. S.* xxi. 321, fig. 3.
O. 25 from *Cat. Arch. Exhib. Edinburgh* (1858), pl. iii.
O. 28*c* from Hoare, *A. W.*, pl. xv.
O. 32, 32*b* from Greenwell, *B. B.*, figs. 37, 38.
O. 33 from Mortimer, *Forty Years*, fig. 500*b*.
O. 34*a*, *b*, from Bateman, *Jour. Arch. Ass.*, vii. 217.
O 35, 36 from Greenwell, *B. B.*, figs. 108, 125.
O. 38, 39, 40, 44, 45 from Thurnam, *Arch.* xliii, pl. 33, 34 and fig. 38.
O. 41 from Bateman, *Diggings*, 39.
O. 42 from Mortimer, *op. cit.*, fig. 203.
O. 43 from *Cat. Sheffield Museum*, p. 66.

O. 45. Bronze blade, unsymmetrical. Dow Low, Church Sterndale, Derby. Bateman, *Vestiges*, 96. *Sheffield*.

O. 46. Ten stone beads. Belmore Mount, Fermanagh. *P. R. I. A.*, 3 ser., iv. 660-2. *Dublin*.

O. 47. Bronze knife. Corky, Antrim. *J.R.H.A.A.I.*, no. 79 (1889). *Mr. Knowles' collection*.

O. 48. Bronze spiral bracelet. Lug na Curran, Queen's County. *Dublin*.

O. 49. Stone celt. Rathbarran, Co. Sligo. *J.R.H.A.A.I.*, 4 ser., viii. 271-2. *Dublin*.

O. 50a, b. Stone celt and bone plate with hooks. Killicarney, Co. Cavan. *J. R. H. A. A. I.*, 4 ser., v. 191-2. *Dublin*.

O. 51. Bronze blade and gold mounting. Toppet Mountain, Co. Enniskillen. *P. R. I. A.*, 3 ser., iv. 657. *Dublin*.

O. 52. Stone hammer. Glenhead, Doune, Perth. *P. S. A. S.* xvii. 452. *Edinburgh*.

O. 47 from Knowles, *J.R.H.A.A.I.*, no. 79 (1889).
O. 49 from *J.R.H.A.A.I.*, 4 ser., viii. 271, fig. 254.

O. 50a, b from *J.R.H.A.A.I.*, 4 ser., v. 191, fig. 255.
O. 52 from Anderson, *op. cit.*, fig. 102.

PLATE I

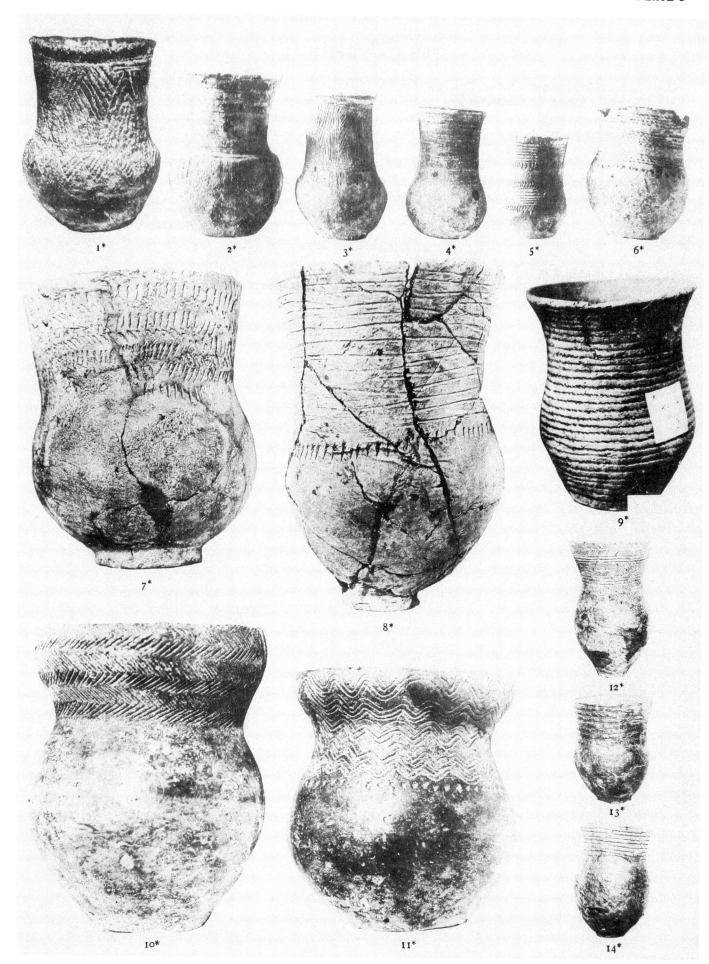

CONTINENTAL BEAKER

1* Benndorf, 5½". 2* Polleben, 8". 3* Querfurt, 7⅛". 4* Mittelhausen, 6½". 5* Aeberode, 5¾". 6* Eisleben, 3¾". 7* Holstein, 6⅝". 8* Holstein, 7¼". 9* Drenthe, Holland, 4¾". 10* Holstein, 6¾". 11* Holstein, 5¾". 12* Ribe Amt, Denmark, 8". 13* Jutland, 7½". 14* Jutland, 8¼".

PLATE II

CONTINENTAL BEAKERS

15* Sicily, 3″.   16* Millares, Spain, 4″.   17*, 18*, 19* H. Pyrénées.   20*, 21* Ciempozuelos, Madrid.   22* Brittany.   23* Carnac, 5¼″.   24* Carnac, 5″.   25* Brittany, 5¹⁄₁₆″.   26* Brittany, 4½″.   27* Buda-Pest, 4″.   28*, 29* Rottleben.   30* Bitterfeld.   31* Wanzleben.   32* Ober-Olm. 33*, 34* Horchheim.   35*, 36* unknown.   37*, 38* Andernach.   39*, 40* Urmitz.   41* Frankenthal.   43* Herrensheim.   44* Andernach.

PLATE III

CONTINENTAL BEAKERS

42* Urmitz. **45*** Holstein, 5⅞″. **46*** Holstein, 6½″. **47*** Holstein, 6½″. **48*** Holland, 6½″. **49*** Holland, 5¾″. **50*** Holland, 5¾″.
51* Holland, 6⅝″. **52*, 53*** Holland, 5¼″, 2¾″. **54*** Finistère, 7¼″.

PLATE IV

Andernach.

Andernach.

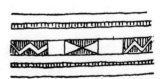

Ober Olm.

Urmitz.

Urmitz.

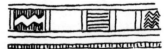

Trebnitz.

Horchheim.

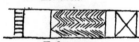

Urmitz.

Herrensheim.

Horchheim.

Liboc.

Litoměřice.

Litoměřice.

Kralupy.

Eisleben.

Gr. Osterhausen.

Dessau.

Erfurt.

Leiselheim.

Erfurt.

Bitterfelt (?).

Rothleben.

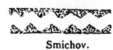

Smichov.

Smichov.

Pr. Saxony.

Bylany.

CORD BEAKERS

Bedersleben.

Kötschen.

Rothmansdorf.

Kötscher.

Ammendorf.

Trebnitz.

Kuckenburg.

Nickelsdorf.

ORNAMENTATION ON FOREIGN BEAKERS

PLATE V

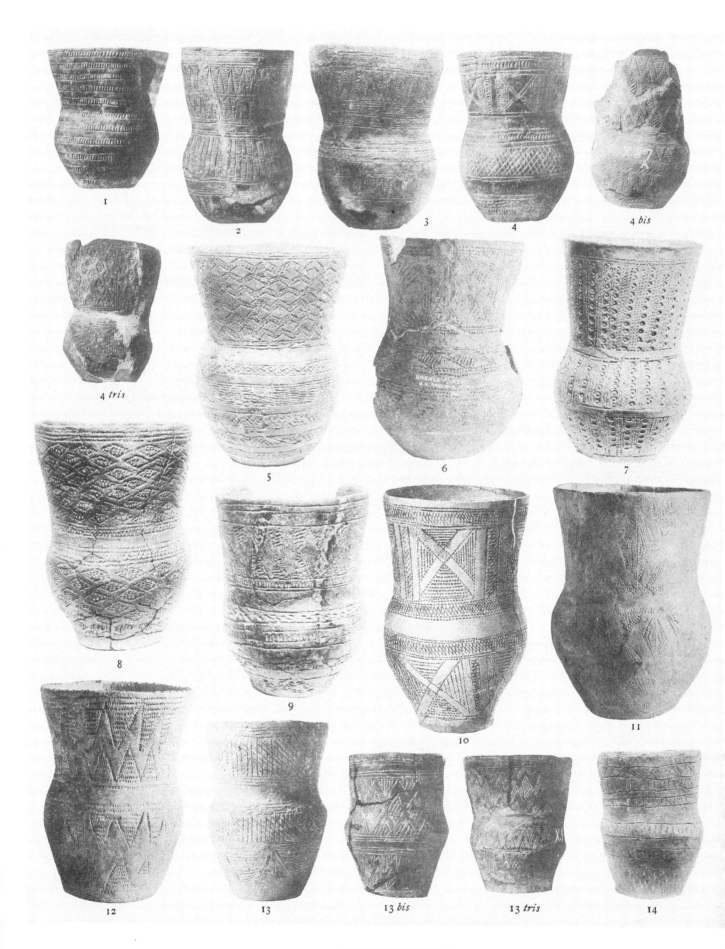

ENGLISH BEAKERS

1 Wilts, 5¾″. 2 Wilts, 7¾″. 3 Wilts, 8¼″. 4 Wilts, 7½″. 4 *bis, tris* Wilts. 5 Wilts, 7¼″. 6 Kent, 6¼″. 7 Berks, 7¼″. 8 Wilts 8″.
9 Wilts, 6″. 10 Wilts, 7½″. 11, 12 Somerset, 7¼″, 6½″. 13 Devon, 7⅜″. 13 *bis* Wilts. 13 *tris* Wilts. 14 Wilts, 7″.

PLATE VI

ENGLISH BEAKERS

15 Dorset, 6″. **16** Devon. **17** Dorset, 5½″. **18** Wilts, 5½″. **18** *bis* Wilts, 7¼″. **19** Wilts, 6″. **20** Somerset, 6 3/16″. **21** Wilts. **22** Berks, 6″. **23** Dorset, 7½″. **24** Wilts, 8½″. **25** Dorset, 8″. **26** Dorset, 8¼″. **27** Wilts, 8½″. **28** Wilts, 7¼″. **29** Wilts, 6⅜″. **30** Dorchester, 7″. **31** Dorset.

PLATE VII

ENGLISH BEAKERS

32 Dorset, 4¾″.   33 Wilts, 6⅝″.   34, 35 Kent, 4″.   36, 37 Kent, 5½″, 5⅜″.   38 Sussex, 5″.   39 Somerset, 6¼″.   40 Dartmoor, 9¼″.
41 Berks, 5¾″.   42 Somerset, 9½″.   42 bis Somerset, 6½″.   43 Berks, 4⅜″.   44 Norfolk, 6″.   45 Suffolk, 7½″.

PLATE VIII

ENGLISH BEAKERS

46 Suffolk, 5¾″. 47 Suffolk, 6¾″. 48 Derby, 7¼″. 49 Derby, 9″. 50 Derby, 4½″. 51 Derby, 6½″. 52 Derby, 6½″. 53 Derby, 7″. 54 Derby, 7¼″. 55 Stafford, 8″. 56 Stafford, 6½″. 57 Derby, 7¾″. 58 Lincoln, 6″. 59 Stafford, 7″. 60 Stafford, 8¼″. 61 Suffolk, 7¼″. 62 Derby, 7½″. 63 Derby, 6¾″. 64 Oxford, 4½″. 65 Cambridge, 5⅛″.

PLATE IX

ENGLISH BEAKERS

66 Northampton, 7½″. 67 Lancs ?, 6″. 68 Derby, 8¼″. 69 Cambridge, 7¼″. 70 Suffolk, 5″. 71 Stafford, 7″. 72–74 Bucks, 4″, 3¾″, 4½″. 75 Oxford, 7¾″. 76 Hunts, 10⅘″. 77 Oxford, 6³⁄₁₆″. 78 Suffolk, 6″. 79 Oxford, 4½″. 80 Norfolk, 5½″. 81 Norfolk, 5″. 82, 83 Suffolk, 4″, 5″. 84 Ipswich, 5¾″. 85 Essex, 5⅝″.

PLATE X

ENGLISH BEAKERS

86 Suffolk, 5″. **87** Essex, 4¾″. **88** Derby, 7″. **89** Cambridge, 7½″. **90** Norfolk, 5″. **90** *bis* Derby, 7½″. **91** Norfolk, 8½″. **92** Norfolk, 6½″.
93 Suffolk, 5⅜″. **94** Glamorgan, 6½″. **95** Denbigh, 4⅞″. **96** Montgomery, 4″. **97** Carnarvon, 5⅝″. **98** E. Riding, 6¼″. **99** E. Riding, 8⅜″. **100**
E. Riding, 7″. **101** E. Riding, 7¼″. **102** E. Riding, 8½″. **103** E. Riding, 8¾″. **104** E. Riding, 7½″. **106** E. Riding, 7¼″.

ENGLISH BEAKERS

105 E. Riding, 7". **107** Yorks, $9\frac{1}{8}$". **108** E. Riding, $7\frac{1}{4}$". **109** W. Riding, $6\frac{5}{8}$". **110** E. Riding, $5\frac{7}{8}$". **110** *bis* E. Riding, $5\frac{7}{8}$". **111** E. Riding, $5\frac{3}{8}$". **112, 113, 114** E. Riding, $5\frac{7}{8}$", 6", $5\frac{5}{8}$". **115, 116, 117** E. Riding, $8\frac{1}{4}$", 7", $7\frac{3}{4}$". **118, 119, 120, 121** E. Riding, 5", $4\frac{5}{8}$", $2\frac{1}{2}$", $7\frac{1}{2}$". **122** E. Riding, 9".

PLATE XII

ENGLISH BEAKERS

123, 124 E. Riding, 9¼″, 6¼″. **125, 126, 127** E. Riding, 8½″, 5″, 6½″. **128, 129** E. Riding, 8½″, 7½″. **130, 131** E. Riding, 6¾″, 7¾″. **132, 133, 134** E. Riding, 8″, 5½″, 6⅞″. **135, 136, 137, 138, 139** E. Riding, 7¾″, 8½″, 7¾″, 6″, 6¾″. **141** E. Riding, 5½″.

PLATE XIII

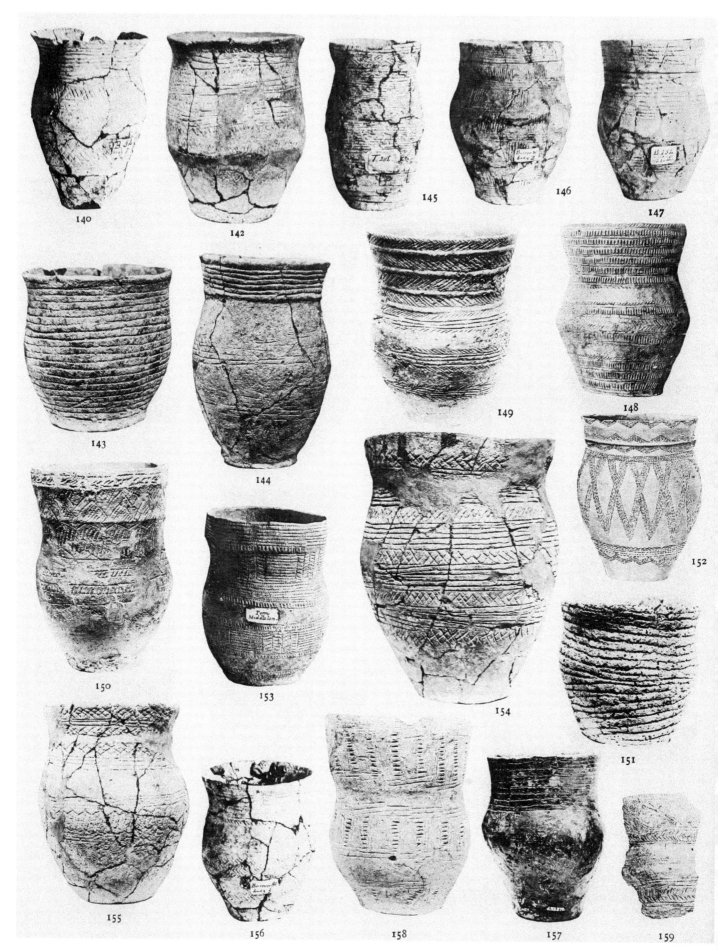

ENGLISH BEAKERS

140 E. Riding, 7″. **142, 143** E. Riding, 4⅞″, 4¼″. **144** E. Riding, 7⅞″. **145** E. Riding, 5⅝″. **146** E. Riding, 9″. **147** E. Riding, 8¼″. **148** Yorks, 7″. **149** E. Riding, 7″. **150** E. Riding, 9″. **151** E. Riding, 4½″. **152** E. Riding, 8⅝″. **153** E. Riding, 7½″. **154** E. Riding, 8¼″. **155** E. Riding, 7¾″. **156** E. Riding, 7½″. **157** N. Riding, 7½″. **158** Northumberland, 6⅝″. **159** Northumberland.

PLATE **XIV**

ENGLISH BEAKERS

160 Northumberland, 6½″. **161** Cumberland, 7½″. **162** Northumberland, 7½″. **163** Westmorland, 7″. **164** Northumberland, 6″. **165** Westmorland. **166** Northumberland? **167, 168, 169, 170, 171** Northumberland, 5⅝″, 5¼″, 5½″, 5″. **172** Northumberland, 9¾″. **173** Northumberland, 7¼″. **174** Northumberland, 6⅛″. **175** Cumberland, 8½″. **176** Westmorland, 7¾″. **177** Durham, 6¾″. **178** Northumberland, 8″.

PLATE XV

ENGLISH BEAKERS

179 Northumberland, 5″. 180 Northumberland, 6¾″. 181 Northumberland 5½″. 182 Cumberland, 6″. 183 Northumberland, 7″. 184 Northumberland. 185 Argyll, 7″. 186 Lanark, 7½″. 187 Berwick. 188 Roxburgh, 8¼″. 189 Midlothian, 6½″. 190 Fife, 7⅛″. 191 Argyll?, 6¼″. 192 Perth. 193 Unknown. 194 Perth, 5¾″. 196 Fife. 197 E. Lothian, 7¾″.

PLATE XVI

ENGLISH BEAKERS

195 Linlithgow, 5⅝″.   **198** Argyll, 9″.   **199** Ayr, 9″.   **200** Perth, 5¾″.   **201** Fife, 5″.   **202** Linlithgow, 5½″.   **203** Stirling.   **204, 205** Fife, 7″, 9″.
206, 207 Midlothian, 6¾″, 7½″.   **208, 209** Lanark, 7½″, 6¾″.   **210, 211** Berwick.   **213** Lanark, 6″.   **214** Kinross, 5¾″.   **215** Perth, 5″.   **216** E. Lothian, 6½″.

Plate XVII

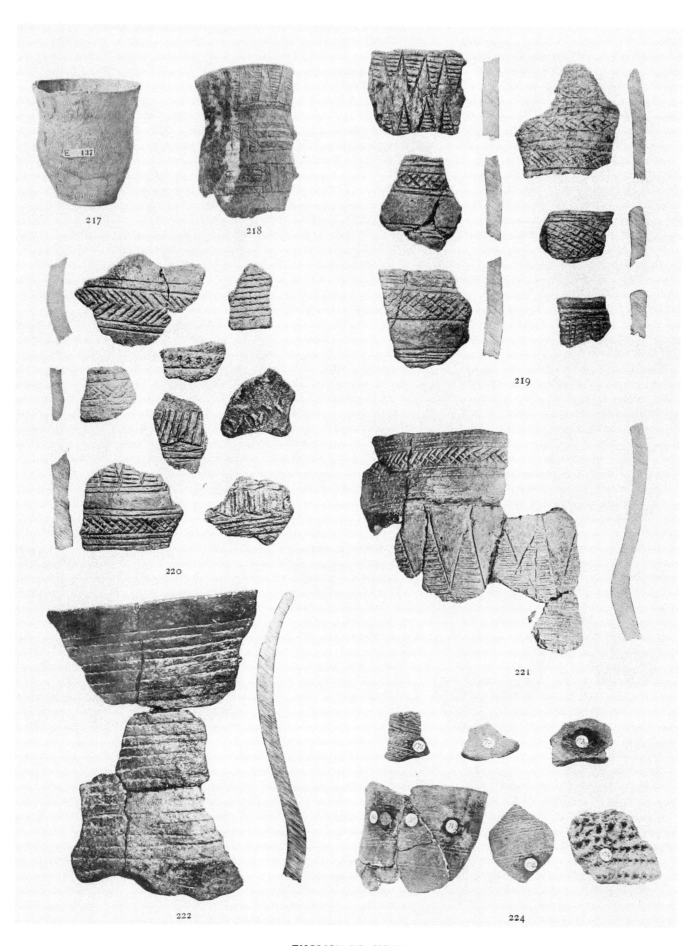

217

218

219

220

221

222

224

ENGLISH BEAKERS
217 Mull, 6½″.   **218** E. Lothian.   **219, 220, 221** E. Lothian.   **222** E. Lothian.   **224** Sligo.

PLATE XVIII

ENGLISH BEAKERS

223 Down. **225** Aberdeen, 4¾″. **226, 227** Aberdeen, 6″, 7″. **228, 229** Aberdeen, 7⅜″, 5¾″. **230, 231** Aberdeen, 5¼″, 4½″. **232, 233** Aberdeen, 6½″, 8″. **234, 235** Kincardine, 6″. **236** Forfar. **237** Aberdeen, 6½″. **238** Aberdeen, 7½″. **239** Aberdeen, 7⅞″. **240** Forfar, 8¼″. **241** Aberdeen, 7″. **242** Forfar. **243** Aberdeen, 7⅞″. **244** Aberdeen, 7¼″. **245** Aberdeen, 6¼″. **246** Aberdeen, 5⁷⁄₁₆″. **247** Aberdeen, 6⅛″.

PLATE XIX

ENGLISH BEAKERS

248 Aberdeen, 8″.   **249** Aberdeen, 6½″.   **250** Forfar, 6½″.   **251** Aberdeen.   **252** Aberdeen, 8″.   **253** Aberdeen, 5½″.   **254** Aberdeen, 5¼″.   **255** Aberdeen, 5″.   **256** Aberdeen, 6¾″.   **257** Aberdeen.   **258** Aberdeen, 6½″.   **259** Forfar, 8″.   **260** Aberdeen, 4¾″.   **261** Aberdeen, 8″.   **262** Forfar, 7″.   **263** Aberdeen, 4⅜″.   **264** Aberdeen, 6″.   **265** Sutherland, 5½″.   **267** Banff, 7½″.

PLATE XX

ENGLISH BEAKERS

266 Nairn, 7″. 268 Elgin, 5½″. 269 Ross, 6″. 270 Banff, 8″. 271 Elgin, 6¾″. 272 Banff, 6″. 273 Nairn, 6¼″. 274 Banff, 5″. 275 Elgin, 5¾″.
276 Banff. 277, 278, 279 Banff, 6½″, 6⅛″, 7¾″. 280, 281, 282 Banff, 7¾″, 5¼″, 7½″. 283 Banff, 6⅜″. 284 Elgin, 6¼″. 285 Elgin ?

PLATE XXI

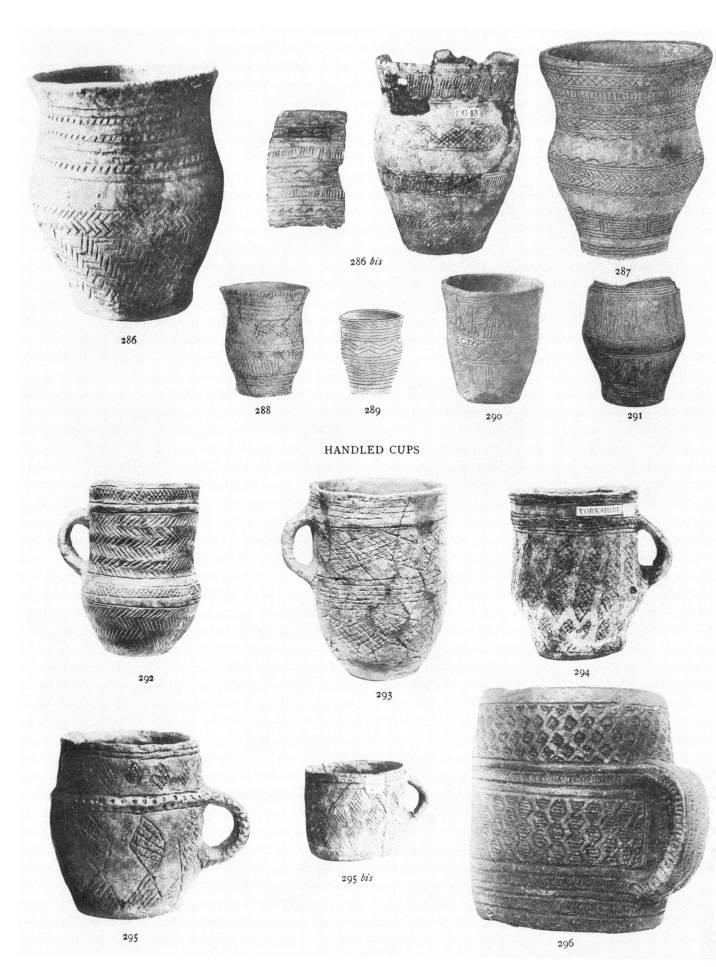

286 bis

287

286

288 289 290 291

HANDLED CUPS

292 293 294

295 295 bis 296

ENGLISH BEAKERS AND HANDLED CUPS

286 Sutherland, 7″. **286** *bis* Caithness, 7¾″. **287** Banff, 7″. **288** Inverness, 5½″. **289** Ross, 5″. **290** Ross?, 5½″. **291** Banff. **292** Berks, 6″. **293** E. Riding, 7¼″. **294** N. Riding, 5¾″. **295, 296** Northampton, 5″, —. **295** *bis* E. Riding, 4½″.

PLATE XXII

ENGLISH HANDLED CUPS

296 *bis* Northampton, 7″. **296a** E. Riding, 5½″. **296b** E. Riding, 5½″. **297** Norfolk, 4″. **298** Dorset, 4½″.
299, 299a Dorset, 4½″. **300** Dorset, 2⅝″. **301** Cornwall. **301** *bis* Derby, 1¾″.

PLATE XXII

Wilts fig. 2.

Wilts fig. 2.

Wilts fig. 3.

Wilts fig. 4.

Wilts fig. 4 a.

Wilts fig. 5.

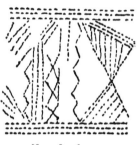

Kent fig. 6.

Berks fig. 7.

Wilts fig. 8.

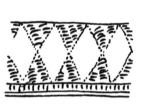

Wilts fig. 9.

Wilts fig. 9 a.

Somerset fig. 12.

Dorset fig. 15.

Wilts fig. 21.

Wilts fig. 24.

Somerset fig. 39.

Kent fig. 34.

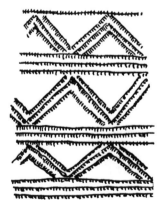

Berks fig. 41.

Norfolk fig. 44.

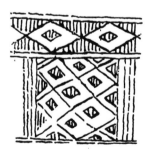

Suffolk fig. 45.

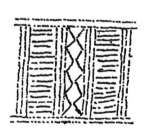

Suffolk fig. 46.

ORNAMENTATION ON ENGLISH BEAKERS

PLATE XXIV

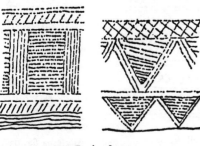

Derby fig. 49.

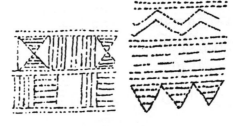

Derby fig. 50.

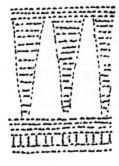

Derby fig. 51.

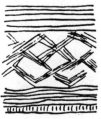

Derby fig. 52.

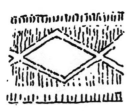

Derby fig. 54.

Stafford fig. 55.

Stafford fig. 56.

Derby fig. 57.

Lincoln fig. 58.

Stafford fig. 59.

Stafford fig. 60.

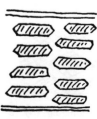

Lincoln fig. 60 a.

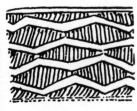

Suffolk fig. 61.

Derby fig. 63.

Oxford fig. 64.

Northampton fig. 66.

ORNAMENTATION ON ENGLISH BEAKERS

PLATE XXV

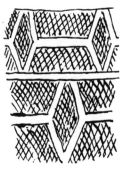

Lancashire fig. 67.

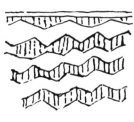

Cambridge fig. 69.

Suffolk fig. 70.

Norfolk fig. 91.

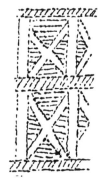

Anglesea fig. 93 a.

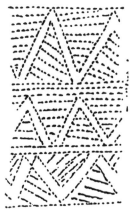

Glamorganshire fig. 94.

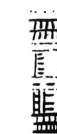

Anglesea fig. 94 a.

E. Riding fig. 98.

E Riding fig. 95.

Denbighshire fig. 95.

E. Riding fig. 101.

E. Riding fig. 104.

E. Riding fig. 107.

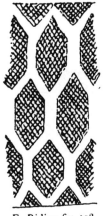

E. Riding fig. 108.

E. Riding fig. 110.

E. Riding fig. 111.

E. Riding fig. 112.

E. Riding fig. 118.

E. Riding fig. 122.

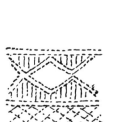

E. Riding fig. 124.

E. Riding fig. 128.

E. Riding fig. 116.

E. Riding fig. 121.

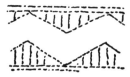

E. Riding fig. 130.

ORNAMENTATION ON ENGLISH BEAKERS

PLATE XXVI

E. Riding fig. 131.

E. Riding fig. 132.

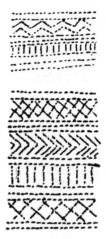

E. Riding fig. 136.

E. Riding fig. 137.

E. Riding fig. 138.

E. Riding fig. 152.

E. Riding fig. 155.

E. Riding fig. 155.

Northumberland fig. 158.

Northumberland fig. 160.

E. Riding fig. 150.

Northumberland fig. 161 a.

Westmorland fig. 163.

Westmorland fig. 165

Northumberland fig. 168.

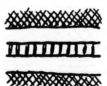

Northumberland fig. 173.

Northumberland fig. 174.

Cumberland fig. 175.

ORNAMENTATION ON ENGLISH BEAKERS

PLATE XXVI

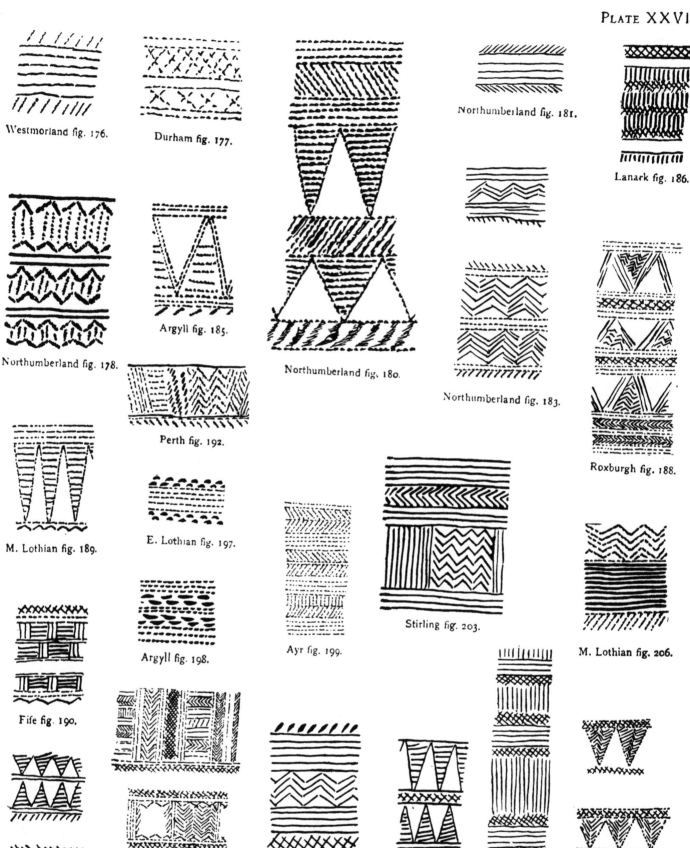

Westmorland fig. 176.

Durham fig. 177.

Northumberland fig. 181.

Lanark fig. 186.

Northumberland fig. 178.

Argyll fig. 185.

Northumberland fig. 180.

Northumberland fig. 183.

Roxburgh fig. 188.

Perth fig. 192.

M. Lothian fig. 189.

E. Lothian fig. 197.

Stirling fig. 203.

M. Lothian fig. 206.

Argyll fig. 198.

Ayr fig. 199.

Fife fig. 190.

M. Lothian fig. 207.

Lanark fig. 209.

Berwick fig. 211.

Lanark fig. 213.

Kinross fig. 214.

Isle of Mull fig. 217.

ORNAMENTATION ON ENGLISH BEAKERS

PLATE XXVIII

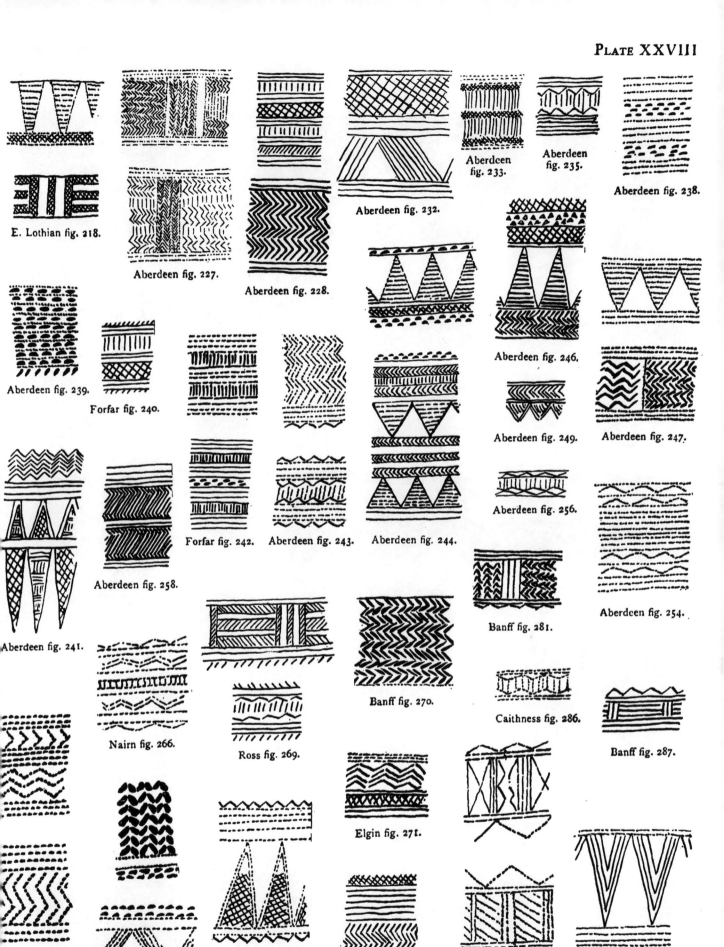

E. Lothian fig. 218.

Aberdeen fig. 227.

Aberdeen fig. 228.

Aberdeen fig. 232.

Aberdeen fig. 233.

Aberdeen fig. 235.

Aberdeen fig. 238.

Aberdeen fig. 239.

Forfar fig. 240.

Aberdeen fig. 246.

Aberdeen fig. 249.

Aberdeen fig. 247.

Forfar fig. 242.

Aberdeen fig. 243.

Aberdeen fig. 244.

Aberdeen fig. 256.

Aberdeen fig. 258.

Banff fig. 281.

Aberdeen fig. 254.

Aberdeen fig. 241.

Banff fig. 270.

Caithness fig. 286.

Nairn fig. 266.

Ross fig. 269.

Banff fig. 287.

Elgin fig. 271.

Aberdeen fig. 261.

Banff fig. 283.

Elgin fig. 284.

Ross fig. 290.

Banff fig. 291.

Banff fig. 267.

ORNAMENTATION ON ENGLISH BEAKERS

PLATE XXIX

FOOD VESSELS

1 Dorset, 6$\frac{1}{16}$". 2 Unknown. 3 Oxford, 5$\frac{1}{4}$". 4 Somerset, 4$\frac{3}{4}$". 5 Unknown. 6 Oxford, 6$\frac{3}{4}$". 7 Oxford, 4$\frac{1}{4}$". 8 Dorset, 6". 8 *bis* Berks, 3$\frac{1}{4}$". 9 Oxford, 5$\frac{3}{4}$". 10 Essex, 4$\frac{1}{2}$". 11 Wilts, 3$\frac{5}{8}$". 12 Wilts, 1$\frac{1}{2}$". 13 Sussex, 2". 13 *bis* Northampton, 5$\frac{1}{4}$". 14 Dorset, 6". 15 Dorset, 4". 16 Gloucester, 3$\frac{3}{4}$". 17 London, 3$\frac{3}{4}$". 18 Hants, 3$\frac{3}{4}$".

PLATE XXX

FOOD VESSELS

19, 20 Colchester, 4″, 2¾″.   **21** Thames at Kew, 2¾″.   **21** *bis* Wilts, 3½″.   **22, 23, 24** E. Riding, 4″, 5″, 5⅝″.   **25** E. Riding, 6″.   **26** E. Riding, 4″.
27 E. Riding, 5½″.   **28, 29, 30, 31** E. Riding, 6½″, 3¾″, 4⅞″, 2¼″.   **32, 33, 34** E. Riding, 4½″, 5½″, 3⅜″.   **35, 36** E. Riding, 3¾″, 4½″.   **37** E. Riding, 5½″.

PLATE XXXI

FOOD VESSELS

38 E. Riding, 4″. **39, 40** N. Riding, 4″, 5″. **41, 42** Derby, 6″, 6″. **43, 44** Yorks, 5½″, 4¼″. **45, 46** E. Riding, 6½″, 5½″. **47** E. Riding, 4½″.
48, 49 E. Riding, 5″, 4⅛″. **50, 51** E. Riding, 4½″, 5″. **52, 53** E. Riding, 4⅖″, 6 1/10″. **54, 55** E. Riding, 5½″, 2¼″.

PLATE XXXII

FOOD VESSELS

56, 57, 58 E. Riding, 6″, 5″, 6″.   **59** E. Riding, 5½″.   **60, 61** E. Riding, 6½″, 2½″.   **62, 63** E. Riding, 4¾″, 5″.   **64** E. Riding, 2¾″.   **65, 66, 67, 68** Derby, 6″, 6″, 3½″, 4¼″.   **69, 70** E. Riding, 6½″, 6¼″.   **71, 72** E. Riding, 6½″, 5½″.   **73** E. Riding, 2⁴⁄₁₀″.   **74, 75** E. Riding, 4⅜″, 3″ without the lid. **76, 77** N. Riding, 5¼″, 5″.

PLATE XXXIII

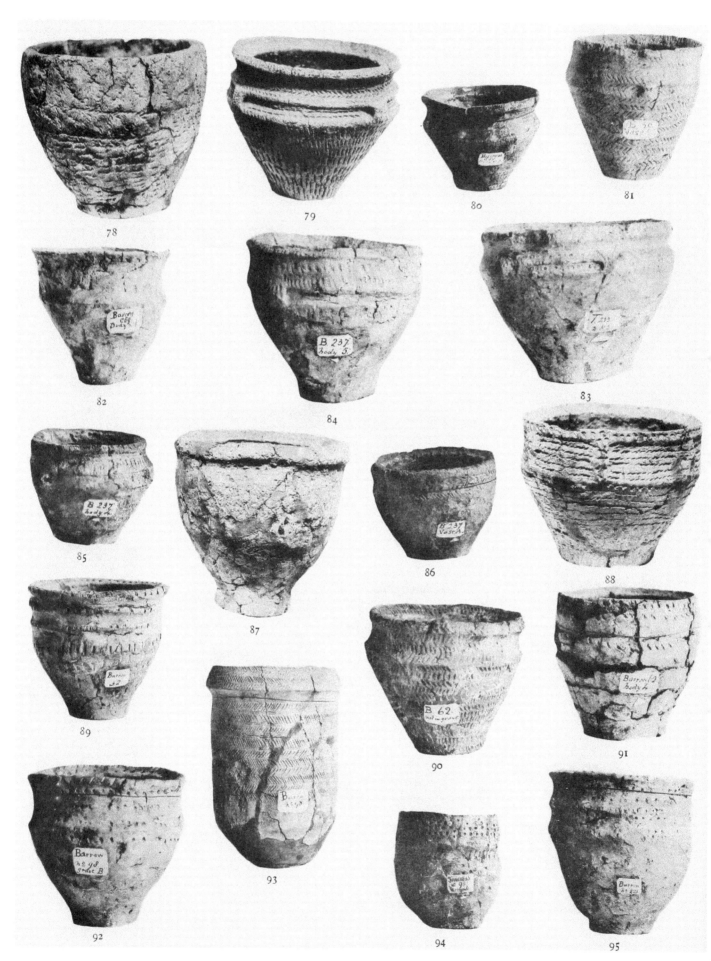

FOOD VESSELS

78, 79 E. Riding, 5¼″, 4¾″.   80, 81, 82 E. Riding, 4″, 4½″, 5″.   83 E. Riding, 4⅕″.   84, 85, 86 E. Riding, 6½″, 4₁₀³″, 3¾″.   87, 88 E. Riding, 6½″, 4⅕″.   89 E. Riding, 6⅝″.   90, 91 E. Riding, 4⅞″, 5½″.   92, 93, 94 E. Riding, 7″, 8″, 5″.   95 E. Riding, 10″.

PLATE XXXIV

FOOD VESSELS

96, 97 E. Riding, 2⅝", —. 98 Northumberland, 3¾". 99, 100 E. Riding, 5½", 5". 101, 102 Derby, 5¼", 4½". 103 E. Riding, 5½".
104 W. Riding, 4¼". 105 E. Riding, 4¾". 106, 107, 108, 109 E. Riding, 5⅝", 3⅜", 5⅛", 4¼". 110 E. Riding, 5⅝". 111 E. Riding, 4¹⁄₁₀".

PLATE XXXV

FOOD VESSELS

112, 113, 114 E. Riding, 4¼″, 5″, 4¾″. **115, 116, 117** E. Riding, 5½″, 4¼″, 5″. **118, 119, 120, 121, 122** E. Riding, 3⅝″, 8½″, 3¾″, 4½″, 4″.
123 N. Riding, 4⅛″. **124** Northumberland, 6¼″. **125** Northumberland, 3¼″.

PLATE XXXVI

FOOD VESSELS

126 E. Riding. **127** Derby, 4″. **128** Yorks, 3¼″. **129** E. Riding, 1⅝″. **130** E. Riding, 4″. **131** E. Riding, 4¾″. **132** unknown, 4½″. **133** E. Riding, 4⅝″. **134** E. Riding, 3¼″. **135** Yorks, 3½″. **136** E. Riding, 4½″. **137** E. Riding, 4½″. **138** E. Riding, 4⅝″. **139** N. Riding, 5½″. **140** unknown, 5″.

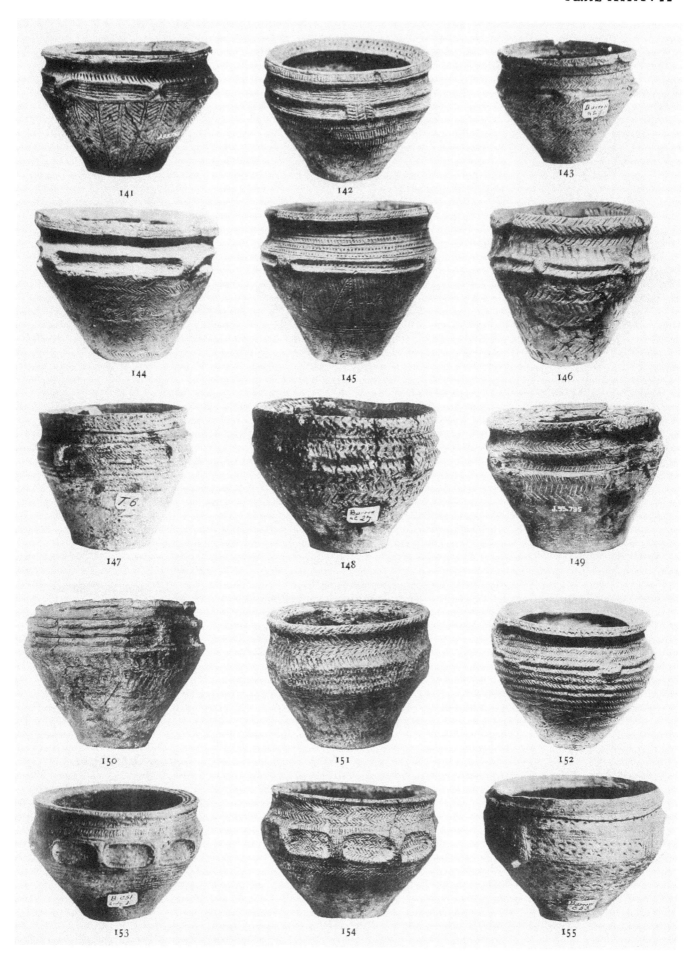

PLATE XXXVII

FOOD VESSELS

141 N. Riding, 4″. **142** E. Riding, 4¼″. **143** E. Riding, 3″. **144** N. Riding, 5″. **145, 146** Northumberland, 4⅞″, 4¾″. **147** E. Riding, 4¾″.
148 E. Riding, 6″. **149** Yorks, 6¼″. **150** Yorks, 6″. **151** E. Riding, 4¼″. **152** E. Riding, 4¾″. **153** E. Riding, 3⅜″. **154** E. Riding, 4¾″. **155**
E. Riding, 5½″.

PLATE XXXVIII

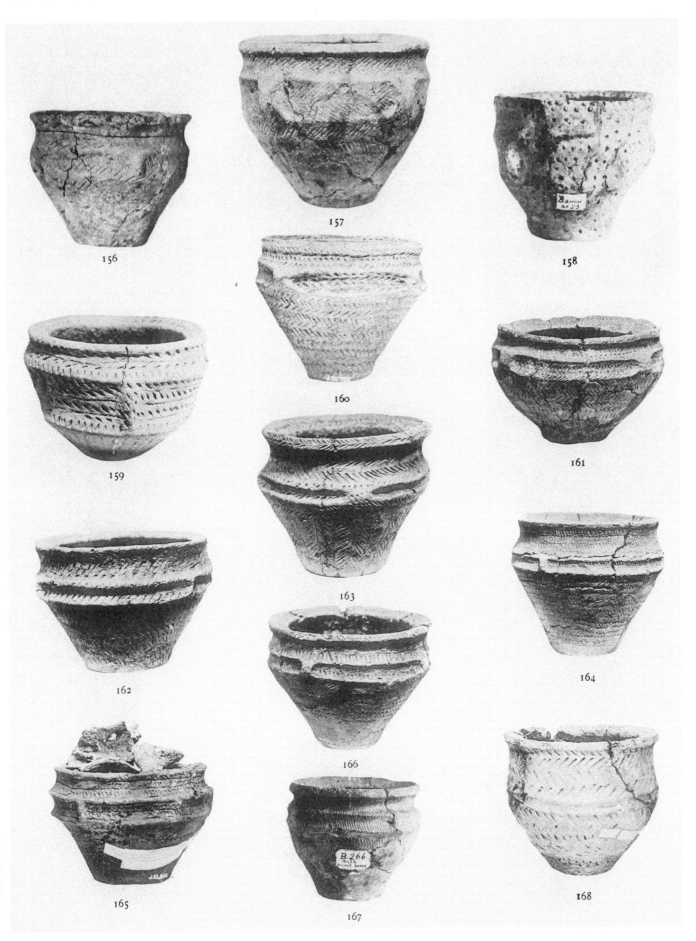

FOOD VESSELS

156 Yorks, 5¼″. **157** E. Riding, 5¾″. **158** E. Riding, 6″. **159** Northumberland. **160** Derby, 5″. **161** E. Riding, 4½″. **162** E. Riding, 4″. **163** Northumberland, 4″. **164** Cumberland, 5½″. **165** Derby, 4¼″. **166** N. Riding, 4½″. **167** E. Riding, 4¾″. **168** Derby, 5½″.

PLATE **XXXIX**

FOOD VESSELS

169, 170 Derby, —, 4¾″. **171** Northumberland, 4⅛″. **172** E. Riding, 5¼″. **173** Derby, 4¾″. **174** N. Riding, 4¼″. **175** Derby, 4¾″. **176** E. Riding,
5″. **176** *bis* E. Riding, 5¾″. **177** Yorks, 4¼″. **178** Derby, 4″. **179** E. Riding, 5″. **180** Northumberland, 4⅞″. **181** E. Riding, 5½″.

PLATE XL

FOOD VESSELS

182 Derby, 5¾″. **183** E. Riding, 6¼″. **184** Derby, 6¼″. **185** E. Riding, 6¾″. **186** Stafford, 6″. **187** Stafford, 5″. **188** N. Riding, 6¼″.
189 E. Riding, 7″. **190** E. Riding, 7¾″. **191** Derby, 6¾″. **192** N. Riding, 5⅝″. **193** E. Riding, 5½″.

PLATE XLI

FOOD VESSELS

194 Stafford, 5½″. **195** E. Riding, 5⅜″. **196** E. Riding, 6½″. **197** E. Riding, 6″. **198** E. Riding, 5½″. **199** Lincoln, 3¾″. **200** Northumberland, 6″. **201** Yorks, 5¾″. **202** E. Riding, 6″. **203** E. Riding, 4¾″. **204** Derby, 4¾″. **205** Northumberland, 6″. **206** Northumberland, 5⅜″. **207** E. Riding, 6¼″. **208** E. Riding, 5″. **209** N. Riding, 5½″.

PLATE XLII

FOOD VESSELS

210 E. Riding, 5¼″.   **211** E. Riding, 4½″.   **212** Northumberland, 5⅜″.   **213** E. Riding, 6¼″.   **214** Derby, 4½″.   **214** *a* Argyll, 4″.   **215** Derby, 4¾″.
216 unknown, 4″.   **217** Northumberland.   **218** N. Riding, 4½″.   **219** Yorks, 4″.   **220** unknown, 4⅛″.   **221** E. Riding, 3¼″.   **222** E. Riding, 3⅜″.
223 Northumberland, 3¼″.   **223** *bis* N. Riding, 2½″.

Plate XLIII

FOOD VESSELS

224 E. Riding, 5″. **225** Stafford, 4¼″. **226** Northumberland, 6¾″. **227** Northumberland, 5¼″. **228** E. Riding, 5″. **229, 230** E. Riding, 2″ without the lid, 3½″. **231, 232** Antrim, 4¾″, 3″. **233, 234, 235** Down. **236** Argyll, 3¾″.

PLATE XLIV

FOOD VESSELS

236 *a*, **237, 237** *a* Argyll, 3¼″. **238, 239, 239** *a* Argyll, 5″, 5″. **240, 241, 241** *a* Fermanagh, 3¼″, 3¼″. **242, 243** Donegal, 4″, 4″. **244** Dublin, 6″. **245, 245** *a*, **246** Meath, 4″, 4⅝″. **247** Antrim, 4″. **248** Queen's County, 4⅜″. **249** Arran, 5″. **250** Bute, 7″.

PLATE XLV

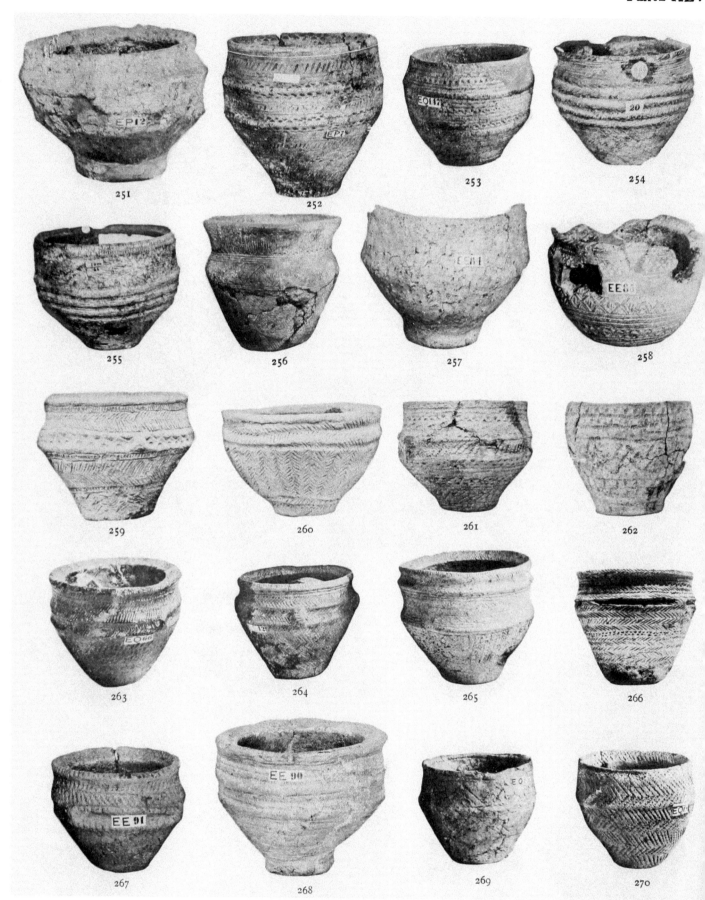

FOOD VESSELS

251 Arran, 5″. **252** Arran, 7½″. **253** Kincardine. **254** Sligo, 4¾″. **255** Cavan, 6″. **256** Enniskillen, 5⅝″. **257, 258** Edinburgh, 4¾″, 3½″. **259, 260** Antrim, 4½″, 3¾″. **261, 262** Lanark, 4¾″, 5½″. **263** Perth, 4½″. **264, 265** Fife, 5″, 5¾″. **266** Bute, 5½″. **267, 268** Fife, 4″, 5″. **269** Forfar, 5½″. **270** Forfar, 5″.

PLATE XLVI

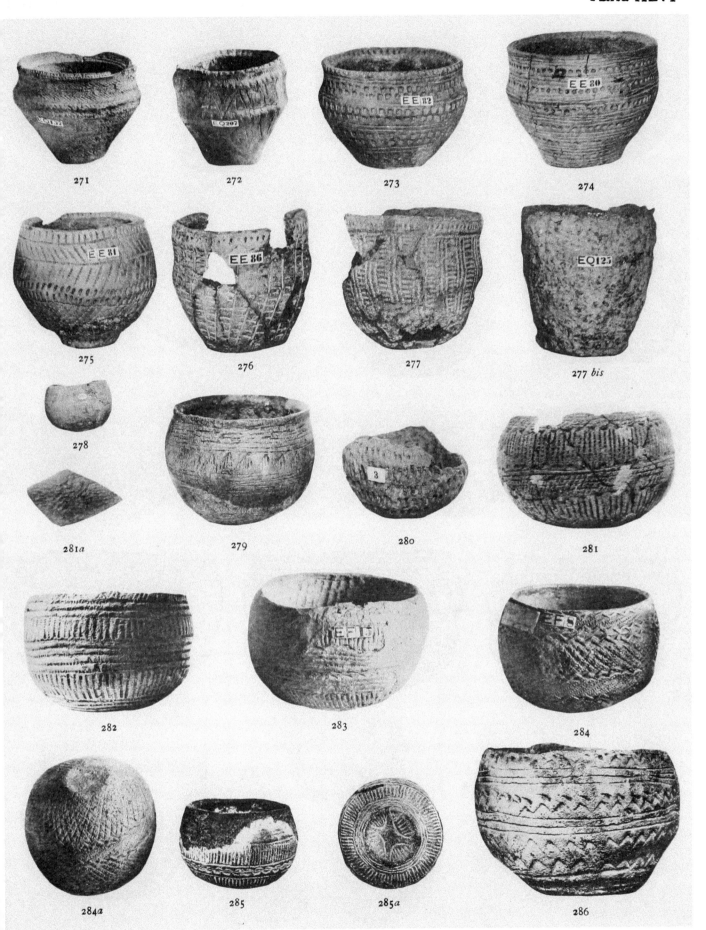

FOOD VESSELS

271 Midlothian, 4¾″.   272 Forfar, 6¼″.   273, 274, 275 E. Lothian, 4¾″, 4¼″, 5½″.   276, 277 Perth, 4¾″, 5″.   277 *bis* Banff, 6″.   278 Antrim, 3¼″.
279 Kilkenny, 4¼″.   280 Antrim, 3⅜″.   281, 281*a* Tyrone, 3¼″.   282 Antrim, 4″.   283 Ulster (?), 3½″.   284, 284*a* Ulster (?), 3½″.   285, 285*a*
Meath, 3⅜″.   286 Kilkenny, 4¼″.

PLATE XLVII

FOOD VESSELS

287, 287 *a* Ulster (?), 4″. **288, 288** *a* Ulster (?). **289** Down, 4″. **290** Down. **291, 291** *a* Tyrone, 4¼″. **292** Unknown, 3⅞″. **293** Sligo, 3⅜″. **294** Kilkenny, 4¼″. **295** Cavan, 3¾″. **296, 296** *a* Ulster (?), 3½″. **297** Sligo, 3⅝″. **298** Unknown. **299** Dublin, 4½″. **300** Dublin, 3⅝″. **301** Antrim, 4⅜″.

PLATE XLVIII

302   302 bis   303   304
302 a   302 b   303 a   305
306   308   309
307   310   311   312
313   310 a   313 a   314

FOOD VESSELS

302, 302 a Antrim.   302 bis Ulster (?).   302 b Argyll, 3½″.   303 Aberdeen, 4½″.   303 a Midlothian, 3 9/10″.   304 Aberdeen.   305 Arran, 5¼″.
306 Argyll, 4½″.   307 Fermanagh, 3⅝″.   308 Ulster (?), 3¾″.   309 Ulster (?), 4½″.   310, 310 a Tyrone, 4″.   311 Wicklow, 3½″.   312 Unknown, 4 1/16″.
313, 313 a Queen's County, 4¾″, 3½″.   314 Dublin, 4″.

PLATE XLIX

FOOD VESSELS

315, 316, 317 Carlow, —, —, 4¼″. 318 Unknown, 4¼″. 319 Unknown, 3¾″. 320 Unknown, 3⅞″. 321 Londonderry (?), 4⅝″. 322 Kildare, 5¼″. 323 Ulster (?). 324 Ulster (?), 4½″. 325, 326, 327 Ulster (?). 327 *bis* Unknown, 4¼″. 328 Tyrone, 4¾″. 329 Down, 4⅜″. 330 Unknown, 3⅝″. 331 Unknown, 3⅝″.

PLATE L

FOOD VESSELS

PLATE LI

FOOD VESSELS

350 *bis* Lanark, 4¼″.   351, 352, 353 Ulster (?), 3¾″, 3¾″, 3¾″.   354 Ireland, 4⅛″.   355, 356 Ulster (?), 4½″, 4½″.   357 Tyrone, 6¾″.   358, 358 *a* Londonderry, 4¼″.   359 Ayr, 3¾″.   360 Arran, 6″.   361 Perth.   362, 362 *bis* Ayr.

PLATE LII

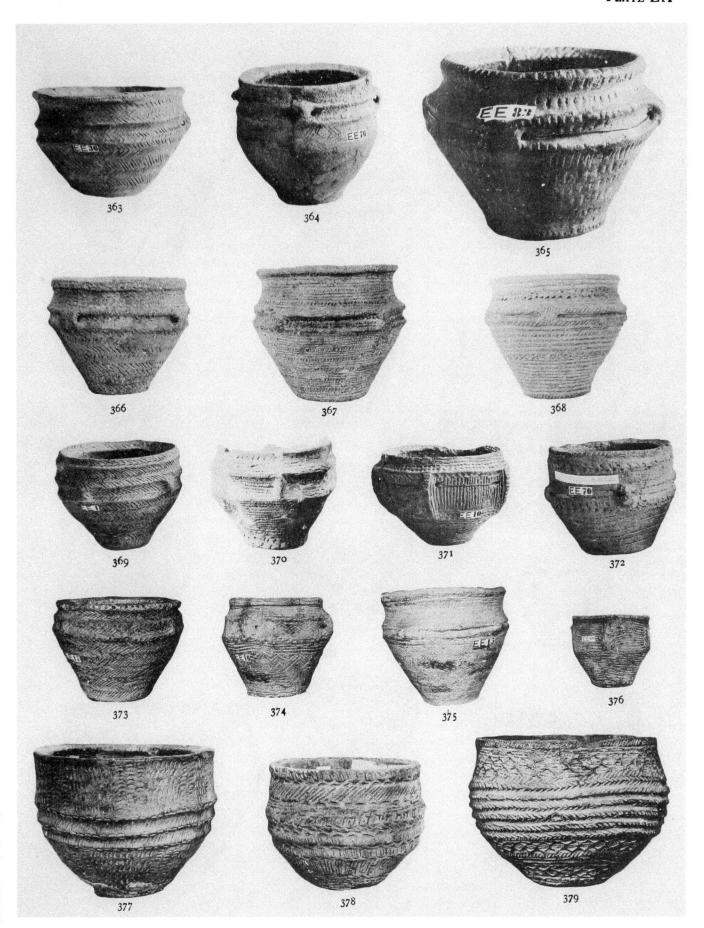

FOOD VESSELS

363 Banff, 5″. 364 Forfar, 5″. 365 E. Lothian, 3¾″. 366 Cumbrae, 4¼″. 367 Ayr (?), 4⅝″. 368 Unknown, 5″. 369 Midlothian, 5″. 370 Stirling, 5¼″. 371 Midlothian, 4¾″. 372 Fife, 5″. 373 Perth, 4½″. 374 Forfar, 4¾″. 375 Unknown, 5½″. 376 Forfar, 5½″. 377 Londonderry (?), 5½″. 378 Meath, 4¾″. 379 Kilkenny, 4½″.

PLATE LIII

FOOD VESSELS

380 Sligo, 5⅜″.   381 Wexford, 3⅞″.   382 Mayo, 5¼″.   383 Galway.   384 Unknown, 6⅜″.   385 Waterford, 7⅛″.   386 Forfar, 5″.
387 Forfar, 5⅜″.   388 Roxburgh, 3¾″.   389 Argyll, 6″.   390, 391 Ross.   392 Galway, 5¼″.

PLATE LIV

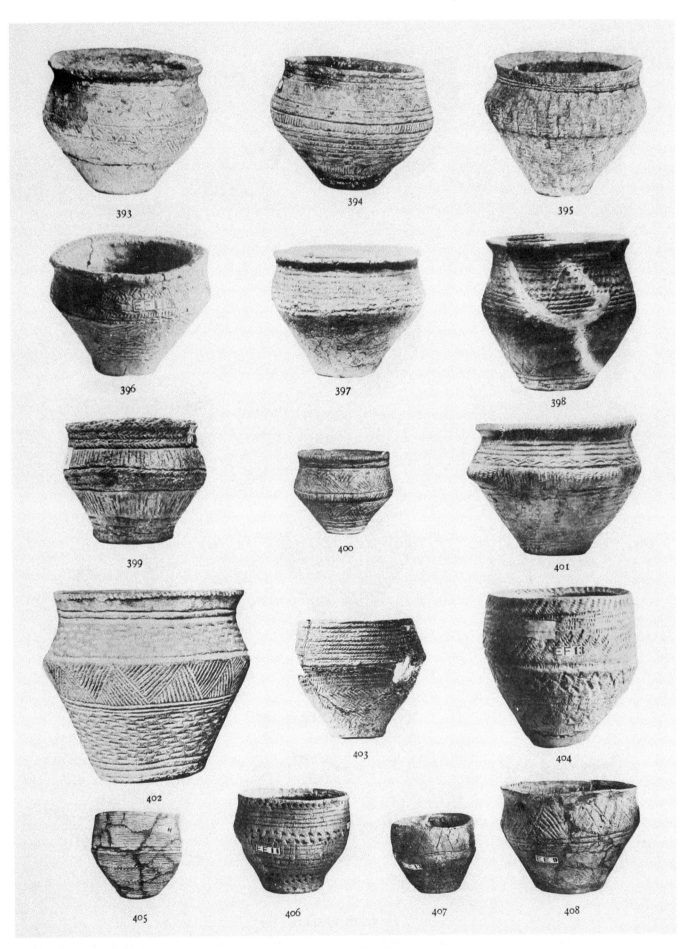

FOOD VESSELS

393 Unknown, 5⅛″. 394 West Meath, 5½″. 95 Donegal, 5″. 396, 397 Ulster (?), 4½″, –. 398 Unknown, 6⅜″. 399 Wicklow, 3¼″. 400 Unknown, 4½″. 401 Cork, 4⅜″. 402 Wicklow, 5¼″. 403 Down. 404 Ulster (?), 5½″. 405 Argyll, 6½″. 406 Midlothian, 5″. 407 Wigton, 4″. 408 Nairn, 4¼″.

PLATE LV

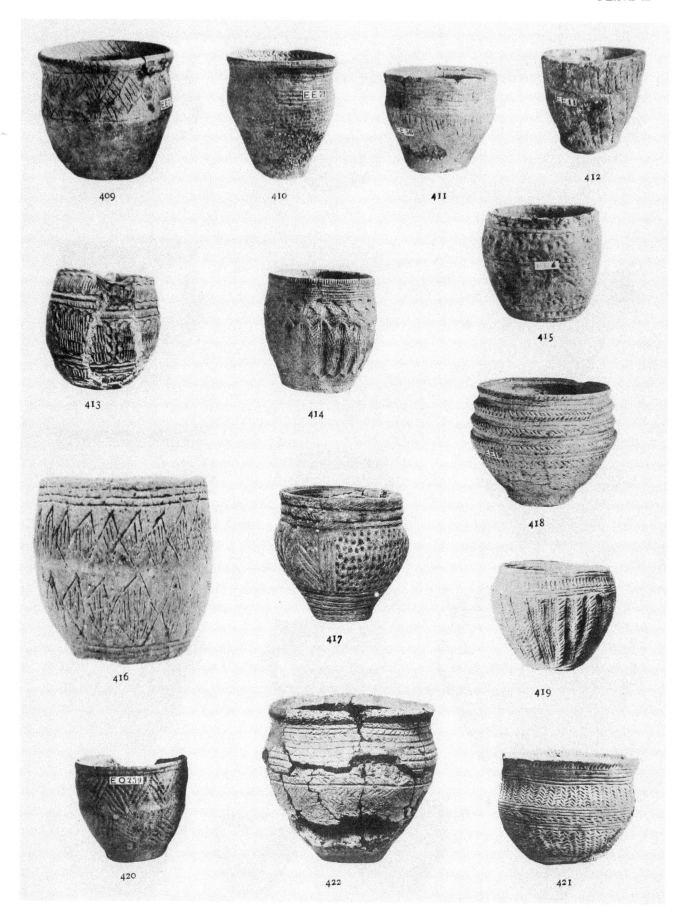

FOOD VESSELS

409 Unknown. 410 Mull, 5½″. 411 E. Lothian, 4¾″. 412 Ayr, 4¾″. 413 Ireland, 5″. 414 Peebles, 5½″. 415 Elgin. 416 Aberdeen.
417 Ireland. 418 Stirling, 5½″. 419 Stirling. 420 Stirling, 5½″. 421 Elgin. 422 Kirkcudbright, 5½″.

PLATE LVI

REGION I

Dorset

Dorset

Dorset

Dorset fig. 1.

Oxford fig. 6.

REGION II

E. Riding fig. 23.

Derby fig. 41.

E. Riding fig. 78.

E. Riding fig. 119.

Northumberland fig. 144.

E. Riding fig. 29.

Northumberland fig. 163.

Derby fig. 169.

Derby fig. 170.

E. Riding fig. 130.

Derby fig. 173.

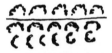

E. Riding fig. 195.

E. Riding fig. 197.

Fig. 141.

Lincoln fig. 199.

N. Riding fig. 201.

Derby fig. 204.

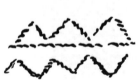

E. Riding fig. 210.

Northumberland fig. 223.

E. Riding fig. 213.

Northumberland fig. 217.

E. Riding fig. 222.

Northumberland fig. 227.

ORNAMENTATION ON ENGLISH FOOD VESSELS

PLATE LVII

REGION III

Cavan fig. 225.

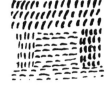

Antrim fig. 231.

Antrim fig. 232.

Down fig. 233.

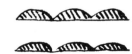

Down fig. 234.

Argyll fig. 237.

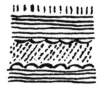

Argyll fig. 238.

Argyll fig. 239.

Donegal fig. 243.

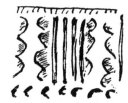

Dublin fig. 244.

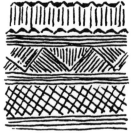

Enniskillen fig. 256.

Edinburgh fig. 258.

Fife fig. 265.

Forfar fig. 269.

Tyrone fig. 281.

Ulster fig. 284.

Ulster fig. 288.

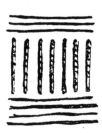

Kilkenny fig. 294.

Ulster fig. 296.

Sligo fig. 297.

Ireland fig. 298.

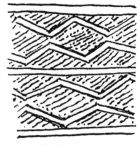

Dublin fig. 299.

Antrim fig. 302.

Aberdeen fig. 303.

ORNAMENTATION ON ENGLISH FOOD VESSELS

PLATE LVIII

REGION III (CONTINUED)

Aberdeen fig. 304.

Argyll fig. 304 b.

Locality unknown fig. 336.

Fermanagh fig. 307.

Wicklow fig. 311.

Carlow fig. 317.

Ulster fig. 325.

Down fig. 329.

Down fig. 332.

E. Lothian fig. 348.

Ulster fig. 351.

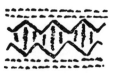

Ulster fig. 352.

Tyrone.

Ayr fig. 367.

M. Lothian fig. 371.

Londonderry fig. 377.

Kilkenny fig. 379.

Sligo fig. 380.

Waterford fig. 385.

Forfar fig. 386.

Forfar fig. 387.

Galway fig. 392.

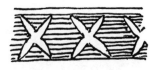

West Meath fig. 394.

Peebles fig. 414.

Elgin fig. 421.

ORNAMENTATION ON ENGLISH FOOD VESSELS

PLATE LIX

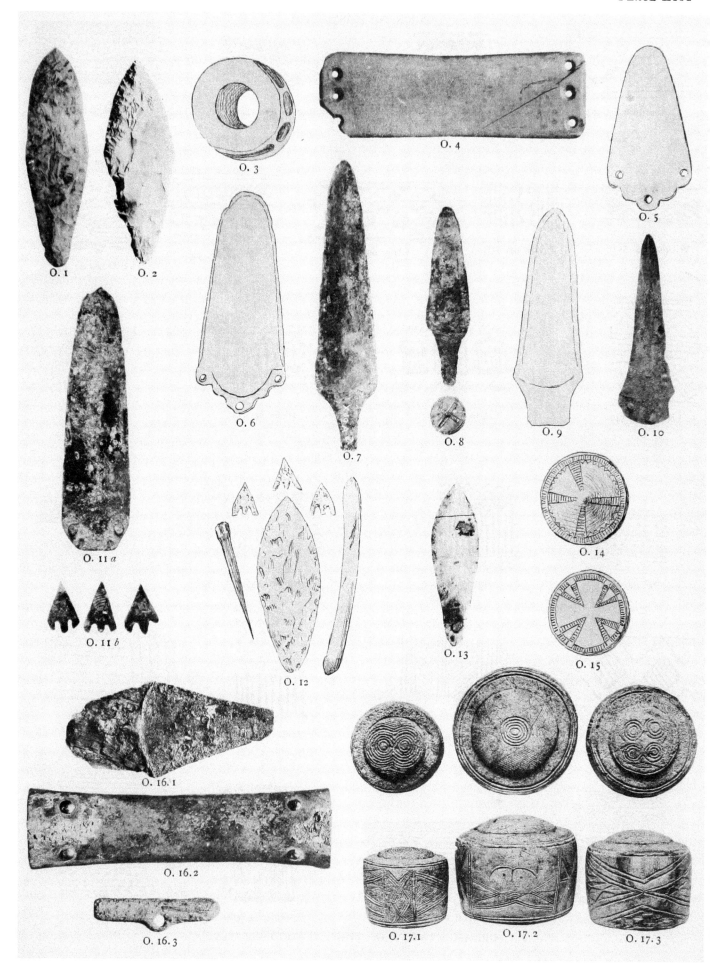

OBJECTS

O. 1 Wilts, 7½″ × 1½″. O. 2 Somerset, L. 5¾″. O. 3 Wilts, D. 1½″. O. 4 Suffolk, 4⅝″ × 1½″. O. 5 Wilts, 4″. O. 6 Wilts, 5½″ × 2⅜″. O. 7 Wilts, 10″ × 2″. O. 8 Wilts, 5″ × 1⅞″. O. 9 Wilts, 5¾″ × 1¾″. O. 10 Wilts, 5¼″ × 1¾″. O. 11 *a* Wilts, 8⅞″ × 2¾″. O. 11 *b* Wilts. O. 12 Derby. O. 13 E. Riding, L. 6¼″. O. 14 E. Riding. O. 15 E. Riding. O. 16 1, 2, 3 E. Riding, 3½″ × 1¼″; 5¼″ × 1¾″; L. 2¼″. O. 17 1, 2, 3, side and top views, E. Riding.

PLATE LX

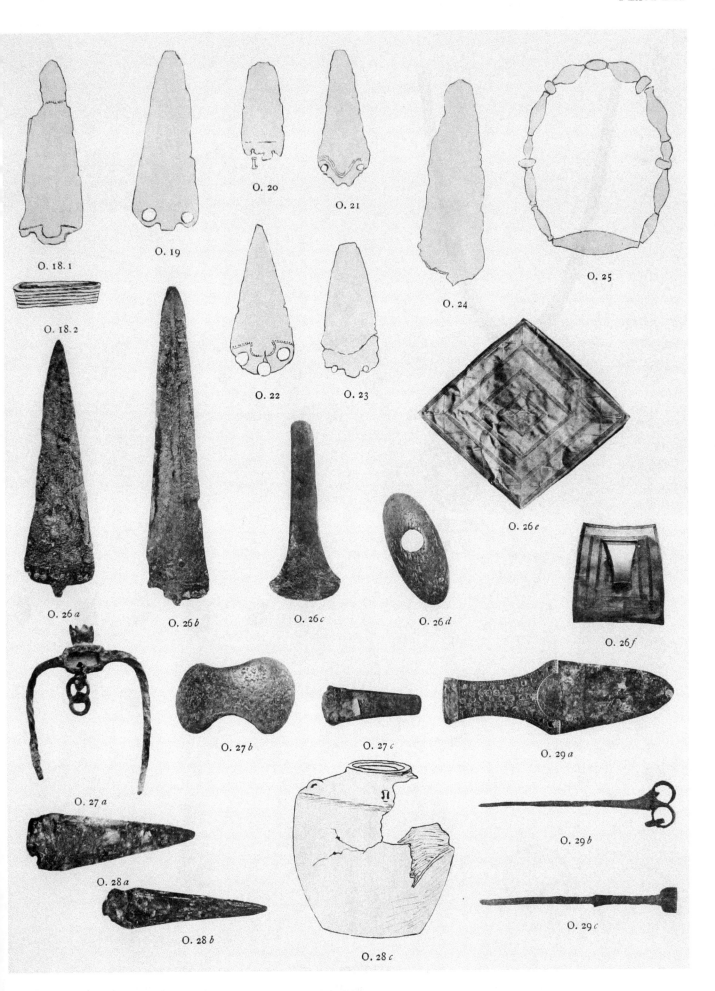

O. 18.1

O. 19

O. 20

O. 21

O. 24

O. 25

O. 18.2

O. 22

O. 23

O. 26 e

O. 26 a

O. 26 b

O. 26 c

O. 26 d

O. 26 f

O. 27 a

O. 27 b

O. 27 c

O. 29 a

O. 28 a

O. 29 b

O. 28 b

O. 28 c

O. 29 c

OBJECTS

O. 18 1, 2 Fife, 6″ × 2⅛″. **O. 19** E. Lothian, L. 5¾″. **O. 20** Perth, 3⅜″ × 1 7/16″. **O. 21** Perth, L. 4½″. **O. 22** Argyll, 5″ × 2¼″. **O. 23** Forfar, 4½″ × 2″. **O. 24** Forfar, 3⅜″ × 1⅜″. **O. 25** Aberdeen. **O. 26** a–26 Wilts. **O. 27** a–27 c Wilts. **O. 28** a–28 c Wilts. **O. 29** a–29 c Wilts.

PLATE LXI

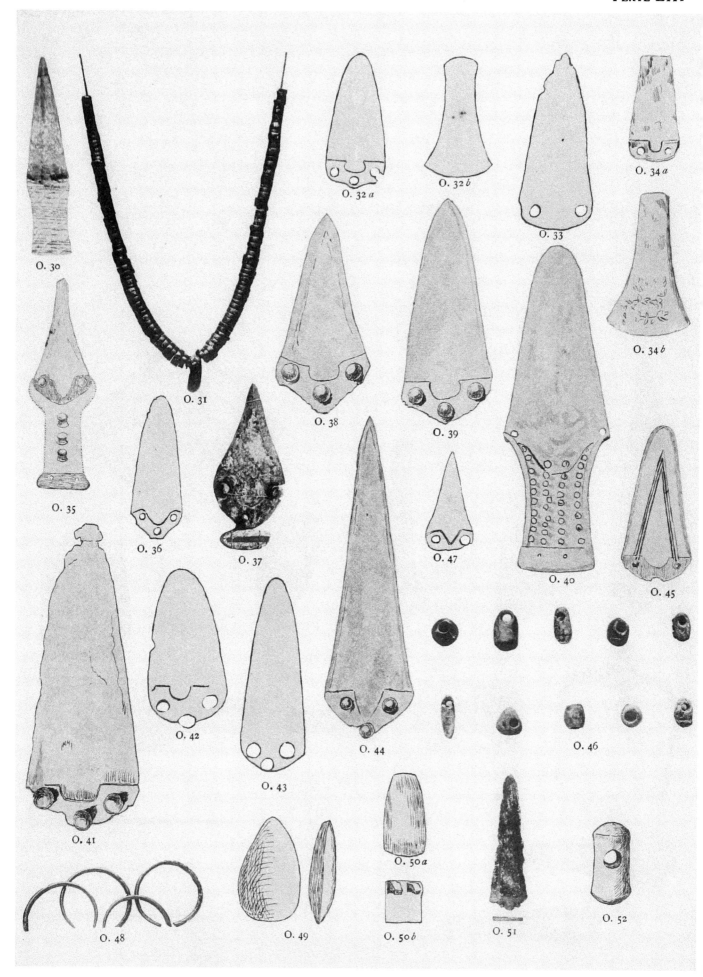

OBJECTS

O. 30 E. Riding, L. 6″. O. 31 E. Riding, L. 11¼″. O. 32 a, b E. Riding, 4½″ × 2″; 4″ × 2⅜″. O. 33 E. Riding, 3″ × 1¼″. O. 34 a, b Derby. O. 35 E. Riding. O. 36 E. Riding. O. 37 E. Riding. O. 38 Derby. O. 39 Derby. O. 40 E. Riding. O. 41 Derby. O. 42 E. Riding. O. 43 Derby. O. 44 Stafford. O. 45 Derby. O. 46 Fermanagh. O. 47 Antrim. O. 48 Queen's County. O. 49 Sligo. O. 50 a, b Cavan. O. 51 Enniskillen. O. 52 Perth.

For EU product safety concerns, contact us at Calle de José Abascal, 56–1°,
28003 Madrid, Spain or eugpsr@cambridge.org.

www.ingramcontent.com/pod-product-compliance
Ingram Content Group UK Ltd.
Pitfield, Milton Keynes, MK11 3LW, UK
UKHW051027150625

459647UK00023B/2848